Flying *in* Coffin Corner

We have to remember that in the future we will want to keep before our children what this war was really like. It is so easy to forget; and then, for the younger generation, the heroism and the glamour remain, while the dirt, the hardships, the horror of death and the sorrow fade somewhat from their consciousness.

—ELEANOR ROOSEVELT

ALLIED FORCE HEADQUARTERS
Grand Quartier Général des Forces Alliées
N RTH AFRICAN THEATER OF OPERATIONS
Théâtre d'opérations Nord-Africain

OFFICIAL WAR PHOTOGRAPHER

Photographe officiel

ARMED FORCES SERVICE PERSONNEL
Personnel des Forces Armées

HIS IDENTIFIES ROBERT THOMPSON, S/SGT, A C SIGNATURE *Robert L. Thompson*
le carte identifie
RIAL N° 6914143 DATE FEBRUARY 26, 1944
tricule N°

ALL UNIT COMMANDERS : YOU ARE DIRECTED TO EXTEND ALL NECESSARY COOPERATION TO THIS CAMERAMAN TO ENABLE HIM TO COMPLETE HIS PHOTO
ous les commandants d'unités : Toute l'aide nécessaire dev être apportée au titulaire de cette carte pour lui faciliter sa mission de prises de vues photographiques ou cinématog
SSION.

S MISSION IS :
e mission est :

— TO CONVEY INFORMATION TO THE WAR AND NAVY DEPARTMENTS, WASHINGTON, D.C. AND TO THE WAR OFFICE, ADMI-
RALTY, AND AIR MINISTRY, LONDON.
— de transmettre toutes informations aux Départements de la Guerre et de la Marine à Washington, D.C., ainsi qu'aux Ministères de la
Guerre, de la Marine et de l'Air à Londres.
— TO PROVIDE NEWS PICTURES FOR RELEASE TO T E PUBLIC.
— de prendre des photographies d'actualité destinées au bic.
— TO PROVIDE OFFICIAL PICTORIAL WAR RECORDS
— de prendre des photographies destinées aux Archives of cielles de la guerre.

NSORSHIP OF ALL PHOTOGRAPHS WILL BE CARRIE OUT IN ACCORDANCE WITH ALLIED FORCE HEADQUARTERS OPERATIONAL MEMORANDUM #43
Censure des photographies ou des prises de vues sera eff ctuée suivant les instructions du Grand Quartier Général des Forces Alliées, telles qu'elles sont destinées dans l'O
morandum...

PROVED BY : *J.A.H. Gammell*
Signé :
LIEUTENANT GENERAL.
N 424
CHIEF OF STAFF, ALLIED FORCE HE DQUARTERS
Chef d'État-Major, Grand Quartier Général des Forces Alliées.

Here are my credentials, which I carried at all times and got me into places I probably shouldn't have been.

Flying
in
Coffin
Corner

ROBERT "BOB" THOMPSON

McAlister Press
SAHUARITA

For my beautiful wife, Wilma, whose waiting was harder than being there—and in memory of my dear friends Ernie Pyle and "Duck" Pond, who were there.

Flying in Coffin Corner

Library of Congress Catalog Card No. 95-60453

ISBN 0-9639519-1-2

Published by McAlister Press, Sahuarita, Arizona

Copyright © 1995 by Robert L. Thompson

All rights reserved.

Manufactured in the United States of America

∞ This book was printed on acid-free, archival-quality paper.

Additional copies of this book may be purchased at military bookstores and other selected retail outlets for $19.95 plus tax. Or you may order directly from the distributor:

McAlister-Nash Military Publications
Post Office Box 241
Sahuarita, AZ 85629

Please include $3.75 for shipping (total $23.70), and for faster service include a cashier's check or money order.

Contents

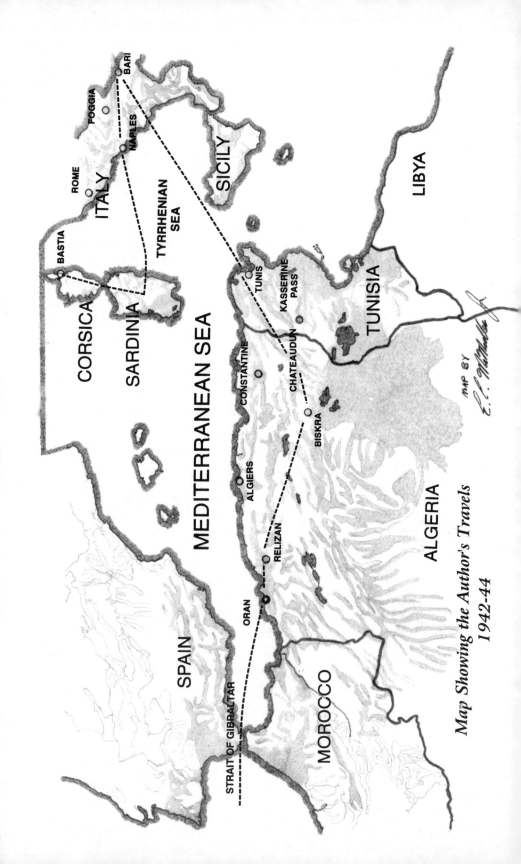

Map Showing the Author's Travels
1942-44

MAP BY
E. L. Wilkinson Jr

Preface

ALL OF MY WORLD WAR II BUDDIES have been reluctant to rehash the unpleasant episodes of their overseas services. I myself have kept some things locked up in my memory for half a century.

We try not to talk about the sad parts of the war, only the fun parts. When old soldiers gather every few years for a reunion, our wives and kids hear *only* the funny stories. Our kids have begun to think that the war was all fun and games. They shouldn't. It is about time they are told the rest of the story.

Recently, a concerned confidant told me, "If something has been bothering you all these years, *get it out.* It will be a catharsis. Anyway, you were a witness to history and the first duty of a witness is to testify. *Write what you saw!*"

This is not a war history in the strict sense of the word—and certainly not on the broad level of General Eisenhower's book, *Crusade In Europe.* This book is simply the reminiscing of a few old warriors who have "come in from the pasture" long enough to tell you about some of their necessary, thankless jobs in a sinister war —World War II.

There are undoubtedly some misspelled words, especially the names of places in Africa that were only heard—not read. If an occasional time sequence is out of sync, or the facts misplaced, it is because of the passage of time and the rigors of age.

You'll discover that the simple "dog face" (enlisted man) is the hero here, not the "brass hats." The brass were given most of the credit and glory while the dog faces were "pawns or numbers" who fought and died anonymously. This book recalls the experiences of some of those unsung heroes.

I accept in advance all the reproaches you may voice about my candid opinions of certain well-known individuals and brass hats. My recollections will probably not sit well with everybody, and might even be controversial. It is not my intention to modify this minute slice of history to clean up somebody's act or to close my eyes to the blunders I witnessed. This is the way I saw it, not the way a Hollywood script-writer might imagine it.

There are some harsh and vicious scenes in this story I felt had to be included to give you a feel for the sights and sounds of battle: The constant danger and the picture of men whose lives were snuffed out in just a millisecond.

The ending of this story may seem anti-climatic; after the excitement all the way through, it will suddenly stop. But that's the way it happened. One second it was bedlam and a buddy was fighting for his life—and the next second it was all over and peaceful.

A few good men have cooperated in validating and telling this bit of history—only on the promise that it be told "as it was." You'll meet these gentlemen later.

My main sources were the detailed notes I made in a large journal purchased in England, and my penciled notations in the margins of the pocket-sized New Testament given to me by my wife, Wilma, as we said goodbye when I was shipping out.

Finally, it is possible only now to tell the *complete* story of my part in this unreasonable war—about one of the most implausible tragedies, in which I was involved, resulting in an inquest where all attendees were placed under a 50-year "Gag Order." We've served our 50 years of silence, so here's where "the kitty comes out of the sack . . . ."

Written sincerely,

ROBERT L. THOMPSON
Technical Sergeant
U.S. Army Air Corps
6914143 1939–1945
Green Valley, Arizona 1994

The yellow flames streaking back from our number two engine were melting the aluminum bomb bay door and blistering the camouflaged skin under my waist gun window. Our B-24 was in serious trouble! And we were still climbing at 10,000 feet over the Mediterranean Sea halfway between Italy and the southern coast of France!

For two years, since 1942, I had survived countless terrifying episodes in this moronic war and now wondered if this one would finally "close the book."

The pilot had called us on the interphone and given us a choice—ditch with him or jump. I ran a quick prayer through my mind, "God, I know you're very busy right now, but what should I do...?"

PART ONE

England

It was a sobering experience to watch the shattered bodies of little children being removed from the rubble of a London apartment building (see page 39).

Convoy To Scotland

UNTIL I ARRIVED AT THE NEW YORK HARBOR, the biggest dock I had ever seen was about fifty feet long and ten feet wide—a narrow finger jutting out into the calm waters of Pine Lake, about twenty miles from Michigan's capital city, Lansing. Boats were fascinating to a ten-year-old.

Of course I was a great movie buff and especially enjoyed films where most of the action took place on luxury liners; where the passengers on these floating cities dressed formally and dined on gourmet food at the captain's table. Their quarters were always elegantly appointed.

Now it was the early part of June, 1942, and I stood looking upward at *my* "luxury" liner, the *Argentina*. She must have been eight or ten stories high. I was awestruck. Pine Lake would have to be enlarged a hundred times before this section of the New York docks would even fit in it.

To the left and to the right, ships were lined up as far as I could see. Within two days, these converted liners, now disguised with dull sea-gray camouflage, would be rearranged at sea to form a convoy.

I was a twenty-two-year-old recent graduate of the Air Corps photo school in Denver when I was ordered to board the ship. It took two full days and nights to bring all the men and material aboard. When the *Argentina* finally pulled out of the harbor, she was crammed with over 5,000 men. Like me, most of them had probably never seen a ship such as this before, and I had never crossed a body of water wider than the Detroit River.

There was an aura of excitement in the air. I guess most of us really had mixed emotions. Some of us were looking forward to this new and fascinating adventure, the devil's madness - war. I was anxious to get on with it.

It seemed like everybody on deck was watching the New York skyline slowly disappear. Someone in our group pointed out the Statue of Liberty and bets were made as to how long it would take her to vanish. Soon we were rolling in open water and the city was history.

The *Argentina* certainly didn't resemble any of the luxurious cruise ships I'd seen in the movies. Where were the small round tables with flowers and fine china? Where was the string ensemble playing the Strauss waltzes?

Our squadron and about 500 other men from various corps of the Army were herded down some steps and directed into a square compartment. I thought this was probably the way cattle were controlled on their way to a slaughterhouse.

There were rows and rows of white canvas hammocks hanging five deep from the floor to the ceiling with not a whole lot of room between them. I wondered how the men were going to reach the upper hammocks.

I immediately threw my barracks bag on the nearest bottom hammock. Other men were also racing around between the hammocks trying to find a bottom bunk.

Since we had eaten before leaving Fort Dix, we weren't expecting chow, so we concentrated our efforts on setting up housekeeping. There was one blanket and a pillow on each hammock.

The lower bunks had been taken fast. First, the bottom ones were grabbed, then the second tier, and so on, until they were all occupied. I sat down on mine and the hammock sagged until I was practically sitting on the floor. A fellow whom I didn't know stepped on the edge of mine and boosted himself up into the one above me. When he stretched out on it, his "empennage" came down to within six inches of my nose! The fellow above him got into *his* hammock and the same thing happened. The guy above me exclaimed, "Hey, I can't get out of my bunk. I'm squeezed in!" He couldn't raise up to get out. He had to roll over the side and grab his hammock to keep from falling! This was obviously not the First Class section.

The loudspeakers blared in a metallic voice that the lights would go out in ten minutes. Then it was black except for a faint blue glow from the steel ceiling above us. Things had quieted down, and I lay back in my hammock and began thinking about the events of the last few days. My wife, Wilma, was foremost in my mind.

Wilma had come to Trenton hoping we would have a chance to see each other before I left. Thousands of other wives had the same idea and we were surprised there had been enough hotel rooms for all of us.

We were free to leave Fort Dix anytime we wanted to, just so we checked in every morning for further orders. Soon, we were restricted to the post, and could only make phone calls to our wives. That meant only one thing—port of embarkation!

Several of the men in our squadron, thinking they would not see their wives again before leaving Fort Dix, went to the post barber and got Mohawk haircuts. They had their heads clipped down to the skin, all except for a two-inch ridge starting at the forehead and running all the way to the back of their necks. They were the most absurd and comical-looking soldiers in the U.S. Army!

Then our departure orders were changed. We were again allowed to go into Trenton and visit our wives. Sudden humiliation! Embarrassment! The "Mohawks" had acted too quickly! One of them said, "I'll go back to town and spend a couple of more nights with my wife, but I'll be damned if I'll take my cap off!"

Someone had started calling us "dogface" after JoJo, the dogface boy. And we wore tags, *dog* tags, so from then on we were dogfaces. We preferred to be called GIs. GI meant government issue. Everything was GI. GI garbage cans, GI trucks, GI uniforms —so a soldier was either a dogface or a GI.

Before the war, civilians despised the dogfaces. We were *less* than dogs. In the summer of 1939, when I was a new recruit at Chanute Field, in Rantoul, Illinois, there was a sign posted in a yard near the field. It said, "Soldiers and dogs—stay off the lawn."

In the old Army, and it was still old at that time, an enlisted man had no privileges. A soldier practically gave up his rights as a citizen. He couldn't vote. He had better not say anything against an officer or a politician, because it meant six months in the guardhouse.

A new dogface earned $21 a month, but after laundry money and the mandatory deduction for the old soldier's home was taken out of his pay, he had about $12 to last for the rest of the month. He got along, however, because for twenty-five cents he could take in a GI movie, eat a bag of popcorn, then go to the Post Exchange (PX) and have a "brown cow"—an RC Cola with a scoop of vanilla ice cream.

Dogface recruits were still getting regular infantry drilling at Chanute Field, wearing World War I campaign hats and given the dirtiest jobs on the post. I was assigned to the coal pile. It was my job to shovel coal from a menacing black mountain into a "donkey cart" and wheel it over on little tracks to old John, a husky civilian who threw the coal into monstrous furnaces in the central heating plant, which sent steam to every building on the post.

My new friend, Roy P. Moore, was put on permanent KP. It wouldn't have been so bad if he had been learning how to cook, but he was the "G" man, which meant he collected all the garbage, saw that all the cans were emptied by the pick-up trucks, and then scrubbed out the cans with GI lye soap.

Moore got fed up one day and asked the mess sergeant for a day off. He was turned down. "The captain sent you over here, and I can't change that," he said.

Roy blew his top! He went straight to the squadron office and stormed in. Without saying a word, he shoved a heavy black typewriter across the first sergeant's desk into his lap. He then banged the captain's door open, rushed in and grabbed the CO by his necktie, pulled him out of his chair, and dumped the contents of a wastebasket on his head.

Poor Roy was arrested and put in the guardhouse to await a Section 8. A Section 8 was the paragraph in the U.S. Army Articles of Discipline, which stated that when a soldier was "unadjustable to military service," he would be kicked out with a dishonorable discharge.

There was a court-martial, of course, and a young second lieutenant, right out of law school, was assigned to defend Roy. The lieutenant did a good job. He got Roy off because he had proved that Roy had been subjected to cruel and inhuman treatment.

Our commanding officer now thought he had better do something nice for Roy, so he sent him to the aircraft engine school. Roy was delighted. This is why he had enlisted in the first place.

Roy came into the barracks one day after school, and bragged that his initials, RPM, were stamped on a little metal plate on *every* aircraft engine. We all thought RPM meant Revolutions Per Minute, but Roy insisted that they were *his* initials.

Civilians had been looking down upon soldiers since time immemorial. My favorite author, Rudyard Kipling, described the civilian-soldier problem very well in his barrack-room ballad, "Tommy:"

> *I went into a public-'ouse to get a*
> *pint o' beer,*
> *The publican 'e up an 'sez, "We serve*
> *no red-coats here."*
> *The girls be'ind the bar they laughed*
> *an' giggled fit to die,*
> *I outs into the street again an' to myself*
> *sez I:*
> *O it's Tommy this, an' Tommy*
> *that, an' "Tommy, go away;"*
> *But it's "Thank you, Mister Atkins,"*
> *when the band begins to play . . .*

Just after I finished photo school in Denver and was sent to Savannah, where a new Army air base was being established, "the band began to play." War clouds were on the horizon. "Keep off the grass" signs disappeared. Civilians smiled at soldiers on sidewalks. Suddenly the "feather merchants" (civilians) were looking for ways to say, "Thank you, Mister Atkins." It was the spring of 1941.

Savannah's city fathers decided that "Mister Atkins" could be thanked by inviting him into their homes on Mother's Day, which was a month away. All of the radio stations cooperated by appealing to the good people of Savannah to, "Invite a soldier into your home for Mother's Day dinner. This will be the first Mother's Day away from home for many of our soldier friends."

This turned out to be the best thing that ever happened to me. "Pop" Durham, my barracks-mate, sat down on my bunk and said,

"Tommy, I've got this girlfriend downtown, and *she* has a girl-friend. They want me to bring a guy over for Mother's Day dinner."

"Well, why me?" I asked.

"Because my girl said it would be nice if I could bring a fellow who has a camera *and* a car."

"*I* have a camera and a car," I said.

"You are the only soldier on this field who *does* have a camera and a car," he replied.

The date was arranged. As the day drew closer, I began to have second thoughts. I was still a bashful, innocent young 21-year-old who had been too shy to go to his high school senior prom. Girls *terrified* me!

"Come on," Pop said, " 'bout time you get your nose out of your books and come out into the *real* world."

It was Sunday—Mother's Day. I put a fresh roll of film in the camera and a dollar's worth of gas in the tank of the 1928 Dodge I had inherited from my father. (Gas was nine cents per gallon on the post) And then we were off to Savannah.

We walked up the long, creaky steps of an ancient Civil War-period apartment house. Pop rang the bell. The door opened and the most beautiful green-eyed brunette I'd ever seen was smiling at us. I swallowed hard.

"Wow!" I thought. "Is *this* one mine?" She wasn't. Mine was out of sight in another part of the house. The rooms were cozy and tastefully restored to look like they did a hundred years ago. Then the disarmingly smooth talk of a real "southern belle" started.

"Did Pop tell you we're having southern-fried chicken?" she asked.

"Yes, he did," I replied. In fact *this* was the main reason I had been motivated to embarrassingly face a couple of strange girls. I'd heard of southern-fried chicken all my life, but being a Yankee, I'd never been *close* to one.

My blind date joined us and said shyly, "I'm Willie." "Not bad," I thought.

The dinner was already on the table and we dug in. It was as good as advertised. The only thing I didn't like was the sweetened iced tea. We didn't pre-sweeten our iced tea at home. In fact, we didn't sweeten it at all.

The girls were nice. I was beginning to loosen up but couldn't take my eyes off Pop's date, Wilma.

"I like your car," Wilma said. She had been the green-eyed apparition in the doorway. This was probably a hint, but her hint was my desire.

"Let's ride around," I said. "Where should we go?"

"Well," Wilma replied, "the azaleas are in full bloom, so let's go to Bonaventure Cemetery."

Cemetery! My very first date and we're going to a *cemetery?*

Wilma continued, "You can get some good pictures of the azaleas there, and see the beautiful Spanish moss hanging down from the trees."

For the next three months I couldn't concentrate on azaleas, Spanish moss, photo lab work or *anything*—only on Pop's girlfriend. I started using every devious and sneaky trick in the book to ease Pop out of the scene. And finally, it happened.

At six o'clock in the evening, August 12, 1941, we said our "I do's" in the First Baptist Church. We and the minister were the only ones there. We went to Morrison's cafeteria for dinner, but I don't remember what we ate. I couldn't believe this had happened to me. My friends back home had selected me to be the least likely to ever get married.

During the meal, my brand-new wife casually mentioned that Willie had fried the Mother's Day chicken.

"She did *what?*"

"Why, Willie fried the chicken, didn't you know?"

"No. I thought *you* did!"

"Oh, Lord," I thought, "I just gave two hard-earned bucks to the preacher and now I find out it was the *other* girl who fried the chicken!"

In two weeks, just as we were settling down to married life, our squadron was invited to participate in the Louisiana maneuvers. Yes, Uncle Sam was beginning to put on his military shoes. The war clouds were getting darker. A foot soldier—ground-pounder —by the name of Colonel Dwight D. Eisenhower had been given the task of getting the troops ready to spring into action when the storm finally hit.

After the hot and tedious trip in a truck convoy from Savannah to Lake Charles, Louisiana, we set up our tents in a large field and dug in to stay for a month.

We quickly erected clusters of pyramidal tents that spread across the field like giant brown anthills. There were latrines at the end of each squadron or company street. GI cans were distributed down the middle of the dirt streets during the hours of darkness, to avoid long trips to the latrine.

Since the nights were cool, and often rainy, we had a little stove in the middle of the tent that looked like an upside-down metal ice cream cone.

The Army Air Corps had flown a few old 1935 B-18 bombers down to attack the Blue Army. This was the type of plane we had used for aerial photo training in Denver. I was to photograph the bomb strikes. It was easy because they dropped five-pound sacks of flour and the white circular splatters really stood out on the red Louisiana soil.

The brass hats tried to feed us some ungodly stuff that might be forced on us in a *real* war. We would have none of that. The feather merchants from town came out to gawk and watch us play soldier. They soon got our message. We wanted *real* food and they were very obliging. I don't remember what the mess sergeant was slopping down on the mess kits, but *I* was eating Oreos, Milky Ways, Cracker Jacks, and all the good stuff I had always loved. The drinking guys were also enjoying bottles of cold Falstaff beer.

The maneuvers were ridiculous—no, laughable—no, *pitiful!* Rain clouds would form every day, followed by a short deluge that turned the red clay to gumbo—then the sun would come out and bake the ground hard again.

The pitiful part, however, wasn't the weather, it was the way we were fighting our mock battles. The ground-pounders didn't all have real guns to train with. Some of the "rifles" were saplings cut from small trees. Some of the machine guns were forked branches with small logs placed across the crotch to make a "gun." The "hand grenades" were cloth Bull Durham tobacco sacks filled with sand.

We weren't much better off in the air corps. We dropped five-pound bags of white flour on the airport runways—or *tried* to. They let me use *real* film in the camera, however.

When we came in to attack the airfield and splattered some flour on a runway, the field was deemed "out of commission." The circular white "hits" were easy to see and photograph.

I wondered if our potential enemy had Bull Durham sacks filled with sand to use in their training.

It was at Fort Dix, our last stop before going overseas, that we took care of a few things. We signed up for $10,000 GI life insurance policies. We filled in the blanks on short pre-printed wills. Our metal dog tags were stamped out on a press and given to us—two tags, one to remain on the dead body and the other for the quartermaster graves registration unit.

Private First Class Hymie Waxman was the only Jewish fellow in our squadron—at least the only one I knew personally, and everybody liked him. He was concerned about the letter "H" (for Hebrew) that had been stamped on his dog tags. We saw him obliterating the letter with his jackknife and asked him why. "Just in case. Just in case," he answered.

One morning while walking on the post, I passed Joe Louis, the heavyweight boxing champion of the world. He was alone and this would have been a fine opportunity to stop and shake his hand, but being a little shy, I passed him without even a smile. He was a private.

Joe was one of my heroes because not only was he from *my* state, but he had "done a job" on Hitler's superman, Max Schmeling, in the ring in New York City in 1938. Schmeling, a German paratrooper and Germany's boxing champ, had made some disparaging remarks about Americans in general and Negroes in particular. Louis was in a rage when he and Schmeling squared off. After two minutes and four seconds, Schmeling was taken to a local hospital in a wretched condition where he recuperated before returning to Germany and the paratroopers.

We boarded a truck convoy at Fort Dix and were driven through downtown Trenton. People lining both sides of the street stood waving and cheering. The good folks of Trenton had set up loudspeakers along the route and "Jersey Bounce" was being played. What a great idea! It was number one on "The Hit Parade" and we were leaving Jersey.

Our trucks stopped at the railroad station, and we jumped out. We were ordered to form in a single file and board the passenger cars. It was impossible to keep everybody heading in the right direction because many of us were looking for and finding our loved ones standing on the platform. I spotted Wilma and ran to her. She was smiling and crying at the same time. I was choked up, but soldiers don't cry. It was a struggle, though, and my first experience of knowing hurt that comes by keeping feelings inside. Feelings not only for Wilma, but for the little addition to our family she was carrying.

I grabbed a window seat on the platform side of the car and stuck my head out to watch my lovely wife slowly fade away. Soldier or no soldier, I had to let the sobs and tears come forth.

I was jolted out of a sound sleep when blinding lights flashed on and a loud metallic voice announced, "Reveille . . . Reveille." The four men swinging in their hammocks above me started climbing down and our first day at sea began.

The mess hall occupied a large area in the middle of the ship three decks above our sleeping quarters. It extended from one side of the ship to the other. Hundreds of hammocks were suspended over the long tables. The clatter of steel mess trays and the constant chatter of hundreds of men made the place sound like a boiler factory. They called this a dining room? Later, thirty of us stood shoulder to shoulder in a small square gray cubicle with cold salt water spraying over our bodies. The soap wouldn't lather. They called this a shower?

The first week out was uneventful. There was a lot of visiting and card playing. Nobody was seasick. We were starting to do a lot of zigzagging, though. There must have been a dozen or more ships in our convoy visible on the horizon. They were *all* zigzagging and constantly changing positions. Cruise ships don't do this.

But then, there are no German submarines stalking them. They played "Jersey Bounce" on the P.A. system. A happy tune, reminding me again of the recent goodbye in Trenton.

We knew we were going to the British Isles. That was the good news. The *bad* news was the "Krauts" knew also. We were all praying they didn't have a torpedo with *Argentina's* name on it.

During this time, I met the guys who were going to be in my photo section. They were Corporal Bennett Tucker, Private Harold Harrington, Private First Class Otto Zinkgraf and Private First Class John Martini. They were all photo lab technicians who had been given to me when our photo officer, Lieutenant Wezak, was reassigned. I was promoted to "acting photo officer."

I was a staff sergeant and had completed all of the ground and advanced aerial photography courses in the Army Air Corps schools at Lowry Field in Denver, Colorado. Wezak never returned. He became the squadron censor.

Lieutenant Wezak had earned his gold bars in a New York City reserve officer's training program in high school. All of our other officers got their commissions in college. After high school, Wezak looked for and found his "dream job," selling peanuts at Yankee Stadium. Although he knew nothing about photography, he got the photo officer job because the table of organization called for this rank, and he was hanging around the squadron office the day that fact was discovered. So much for Army logic.

A few days later, just before midnight, we made our way slowly into the Firth of Clyde and docked. It was raining. We had arrived on Scotland's northwest coast and were now in the land of Macbeth. We had been ordered to have our barracks bags and submachine guns with us on the main deck so we could disembark quickly and board a troop train waiting alongside.

It was midnight when we started going down the gangplanks. It was hard to see much in the darkness, but we could make out *many* gangplanks with lines of men coming down each one. Huge cranes immediately started lowering boxes, trucks, guns, airplanes, and supplies down to the dock. A long train was just a few steps from the ship, and the side doors in each passenger car were open. We shuffled along in single file.

As we shuffle-walked toward the train, a soldier counted us. When the correct number of men to fill a car was determined, he stuck his arm behind the last man and directed the next man, and those following, to another car.

This troop movement went so smoothly and quickly that it seemed like it had been rehearsed. After we were in the car and seated, we noticed that there was another troop train on the next track pointed in the same direction. There was probably a third train to carry the freight, but we couldn't see it.

It had taken two days and two nights to load the *Argentina*, but it looked like they were going to *unload* before daylight.

The train started rolling slowly through the unlighted dock area and into the darkness of the countryside. There were no lights visible anywhere. We couldn't see a flicker of light outside the windows, and only dim blue overhead lights remained on in the car's ceiling.

In the darkness, we heard an English voice say, "Jerry's looking for us, so don't even *think* of turning on a flashlight." Then an American voice, "Boy, we're in a *war* zone. Wonder when we'll see some bombing or something?" English voice again, "Remember, we're under blackout rules. The Jerries like to strafe trains."

The coaches were crowded with soldiers sleeping on top of each other and our car was reeking with the smell of soot, sweat, and tobacco breath. Suddenly we felt the jamming of the brakes, heard the hissing of compressed air, and we were thrown around the jolting coaches.

A Limey voice said, "Air raid alert," and the blue lights went out. We sat there in silence for ten minutes . . . twenty minutes . . . no movement, cold silence. Then the English voice said, "All clear." The blue lights came back on, and there was a short blast of the whistle and jolting of the coaches as the train continued its eastward journey.

The train continued creeping along. The engineer probably couldn't see more than a few feet ahead in the rain and total blackout. We couldn't see lights in houses, cars, or even any railroad signals. Scotland was completely blacked out.

About two hours later the train shuddered to a halt. We could just barely see what was happening. We were in a railroad station and an Englishman on board told us we were in Edinburgh. We pushed the wooden windows down and stuck our heads out. It was still raining. Dozens of women wearing long glistening raincoats were standing on the wooden platform close to the train. They were holding up baskets of cookies and trays of steaming tea. We leaned out the windows, reached down, and eagerly accepted their offering. The smiling women kept repeating, "Welcome, Yanks. Welcome to the war."

We were being welcomed with affection and gratitude. We were among the first Americans over there. We were so new that later on people on the street would stare at us in curiosity.

The night wore on. We slouched in our seats, squirming, trying to get some sleep. When we came to another station and stopped, we pulled the windows down and looked out into the night. All the signs had been removed to confuse any German paratroopers who might have dropped in. When we asked a civilian on the platform where we were, his answer meant nothing to us.

Sometime later dawn brought ghostly gray images into focus. We could now see farm houses, some with thatched roofs, hedgerows, sheep, and camouflaged army trucks called "lorries." We slowed down and finally stopped at another station. The rectangular sign on top of the station house had been painted to remove the name of the place. Word soon spread that we were about forty miles north of London in the town of Molesworth. A fellow standing on the platform shouted, "This is the end of the line, Yanks!"

It was on that troop train that I heard the English being called "Limeys." We learned it was a term used centuries ago to refer to a sailor who sucked on limes while at sea to prevent scurvy. From then on, the English were Limeys, and the Americans were Yanks. No disrespect was intended.

Molesworth Royal Air Force Base

A CONVOY OF TRUCKS WAS WAITING for us at the station—English lorries and a few American 2½-ton 6x6's. My boys and I threw our bags into a lorry and crawled in.

Our trucks dropped us off at the large mess hall on Molesworth's Royal Air Force (RAF) base. It was run by the English RAF, and this was to be our first experience eating English food. Kidney pie for breakfast, and bread and tea, of course. The pie not only *smelled* like the kidneys hadn't been properly drained before cooking, but *tasted* like it. We ate the bread and drank the tea. The putrid-smelling pie was consigned to garbage cans.

We wondered if *all* the meals would be like this. They weren't. They were monotonous, though. Every day we were served boiled mutton, boiled cabbage, boiled potato, boiled brussel sprouts, bread, and tea. Later we got orange marmalade to spread on our bread at breakfast. This was the first I'd ever had. It was delicious.

While we were eating breakfast, a radio connected to loud-speakers kept us in a happy frame of mind. We were listening to the latest music from "Your Hit Parade"—good American music. It stopped and a lady with an "American girl next door" type voice said, "Welcome to Molesworth, Yanks! We've been expecting you since you left New York. Oh, and by the way, don't you think that chap over behind the serving line should stop smoking while he ladles out the kidneys?" We all turned toward the serving line. The chap with the cigarette waved and grinned. What a shock! What *is* this?

The music started again and in the middle of "Don't Sit Under the Apple Tree," sung by the Andrews Sisters, the radio clicked off. An English accent came over the speakers. "Sorry you chaps heard that. We tuned into Axis Sally because she was playing American music. We meant to cut her off before her message. Don't let this bother you. Just enjoy Sally's music and ignore her threats." We all started mumbling to each other, "But she knows we've arrived at Molesworth, and we haven't even been here for more than an hour. If the German spy system is *this* good, we're dead ducks." But during the rest of our stay in England, Axis Sally became our favorite disc jockey, and we learned not to take her threats too seriously.

We were introduced to our new home. It was a long, narrow, tarpaper-covered wooden building with a round tin pipe projecting up from a crude-looking space heater, which was not much more than a swelling in the pipe. It was called a hut and the "stove" was called a "tortoise." The bunks were double-decked, narrow, spaced about four feet apart, and made of two frames of angle iron. The crossbars were also iron; they supported three excelsior-filled canvas squares that were placed end-to-end to form a mattress. These were called "English biscuits." As we rolled over during the night the biscuits would separate with the top and bottom ones sliding off the rack. This would leave us draped over the center one. We wanted to fasten them together but were told we could not alter British property. "Mess with those biscuits and your head will roll and your hide will be nailed to the door of the hut!" Good old Lieutenant Bubba Goik. Bubba was the lowest-ranking officer in our squadron and we all suspected that he had also been a low-ranking civilian.

No fires were started in the tortoises and the nights were very cold and damp. There were two blackout curtains at each door. We were instructed to let the first one drop, stand between them until we couldn't see any light, then open the other one to go out into the darkness. We had to walk over a half mile to the mess hall.

The next day was somewhat more exciting. We spotted our A-2 aluminum photo lab trailer parked next to a small building. On further examination, we found that the building was the RAF base photo lab. We went inside and found Sergeant Helms, the base photographer, sitting at his desk.

"Welcome to the war, Yanks." Seems like we had heard that before. "Nice lookin' trailer ya got out there. Do ya all sleep in it?"

"Wish we could, but it's not for sleeping, it has two air-conditioned labs in it—one for processing film and the other for printing." Helms was impressed.

Sergeant Helms spent the next hour explaining the English lab equipment and introducing us to their method of drying film, identifying negatives, and most important of all, what a Naafi wagon was. The Naafi wagon, Helms explained, is a "mobile slop shop" that parks near the photo lab every afternoon at four o'clock and sells tea and cookies.

"Naafi? Is that the make of the vehicle?"

"Blimey, Yank, ain't ya never heard of the Naafi?"

"No."

"You Yanks have a thing called USO and they pass out cookies to servicemen, don't they?"

"Yes, we have a USO and they pass out cookies."

"Well, Naafi is like that. Naafi stands for Navy, Army, and Air Force Institute."

"Now if ya will excuse me, I'm trottin' off to me new assignment in Podington. I 'ave officially turned this mess over to you. Keep your socks up, mates. Cheerio."

He left, and one of the men remarked, "Wasn't it interesting the way Helms quick-dried that negative? He took it out of the wash, threw it into a tray of grain alcohol briefly, held it up, and set fire to it. The fire burned so fast that the emulsion didn't reticulate and his hand wasn't burned. *That's* something they didn't teach us in photo school."

The meals didn't improve. Now we were getting the same old thing every day—"victory pie." It consisted of potatoes, carrots, parsnips, and turnips. We would visit various towns looking for hamburgers, but the Brits didn't know what we were talking about.

The Salvation Army passed out pocket-sized New Testaments. The Ten Commandments were printed in the front. "Thou Shalt Not Kill" had not been edited out. We thought they were great gifts. One fellow said, "The pages are just the right size for rolling cigarettes."

Things were improving in the huts. We now had pictures of Chili Williams in her two-piece polka-dot swimsuit posted all over the place. She had suddenly jumped ahead of Betty Grable as our "number one pinup."

British Broadcasting Company: Berlin radio last night broadcast this appeal to the German People. "The crews of many planes shot down during flights over German territory and compelled to make a forced landing have recently, in many cases, attempted to escape being taken prisoner by clever camouflage or flight!

"The German civil population are asked to render active assistance and to maintain greatest watchfulness. All incidents, even the seemingly unimportant ones, may be of the greatest possible value for the defense of the country."

Sightseeing

WHEN WE GOT TO MOLESWORTH, a story was going around that the commanding officer at a nearby air base, a reserve lieutenant colonel, newly arrived in England and fresh from his job as a postmaster in Kansas, had done some lousy flying and had "washed out" an airplane. He was relieved of his command and promoted to the rank of full colonel and given the job of developing vegetable gardens around the area bases. He was a personal friend of Vice-President Harry S. Truman.

We were seldom bombed, but frequent bombings nearby gave us a spectacular light show with the flash of bombs and an occasional Jerry plane going down in flames.

There was very little photo work to keep us occupied during the next four months and we used this time for sightseeing. Fortunately, the officer in charge of each section was issued a jeep, and I was the acting officer in charge of our little photo section. "Jeep" was the shortened version of General Purpose, or G.P., the vehicle's official designation.

One morning I asked Hal Harrington to accompany me to the city of Cambridge. This was the home of 850-year-old Cambridge University. We had both studied about Cambridge in English history and hadn't thought we would ever have a chance to see it.

We drove the jeep over to the fuel dump (a GI gas station), filled it up and were on our way.

When we arrived in the city, the first stop we made was at a bookstore where we bought some books about the history of Cambridge and a couple of large notebooks. Harrington and I had decided to keep an accurate account of our overseas tour so we would have something to show our folks when we got home. I had already started making marginal notes in my pocket-sized Bible, but could go into much more detail with a notebook.

Cambridge was a beautiful place with dozens of ancient ivy-covered brick buildings and footpaths cutting across the campuses. We had just left and started walking toward town when a tall, imposing-looking gentleman with gray temples and a dark business suit came up from behind us, placed his hands on our shoulders and said, "Hello, soldiers, are you ready for lunch?"

"Yes, as a matter of fact we were on our way to find a restaurant."

"Come with me. Be my guest at the Rotary Club luncheon. I was just on my way." We accepted his surprising invitation.

During the five-minute walk to the club, the gentleman explained the Rotarians had agreed that the first American soldier any of them spotted was to be brought to a meeting as the guest of honor. He asked us about our trip to England and a few questions about our impressions of "the old country." I did all the talking because Harrington usually avoided conversation due to his stuttering.

Some children ran up to us and asked, "Any gum, chums?" The gentleman said, "We have no chewing gum here and the little beggars have already heard you Americans *always* have some in your pockets."

"Sir, how do you keep your lawns looking so beautiful? Our *golf courses* aren't this nice."

"Very little effort. Regular fertilizing, regular cutting and at least 300 years produces a fine lawn."

Harrington and I were probably the first American GIs to visit Cambridge. We were among the first Americans to arrive in England, and the great majority of the troops who had arrived with us were out looking for pubs, not culture.

We were just a couple of "dog faces"—only *pawns* on the chessboard of war—not knights or bishops. Surely, we thought, the gentleman would rather have taken a captain or a major with him.

We were led into a stately looking two-story vine-covered brick building with no identifying sign of any kind on it. At the top of a flight of stairs, we saw open double doors with a uniformed character right out of a Dickens novel wearing knickers and long white stockings standing there stiffly, greeting the members as they entered. The character smiled, bowed his head slowly and said, "Good afternoon, gentlemen."

Instant culture shock! It was a quantum leap from the crowded, noisy Molesworth mess hall to this stately quiet Edwardian hall. It was long and narrow, with large paintings on the walls of noble-looking gentlemen wearing wigs and fancy fluted white collars. The long oak table had been set with tall sterling candelabra, finger bowls, fresh flowers and other things we had seen only in movies of the rich and famous.

Our smiling sponsor bowed slightly, motioned with his arm, indicating two chairs for us, and sat down on our right. A gentleman at the head of the table asked us to rise. He bowed his head, as did everybody else, and recited a Rotarian's prayer.

The meal was served in a regal and formal manner. Uniformed waiters dressed like the doorman brought silver platters to our sides, removed the domed covers and lowered them so we could see if the roasted Cornish hens were suitable. They were, of course. And so was everything else during the hour-long meal. Harrington put his lips close to my ear and whispered, "G-g-g-good Lord, the w-w-w-war could be l-l-l-lost while these guys are e-e-e-eating their chow."

The dishes and finger bowls were quickly cleared and crystal chalices were placed before us. Then came the pouring of the wine, a show within a show. The wine stewards retreated, and the gentleman at the head of the table stood and raised his chalice to eye level. The rest of us did the same.

Head man: "God save the King!"

A chorus from the room: "God save the King!"

Head man: "God save President Roosevelt!"

Chorus: "God save President Roosevelt!"

Head man: "God save our American guests!"

Chorus . . . They were asking God to save *us,* and we were too embarrassed to join them, but we felt very honored, special and appreciated.

We walked down the stairway hardly believing what we had just experienced. War rationing had reduced the average British table to the bare fundamentals for survival. But this had not been an average British table by any stretch of the imagination. We had talked to some of the civilians and learned that they were each rationed one pint of milk every other day, two eggs per week, one-half pound of sugar and a few ounces of tea each week.

God save that fine old English gentleman who took us up to fantasyland on that unforgettable day in Cambridge!

Axis Sally was still taunting us with her broadcasts. One day we heard her telling us that since we had ignored her advice about going back to the States, she might as well tell us where the best pubs were in our area and which girls had the "social" disease called "the clap." She did.

We were amused, but not surprised, when Sally asked us if we were enjoying the SOS (Slop On a Shingle) we were now getting for breakfast. SOS was an American invention consisting of creamed chipped beef on toast. It was better than the Limeys' kidneys and mutton. We were thankful that the Limeys had turned their kitchen over to American cooks.

London Daily Express: "Forts" Bomb Ports By Day—Masses of Allied planes were masters of the skies over a wide area of Northern France yesterday during a dual offensive in which U.S. Flying Fortresses and Bostons made their biggest daylight attack across the Channel.

One afternoon, the five of us left the base in our jeep for some more sightseeing. It was fun driving on the "wrong" side of the road. The English said that *we* drove on the wrong side in the States. After all, *they* had traveled like this for hundreds of years. Why?

"Well, Yank, it's like this. Way back in medieval times when men on horseback traveled through the countryside, they were all armed with swords because of dangerous highwaymen and other undesirable characters. Nearly everyone was right-handed and when they passed another horseman on the road, they could grab their swords in their right hands if need be, and start swinging."

We had already learned that the English were doing things *their* way long before the Americans did—speaking English, for instance, and riding or driving on the "wrong" side of the road.

Before heading out into the countryside, we drove to Molesworth to see the damage left by a German bomber that had gone straight down with a full load of bombs. It was awesome. A whole square block had been leveled. We photographed a two-story house with nothing remaining but the back and a side wall. A stairway went nowhere and a fireplace was hanging in the air. An undamaged vase was on the mantle. We then headed east to see the countryside and drove until we were lost.

We had lost track of where we were because all road signs and markings had been removed so that the Jerries who dropped in by parachute would have a hard time knowing where *they* were. By now it was completely dark, and to make bad matters worse, one of the famous "pea soup" fogs had settled down, making driving impossible. There were no other vehicles on the road. Only a dumb Yank would be out in this stuff. Of course no lights were visible because of the total blackout.

I was driving, and had Harrington sitting on the hood getting directions from Tucker, who was walking in front feeling his way along the side of the road. We crept along for about thirty minutes and seemed to be getting nowhere. Suddenly, and without knowing why, I said, "Tucker, we're in a village and are coming to a street corner. Guide us to the right and we'll stop because there is a police station there."

I stopped the jeep, got out and walked to a building I couldn't see, and felt my way up three steps and knocked on the door. A policeman parted the blackout curtains and invited me in. There was another policeman in the room removing his coat and cap. Two steaming cups of tea were sitting on a desk.

"I'm Constable Weaver," said the gentleman who let me in, "and this cop's name is Havens. He came in just ahead of you."

I introduced myself and mentioned that this was the first time I had ever heard a policeman use the word "cop." "I thought that was sort of a disrespectful name someone in Chicago had probably tagged the police with," I said. "We used to play cops and robbers when I was a kid."

"Well, you chaps got it from us," Weaver said. "Cop stands for Constable On Patrol, so you see, it isn't disrespectful at all."

I explained that four of my buddies were sitting in a jeep outside in the dark. Cop Weaver picked up a blackout flashlight and led me down the sidewalk and over to the jeep. The boys came in and we were all offered cups of tea. The cops didn't poke fun at us for being out on a night like this as we had expected, but gave us a comfortable cell where we spent the night.

It was crystal clear the next morning. We thanked the officers for their kindness and returned to our base at Molesworth. I felt that finding that police station was more than coincidence.

Thick fog rolling in over the airfields had caused many deaths of airmen trying to land after a mission. The English solved this problem with "FIDO."

FIDO, or Fog, Intense, Dispersal Operation, consisted of large burners placed along the runways. The tremendous heat generated by them created clear "tunnels" through which planes could land safely. When the FIDO was turned on it roared like a hundred blast furnaces and the illumination created an eerie glow in the fog over the runways.

Express Air Reporter: Fighter pilots of the RAF yesterday gave new praise to the crews of the American Fortress and Liberator bombers for the skill they showed in fitting into the Anglo-American tactical plan in the raid on Lille last Friday.

The way that plan was followed—105 German fighters were destroyed or damaged for the loss of four bombers—makes one of the most fascinating stories of the air war.

My boys had been assigned to me just a short time earlier and I didn't know them very well. I was curious, so one day when we were eating our chow, I asked them about themselves.

"Martini, you say you had never been out of New York City before being drafted?"

"Never out of Queens."

"What did you do after high school?"

"Hawked long-stem roses at subway stations."

"Harrington, you were drafted too, weren't you?"

"Wa-wa-well sort of. My da-da-da-dad was the chief of po-po-police in Ca-Ca-Carterette, but one day a judge a-a-asked me if I'd rather get six mo-mo-months in the pokey or go to the A-A-A-Army."

"Tucker, how about you?"

"Wasn't doin' much so I enlisted."

"Zinkgraf, what's your story?"

"I was working for a supplier to the cheese industry when Pearl Harbor came along. Decided not to wait to be drafted, so I enlisted January 2, 1942. Six months later after we got over here in England, I got my draft notice."

It was time to start trading the photo supplies we didn't think we would need for anything else in the photo line we probably *could* use. After loading the jeep with surplus odds and ends, I drove to the nearby base in Podington. This was another RAF base that had been turned over to the Americans.

I was entering the photo section when someone a couple of buildings away shouted, "Hey, Tommy, where did *you* come from?" It was John "NMI" Kucer, the private who had worked for me in the photo lab in Savannah. We had kidded him about the NMI because this is what the Army placed on a man's record when he had "No Middle Initial."

I was surprised to see John, especially the way he was dressed, because he was now wearing an officer's uniform. We went inside and sat down at his desk. John then explained that he had been in the ROTC program in high school in Rochester, New York, and had suddenly gone from a private to a second lieutenant because of a shortage of officers.

"Tommy, I'm in big trouble," he said softly so his men couldn't hear him. "You remember that you had me ferrotyping prints and cleaning up after you in Savannah, but I knew *nothing* about aerial cameras. Now I'm stuck with the installation of K-17s and intervalometers and electrical cables and things I've never *seen* before.

Will you stick around for awhile and check me out on those things in a B-17?"

"John," I said, "I really came over here to see if I could trade some things, but you've got a bigger problem than *I* have, so give me a couple of your men and we'll try to check them out."

"The guys think I know all about this stuff," he said, "so let's just take a camera, an intervalometer and the cables out to a B-17 and you install them and I'll take notes."

At the plane, we went up into the radio operator's compartment and lifted the trap door in the floor exposing the camera well and I explained the installation of the K-17c camera and accessories. We had to go over the electrical wiring and cables a few times while John took notes, but finally he had it.

It took the rest of the day, but by the time I left, John was a more confident photo officer than he had been before we ran into each other. I was pleased with myself.

London Daily Express: United States Flying Fortresses and Liberator bombers destroyed 48 German planes in the raid on Lille on Friday, it was officially disclosed last night. Many more were probably destroyed and damaged.

Last night checking up on the stories of pilots and crews was still going on, and a U.S. Army Headquarters spokesman said, "When the final count is taken the total German losses will be found to be staggering."

The Black Swan

EVERY SQUADRON HAD A "CHARACTER." We were lucky—we had *two*. They were Stanke and Sturm, an inseparable couple of privates with burlesque-sounding names. Stanke and Sturm, however, saw nothing funny about it. They said, "With names like ours, we'll probably form a law partnership after the war."

By the time the sun set on paydays, Stanke and Sturm were broke. They would find a blackjack game going on in one of the barracks and join in. We were paid in English pound notes which were worth $4.03 each, and the guys, not being used to this, would throw a pound note down on the table as though it was a dollar. So a fellow could blow his entire month's pay in a matter of minutes. Stanke and Sturm didn't have a chance. Not only were they lousy blackjack players, but they never did figure out the exchange rate of their money.

One payday, after they had lost their money in a game, our characters told John Martini that even though they were penniless, they were going to The Black Swan and have a couple of pints. Martini doubted that stingy old Perkins, the publican over there, would give a pint of beer to his own mother.

"Okay, Martini, come on along tonight, and we'll show you," said Sturm. "We've got a plan." Martini came to me and said, "Hey, Sarge, Stanke and Sturm are going to try to pull a fast one on old Perkins tonight at The Black Swan. Let's go along and see if they can do it."

The Black Swan was one of our favorite watering holes. It was an ancient pub a quarter of a mile from our front gate, in the tiny village of Old Weston. There were about ten houses, a store, a church and The Black Swan. Nobody knew the age of the pub, but the Shadbolts, who lived next door, told us their house had been built in 1622 and The Black Swan was old at *that* time.

That evening, an hour after sundown, the four of us started down the road to Old Weston—Stanke and Sturm, Martini and I.

That afternoon at six we walked down the road to The Black Swan

We walked leisurely along the hedgerows and noticed that aerial bombs had been placed end-to-end close to the hedges so Jerry couldn't spot them from the air with his reconnaissance cameras.

We arrived at The Black Swan, pushed the blackout curtains aside, and went in. Cigarette smoke was so thick in the dimly lit interior that it resembled the infamous London fog. On our right was a long bar running half the length of the room. Perkins, the publican, stood behind the bar with three tall levers sticking up in front of him. When he drew a pint of beer into a mug, he placed one hand on top of the desired lever, tilted it slightly toward himself, and the dark, warm, uncarbonated beer (or ale) drained into the mug that he held in his other hand. We had learned that it was no use to order a glass or bottle of beer, because a pint in a mug is what you'd get anyway.

"Pints have been served in our pubs from time immemorial, and we're not about to change it simply because you Yanks come over here and ask for a bloody bottle."

To the left of the bar, and filling the rest of the room, were a dozen or so round wooden tables. A dart board hung on the back wall. Blackout curtains covered the windows.

There was another employee in The Black Swan, the barmaid. She delivered pints from the bar to the tables. She was obviously frustrated and fed up with the constant "cute" remarks coming from the Yanks.

The publican sold cigarettes singly over the counter. The barmaid was not allowed to bring them to the tables.

Stanke and Sturm ambled up to the bar and stationed themselves directly in front of old Perkins and his levers. Our two characters then initiated their plan.

Stanke: "There's two pints in a quart."

Sturm: "You're crazy. There are *four* pints in a quart."

Stanke: "Bet you a shilling there's *two* pints in a quart."

Sturm: "Ya got a deal. Hey, pub, how many pints in a quart?"

Publican: "Blimey, Yank, there's two pints and always *has* been."

Stanke thanked the publican and the two of them wandered over to a table near the far wall. As they were sitting down, Sturm held up his hand, snapped his fingers and said, "Hey, barmaid."

When the barmaid arrived at their table, Sturm said, "Give us two pints on the house."

The already frustrated barmaid said, "Wot ya mean two on the 'ouse?"

Stanke: "That's right, woman, two pints on the house. That's what the pub told us."

Stanke stood up, faced the bar, held up two fingers and shouted, "Hey, pub, didn't ya say two pints?"

Publican: "Yes, that's right—*two*."

This brilliant scheme had worked so well that Stanke and Sturm started making the rounds of *all* the pubs in Northamptonshire. It always worked.

London Daily Express: United States Flying Fortresses made their biggest daylight raid on occupied France yesterday, rounding off a continuous day and night blitz by Allied planes on enemy targets.

In the raid on France three squadrons of Flying Fortresses pounded the Nazi Marshalling yards at Rouen, while Bostons sent a rain of bombs on Le Havre docks. Many fires were started.

The President's Son and the Vicar's Daughter

ONE MORNING, CAPTAIN VAN CLEAVE, our squadron commanding officer, called me into his office. I was just beginning to know this man and already respected him. He was tall and slender and wore horn-rimmed glasses. Van Cleave had been called to active duty from his position as dean of students at a small midwestern college. It was probably his work with men our age that made him so popular as our commanding officer (CO). He "went by the book" but was always fair and honest with us.

"Sergeant Thompson, I'd like you to gather up your paperwork and move over to the base headquarters building. You'll be sharing an office with three other heads of photo sections. By the way, one of them is Lieutenant Colonel Elliott Roosevelt, the President's son."

"Sir, do you mean I am to sit in with some officers?"

"Don't let it bother you. You are an *acting* photo officer and they will accept you."

Captain Van Cleave adjusted a gold ring on his finger, held his hand out toward me and said, "By the way, I'd like you to see if Colonel Roosevelt is wearing a Masonic ring. There will be an emblem on it like this. His father is a Mason and so is King George and Prime Minister Churchill. I'm just curious."

"Yes, Sir."

I located the office and went inside. It was a square room with a desk in each corner. At first I felt a little out of place because the other men were all commissioned officers, and I was a non-commissioned officer. Since I was an *acting* photo officer, however, and the base commander wanted all of the unit heads to be together, I fit that category so didn't let it bother me.

It usually happens that a "rotten egg" shows up in every group. The rotten egg sitting in one corner was Lieutenant Colonel Elliott

Roosevelt. It soon occurred to me that he had not achieved that lofty rank because of a knowledge of photography, but because he was the son of the President of the United States.

I wasn't sure why Captain Van Cleave was so interested in finding out what kind of rings Colonel Roosevelt wore, but I was able to report that he wore *no* rings.

Roosevelt had a habit of disappearing for three or four days, and then returning long enough to put his feet up on his desk, lean back, lace his fingers behind his head and relate the details of his conquests in London. I knew that rank had its privileges, but I was not impressed.

I had brought our K-20 aerial camera into the office for disassembly and cleaning in preparation for future use. The three officers, who had never been near a photo school, were impressed. I had taken the compur-rapid shutter apart and spread the 109 pieces out in sequence on the desk top. Breathe a little hard and a fragile brass diaphragm leaf might disappear. Watchmaker-type work. Mix up the layout sequence and you've *had* it.

Returning to the desk after a five-minute break, I felt that all eyes in the room were on me. It didn't take long to understand the reason. The 109 pieces weren't going back into place the way they had come out. I *knew* I hadn't made a mistake in the layout. I sat there pondering the problem when suddenly Roosevelt jumped to his feet and started roaring with laughter. He left the room still laughing. One of the other officers, a captain, walked over to my desk, placed a hand on my shoulder and said, "You didn't make a mistake, Sergeant, the colonel mixed up the pieces. I'm sure you didn't know it, but the President's son is a practical joker."

And I had thought all Roosevelts were nice people.

London Daily Express: On Friday approximately a thousand American bombers and fighters attacked Bremen, whose shipbuilding yards have one of the largest outputs of submarines in the Fatherland.

Some of the Fortresses and Liberators fought it out with as many as a hundred enemy planes. For a loss of 39 of our own planes, 56 Luftwaffes were destroyed.

Zinkgraf and I visited the beautiful ancient church in Old Weston one Sunday afternoon. We walked along the high bushy hedgerows that formed the fences along every field and lined every road. As usual, large aerial bombs were lying end-to-end against the hedges, even in the church yard.

We were looking at the graves of four Royal Canadian Air Force airmen who had recently been buried near the church wall when the Vicar, who lived in an adjacent stone house, came over and introduced himself. He told us the church building was between five and six hundred years old.

It was a classic old English structure. The walls were constructed with large stones, which had been brought down from a quarry in Wales and hand-hewn into perfect cubic ashlars. The pointed steeple rose to about 70 feet.

We walked inside and found that the aisle from the front door to the altar was covered with a sprinkling of straw. The Vicar explained, "Around three hundred years ago, a parishioner died and left a great amount of money to the church. He made one request, however. Straw must be spread in the aisle the day of his funeral and each year on the anniversary of his funeral."

"Why do you suppose he did that?" Zinkgraf asked.

"Well, the story has been passed down that the old chap had always been annoyed by the noise made by men wearing hobnailed boots clomping down the stone aisle to their place in the congregation."

"How long will this custom continue?" I asked. "Indefinitely," he answered.

By this time, the Vicar's daughter had joined us. She was probably eighteen years old. The Vicar introduced her as Mavis and told us she would show us around. He then left the building. Mavis said, "Welcome, Yanks. I'm not married." "Oh, boy," I thought, "this one is looking for a rich American and didn't waste a minute letting us know she's available." She was simply dressed and homely with a pinched face and a pointed nose. She was spare and lean—almost emaciated. She had no bosom and no bottom.

The Vicar's daughter said, "I'd like to take you chaps up into the belfry so you can see the countryside. You can even see your air field from up there." Otto and I thought this was a good idea and followed her to a small narthex at the front of the church below the steeple. There was an ancient wooden ladder going straight up into the bell tower.

Mavis explained, "I won't be able to ring the bells for you. There's a government order that the bells can be rung only for an invasion warning. I'll go first and you chaps follow me." As she started up the ladder, her full skirt filled out from the draft. Zinkgraf and I looked up at this unbelievable scene and I said, "Otto, you go first."

"I'm not going up that ladder behind her, *you* go first," he replied. We looked at each other and slowly shook our heads. *No way!* Otto called to the girl, who was already pretty far up the ladder, and yelled, "Thank you very much, Mavis, but we just remembered we have to get back to the field right away."

The Black Troops

WHITE AND NEGRO SOLDIERS WERE SEGREGATED. Our facilities were several miles apart. None of the Negroes were combat soldiers. We had heard the brass thought they couldn't be trusted in combat situations. They drove trucks and worked in supply depots and on the docks. Their officers, however, were always white.

At first we were overwhelmed with disbelief when we saw Negro dogfaces strolling arm-in-arm down city streets with white English girls. Our deep south buddies were *livid!*

What could we do? The Negroes had told the naive, gullible girls that they were American Indians—and they had money to throw around. We were paid three times as much as our British counterparts and the "Brylcreem boys" were losing out. Brylcreem was an English hair cream that slicked hair down like Rudolf Valentino's and the British ground troops used this sarcastic way of referring to the RAF boys.

"Just look at that buck," one of our South Carolina buddies said, "he's got a blonde on his arm and a grin so wide all of his ivories are showing."

"Do what *they* do, stupid," his companion said. "Show 'em a wad of money and tell 'em *you* are a *white* Indian."

We heard another southern fella shout at a Negro soldier walking with a white English girl, "Hey, ya dumb broad, don't have nothin' ta do with them Nigras. They got tails and they howl at the moon."

The southerner knew he was safe. The military police—MPs— had been ordered to shoot Negro soldiers if they "got out of line." This was only a rumor so I asked an MP.

"You mean you would actually shoot a Negro soldier just because he's black?"

"Yeah, why not—just another nigger."

I couldn't believe this was happening. The only Negro I'd known before going into the Army was Louis Woodman, a *great* athlete in high school. He was one of my heroes. He was smart in class and could out-run and out-jump *everybody*. I used to wish I was black and could be like him.

Also, wasn't the Heavyweight Boxing Champion Joe Louis, "The Brown Bomber," everybody's hero? Had the brave "Buffalo Soldiers who helped tame the west" been forgotten?

The Limey soldiers had three things against the bloody Yanks. "They are oversexed, overpaid—and over *here.*"

High Wycombe

THE NAAFI WAGON NEVER MISSED. Every day at four o'clock it parked near the photo building, and we had our tea and cookies. I always used this opportunity to leave my office in the headquarters building and meet the photo boys to see how they were doing. The tea wasn't made like we had it at home. It was prepared with milk and sugar and we couldn't fix it the way we wanted it. Everybody in the vast British Empire probably made their hot tea the same way. Sort of held them together, I supposed.

The boys were all happy they were "splashing hypo" again. In fact, they had gone into the portrait business. All of the air crew members had come in to the lab to have ID shots made of themselves wearing civilian clothes. Our raids had already started over France. The boys weren't at all sure the military ID photos made the Americans look like French farmers.

Captain Van Cleave asked me to prepare for a few days away from the base and advised me to take a camera and a lot of film. I gassed up the jeep and headed for High Wycombe, a village where the British Bomber Command was located. American Brigadier General Ira C. Eaker was in the process of setting up our headquarters operation there also.

I drove through the checkerboard squares of the English countryside, which were dotted with sheep. Right from the start I liked England. I had expected it to be green because our school books *said* it was green, but I hadn't expected it to be *this* green. I was in awe of this age-matured country where buildings less than 500 years old were called "new." And, for the first time in my life, I understood that foreign people look just like we do but act and think differently.

I wondered if the Germans were really as different from the English and Americans as our propaganda peddlers and politicians claimed them to be. It seemed to me that with men like Beethoven and Mozart from that area, the *present* generation couldn't have deteriorated too far. The exception, of course, was Hitler.

The beautiful village of High Wycombe was about twenty miles west of London. Bomber headquarters was situated on the most lovely grounds I had ever seen. The large headquarters building was formerly an exclusive girls' school called Wycombe Abbey. There was a green sweep of lawns sloping gently down to a reflecting lake, bordered with weeping willow trees whose branches touched the water. Several graceful white swans glided leisurely along in this peaceful picture-postcard setting.

I found the billeting office and was shown to my room. It was a small cubicle with a bed, a dresser, a large wooden wardrobe, a desk and chair. Lace curtains covered the window.

Each bedroom, still dainty and feminine, was unchanged from the time girls from "upper-crust" families had occupied them. There was a little electric bell button on the wall beside each bed. A small card beneath the button said, "Ring twice for mistress." I later learned that the first night the Americans occupied the rooms, they kept the duty officer awake all night ringing the bells.

It was already getting dark, so I found the dining room and had a good American supper. After the meal another staff sergeant and I walked out to the edge of the lake and sat down. He had told me we would see a light and sound show in the sky over London.

In less than an hour it was completely dark with millions of stars visible in a cloudless sky. We heard the distant droning of engines.

"Here they come," the sergeant said.

"Germans?"

"Yes, and they are high tonight."

The London air raid sirens started wailing and long slim fingers of light stabbed the sky, weaving back and forth. In about five minutes we heard the muffled sound of bombs exploding and saw the flashes of anti-aircraft shells high in the sky. In another five minutes the "show" was over and the air raid sirens wailed all clear.

The alert sirens made an up-and-down wailing sound that

lasted about three minutes. The all clear was a long single note without any wailing.

The next morning I reported to the office and was told that the officer I needed to see had not returned from a short trip.

"Been to London?" a lieutenant asked me."

"Not yet," I replied.

"Why don't you drive in and look it over? Come back tomorrow and Major Lay will be here. He's the officer you will be working with."

I had heard about the damage in London and was anxious to see it. I really wasn't prepared for the massive and overwhelming destruction that spread before me as I drove into the center of the city.

Whole blocks of buildings were skeletons with debris lying in the streets. Coils of barbed wire were strung around some of the buildings—probably government facilities. Sandbags piled up on sidewalks rose slightly above store windows. Camouflaged Army lorries and cars were creeping up and down the littered streets. There were more people wearing uniforms than civilian clothing.

Fire hoses were spread around like giant spaghetti. The odor of death—people or animals?—rose from beneath the deep rubble. Barricades were placed across streets to keep people away because crazily tilted buildings threatened to collapse at any moment.

Stacks of rubble and wreckage were everywhere, jagged half-standing walls, empty houses that could be seen through. Roofless homes. Deep craters in the gardens. Cars and doubledecked buses twisted into grotesque shapes. I wondered how so many people could have survived such a maddening holocaust.

My question was answered when I began to notice shelter signs posted on lamp posts and buildings everywhere. They were black metal plates with a big white letter "S," and underneath the word "Shelter" was printed. Each sign also had a white arrow pointing to a building or tube (subway station). There were also signs pointing to fire stations and first-aid posts.

There was a lot of military activity in the parks and on the large grounds surrounding some of the buildings. Barrage balloon stations and anti-aircraft units were dug into circular pits with sand

The Limey ack-ack crews were spread around in Hyde Park and Kensington Gardens.

They were sprawled all over the floor in the Picadilly Underground Station.

bags piled up around them. We had seen the balloons and heard the ack-ack fire from High Wycombe, so I thought it would be interesting to see them up close.

The balloons were being operated by Army Territorial Service (ATS) girls. The Limey soldiers had substituted a shorter word for Territorial. I spoke to one of the brown-uniformed ladies and asked a few questions. Before going into the technicalities of her job, however, she told me boastfully that before the war started, she had been a student actress at Leslie Howard's studio.

"Leslie Howard," she said, "is the star of "Gone With the Wind." This was a new movie, and I had thought that *Clark Gable* was the star—but over here, it was *Mr. Howard.*

The ATS girl told me that hundreds of balloons like hers floated over London. I looked up and saw her silver balloon above the scattered clouds. "It's up there about 7,500 feet on its steel cable," she said. "We do this to discourage low-flying German aircraft."

I then walked over to a large anti-aircraft gun. Three others were in the park and were separated by about 20 yards. The gun barrels were sticking nearly straight up. There were several men around each gun pit.

I approached a sergeant who was wearing a headphone and asked him to explain how they operated. I told him we had probably seen some of his work from the safety of High Wycombe.

"About a dozen men are stationed at each gun—sometimes more. There are four guns in our battery. The gunman sits here in this metal bucket seat on the gun platform. Some of the men work the dials here on this panel, and others load and fire the gun. Other men carry the shells from the lorries to the storage pits."

I looked at a stack of shells and was surprised by their size. They were smaller than I thought they would be. They were about as long as my arm, but only three or four inches or so in diameter. I asked about this.

"Actually these are the big ones," the sergeant explained. "They are 90 millimeters and we use them for high altitude work."

There were also six huge searchlights mounted on lorries in the park. We had seen their thin beams stabbing and sweeping the black sky 20 miles away in High Wycombe. One of the searchlight operators said, "Sometimes we catch handkerchief bombs drifting slowly down through the beams of our lights and there is nothing we can do about them but just follow them down until they explode."

A tall, thin civilian with long, black hair and a full beard was standing on a box in the park preaching from a sheaf of papers that he held in his left hand, raising his voice and shaking his right fist in the air. Everybody was walking past without even glancing at him. I slowed down and looked at him as he was raising his cool and precise English voice and saying, "You must realize the inevitability of the future!"

In a different part of the park another man on a box was also preaching to nobody in particular. I left the park and walked past a cinema where a line of men and women in uniform and a sprinkling of civilians were queued up in front of a theater. A "barker" was standing by the curb holding up an orange and shouting that it would be auctioned off inside.

Since there were still very few Americans in London yet, it was interesting to see people on the streets stop and say, "Look, there's an American." It made me feel like a celebrity.

When I got back to the jeep, I found two English soldiers standing next to the flat hood. They were using the front of the jeep for a table. They were eating fish and chips that had been placed on newspapers. One of them said, "Whadda ya say, Yank— trade a pack of Camels for a box of Players cigarettes?"

Later that afternoon I saw many English soldiers and civilians strolling casually down the streets holding newspapers containing this typical English fish delicacy. They had bought them from street corner vendors who fried the fish and potatoes right on the spot and dumped each portion onto a few pages of old newspapers for easy carrying and to absorb the oil.

The next morning, I reported to Major Beirne Lay, Jr., and as soon as I met him, I remembered where I had heard his unusual name. He was a Hollywood screenwriter and had written one of my favorite aviation films, "I Wanted Wings." It was about his Air Corps training at Randolph Field in Texas.

Beirne (pronounced Bernie) and I covered Bomber Headquarters, now the 8th Air Force Headquarters, from top to bottom. He wrote about what we saw and I photographed it for the historical archives of the new 8th Air Force. This took several days.

I told Major Lay that I had been in London and how it would be impossible to visualize New York City or Chicago in such a condition. Beirne had been there, and he agreed.

One afternoon after work, Beirne asked if I would like to go to London with him to attend a concert by the London Symphony Orchestra in Albert Hall. We had discovered that we were both Mozart lovers. I doubted that his officer friends were. I told him I would like nothing better, but Nazi bombers were pounding the city practically every night. He laughed and said, "Well, maybe they'll bomb High Wycombe tonight while we are in London."

Beirne had a jeep. He wanted to drive because he said he liked to drive in England.

Since London was not far from High Wycombe, we were at the outskirts of the city in a short time. It was still daylight. The concert would start at 8 p.m., so this gave us plenty of time to drive around the city for sightseeing.

We saw very little damage until we got close to the Paddington Underground Station. From there all the way into the central city we had to drive around huge piles of debris. The streets were full of rubble, but most of it had been pushed to the sides.

On the way to the city center, we drove around the famous Picadilly Circus. Hundreds of "Picadilly Commandos"—GIs—were strolling around. A statue had been encased in a concrete shelter for bomb protection. Major Lay had been there before and knew where there was a nice fish-and-chips shop. We went in and took a number. The table top was greasy from the soaked newspapers on which the fish and chips were being served. A sign posted on the wall proclaimed, "Waste the food and help the Hun." Finally a woman leaning through an opening in the wall from the kitchen called out, "Thety foah-thety foah." Thirty-four was our number so I walked to the window and was handed our fish and chips, each on a folded page from a newspaper. The grease soaked through to the table top. Beirne laughed and said, "Great way to eliminate dish washing."

Beirne and I amused ourselves by eavesdropping on two elderly English women sitting at the next table. We were fascinated by their accents.

"If there was a God, He would show some *mercy* on us," one woman exclaimed, slapping the flat of her hand down on the tabletop.

"Leave God out of this," her companion replied, "*men* make war, not God."

While we were returning to our jeep, we saw the early evening parade of tired-looking men, women and children carrying their bedclothes and pushing baby carriages, heading for the underground stations where thousands slept every night.

We jumped into the jeep, parked it three blocks from Albert Hall and walked inside thirty minutes early. The lobby was packed with civilians and men and women in uniform. Many were standing around the bar drinking sherry out of tiny glasses. There was a long narrow sign over the bar that read, "Grin and bear it." We had seen similar signs around town. Typical British dark humor.

Before the concert started, a gentleman wearing a tuxedo came through the curtains and told the audience to remain seated in the event of an air raid.

The concert lasted a little over two hours. At intermission many people went back into the lobby for some more sherry. The orchestra played several of our favorites. Beirne especially enjoyed excerpts from "The Magic Flute." While they were playing "Laudate Dominum," the thought flashed through my mind that if a bomb with my name on it came crashing through the roof while those ethereal sounds had me hypnotized, I couldn't complain.

There was no air raid. We were very lucky.

We left the hall and walked back to the jeep. Beirne said, "Let's go back to Picadilly and eat some more fish." We returned to the restaurant and took a number. While we were waiting, we heard the wail of sirens. We saw the groping fingers of search lights, and heard the grunt of anti-aircraft guns.

People started rushing out. They seemed to know where they were going, so we followed. They ran straight over to the Picadilly underground station and hurried down the steps. We beat a lot of them. We carefully stepped over the arms of sleeping children. It was very hot and stuffy down there and smelled of unclean bodies.

While seated in the underground, I read some of the signs posted on the walls. One of them said, "Everybody should learn to take air raids and air raid alarms as if they were no more than thunderstorms." It was signed by Winston S. Churchill.

The "tube" was oval-shaped with steel walls. Wooden benches lined one wall and train tracks ran along the other. We were down seventy feet in the bowels of the underground and hundreds of fully dressed people were sprawled around in every direction, sleeping on the concrete floor.

We heard the "drone of death," as the English called it, in the sky. Somebody remarked they were Heinkels because their engines were out of sync. The bombs were being dropped in sticks of five or six. We could hear every one of them hit. One landed very close to the entrance of the station and there was a terrific blast of hot air and a roaring noise. The lights blinked and went out. We looked up the stairway and saw the reflections of red flames. The woman sitting next to me was softly singing, "We'll Meet Again." The lights flickered back on.

A little old gray-haired lady sitting on the other side of the singing woman was holding a small, square wooden bird cage in her lap. She had her forehead resting on top of the cage and her eyes were closed. A yellow canary was lying on the bottom of the cage.

The near hits sounded sharp and crashing. The ones falling far away were soft and muffled. The English people were taking it but I didn't think I could stand it much longer. One old gentleman was rocking back and forth and hugging a dirty pillow with his head buried in it. Little girls cradled dolls in their arms. Small boys pointed their toy guns to the ceiling and shouted, "Bam! Bam!"

Most of the English people were calm and unruffled. Beirne, being a professional "word man," said they were imperturbable. But not *one* toothless old woman. She stood in the middle of the prone bodies screaming and waving her arms, "I've lost me brolly! I've lost me ruddy brolly!"

"Oh *brother*," I thought, "some of these poor people have lost their houses, dogs, even *spouses*, but *she* has lost her umbrella!"

There was a loud explosion near the entrance of the subway. Chunks of concrete smashed down the steps, creating a cloud of choking dust. Little girls clung to their mothers and screamed uncontrollably. Many people were praying aloud. Men and women began to sob.

We waited for another explosion, but it never came. The all clear was sounded just as a wall of water came gushing through the station over the sunken tracks. I thought that now we had survived the bombing, we would probably drown! The water was up on the platform and ankle deep as Beirne and I ran up the stairway.

Up on the street level it looked like the whole world was burning. A woman in the crowd was screaming that somebody had stolen the lid to her tea pot. I couldn't believe it!

I didn't understand the rules of war and the law of reprisal. I couldn't grasp the military advantage of such devastation. This horror had caused the British to clench their fists and join together under Churchill to "Beat the Hun!" Beirne observed wryly, "The English are fighting for their gardens, their Ceylon tea and their weekends. And those Germans up there—they are just ordinary guys overcoming terrible obstacles—even self-doubt and paralyzing fear—to do what they have been ordered to do. As much as I try, I cannot hate them—only their cause."

The Germans had dropped tons of fire bombs. Flames seemed to be leaping hundreds of feet into the air. The sky was red. The barrage balloons were standing out as clearly as they had been in daylight, but now they were pink instead of silver.

I should have been ashamed for thinking it, but the whole horizon of London was circled with fire, and I thought it was the most horrible, awesome and *beautiful* sight I'd ever seen.

Beirne and I picked our way through the streets glowing from red flames, and found our jeep—safe and sound. The flames had turned everything into a soft glow, so we didn't have to turn on the blackout headlights until we were in the outskirts of London. We were able to stay on the left side of the road because of the white painted lines.

The next morning "Lord Haw Haw" broadcast his daily venom. "Thousands of you were killed last night. Rise up and demand a new government, one that will make peace with Germany." Then the nasty little English traitor, William Joyce, started chanting, "There's going to be a bombing, there's going to be a bombing." He did this in the same rhythm and tempo that we used as kids when we taunted, "I'm going to tell your mother, you're going to get a spanking."

High Wycombe was far enough from London so the noise of the nightly air raids didn't seem to be life-threatening. The exploding bombs weren't near enough for the sound to be crashing like it had been in the city. It sounded more like the low growl of an approaching thunderstorm. The distant rumbling and flashing reminded me of the pleasant times my parents and I had spent while sitting on our front porch, enjoying the sights and sounds of summer showers. Of course, we didn't hear the mournful and spine-chilling wails of air raid sirens from our porch.

While in High Wycombe, I learned that the 8th Air Force had been brought into existence on January 28, 1942, in Savannah, Georgia. What a coincidence—my married life with Wilma had also been brought into being in that very place only five months earlier.

London Daily Express: **Whether this daylight bombing with American planes will be so successful when deep penetrations are made without fighter escort has yet to be proved. Fighters have already been operating to the limit of their range.**

Brigadier General Ira C. Eaker, a constant pipe smoker, had been an American observer with the Royal Air Force before we entered the war. Now that we were *in,* he had been given this large and beautiful girls' school. Here, he established "Pinetree," the code name of the 8th Bomber Command.

The last day I was at High Wycombe, Beirne and I were ordered to attend a meeting to cover General Eaker's speech to high-ranking British Air Force officers. The British were trying to persuade Eaker that if he made daylight bombing missions over France and Germany the cost in casualties would be too high. It was impossible, they said. Eaker said that precision bombing missions where you could see what you were hitting were far better than going over there after dark and dumping on the first flicker of light you saw. A dig at the RAF.

General Eaker's main English antagonist was their top airman, RAF Air Marshal Sir Arthur Harris. The English called him "Bomber" Harris and Hitler referred to him as "Butcher" Harris. These two top airmen were worthy and well qualified to lead their air forces. Harris had been knighted by the King and Eaker was not only a West Pointer, but had earned a law degree and studied journalism during his off-duty hours in the Army Air Corps.

General Harris told General Eaker, "We have to use saturation bombing. We kill lots of workmen, true, but may I remind you, when *you* destroy a fighter factory it takes the Germans six weeks to replace it. When *I* kill a *workman* it takes twenty-one years to replace him."

General Harris was also less than pleased with our remarkable new Norden bombsight. Eaker had told him, "With this sight we can drop a bomb in a pickle barrel from 20,000 feet." Harris replied, "Yes, but with clouds and smoke screens you might not see your bloody pickle barrel."

Following a fine luncheon, General Eaker stepped to the podium and made his famous remark to the British.

"Gentlemen, you've been telling me my plan is impossible. The difficult we'll do immediately. The impossible will take a little longer."

Eaker was a very diplomatic officer and also fair to his troops, which was not always easy. A story made the rounds that President Roosevelt's plane was on its final approach for landing at an English airfield when a badly shot-up fighter cut it out of the traffic pattern. The pilot could have bailed out but was trying to save a plane, which he just barely did.

There was a big stink about this incident and General Eaker was ordered to reprimand the poor fellow. Eaker allegedly wrote a letter to the fighter pilot in which he said, "I am reprimanding you for saving our taxpayers the cost of an $80,000 airplane and also for saving your own life. By your action, you cost our Commander-in-Chief an extra three minutes in the air. Acts like this cannot be tolerated."

It was my last night at High Wycombe. I sat beside the lake watching the sky. The night was clear and the stars were bright. Every light on earth was out. A falling star streaked through the sky leaving a fiery trail behind it. The faint sounds of the London air raid sirens started. Then I heard the unsynchronized droning of German engines. They were coming directly over us and heading east toward London. They were probably already on their bomb run. Slim shafts of light started probing the black sky above London in an effort to catch and hold a bomber long enough for the ack-ack batteries to open up on it. I heard the distant rumbling of the exploding bombs. The sky over London glowed red. Two GIs with English WAAFS walked arm-in-arm, stopping at the edge of the lake occasionally to toss chunks of bread to the ducks and swans. In less than ten minutes it was all over. The all-clear sounded. I watched the beautiful clear sky and the bright stars for awhile longer, then went to bed.

My thoughts drifted back to a year ago today when Wilma and I were married. It was the smartest thing I ever did.

Every morning after the punishing raids, Lord Haw Haw would broadcast his regular radio message to the British people. "Throw down your arms. Give up. Can't you see it is useless? You are dying by the thousands every night. If you don't soon give up, you will be on your knees begging for mercy."

A better example of Haw Haw's meanness: He said, "The seven million Londoners have completely lost their self-control. They run aimlessly about in the streets, ragged, wild-eyed and frightened into insanity."

"Oh, *shut up*," I said to myself, "turn your microphone over to Sally. She exaggerates a little, but at least she'll follow up with 'Moonlight Serenade' or 'The Beer Barrel Polka' or something nice."

Our impression of the English people in London was 180° from Haw Haw's. They were staunch and defiant. They were prideful and dignified. And give up? *Never!* We even saw tiny British flags sticking in the ruins of their homes.

Back at Molesworth, I anxiously tore open the letter that was waiting for me from Wilma. My heart was broken when I read that she had lost the baby. She hadn't wanted to know if it was a boy or girl.

In this letter she wrote the words to a song—"I'll Get By As Long As I Have You . . . there may be rain and darkness, too, I'll not complain, I'll see it through. Though you may be far away, that's true . . . I'll get by as long as I have you." It was a comfort to her and a reminder that not all is lost as long as we had each other.

I put the letter down and continued listening to Axis Sally. Sally stepped in right on cue. Her timing *couldn't* have been more perfect! She played, "I'll Get By." I turned to jelly.

"Sally," I thought, "you really *are* doing your job for the demoralizing department of the Nazi propaganda campaign. You're right. I don't want to be here—I want to go home and be with my beautiful bride."

Our Flying Fortresses—B-17s—were being flown to England over the northern route. One was forced down on a Greenland ice cap by a storm. Supplies were parachuted to the crew, including cigarettes and whisky. The downed pilot radioed, "Now drop us a couple of blondes and leave us alone."

We were ordered to clear our equipment out of the RAF photo lab, write our last letters home and get ready to move on. By this time, our B-17s had flown about fifteen missions—all high altitude. The British thought that American crewmen flying at 20 to 30,000 feet were specially selected superior physical specimens. They were *sure* of it when one of their flight surgeons went along on a raid to study the effects of high-altitude flying and passed out. He hadn't properly adjusted his oxygen mask.

PART TWO

Africa

I was in awe of Eddie Rickenbacker, my World War I flying hero (see page 103).

Convoy to Africa

AS USUAL, IT WAS RAINING when we threw our gear on a truck, loaded and locked our A-2 photo trailer and headed for Newport Harbor to board the *Rangatike*. This was a New Zealand cattle boat that had been converted to a troop carrier. This time our destination was a secret. Rumors had us going back to the States, to northern Russia and even on an invasion of France. We would be sailing into the unknown.

The docks at Newport had suffered greatly from the Luftwaffe blitzes. The English were working twenty-four hours a day to keep them open and operating.

We stood cold and shivering on the dock waiting to fall in line and move up the slippery incline to the deck. It was a typical English day, cold and with a driving rain. The long olive drab raincoat had, by now, become my favorite item of government issue. Finally we splashed our way over to the gangplank and, laden with tommyguns and barracks bags, made our way up to the deck.

Our convoy was made up of both British and American troop ships. We had a heavy escort of Royal Navy fighting ships. We moved fairly fast. Now it was all up to God and the British navy.

On our first morning at sea, we were all startled when every ship in the convoy opened fire to test their guns. At this point the invasion of France seemed to be a possibility. We still didn't know where we were going. Rumors started again. We were going to Norway. We were going to Iceland. Some still thought we were headed back to the States.

All of the cattle compartments had been cleared out and we were packed into them. We slept in white canvas hammocks on E deck, which was toward the bottom of the ship, and it reeked with the sickening odor of stale kitchen grease and bilges. Our hammocks hung directly above our mess tables. We were stuck with that dreadful English food again. The kidneys *still* smelled like they hadn't been drained.

My boys and I couldn't eat for days. Because of a lack of hot water, the dishes were greasy and dysentery spread like the plague. As on the *Argentina,* we were ordered to take cold salt water showers every three days. This time, however, we had no soap.

We were told that there were probably fifty or more ships in our convoy. Some were close to us—about a half mile—and others were spread all the way to the faint line that separated the ocean from the sky—about fourteen miles away. They were tiny specks that kept appearing and vanishing as the ships changed their positions. We were somewhere in the center of the armada at this time and a Limey sailor said the ones in the outside corners of the square were the most vulnerable to the German U-boats. He said they were in "coffin corners." We would eventually work our way there. The sailor continued with another happy thought. "When the Huns sink one they hang around for rescue ships to pick up the survivors and then sink *them.*"

Two canteens were opened for the troops. One sold hot tea and "arf-'n-arf," the dreadful coffee and milk mixture the British called coffee. We jokingly referred to it as the wet bar. The other canteen sold cigarettes, candy and so forth. If it hadn't been for *this* one, we would have starved. There were constant long lines at each one. Sometimes we had to stand in line for two or three hours, but there was nothing *else* to do.

The fifth day out, we were each given a little blue book that removed all doubt. We were no longer sailing into the unknown; we were bound for North Africa. The little "Welcome to North Africa" book wasn't about how to fight after we got there; it gave advice about how to conduct ourselves in a strange Arab land.

"Boy, these Ay-rabs are really strange. Couldn't get *my* wife to walk ten paces in front of me." It turned out that Arab men weren't so dumb. Their wives would set off the land mines in time for old dad to hit the deck. Traditions change fast in wartime.

We slowed down and finally stopped—then dropped anchor. We pitched and wallowed, soared and plunged in heavy seas for a full day. The first weak ones were getting sick. I tried to tough it out, but with all the liquid sickness splashing around on the decks and even on the bulkheads, I became a basket case.

There was very little to do. Those who could still hold their heads up squatted on the deck and played cards or spent hours talking about home or their experiences in England.

We were told that a tough old Air Corps colonel was the commanding officer of the troops on board. He got on the loudspeakers and warned us about smoking or using flashlights on deck at night, and about throwing cigarette butts and candy wrappers overboard. "The Germans can track a convoy for hours by following floating debris, and one little light on deck could kill us all."

We were ordered to wear our "sandbags" night and day. This is what the Limeys jokingly called their life preservers. They did resemble a couple of bags tied together. In addition to the sandbags, we had to wear our web pistol belts with full canteens of water hanging from them. We looked a lot more like fighting men now than we did on our convoy to Scotland.

We were approaching the Strait of Gibraltar. The radio reported that a large German U-boat wolf pack was concentrated around the narrow strait. It was said that fifty or more subs were "loaded and locked." They were patiently waiting for us like eager hunters in a duck blind.

The convoy started closing up. We were now going faster than we had before. A man fell overboard and started waving and splashing. The ship didn't stop.

One hardened individual who had seen the man fall overboard turned to the guy next to him and casually remarked, "I'm gettin' tired of this sea air. There ain't no smells. My nose is bored."

An officer came down to our "stateroom" after dark and gave us a real morale-building talk. The ship's captain, he said, had called the officers together for a meeting to discuss a few things we needed to know about docking. He had also mentioned that in case we were torpedoed and sunk, there wouldn't be enough lifeboats and rafts to go around.

"Now hear this, men," the officer continued, "the captain said there *might* be enough life rafts if you *do not climb in,* but just cling to the sides."

"Oh, *great!*"

All of the lifeboats had been let down to deck level and the rafts were unleashed and placed along the rails. We were supposed to stay down in our compartments during the hours of darkness, but I was curious about what was going on topside and shuffled along the black passageways and stumbled up the stairways, or ladders as they were called, to the main deck. In a running sea it was a real sensation groping around the deck in the blackout.

This was the perfect time for some light entertainment. It is impossible to assemble thousands of men from every walk of life and not find talented entertainers among them. An enlisted men's variety show was put together. An accordionist was dug up from somewhere down in the "dungeon." Then a couple of banjo pickers, then dancers, singers, a trumpeter—all professionals.

The entertainers had rehearsed a couple of times before we approached Gibraltar. Now it was time for the show. A compartment down below was cleared out. We sat on the floor squeezed tightly together, and the show started.

It was terrific! Real talent. A lot of loud burlesque jokes and shenanigans mixed with concert violin and piano playing. The act I enjoyed the most was the three hairy-legged GIs who wore skirts made from bath towels and had white mop strings hanging over their heads for long hair. Some canned music started, and we instantly recognized the three Andrews Sisters singing, "Boogie-Woogie Bugle Boy of Company B." The one in the middle looked pretty good.

Then a fat corporal did a strip-tease routine of Gypsy Rose Lee. His movements were amazing. I doubted that Gypsy herself could be more sensuous. The guy danced and stripped, danced and stripped. Finally he was down to his long olive drab GI underwear. He whirled over to the front row, lifted his veil, and planted a kiss on top of a bald-headed colonel!

The tension and anxiety that had been building up was gone. We roared with laughter. The timing couldn't have been better.

Still, nobody on the ship expected the night to pass without being blown into the water. We seemed to be heading for a certain rendezvous with death.

Men who had never seen the inside of a church were now beginning to join their religious buddies in circles around chaplains of various faiths. It was rumored that one confused fellow was attending services with the Catholic chaplain, Jewish chaplain, and Protestant chaplain. He didn't want to take any chances. He had covered all the bases.

Although our own squadron chaplain, a Protestant from Oklahoma City, had gone "the way of all flesh" while we were in England, I couldn't see myself splashing Holy Water or lighting Jewish candles, so I joined his group. My good wife, Wilma, had given me a small, palm-size New Testament just before we left the States and it had been in my left shirt pocket since then. I, too, needed to cover the bases.

I had decided to keep a diary and was already making penciled notes in the margins of the Bible. Little did I realize that fifty years later, I would locate the Bible in the bottom of a dusty old box of war mementos and find enough detailed information in the margins to write a book.

We got closer to Gibraltar. We were still zigzagging and now the ship was turning so suddenly and so sharply that it would heel over and send loose objects and men sliding across the wet deck. We were in submarine-infested waters. Later, Ernie Pyle, the columnist, told us that he had spent the night on the bridge and had seen silvery wakes in the moonlight left by torpedoes. There were several near misses, but fortunately, none made contact. The only regret I had was that if there was any action, my camera was somewhere down in the hold.

The deck continued heaving as the ship surged forward, then sinking beneath us as the ship fell back. I grabbed a big trash can in the middle of the deck to support myself. Four other men were clinging to it, retching and puking into it. I hung my head over the can and lost most of what was left in my stomach.

I crawled over to a bulkhead, sat down and leaned against it. It was lined with men holding small heave buckets between their knees. Every one of them was retching and moaning. I thought I was going to die. Then I thought I *wasn't* going to be put out of my misery. I leaned over the rail to feed the fishes. There wasn't a place along the rail where men were not doing the same thing.

At last we started through the Strait of Gibraltar. There were a few lights on our right in Spanish Morocco and the Mediterranean Sea was calm. It was like reaching a smooth concrete highway after bouncing along on a country road. We were still in dangerous waters, but had made it safely through the strait, which was only eleven miles wide. A peculiar sense of relief came over us.

Nobody on the ship slept that night. We had been ordered to stay up on the main deck. When dawn came, we couldn't see land on either side of us. We had left the strait during the night and were heading east in open water.

We were well into our last night at sea and heading for a port on the northern coast of Africa. A British sailor said we were going to dock behind the invasion force.

Our convoy closed ranks and started the slow docking maneuvers. The moon was still full, and we could see white buildings stacked up a hill leading into the city of Oran.

The fascination of seeing our first African city was changed abruptly into one of terror. We heard the sound of many powerful engines coming in from out at sea. Then, the war started. Bombs started exploding along the docks, on the ships and all over the area. We didn't see the German planes; we were too busy scrambling down the gangplanks and running up the hill into the city.

I was still too sick and weak with dysentery to run with my barracks bag and Thompson submachine gun, so I threw them under an ambulance that was parked between the *Rangatike* and a high concrete retaining wall and slithered in behind them.

The sailors on our ship and all the others were firing their guns straight up into the darkness. Ack-ack guns on the docks were also in action. Flak was falling on us from our guns and shrapnel from the German bombs was tearing into the men and equipment.

The explosions from the Stuka dive bombers were deafening! The black ground near the ambulance heaved and flashed an angry red. Men were shouting and screaming! Flak from the Limeys' ack-ack guns still rained down like a metallic hailstorm. The cordite fumes from the exploding bombs were stifling. "Oh *Lord*," I thought, "I hope the ambulance doesn't drive away and leave me exposed!"

The retaining wall crashed down on top of the ambulance, practically burying it with crumbled chunks of shattered concrete. I was *petrified* with fear! "Oh well," I reasoned, "at least I won't lose my protection now." Flames shot up from wooden storage buildings all along the dock area.

Operation Torch was off and running!

The mind can play strange tricks at times. I started thinking about my old pal, Laddie, a shaggy collie, who was so terrified on the Fourth of July when firecrackers were going off, that he would run in every direction not knowing where he could find safety. Then my mind switched from Laddie to the reality of what was happening here and now. Mentally I pleaded, "God help me!"

The explosions and shooting finally stopped. Troops that had been caught aboard their ships when the madness started began hurrying down the gangplanks, forming up on the docks and marching up the hill into the city of Oran. The wounded were taken away in ambulances. Bodies and pieces of bodies were tossed up into trucks. I pushed my belongings out from under the ambulance, crawled out between the chunks of concrete, stood up, brushed myself off and contemplated my future.

Numerous groups of men were starting to become organized in the dock area, but mine was not one of them. I wandered around like a lost child trying to find my squadron. Then it dawned on me that I had last seen them running up that hill into Oran.

I wandered aimlessly along the dock and up the hill toward the city, helplessly lost. Every few seconds I called out for my squadron. Many other dazed and confused soldiers were doing the same.

It wasn't until sometime later that we learned about the important role Colonel "Wild Bill" Donovan's Office of Strategic Services (OSS) played in the successful invasion of North Africa.

Most of the French navy and a large part of their army were stationed in North Africa. There was a lot of unrest and dissension in their military. Donovan's OSS was successful in helping to enlist the support of the dissidents. He also won over the support of the Arabs' most powerful tribal leader by paying him 50,000 francs. Ten thousand of Morocco's Arab tribesmen, although usually hostile to Westerners, then gave their support during the invasion.

The French established a communications network across North Africa, and secret agents in Morocco, Algeria and Tunisia sent valuable information to the OSS headquarters in Washington, D.C.

Donovan urged the French underground to sabotage communications and railroads, and if necessary, perform assassinations. The OSS fooled the Germans into thinking the invasion would be 1,500 miles south of the northern coast at the French West African city of Dakar. Most of the German U-boat fleet was in the waters off Dakar when our invasion force landed on the northern coast.

Thanks to the OSS, our landings in North Africa were not as bloody as they would have been without their invaluable work. Hitler began calling Operation Torch his worst nightmare.

London Daily Express: In the biggest victory since the Dieppe raid, 98 German planes were shot down, to make the best total since the Battle of Britain.

This is something new in air warfare, writes the 'Sunday Graphic' air correspondent, and once again supports the United States claim that their Flying Fortresses are more than a match for any fighter the Germans are known to possess.

Oran

I HAD LEFT THE *RANGATIKE* SICK as the proverbial dog—sick from dysentery, the Limey food and the motion of the ship; I was a real stretcher case, but I knew that I now had to summon up the strength to rejoin my squadron. But where was it? I was lost. My squadron had run off somewhere to find a safe place while I was on the dock. Now it was time to find them. Where would they be? Probably at the nearest airfield.

A military policeman (MP) told me how to get to Tafaraoui Airfield, which was a couple of miles south of the city. I bummed a ride. On the way, I noticed that the people were carrying on as though the war was a thousand miles away. Tall stately palm trees lined both sides of the entrance to the airfield.

The driver slowed down so he could stop at the guard gate and whisper the password of the day. He told me the word was changed every day, and today it was, "Hi-Yo Silver." We stopped between the guard and about a dozen little Arab kids also standing there. When the driver leaned over to whisper the password to the guard, the kids all shouted in unison, "*Hi-Yo, Silver!*"

As we were driving in, I made a remark about the beauty of the entrance. The driver said, "Yeah, but the enemy spoiled it by stretching piano wires tightly across the road just high enough to cut off the heads of the first jeep passengers to drive in there."

Our foes had strung piano wires at neck height across the roads. A jeep would come speeding along with the windshield usually down for better vision. The wire would pass over the hood of the jeep and catch the occupants at throat level. Several drivers and front seat passengers had been decapitated before the engineers modified the jeeps.

Tall steel bars, slightly over head level, had been welded to the front bumpers. "V" notches were cut at neck height to break the piano wire. Every jeep in the area sported this new "after-market" accessory.

I felt so sure that *this* was where I would find my squadron that I told the jeep driver to continue on and not wait for me. I wandered all over the area, in and out of hangers and the other buildings, but nobody had heard of my outfit.

This was an interesting place. There were still some German flags hanging on office walls, French and German bombers and fighters lined up on the ramps, and trucks and motorcycles parked everywhere. It looked like the German planes were not flyable. Some of the engines were off and maintenance stands were against the fuselages. Evidently the Krauts had flown every one they could get airborne to another location. There was a weird-looking machine that looked like a motorcycle, except that the back end ran on two small caterpillar tracks instead of wheels.

Jerry had evacuated *this* place in a hurry! I wanted to crawl inside a German bomber, but MPs were stationed beside every one of them and wouldn't allow me to do it. Most of the aircraft were French.

A fellow in a 6x6 - 2 ½ ton truck was heading into Oran, and he let me sit in the back and ride in with him.

Back in town I found a fellow in another deuce-and-a-half who was heading for La Senia, the airport on the west side of Oran, and I thought I might find my outfit there. We drove out there and I observed that all of the military planes at La Senia were French. There was a long row of large white gasoline storage tanks on the field with big yellow sea shells painted on the sides—Shell Oil Company. French Zouaves, who had joined forces with the infantry, were walking guard duty around them.

My driver friend headed back to town, and since I hadn't found my outfit, I rode with him.

Oran was a big place. It reminded me a little of Detroit. There were modern office buildings and six- or seven-story apartment houses. In the center of the city, there was a Renault automobile showroom with brand new black cars still in the windows.

We had been issued invasion money on the *Rangatike,* so I thought I would spend some of it on a French-English dictionary.

There were none left in town. Our bills looked exactly like regular money, except for a yellow stamp, so if the money fell into German hands it would be useless to them. Later, when I started using the bills, they were accepted everywhere, but the change was always in French francs.

The large Renault store windows, and a lot of other store-front windows, had been taped with "shatter tape" to save them during German and American bombings. We had seen the same window treatment in London. A few stores had sandbags stacked up on the sidewalks close to their windows.

I was lost. My squadron had found refuge somewhere, but Oran was a large city and, like Laddie, I didn't know which way to go. It seemed logical that I should attach myself to *any* friendly group, then figure out my next move.

I started wandering around the city dragging my bag and gun. I wondered why we had been issued gangster-type machine guns because we weren't "ground-pounders." I suddenly realized that my weakness had disappeared. The trips to the two airfields must have helped.

I could look forever and not find my squadron in all this confusion, so I followed several soldiers into a large three-story building. It was immediately clear to me that I had placed myself right in the middle of a bunch of tough infantrymen. They were playfully tossing hand grenades around like softballs and acting very macho.

One of them decided to have some fun with this "fly boy." He pulled the pin on a hand grenade and handed it to me. I squeezed it as if my life depended on it. Finally when it didn't go off, and my blood pressure returned to nearly normal, the laughing soldier told me the secret. "This is a Limey grenade, fella, and it has to be fused before it can explode. If ya don't fuse it, the pin don't make no difference."

They were the First Infantry Division and had big red "1s" on their shoulder patches. These guys had just taken Oran away from the hostile French, and I guess their adrenaline was still shooting around in their veins.

A staff sergeant saw similar chevrons on my sleeves and acted as the official "greeter."

"Ya lost, buddy?"

"Sure am. Can't find my squadron."

"Oh, one of them flyboys, eh?"

"I'm in the Air Corps."

"Well, ya ain't now. Yer in the Infantry."

"Take me to your leader. I have no intention of joining the Infantry."

A young, pink-cheeked second lieutenant in the orderly room relieved my anxiety. He asked me to bed down for the night and have Thanksgiving dinner with them tomorrow. He would then show me how to get to Invasion Headquarters where they would surely help me find my squadron.

While I was in the orderly room, I flipped through the notices and orders thumb-tacked to the bulletin board. One of them caught my eye:

"Soldiers will not enter, smoke, sit, loiter or stop in front of mosques; make noise or stare while Moslems are praying; drink liquor in front of Moslems; make fun of the natives; show disrespect to Algerians; or wear the uniform improperly."

Evidently, this was something the brass forgot to include in the blue "Welcome to North Africa" book.

It was high noon and time for our first Thanksgiving dinner on foreign soil. The lieutenant told me to go to the third floor and join the officers and non-commissioned officers. When I entered the large dining room, I noticed that only staff, technical, and master sergeants were there on the enlisted men's side of the room —no lower-ranking non-coms or privates.

We sat down at long tables with white tablecloths and some flowers as centerpieces. Soon, French waiters started appearing with trays of food. Turkey, cranberries, mashed potatoes, vegetables and red wine. I had never seen anything nicer in a Stateside mess hall.

After finishing my pumpkin pie, I left the table and walked over to a window to watch the rain. Looking down, I saw the lower ranking non-coms and privates standing flat against the building trying to avoid the rain as they ate out of their mess kits. After all, they were the lower ranking "dogfaces."

I went back to the table and sat down. The other non-coms were drifting away and I started to reflect back to the time *I* was just a low-ranking dogface.

After the Thanksgiving dinner I walked back downstairs, but I stayed inside because it was cold, wet, and windy. The "tough guys," I learned, had taken Oran from the French—and our guys had been surprised that the French troops were allied with the Germans. This little oversight had been changed suddenly after a hurried diplomatic conference three days later. Now the French troops were shooting at the Germans. They had been *Vichy* French.

The *French*—those *wimps!* They had acted *exactly* like Vonnie Howard, the runny-nosed anemic little kid from down the block where I had lived as a boy. Vonnie always had a dirty face, wore ragged clothes, and walked on his untied shoestrings, but we envied him because he could stick a whole orange in his mouth.

Like the French, Vonnie always wanted to chum around with who he figured were the *strong* guys, so he allied himself with Tommy Korkeski, our neighborhood bully.

One day Tommy got into a loud disagreement with Wesley Eaton over the ownership of a nice blue agate marble. During the ensuing altercation with Wesley, Tommy lost his neighborhood bullyship. Vonnie immediately deserted Tommy and became *Wesley's* shadow.

Then, one day, Heinie Hauptmann came swaggering into our neighborhood from Regent Street, followed by his scruffy little entourage. Heinie had inherited his haughty Bavarian arrogance from his German immigrant father.

As soon as Wesley, *our* new neighborhood bully, and Heinie, the *Regent* street bully, spotted each other, they squared off like two bantam roosters in a chicken yard.

Wesley handed his half-eaten Tootsie Roll to Vonnie, Heinie removed his glasses, and the two gladiators clashed! After about a half-dozen well-placed punches, it was obvious that the Regent Street bully would be victorious.

Vonnie immediately abdicated his allegiance to Wesley and "threw in" with Heinie . . . and he ate the rest of Wesley's Tootsie-Roll.

General Geraud and Admiral Darlan were the French "Vonnies." In a letter to General Smith in London, General Eisenhower said, among other things, "All of the Frogs have a single thought—'me' . . . dealing with little, selfish, conceited worms that call themselves men . . . ." President Roosevelt called Darlan a "stinking skunk."

Later during the African campaign we learned that the French government surrendered when Germany invaded. Another French government was set up with headquarters in Vichy, a health resort. Pierre Laval became Premier, and he favored the Germans. The French army in Algeria, including the French Foreign Legion, was getting orders from Laval in Vichy. This is why the American and British suffered so many casualties from the French army when we landed in Oran.

This also explained the reason we were being shot at by snipers from tall buildings and church steeples in the otherwise peaceful city of Oran. The snipers were civilians who had refused to switch over to the Allied side when Laval gave orders to the army to "get behind the strong guy."

The French, like wimpy little Vonnie Howard, wanted to be on the winning side—with the *big* guys, so they killed American and British troops for three days thinking that Germany was unbeatable. Finally, Allied generals, including Eisenhower, met with Laval in a tunnel under the rock of Gibraltar and convinced the wimpy, teetering Laval that if he stood behind *us,* he would be with the strong guy who would eventually whip the bully. This is when the French army and navy surrendered to the Allies three days later and turned their guns around to face the Germans.

Vive la bloody French!

President Roosevelt had prepared a radio message to be broadcast to the French troops in Algeria simultaneously with our landing. Because of Laval's indecision about which "bully" to stand behind, Roosevelt's message was aired four hours too soon. This destroyed any element of surprise. The President's message had backfired, costing us many casualties, and angry officers loudly cursed him for risking lives this way.

The infantry soldiers had found, in me, an eager listener to their invasion stories. They told how fiercely the French soldiers had fought against them. One French motor launch, they said, went around Oran harbor machine-gunning wounded Americans. Some of the French troops were wearing red fezes. The soldiers thought this was very confusing.

They seemed to especially enjoy telling stories about their officers.

"Tell him about coming to shore on that invasion barge," one of the men said. Everybody burst out in large guffaws.

"Okay, the barge driver thought he was at the shoreline. It was dark and hard to tell. He stopped and somebody let the hinged front end of the barge down too soon. The officer in charge of our barge wanted to be the first one on shore. He was sitting in his jeep with the motor running. When that ramp dropped, the lieutenant stomped on the accelerator, and his jeep shot out into ten feet of water." More laughter.

"Tell him how the colonel captured the 'Frogs' with a package of cigarettes," someone said.

"Well, we have this lieutenant colonel who speaks French like a native, and he captured a bunch of Frog soldiers with one package of cigarettes." The storyteller paused and looked at me to see if I was following him.

"You mean he captured French soldiers, don't you? How did he do it?"

"Yeah, sure, *French* soldiers—*Frogs!* Well, it was kinda accidental. When the colonel walked up the hill from the beach, he found a small building. It was dark and no lights were on inside. The colonel opened the door cautiously with his pistol in his hand. A bunch of Frogs were sitting on the floor. They were startled when the colonel shined his flashlight in their eyes. The colonel started jabbering away in French and made them feel at ease. He passed the cigarettes around and then told them they were captured. After they all finished their cigarettes, they left the building and marched away with their hands in the air and the colonel following them." More laughter.

"We almost had the honor of fighting the famous French Foreign Legion," one of the men said. "They had a column of tanks on the road south of Oran when the Limeys spoiled our chance by scattering them and turning them back with their Spitfires."

A corporal spoke up, "We had a sniper problem in the city. They were in the buildings and church steeples. And they *still* are. Anyway, this major, a West Pointer I think, was walking down a street with me and made me walk slightly behind and on his left. Army protocol, they call it. The lower ranks always have to do this. He said, 'You're going to be my bodyguard.' Well, the enemy wasn't dumb. *They* knew about the lower ranks walking this way. The major got one right through the head, through his helmet and into his head. Clean as a whistle."

The stories went on and on. I couldn't help noticing that not *one* story was told about the bloody and gory parts of their battle. They just wanted to have some good laughs for awhile.

The next morning, the lieutenant gave me directions to the Invasion Headquarters building. I was relieved to be leaving the Infantry.

I started to make a shortcut down an alley between two buildings. A Spanish-speaking Berber was just coming out of the alley, so I thought I'd try my high school Spanish on him. I said the only thing I remembered from two years of bluffing my way through classes.

"Tengo un lapiz amarillo," I claimed.

He stared at me for a moment, shrugged his shoulders and walked on. Evidently he was not interested in the fact that I had a yellow pencil.

The alley, I soon discovered, was where the local Arab workmen came to relieve themselves. The stench was overpowering! Every fly in Oran knew about it and was orbiting the area.

The headquarters building was a madhouse. Officers and men were running up and down the hallways and in and out of offices. Everybody looked confused and mixed up. A master sergeant pointed down a long corridor and told me to go to the end, take a left and ask for Colonel Zartman.

It was obvious that I was the only man in that building dressed for war. I still carried my machine gun, had a canteen and first-aid kit hanging from my pistol belt and wore no necktie. This must have made some of those "desk jockeys" pretty nervous.

Colonel Zartman sat at a desk in front of a wall completely covered with a huge chart. The chart was divided into hundreds of squares. Each square contained the name and number of a unit, squadron, division or any other group of men on their way to war.

I saluted the colonel, introduced myself and told him I had become separated from my squadron. "I'm lost, Sir," I said.

He stood up, turned toward the chart and started scanning the squares to see if he could find my outfit. After satisfying himself that no such squadron existed in the North African Theater of Operations, he said, "Sorry, Sergeant, but we're so new at this war business that I'm afraid everything is snafu—situation normal, all fouled up."

"But Colonel," I said, "when and *if* I find my squadron, I'll probably be shot for desertion."

"Oh, no, you won't," he replied, "I know where *you* are. Your *squadron* is lost. You might say they deserted *you*." I was beginning to like this colonel.

Zartman sat back down at his desk, lifted a sheet of paper out of a drawer and scribbled a few lines. "Here," he said, "this is a note to your squadron commander, whoever, and wherever he is, telling him that *he* is lost but headquarters knows where *you* are. By the way, you tell him I want him to call me *pronto*." I *knew* I liked this colonel.

"One more question, Colonel, which way are most of the units going?"

"Well, General Patton has everything under control west of us and the enemy is east of Oran, so you'd better hitch a ride and go east as far as you can without getting into a lot of trouble."

I folded the colonel's note, stuck it in my pocket, saluted him smartly and left the building with my trusty "Al Capone" gun and barracks bag. A military policeman out front told me how to get to the railroad station. My next adventure in "Operation Torch" was about to begin.

I had been in town just a few hours but had already been pan-handled by dozens of Arab boys. *They* called us Joe.

"Hey Joe, chok-a-lot? Choo-wing-goom?" It certainly hadn't taken the little characters long to discover that many GI Joes had chocolate and chewing gum in their pockets. No doubt they had been begging from the French soldiers a short time earlier in *their* language.

When we gave them a handout, they politely said, "Baraka-baraka." (Blessing, blessing.)

There were thousands of Arab men and boys on the streets, but very few women and *no* little girls.

Union Jack: (The newspaper for the British fighting forces) Our losses during the day were six aircraft. At least eleven enemy planes were accounted for. Thirty German aircraft which attacked an Allied convoy in the Mediterranean were given a hot reception.

Coastal fighters shot down at least eight of the enemy, and the anti-aircraft guns of the convoy accounted for a further one.

The Train Ride

WALKING ACROSS TOWN TOWARD THE RAILROAD yards, I kept a watchful eye on every church steeple. The guys in the infantry barracks had told me that Arabs and Vichy French snipers were still hiding in them and would take a shot at any American they could line up in their sights. I kept my tommygun ready.

This was my first experience moving around in a strange place knowing that somewhere out there, hostile eyes could be watching me and that at any moment a bullet I wouldn't hear, fired by an enemy I hadn't seen, might strike me. It gave me a strange feeling of exhilaration.

Two long trains were on the tracks at the station. One was pointed east and the other west. The one pointed east was probably heading for adventure and excitement, so this is the one I selected. It was being loaded with guns, tanks, fuel drums and ammunition. A military policeman said it wouldn't leave before dark because no Allied trains dared venture out in the daylight. I used this time to "liberate" some canned food from the back of a deuce-and-a-half. It turned out to be "armoured pig" and "bully" (Spam and corned beef).

I walked up and down the track looking for a good place to do my "hobo" act. In about the middle of the train, I found an empty boxcar. All of the other cars were flatbeds piled high with everything necessary to supply our war effort. Since I was a creature of comfort, it seemed only logical to crawl inside this boxcar and be sheltered from the rain and engine smoke. There was no way of knowing how long this would be my living quarters. In went the tommygun, the barracks bag and me.

An Arab sat side-saddle on his skinny-ribbed, flea-bitten donkey and watched me board the train. This Arab, like all the rest I had seen, was dressed in rags.

Somebody with a sense of humor had scrawled "40 hommes et 8 chevaux" on the side of the car. Of course, there weren't 40 men and 8 horses inside. At this point it was empty. I remember my dad telling me about how men and horses were transported to the front in World War I. Each boxcar carried "40 hommes et 8 chevaux."

It was becoming quite dark when I found that I would have a companion on the trip. A smallish French conductor wearing a blue uniform threw a round tin lunch bucket and a large clipboard up into the car and climbed in. I wanted to explain to him why I was there and what I hoped to accomplish, but he just smiled, shrugged his shoulders and said something like, "Defense de fumer, no parlais Anglais." His gestures seemed to indicate I shouldn't smoke and he didn't speak English.

I wondered why there was only one boxcar in the train and why it was empty except for a thin layer of straw on the floor. I never did find out.

Before it was completely dark, the little conductor motioned for me to come up to his end of the car and gestured that it was time to eat. I removed the metal ribbon from the bottom of a can of "bully" while he flipped open the lid of his metal lunch box. He removed a chunk of bread, a clove of garlic and a bottle of red wine. I watched with interest as he ritualistically placed the bread, the garlic and the wine on a square red napkin. He then squeezed the garlic clove and rubbed it on the bread. No wonder I found being close to him offensive while we did our gesturing. He had the most dreadful breath I had ever been subjected to. I thought this *might* explain the empty boxcar. Probably nobody else would ride with him.

We rode the train for three nights, stopping every few miles to unload things. Every time we stopped, I'd jump down from the boxcar and examine the front bumpers on the 2 ½ ton 6x6 trucks nearby. I was looking for my group's painted bar code—three vertical bars—gray, white, gray. No luck.

This boxcar had no sanitary facilities. When the train was on a siding, it wasn't so bad. But when we were moving, the boxcar smelled like we were riding in an open sewer.

We were standing on a siding around midnight while several flat-beds were being unloaded. A Frenchman saw me pacing up and down the tracks near the boxcar, and with gestures pointed to a house a few feet from the tracks. He wanted me to follow him to it.

We walked into a side door that led into a candle-lit kitchen. His smiling wife was placing three steaming cups of coffee on a large round wooden table in the center of the room.

We sat down and did a lot of smiling, not much gesturing, and started sipping the potent black liquid. It was awful! This brew could have been diluted with more hot water and supplied a whole squadron!

I gestured that I had to get back to the train, and said, "Mercy," which was as close to "Thank you" in French that I could come up with. The Frenchman gestured that he would like some cigarettes, but I had none.

Finally, during the fourth night, I jumped out into a heavy rain and practically landed on the front bumper of a deuce-and-a-half. At last! Gray, white, gray! I shouted at the driver to wait for me, crawled back into the boxcar and got my tommygun and barracks bag. I didn't recognize the fellow, but the bumper code meant I was home.

Stars and Stripes: (The newspaper for the American Fighting Forces) In Algiers, the APO, which handles mail not only for its own area but also for the battlefronts was swamped. But the mail crews, most of them former civilian postal employees, routed out the mail with the speed and efficiency of a sausage factory. They also tackled the job of drying, deciphering and dispatching the mail that went to the bottom when a convoy freighter was torpedoed. One soldier who was ready to divorce his wife after no news for three months got 50 letters—at once. The torpedo had hit the stern of the vessel, where the mail bags were stored, and some of them tumbled out of the gaping hole and sank. Most of these bags were salvaged and delivered to the Algiers APO.

Relizan

HOW I MANAGED TO FIND MY BOYS in the dark and in a strange place, I'll never know. I reached into a pup tent and shook Martini out of a sound sleep. When he was awake enough to know what was happening, he exclaimed, "Sarge! You're supposed to be *dead*. Everybody *said* you were."

"Your luck just ran out, Martini, I'm back."

At seven a.m. I found Captain Van Cleave, standing outside his tent shaving out of a steel helmet full of hot water.

"Thompson! Where have you been? We thought you were either a deserter or a cadaver! You've got some explaining to do, and *fast*."

I reached into my pocket and pulled out the note from that nice colonel in Oran.

"Here, Captain, I think this will clear me."

"Holy mackerel! They don't know where we are?"

"Guess not. We're not on Zartman's wall."

We were in the French village of Relizan. It was only one hundred miles east of Oran, and it had taken me four days and nights to get there.

Our photo trailer was parked close to the pup tents where I had found Martini sleeping. The other guys had also been sleeping in their tents but had not heard the Martini greeting.

Zinkgraf welcomed me with open arms. "Sarge, am I glad to see *you*. We thought we'd be stuck with Wezak again."

Martini said, "Sarge, you got here just in time for the big dance." I asked him to explain.

"Well, some Germans had been here for quite awhile before we ran them off. They were very good to the Arab and French people. Our squadron commander got us all together the second day we were here and told us that higher headquarters had ordered us to 'bend over backwards' to show the natives that *we* are good guys, too."

Harrington, who spoke a little high school French continued, "The captain a-a-a-asked m-m-m-me to write down so-so-some French . . . " At this point Harrington was interrupted by Martini, because Martini knew that because of his stuttering, Harrington would take too long to complete his story.

Martini continued, "Everybody has been racing around making arrangements for a dance downtown. There's going to be food, drinks, music and *everything*. Somebody even found a hall for it. Word is being spread around the French community that all the girls are invited, and they are welcome to bring chaperones."

Tucker broke in. "Harrington was going to say that Van Cleave asked him to put together a list of French phrases with the English meaning we can use at the dance. Harrington told the C.O. that Private Bill Rose had been studying to enter the diplomatic service, and had a language major at *Yale,* no less, and spoke French better than the *French.* So *Rose* is going to do it."

Martini again. "The theory is, that we can get a lot of people together, entertain them, feed them, and make things a lot easier for the troops who will be coming through here from now on."

I said, "Sounds to me that an important occasion like this needs to be photographed. I can't dance, and wouldn't even if I could, but I'll ask the C.O. if he wants me to shoot the party. If he does, it'll be one for the *books.* I came over here to photograph a war, and I'll wind up shooting a bloody *dance!"*

Two evenings later, I dug my best "Sunday" clothes out of the barracks bag, rubbed out as many wrinkles as I could, stuck a film pack on the back of the camera, and drove to Relizan. The dance hall was easy to find. Dozens of GI trucks lined the street in front of a long, narrow one-story building. A bunch of soldiers were standing around the entrance watching the local girls and their chaperones enter the place. Bill Rose was in the doorway smiling and welcoming the visitors with his beautiful "diplomatic" French.

I went inside. This had been a regular dance hall, by the looks of it, wide open, with a small stage in the center on the far side. Our mess sergeant and his boys had set up a buffet of food and lemonade on one end of the hall, which broke *all* Army regulations on how GI food should be prepared and served. It was *beautiful!*

Six GI musicians were up on the stage arranging their chairs and instruments. I wondered where the instruments had come from, and especially where the mess sergeant had found all that appetizing food. Too bad he couldn't do the same for us back at the squadron mess tent.

Long lines of straight-backed chairs were lined up against the walls. The raw light bulbs hanging down from the ceiling were decorated to look like the stars we placed on top of our Christmas trees.

The French girls were starting to sit down along the walls. They were dressed up in very nice-looking clothes. They had been told they could bring a chaperone. We thought they would bring either their mother, an older sister, or any adult they could round up. Wrong! Some girls had brought mothers, fathers, brothers, sisters, grandparents—the *whole* family! Why? For the *food,* of course. We hoped the mess sergeant had anticipated this.

The hall was crowded with soldiers who were milling around and *all* of the chairs were occupied. Brothers and sisters and even some of the adult chaperones were sitting cross-legged on the floor in front of the smiling girls.

The orchestra started. It wasn't exactly Glen Miller or Tommy Dorsey, but the music was recognizable even though not all of Hymie's piano keys worked. The guys started reviewing their mimeographed French phrases. Bill Rose had done a good job and every man in the room was dancing around with a copy in his hand. It looked like this:

1 Hello, my name is _____. What is yours?
1 *Bon jour, mon nom est _____. Et le votre?*

2 Welcome to our dance.
2 *Bien venue a notre danse.*

3 Would you like something to eat?
3 *Voulez vous manger?*

4 Would you care to dance with me?
4 *Danser avec moi, s'yl vous plait?*

There were several more phrases on the list, but most of the men didn't get very far beyond number four.

The men were going over to the girls they wanted to impress and reading the French words to the best of their ability. Their pronunciation must have been *atrocious,* because the French people were breaking up with laughter.

One of the guys pushed his way through the couples on the dance floor so he could talk with Bill Rose, our French language expert.

"Hey, Bill, I've lost my French word sheet. How do you ask a girl if she wants to dance? See that cute little brunette over there sitting among all those old folks? I'm going to ask her to dance."

I watched Bill carefully rehearsing the fellow, so he would have it down perfectly. Finally, the guy nodded his head. He *had* it. He started toward the wall where his "pick of the crop" was seated.

While the fellow was on his way, Bill jerked my sleeve and said, "*Quick!* Go over there and be ready to get a real good picture!" I moved through the crowd and had the camera ready when the fellow arrived in front of his girl.

He smiled and bowed slightly, probably like the gentlemen he had seen in the movies, and said, "Mademoiselle, voulez vous coucher avec moi?" There were shocked expressions on the faces of the girl, her mother, father, and little sisters and brothers. They looked at each other with their mouths hanging open. Without saying a word, they all got up and marched briskly toward the door in a single file.

Bill Rose had tipped off several of his friends, and they were there to witness the poor guy's embarrassment. Rose had decided to have a little malicious fun with the unsuspecting fellow.

Our gallant Lothario had asked, "Would you care to go to bed with me?"

The orchestra stopped playing and the musicians started putting their instruments away as Bill Rose stepped up on the stage. He must have told our guests the party was over because they all jumped to their feet and started chanting, "Vive les Americains! Vive les Americains!" until they were hoarse. Our little friendship party had obviously paid off. It would have been good if we could have found a way to befriend the Arabs. Of course this would have been impossible because many Arabs seemed to have have a built-in unfriendly nature and they probably didn't dance.

Back at the camp, we wanted to open up for business and make our contribution to the war effort, but there were no bombers or fighters here to service—not even an airfield. We were told that a German "lease" was about to expire at a place called Biskra on the northern edge of the Sahara Desert and this is where we would establish our operation after they had cleared out.

In the meantime, the first thing I wanted to do was make an inventory of all the photo supplies to see if anything had been damaged during the long trip over here from the States.

After everything was accounted for and properly arranged, there was nothing to do but sit around and wait. "Hurry up and wait," the old Army game. My boys had already checked out the trailer and found that everything worked. They had even fired up the jeep, and it was okay.

I drove into Relizan to see what a small Algerian city looked like. It was probably half French and half Arabic. Business appeared to be going on normally.

One place caught my eye. There was a storefront with a photographic portrait display in the window. I went inside and met the photographer. He was French and probably about fifty years old and was the only one there.

I was becoming quite proficient communicating with gestures by this time. Old "garlic breath" on the train and I had practiced a lot. I learned that the Frenchman was still able to take a few sittings and deliver prints, but he was running out of film and printing paper fast and no more would be available until after the war.

After he had given me a thorough tour of his studio and darkroom, I started feeling sorry for him because he would soon be out of business. I told him I would give him some of my supplies and he was very pleased. He told me to come back the next day, and I could watch him shoot a sitting.

I returned the next day with four boxes of 20x24-inch bromide printing paper. This was 400 sheets, and he could cut them up and print 2,400 8x10 portraits. We would not be able to use the paper, because we had no enlarger. Lieutenant Wezak had requisitioned the paper in the States not knowing the difference between bromide and chloride printing paper, and I was going to burn it to get it out of the way. Wezak had also packed a few boxes of 8x10-inch film that we couldn't use. The French photographer now had enough film and paper to last for the duration, if not his lifetime. He was ecstatic!

Wezak's judgment as a censor was also becoming questionable. When he read my letters to Wilma, sometimes he would add a line or two. I'm surprised he didn't correct my spelling. He had probably done a better job selling peanuts at ball games.

The Frenchman's sitting was still an hour away, so I studied his operation more carefully. He had an 8x10-inch homemade enlarger in his darkroom. A little skylight in the ceiling directly above the enlarger shielded by a bellows-type device provided light for printing. There was no electricity in the lab. A large northern skylight in the studio provided the portrait lighting. Again, no electricity.

It was about time for the photographer's customer to arrive, and he explained that it would be necessary for me to hide behind some drapes as I watched him shoot the sitting. The customer was a wealthy Arab sheik and over the years, after he had traded a camel or a donkey for a young girl to be his new wife, they all came in for a group portrait.

The little brass bell hanging on the front door jingled, and I hid myself. The Arab family walked into the studio and positioned themselves in front of the painted background. This Arab wasn't like any I had seen in Algeria. He was dressed in a clean white robe with elaborate trimming, had a white turban on his head, and was wearing a gold chain that hung loosely around his waist with an ornate dagger hanging from it. He had just acquired wife number six, who looked to be about 12 or 13 years old.

The photographer posed the group. The tall Arab was seated in the center, his new wife stood on his right and the other wives were placed so that there were three standing on each side of the seated Arab. The wives all dropped their veils and then I knew the reason for having to hide. No man was supposed to see his wives, not even another Arab. An exception had to be made in this case, however, so the portrait could be made.

The new wife was a cute little girl. She looked so young that she could have passed as the daughter of an older wife. The ages of the wives ranged from about forty down to the latest child bride. The Arab probably had to fork over his best camel for *this* one.

Back at our camp, the photo guys were anxious to hear about my experience at the French studio. After going into detail about the setup and especially about having seen several barefaced Arab women, Tucker exclaimed, "My God, Sarge, that raghead might have slit your throat and torn your tongue out by its roots!"

Three weeks later Captain Van Cleave called me over to his tent.

"Come in, Sergeant Thompson, and sit down. First of all, the idiots in Oran have finally put their act together and know where we are. Now for some more good news. Pack up your photo gear, hook up your trailer and get ready to join a cadre to Biskra."

Cadre to Biskra

A CADRE, AS EXPLAINED BY WEBSTER, is a nucleus of trained personnel capable of assuming control and training others. So a cadre was formed to travel from Relizan to Biskra, a small city on the northern edge of the Sahara Desert at the foot of the Atlas Mountains. Our ground-pounders had just finished convincing the Krauts that their vacation was over in Biskra, and they would probably enjoy moving east to a new and safer location. Our convoy would have to travel high up through the Ouled Nail Pass in the Atlas Mountains, and drop down into the desert to get there.

Our cadre consisted of one key man from each section—photo, radio, weather, shop and so forth. I was going because I was responsible for the photo section. The boys and I loaded all of our boxes of photo supplies and equipment into the deuce-and-a-half truck and trailer. A master sergeant drove the truck over to our area and was good enough to back it up and help us hitch the trailer. Then, without any instruction about how to drive this monster, he simply said, "Okay, Thompson, she's all yours. Good luck!"

Every truck in the convoy was a GMC. We had been told they were practically indestructible. Power was transmitted to every wheel and if that wasn't enough, in a tough situation, they had power-driven winches on the front.

I had never driven a truck before and was immediately confused because it had two shifting levers. Zinkgraf said he thought the shorter one might be the "thing you use to throw power into the front wheels."

I started the engine and pushed the long lever until it engaged, let out the clutch and the truck leaped forward and quit. "Well," I thought, "*that's* not right." I wanted to jump down and ask for some help, but all the other trucks were starting to maneuver into position, and I was too embarrassed to hold up the parade. After trying a couple of more positions with the lever, I was able to creep into the line that was forming on the road. There were twenty-one trucks and trailers, including mine, and we looked like a camouflaged circus caravan. If I could just manage to get this equipment to Biskra without costing our miserable striking taxpayers a ton of money (we detested the U.S. factory workers who went on strike while we were fighting) somebody else would have the responsibility of returning the truck to Relizan.

We headed southeast into the mountains and drove all day and into the twilight before reaching Ouled Nail Pass, near Djelfo, where we would camp for the night. We were high up and it was cold. The sun had just set behind a hill, painting the low-lying clouds a beautiful golden hue. I wandered around the hills for awhile and made a few shots with my camera.

When I got back to the truck and trailer, it was just barely light enough to see a dozen or so Arab men and boys standing in a line a respectful distance from the road watching us. Two boys, probably 12 or 13 years old, were standing a little closer to the trailer. They were barefooted and their ragged garments were hanging loosely over their shoulders. They looked like walking skeletons, starved, hardly any flesh covering their bones; arms and legs so thin it seemed that only their skin was left to cover them.

We had been told by Captain Elmer Davis, the convoy commander, not to feed the natives. I didn't care *what* Davis told us, these boys were near *death*. I reached inside the truck and got a Baby Ruth candy bar. When I was moving toward them, holding the bar out to them, they started walking backward slowly, not removing their wide black eyes from me. I stopped, unwrapped the candy, broke the bar in half, and held the two pieces out to them. "Here," I said, "this is *food*. This is *candy*." They came forward, snatched the candy out of my hands, and crammed the pieces into their mouths. They didn't act like children who wanted a candy bar, but like children who were *very* hungry!

It was dark. I went inside the trailer, turned on the flashlight, and opened a can of armoured pig. After I had finished eating, I stepped back outside to see what the other men were doing. Most of them had wrapped themselves in blankets and crawled under their trucks to go to sleep.

When I returned to the trailer, the beam from the flashlight caught a small Arab boy. He was wearing a red fez and was standing right in front of the door. He squinted in the light but didn't move or say anything. I said a few words in English and even used the few words of French I had picked up. No response. Deadpan expression. It was gesturing time again—the universal language.

"Here is my jackknife. I'll trade it for your fez." The fez was quickly removed, and he held out his hand for the knife. I put the fez on my head, and the boy turned and ran into the darkness with his new knife.

I went back inside the trailer, stretched out on the floor, and covered myself with everything I had to keep from freezing. Before I was hardly settled, there was a loud pounding on the door. I opened it, turned on my flashlight, and found the fezless boy standing there with his father. The old Arab was *furious!* He was shouting in his guttural language, shaking his fist in my face and thrusting the knife at me. I got the message *fast!* The little blue "Welcome to North Africa" book *had* warned us about the treachery of some of these people and how little a human life meant to them. I wasn't *about* to test him, because my machine gun was up in the truck.

We exchanged the souvenirs, and the old man grabbed his kid by an arm and dragged him away. *Close call!* I felt like I had just thrown away one more of my quota of nine lives.

It was early, but already all traces of the night's coldness had gone, burned up quickly in the morning sun and the dry wind. We stood by our trucks and had our breakfast of cold C-rations, which we ate out of the cans and washed down with water from our canteens. We had dug a short slit trench at the side of the road to use as our latrine and garbage dump.

We were surprised to see several Arabs squatting on the ground at the edge of the pit. They were picking around in the filth looking for food! A fellow said, "Aagh! My *dog* wouldn't even do that!" I countered, "Did you ever see your dog starving?" If the captain hadn't been watching us, we would have tossed a few cans of food over to them.

We boarded the trucks and continued down the road. Captain Davis was our convoy commander and the only commissioned officer with us. He was responsible for the twenty-one trucks, so his work was *really* cut out for him.

Davis was an elderly gentleman with a sprinkling of gray hair at his temples. He had been a shoe salesman before the war. "I sold *Florsheims*," he bragged. Davis was so old, in fact, that he had been in World War I. His driver said that the captain was so ancient that "he could have been a busboy at the Lord's Supper." He was probably in his late forties. At age 22, it's hard to believe that life *begins* at forty.

Our captain had been called back to active duty from the reserves. It had been a long time since he had done any soldiering. We had to show him how to wear a modern gas mask, where to hang his pistol on his web belt, and even how to use "Mother Nature's" latrine along the side of the road. Mother Nature provides a lot of necessary things out in the boondocks, but not toilet paper. We instructed the captain to use a French 20-franc note like we did. Fortunately, the notes were somewhat larger and softer than our own dollar bills. And they were worth only a few cents each.

Since Davis had been overseas in a war, we were anxious to hear some war stories. He said, rather apologetically, that he had arrived in Paris just two months before the armistice and had been a supply corporal in that peaceful city. He could see we weren't really interested in how he issued sheets and pillowcases, so he told us the fascinating story of how the American expression, "Okay" had worked its way into our conversations. The French, he explained, talked rapidly, but you could often detect the words, "Au quoi." That sounded like okay. The Yanks, then, returned home with an expanded vocabulary—"Okay."

It took one more day to reach Biskra, which is about two hundred and fifty miles southeast of the coastal city of Algiers. We dropped down out of the hills onto the plain that would lead to the Sahara Desert. We passed some Arabs riding their miniature donkeys, but more were on camels. We drove through a village of sun-dried mud huts and a field where a herd of camels was grazing.

Finally, according to the captain's sectional map, we had arrived at the town of Biskra. We brought our trucks to a slow crawl through the streets to avoid hundreds of donkeys, camels and pedestrians.

Biskra—The Edge of the Sahara

BISKRA WAS A MODERATELY LARGE VILLAGE with paved streets, and French and Arab people on the sidewalks with kids and dogs chasing each other. There were no cars, though. No gasoline was available for civilian use.

Somehow our brave leader knew where to take us to set up camp. We left the village and drove over the desert for a few minutes and came to a large date palm orchard. There were *hundreds* of palms standing in straight rows with irrigation ditches between them.

Everything was clean and neat. An Arab was tending the ditches and directing the flow of water. Captain Davis stopped the convoy at the edge of the palms, got out of his truck, looked around and said, "This is the place. Set up anywhere you want to in the grove and be prepared to wait for a couple of weeks until the rest of the men arrive."

According to the map, we were one mile from Biskra in an oasis called Cora. One white two-story building stood alone at the edge of the grove. I reasoned that this would become the headquarters building because headquarters types try to avoid tents, so I detached the trailer from the truck about midway between the first row of trees and the white building, which was about 20 yards from the spot I selected.

The trucks were unloaded in various spots throughout the grove. And then suddenly, and without warning, they got back into a line and disappeared in a cloud of dust toward Biskra. I had enough armoured pig to last for a couple of days, and then I would have to break into the long wooden 14-man "compo" box. I knew there were only a couple of things in the box that interested me— boiled sweets (hard candy), tea, and toilet paper.

The British fed their men with 14-man composites. One compo

box was a complete ration for 14 men for one day. It contained: Beef and kidney stew. No thanks! Steak and kidney pudding. No thanks! Mutton. No! Tinned sardines. No! Bangers (sausages made of cereal that tasted like sawdust). No! Oxtail stew. Ugh! Cigarettes. No! Powdered tea. Yes! Boiled sweets. Yes! Toilet paper. Yes! Yes! The toilet paper would save me a lot of money. The Limey soldiers called toilet paper "Army Form Blanks." I wondered why they hadn't included a British favorite—orange marmalade. And why they were so fascinated with kidneys. Animals must be blessed with more than two.

We had probably been given the English compo box because American and English food was being distributed from a central warehouse in Oran. No doubt some of the Limey soldiers were wondering how Yanks could stand the Spam.

Now, for the first order of business. I wanted to see what was in that building. The other men were nowhere to be seen, and I couldn't even hear them, so I walked over to the building alone. The door was not locked, so I went in.

Somebody had been here recently. There were a couple of abandoned German uniforms, some letters, books, and mess gear scattered around. Bread and tangerines were on some of the desks. This had been an office. On closer examination, I found German newspapers and magazines strewn around. On one desk there was a small picture of a Kraut soldier posing beside an attractive young lady. It was obvious that they had lost no time leaving *this* place.

A German steel helmet was on the floor in one corner of the room and I immediately captured it for a souvenir. No enraged Arab was going to take *this* away from me. I had become the first GI to occupy a former enemy hangout in Biskra! Our captain had told us that a German detachment had been there operating a listening post and a weather station.

I had never experienced such peace and quiet. Not a sound could be heard from any direction. I didn't try to find the rest of the cadre. They were scattered around in the palm grove and maybe in the desert beyond it. No matter, I could amuse myself with the dart board I'd brought from England.

I walked out a short distance into the desert and looked around the horizon. The expansiveness of the sea of sand was overwhelming. No doubt it was full of mystery and danger. I stood there and stared into space. There was something eerie about the whole feeling, something I had never seen or felt before.

I was *completely* alone—my imagination took over. Just think of it, more than a hundred years ago Beau Geste was out there with the French Foreign Legion.

My convoy commander knew that I could sit there forever without any danger, but it hadn't occurred to me until that very moment. My self-confidence mounted and I took a deep breath and sat down. I laid out my tommygun and 50-round ammo drums and for the first time in my life I realized I was in complete control of my destiny.

I was ready for any adventure—ready to be swept into the secrets of the emptiness stretching to the horizon before me. Just like Beau Geste, I would survive.

This was a good opportunity to try something I'd always been too embarrassed to do in public. Sing out loud—*real* loud.

> *"Oh Rose Marie I love you,*
> *I'm always dreaming of you.*
> *Sometimes I wish that I*
> *Had never met you . . . "*

Oh, Lord! There was a raghead over there sitting on a white horse listening to me. Didn't hear him ride up. This guy looked meaner than the little fez boy's dad. I wondered which side *he* was on.

I casually walked over to the trailer. Out of the corner of my eye I could see him just sitting there—not moving. I wondered if this was one of those famous mirages you're supposed to see on the Sahara Desert.

My tommygun was propped up against the trailer. I picked it up and pointed it to the sky as I stared at him. Ah-*ha*, it moved. It was no mirage. The horseman rode slowly toward me, held up his right arm in a Roman salute—or was it a Heil Hitler salute—and dismounted.

This was a dark, handsome native with leathery skin, sharp black eyes and black mustache. There was a menacing-looking scar on his left cheek and one across his nose. He was wearing a long brown coat or uniform of some kind. Leather bandoleers draping from his shoulders formed a "V" on his chest. The sharp points of three brass bullets stuck out of each of several pockets attached to the bandoleers. His rifle was stuck muzzle down in a loop on his saddle.

The Arab walked toward me, his beautiful white horse trailing behind him. He was obviously a soldier, dressed in a Hollywood-type costume. He was wearing a white turban that he had probably formed by winding a long narrow cloth around his head. It covered his ears and no hair was visible.

I set the gun back down against the trailer and stretched out my hand for a handshake. He ignored the gesture as though he hadn't seen it. I did a lot of broad smiling to show him I was a nice guy. His solemn, stoic expression did not change. I knew not what to do.

Suddenly, an inspiration flashed into my head. I wiggled my finger for him to follow me, walked over to the dart board that was hanging against the side of the trailer and said, "Darts anyone?"

He followed me and stood there waiting for some instruction, so I picked up a few darts and started throwing them at the board. I thought, boy, *this* guy doesn't know much more about darts than *I* do. Bet I can beat him.

It was his turn. He took the darts and threw one at the board. It landed on fifteen. Good shot! I pointed to the board and said, "Fifteen." He put his finger on fifteen and said something that sounded like "Homestash." And so it went. We had a fine time playing English darts in the most unlikely place on earth—the Sahara Desert.

The next morning, shortly after I had taken my bath in a nearby irrigation ditch, my dart-playing Arab friend and his white horse returned. This time I invited him to sit down on a wooden chemical crate and make himself comfortable.

He had a leather sheath hanging from a belt around his waist.

A carved dagger handle was sticking out and I wanted to see the blade. It was gesturing time again.

"I'd like to see your dagger."

"I can't remove it unless it's to draw blood."

"Well, nobody's looking."

He removed the long sharp dagger from its sheath, held up a finger and pricked it with the needle-sharp tip. Blood dripped on the sand. He handed the weapon to me for examination. It was an incredible piece of equipment. I handed it back to him. He wiped the bloody tip on his coat and replaced it.

The Arab mounted his horse and rode straight out into the desert. He was out of sight in a few minutes and I wondered what was out there that would interest him. Out of curiosity, I walked in the same direction for about fifteen minutes. I was getting into loose sand and it was hard walking, so I turned around and started back toward the date palm grove. I spotted a peculiar-looking reddish brown rock in the sand and picked it up. It was a hard sandstone and looked like a rose. I later learned that it was called desert rose.

I looked around this time to see of anybody would hear my singing. Nobody, so . . .

> *"I've got sixpence*
> *Jolly jolly sixpence*
> *I've got sixpence to last me all my life.*
> *I've got tuppence to spend*
> *And tuppence to lend*
> *And tuppence to send home to my wife."*

After the fellow with the horse and dagger had disappeared into the desert, a native came by tending the irrigation ditch that ran in front of the trailer. Again, with gestures and a few words of French, I learned some things about him. His name was Mohammed Gazda and he lived in a small house in the date palm grove. He worked as the irrigation technician.

It was good to have some company, especially somebody who smiled and acted a lot more friendly than the horseman with the dagger. I offered him some Spam and he politely refused. I asked him to play darts with me and he accepted. Mohammed was a better player than the other fellow though *he* had never seen a dart board.

Late one afternoon, a sirocco born in the furnace of the Sahara came howling through the area and I quickly took refuge in the trailer. The screeching wind stopped abruptly, and within minutes Gazda was smiling at me and gesturing for me to follow him. We arrived at his little house in the center of the grove, and he waved for me to go in. When we stepped inside, his wife and son dashed into the kitchen. They stayed there without making a sound while we had tea. It must have been tea, but it was strong and syrupy and tasted like nothing I had ever put in my mouth before. To be polite, though, I finished the liquid, stood up, thanked him and walked back toward the trailer.

Just before reaching the clearing at the edge of the grove where the trailer was parked, I heard an aircraft and looked up. There was a small plane at a thousand feet or so flying back and forth. The sun was bright, silhouetting the plane, and I couldn't identify the markings on the wings but assumed it was one of ours. Wrong! It dived down and a spray of bullets kicked up the sand between the building and the trailer. I stood there frozen. It pulled up and made another pass, this time farther down the clearing where I assumed the rest of the cadre was located. Again there was more gunfire. It then pulled up and headed east.

Until now I hadn't cared where the rest of the men had set up camp and had not bothered looking for them. Now, it seemed important to walk down the line of trees to the area that had been under attack and see how *they* had made out.

There was a lot of excited chatter as I joined the group and some of the men were digging to locate German bullets for souvenirs. Nobody had been hit and none of the equipment had suffered. One of the fellows guessed that a photo recon plane had mapped our area while it was flying back and forth and then gave us a couple of short bursts before going home.

Exactly two weeks from the time our cadre left Relizan, the rest of the men arrived at the oasis of Cora. They had taken a French 40 and 8 train to Algiers, dropped back down through the mountains and unloaded at Biskra. This roundabout, backtracking route was necessary because railroad tracks hadn't been run through the high and rugged Ouled Nail Pass. I asked Zinkgraf why they had gone so far out of their way to get here. "Because we had to follow the tracks," he answered. "Okay, Otto, dumb question."

I was very happy to see the boys again. A friend of ours from Relizan, "Duck" Pond, who was a waist gunner on Lieutenant Frost's *Dirty Girty,* came over to show us the small white dog he had bought from an Arab for a package of cigarettes. Duck had named him "Zig-Zig." If it had been *my* dog, I would have named him "Tripod," because he had three legs.

Later, when Ernie Pyle was writing an article about Duck and his dog, he called the pup "Ziggie." Duck read Ernie's dispatch before it was sent back to the States.

"Ernie, my dog's name is Zig-Zig and I named him after that French woman downtown who stands on her balcony and waves at us. As you know, we call her "Mademoiselle Zig-Zig."

"Sure, Duck," Ernie replied, "but the censors wouldn't let that pass so I named him Ziggie just for the article."

"Why would the censor cut 'Zig-Zig' out, Ernie?"

"Because it might not go well with the readers back home who understand French."

The trucks loaded with equipment from the train spread out to various parts of the palm grove and started unloading. All of our photo equipment and supplies were already here because I had brought them with me on the truck convoy. It was like setting up a traveling three-ring circus. Everybody knew what to do and did it quickly.

My boys set up their pup tents behind the trailer and smoothed the ground under them. We moved the chemicals, printing paper and everything we needed to get down to serious business into the trailer. We started the generator to make sure we would have 110 volts to run the air conditioner and processing machines.

Our squadron commander rounded us up and gave us some interesting news. The intelligence people had learned that before leaving Biskra, the Germans had promised the Arabs a $100 reward for every American GI they took out of action. So we now had bounties on our heads. And if *that* wasn't enough, they had probably also poisoned the water wells.

Our medical officer said he would go back to Relizan, scrounge some water trucks, and come back as soon as possible and fill the Lister bags. In the meantime, we were to drink the red wine that was in plentiful supply here. We all filled our canteens with French wine. By the time old "sawbones" got back with the water, the wine had eaten through the aluminum and our canteens were leaking. Just one of the inconveniences when traveling in foreign countries!

The temperature extremes down here on the Sahara were drastic. The days were fiery hot and the nights were bone-chilling cold. Not exactly a good place to "camp out," but we got used to it. Fortunately we had an air-conditioned place to work.

The war started right away—with a *bang!* The first night, just after dark, several German Junkers 88 came over for a visit. They no longer owned this place and wanted to show their displeasure that *we* were here. They had moved their detachment to an undisclosed location, probably in Tunisia, but hadn't left a forwarding address. Tonight they were back dropping 500-pound bombs on us. Welcome to the desert!

We had all dug slit trenches, of course, because it was obvious the Krauts would be back to irritate us. My boys and I had dug ours just behind the photo trailer. Duck Pond had helped us dig the trench because, he said, he had built a darkroom in his basement at home while he was in high school and now wanted to hang around to see how the "pros" operated.

Duck started spending all his spare time with us and would often be in our slit trench during raids. His dog Ziggie was always with him. We liked Duck a lot because he had a great sense of humor and could talk just like Donald Duck, only better. He was also one of our heroes because he had flown on some raids before we left England. We became very close friends.

Our B-17s and P-38s came in by the hundreds. Now we realized why Relizan would not have been suitable for an airfield—too small. The Sahara was sandy but hard and flat around the oasis and large enough to accommodate every aircraft in the world. The newly formed 12th Bomber Command, under the command of Brigadier General Doolittle, consisted of the 97th and 301st heavy bomb groups and two P-38 fighter groups. We called the Boeing 17s "Flying Fortresses" and the Lockheed 38s "Lightnings." Looking out across the horizon, it seemed like every flying machine in the U.S. Air Corps was spread out on the hot sands of the desert. A newly-made brigadier general was our base commander.

The 97th Bomb Group was the first to arrive in England and the first to raid a German target. The 301st Bomb Group followed them and soon started their raids. They had both distinguished themselves before coming to Biskra.

The 12th Bomber Command became part of the Northwest African Strategic Air Force (NASAF).

If we had not been sure why a photo section had been sent down here, the number of planes removed all doubts. Many of the B-17s carried long-lens cameras for bomb spotting and some of the P-38s had been converted to F-5s, which had tri-metrogon camera set-ups.

The three tri-metrogon cameras with six-inch wide-angle lenses were mounted in the nose of the plane. One pointed straight down, one pointed obliquely to the right, and the other one to the left. When we removed the exposed film from the tri-mets and developed and printed it, the photo interpretation people could see everything from horizon to horizon.

There was never a bombardment without aerial photographs afterwards. A good photo interpreter could almost count the bolts of a bridge on a low-level photo run. Low-levels were called "dicing runs" because a recon pilot was gambling with death. These photos were extraordinarily precise and gave as much detailed information as an inspection on the spot—and they were quicker.

It took a trained person to know how to mount these cameras, set the intervalometers and hook up the cables. For an operation this size, it was hard to believe that I was the only trained man on

Mohammad Gazda brought his son over to the photo trailer to show him our dart board.

After showing me his sharp dagger, the Spahee gave me his broadest smile.

Loading and unloading film magazines from the F-5s kept us busy

The irrigation ditch in front of our trailer was a favorite place for a morning bath.

the base. Somebody had dropped the ball by not having more trained aerial photographers here. (They showed up later.)

It was impossible for me to do all of this by myself. It was necessary to set up a small school and train some helpers. *My* boys were lab technicians but knew nothing about aerial cameras, and they were going to have their hands full running the labs. I was able to scrounge some armament guys who were happy to be working with us instead of wrestling with heavy bombs.

Our workload was increasing, and to complicate the problem, our squadron commander threw something else at us! We were to install gazaps on the P-38 fighters. "Gazap" was a quick way of saying, "Gun sight aiming point camera." These little 16-millimeter movie cameras would be activated every time a fighter pilot squeezed his gun trigger.

This presented another problem. Our film developing equipment was designed to handle *only* nine-inch-wide rolls from aerial cameras, and we hadn't come prepared to develop anything else. Motion picture film is developed in large heavy machines and there wasn't one in Africa, unless the Krauts had one.

We unloaded the gazaps from seven planes that had fired at the Krauts and brought the film magazines over to the photo trailer. The pilots had told us they had fired their guns for just a few seconds, so I knew that each magazine would have only about eight or ten feet of exposed film.

"American ingenuity" time. It's a necessity out in the boondocks. Our roll film developing tanks were long and deep and this gave me an idea. I went into the developing lab, stripped to the waist, turned the light off and unloaded the film from a magazine. Just as I had figured, there was about eight feet of 16-millimeter film exposed. I wound the film back and forth between my fingers and elbow, then dunked my arm down into the tank and raised and lowered it for proper agitation. This was done in the developer tank, the rinse tank, the hypo tank and finally the wash tank.

After going through this procedure with the other six magazines, I brought the developed film outside for drying. The boys stretched the wet film out, and it didn't take long to dry in the hot dry desert air.

After the film was dry, we took it to the briefing tent where we had set up the projector that was used to show Hollywood movies to the troops. Now we would see if we had any kills. The pilots crowded up close to the screen to see some *real* war movies.

We could have made a fortune if we'd had the popcorn concession, because by the time we were ready to turn the projector on, word had spread and the long tent was full of eager movie fans.

We showed the gunnery work of all seven pilots. They kept jumping up and down out of their chairs and shouting things like, "Hey Joe, if you had just lifted your nose a little more." "Look at that guy bail out, I almost hit him." "Holy mackerel, I went right through that Jerry's debris and fire." Little did any of us realize that someday, after the war, Hollywood would use film footage like this over and over again in war movies.

Our P-38s were deadly. Each one carried a 20-millimeter cannon and four .50-caliber machine guns. When they were used for bombing, they could carry two 500-pound bombs—one under each wing. Mechanics pasted paper over the cartridge chutes and muzzles to prevent blowing sand from jamming the wing guns.

The first planes to be flown to Biskra were a group of P-40 fighters. They soon disappeared when the newer and more potent P-38s took over. Since the French pilots had become unemployed following their surrender, they were looking for work. General Doolittle gave them some of our old P-40s, which had no armor protection for the pilots. The Frenchmen stole all the stove lids they could find and placed them in the seats of the fighters. This sounded to us like *American* ingenuity.

A tooth filling fell out one morning while I was eating breakfast. I went back to the tent and took a morning bath out of my helmet. By this time, a stabbing pain was getting my attention.

I walked over to the dentist's tent and found him sitting outside playing blackjack with his enlisted man assistant.

I said, "Lieutenant, I have a bad toothache."

The lieutenant said, "We'll have a look at it as soon as Joe finishes cutting that fellow's hair."

Joe was the squadron barber and used the dentist's chair when it was available. He charged 25¢ or two packages of cigarettes for a haircut.

I said, "Joe, hurry up and finish. I have a terrible pain."

Joe said, "Hold your horses. I have another guy waiting for a haircut."

"Well, that's tough," I replied. "The lieutenant said *I* would be next and you're outranked anyway."

Joe put the finishing touches on his customer, removed the towel and shook it just like a Stateside barber.

The dentist asked me to sit in his old-fashioned "gay-nineties"-type wooden chair. When I sat down and leaned back, the sun blinded me. When I complained about this, the dentist said, "I've got the sun right in your mouth where I can see what I'm doing. Pull your cap down over your eyes."

I was concerned about the sand that was swirling around the chair. "Don't worry about it, Sergeant," he said. "It's no more than waist high right now and I've worked in a lot worse than this."

He picked up a long steel pick, wiped it on his sleeve, and started poking around in my bad tooth. He struck a nerve and I nearly hit the nearest cloud. "Oh, yes," he said, "guess we need a little Novocain."

"Okay, Private," he said, "crank up the drill." The assistant placed his foot on the treadle pedal and started pumping. The drill started rattling. The dentist didn't think it was rotating fast enough, so he said, "Peddle faster, Private, and maybe I'll make you a corporal."

After the tooth was filled, the assistant handed me a canteen cup of water so I could rinse the sand and tooth debris out of my mouth, and I spit it on the ground.

The lieutenant said, "Sergeant, you have four wisdom teeth that aren't doing you any good."

"No thanks," I replied, "Joe has another guy waiting for a haircut."

The dentist lit a cigarette. Speaking to nobody in particular he said, "*Damn!* Why are we getting these foul-tasting Wings over here? Our government could improve our morale a thousand percent if they would send us Camels or Luckies like the feather merchants at home are smoking."

The peace and quiet I experienced while playing darts with the Arabs had given way to the roar of hundreds of engines. We heard them day and night. Ours by day and theirs by night.

The Krauts were still coming over for visits every night just after dark. Our slit trenches were getting *deeper* every day! The one the boys and I had dug behind the trailer was about three feet wide, ten feet long and six feet deep. Tucker, who knew about such things, said it reminded him of a long grave. Some of the guys called them "dive" trenches or "foxholes."

We could synchronize our watches with Jerry's arrival. He was never early or late. For some strange reason, Jerry had decided to drop his first string of bombs on us at 6:30 p.m.—*exactly.* Somebody said that Germans are very methodical. At 6:20, the boys and I would pick up our tommyguns, put on our steel helmets and slip down into the slit trench. All around us, the rest of the men would be doing the same thing. At this point we would look around, wondering who among us would still be alive by morning.

Then we would joke and laugh for ten minutes while we were waiting. This attempt at bravado didn't really fool anybody, but it seemed better than complaining. About a minute before the slaughter started, hundreds of voices would fade and stop, something like what happens when the curtain goes up at the ballet.

Faint sounds of unsynchronized engines would let us know that our efforts had not been wasted. Louder, louder, yum-yum-yum . . . ."Why can't Jerry get his RPMs together like our P-38 boys do?" The JU-88s would always come over single file, follow-the-leader style. There were usually three of them. They would be about 1,000 feet, low enough so they couldn't miss, but high enough to be unconcerned about hundreds of tommyguns.

We soon learned that our headquarters building was in the center of their figure eights. It worked like this: They would head straight for headquarters on their way in, drop their first string of three bombs, fly out about two miles, make a wide 180° right turn, come back over headquarters, release three more bombs, fly about two miles in the opposite direction, make a 180° left turn and head back. Their pattern made a figure eight in the sky. They released their bombs on each run.

When the ear-splitting crash of bombs started we would crouch even lower. Palm-sized pieces of jagged red-hot steel howled through the palm trees. One bomb hit with a frightening blast somewhere near the trailer and a red flash of light washed across the walls of our trench. We thought, "Well, there goes our photo operation."

Every time their engines were loud enough and we knew they were directly overhead, we would lower our heads, point the tommys straight up and hold the triggers down. Thousands of .45-caliber rounds would stream up in the direction of the bandits. We seldom hit one, but it relieved the boredom.

Rarely did a bomb hit near our headquarters building. Lucky for us, since we were a stone's throw away.

The noise of the explosions stopped and we heard the Germans flying away from our area. Then the stillness became intense, except for a loud ringing in our ears. Then Ziggie started howling, which broke the tension. One fellow close to us started venting his anger at the Krauts with a loud stream of very forceful expressions because his tent and all of his personal possessions were gone.

One evening, just before 6:30, a private who used a slit trench near ours asked if he could be with us during the raid. Since we had the room, we told him he would be welcome. We didn't know the fellow or anyone else who usually shared the trench with him, and didn't ask him why.

There were some rifles on the base and he had one of them. He brought it with him and placed it up on the ground at the edge of the trench.

When the raid started and the rest of us got down as far as we could, this fellow stood up and pointed his rifle in the direction of his trench. We thought this was a little strange but were too occupied to ask him why he was doing this.

Jerry came over and released his first string of bombs, and we all started shooting straight up. The private, however, was shooting his rifle in the direction of his trench. When Jerry turned to complete his figure eight and it got quiet momentarily, we all stood up to see the damage that had been done nearby. This was our usual routine between bomb runs.

Tucker asked this fellow what he had been shooting at while Jerry was overhead. "My captain," he said, "sticks his head up once in awhile and when he does, I'm going to blow his brains out."

"You idiot!" I shouted. "Get out of here and do your dirty work somewhere else!"

We knew this type of thing was happening, occasionally, and there is no way of knowing how many GIs were deliberately hit by one of our own men during these times.

Because of their lousy aiming, the Jerries were missing the headquarters building and hitting B-17s, palm trees, slit trenches and everything else. Our whole area was wilting into a shamble of splintered trees, shattered earth and twisted airplanes.

Some of the German pilots had a diabolical way of adding insult to injury. Before leaving our area, they would drop their trash on our field. Bottles, cans, garbage from their mess hall and anything else they no longer found useful. Tidying up after the Krauts every morning was something we knew we'd have to do, but pick up their *garbage?*

Bombs and trash were not all that was dropped out of the JU-88s every night. The Germans had a clever way of building booby traps. They would use small articles familiar to Americans for these explosive devices. A nice new Parker fountain pen lying on the ground the morning after a raid was sure to be found and picked up by someone.

When the cap of the pen was unscrewed, however, a detonator would set off a small charge and it would explode. A few hands were lost this way. This didn't have to happen too many times before everybody on the base knew about it. Anything on the ground that looked suspicious or out of place was suspect.

A Limey demolition crew was attached to our base. We had been told to report anything that looked suspicious to them.

One morning, after our evening air raid, Harrington, our squadron practical joker, placed his own Parker pen on the ground a few yards in front of the photo trailer. We all sat down and watched men walk by. Everyone stopped, took a long look at the pen and then carefully stepped over it and went on his way.

About 30 minutes later, the Limey demolition crew arrived on the scene. It would have been interesting to see how they handled the situation, but Harrington spoiled our fun by telling them the pen was his.

We learned one day from a pilot who was returning from a mission that he had spotted the wreckage of a plane—he didn't know what kind—while he was making a straight-in approach to the field. I was ordered to ride out there with several other men from various sections to inspect the plane. My job, of course, was to dig out the camera and bring the film magazine back.

After our truck had driven about five miles, the driver shouted to those of us in the back that the wreckage was ahead. He was shouting because the wind had suddenly started howling. Then it hit! It was one of those desert siroccos that suddenly turn the sky into a howling yellow furnace and wipe out hills, villages and palm groves. The vehicle was uncovered so those of us in back jumped down and huddled against the downwind side of the truck.

We pulled the goggles down from our foreheads just as the wind brought flurries of razor-sharp grains of sand that stung our faces and obscured our view of the wreckage in the distance. The goggles were our equivalent of a camel's second pair of eyelids.

Then, just as suddenly as it had started, the penetrating howl of the hot wind diminished to a whisper.

The driver told us to jump back into the truck and we continued. The heat was rising, bringing shimmering images of mirages into view. Sheets of water vanished as we neared them. A black mass on the sand ahead of us looked like vegetation. It was the shadow of a cloud.

A fellow shouted, "Hey, look! There's a lake!" The "lake" kept retreating as we moved toward it.

I wondered how the aircraft mechanics could save an engine exposed to this punishment. We were lucky because our photo trailer was light-tight and *air*-tight. Our tommyguns were propped against the trailer, but we had protected the muzzles by placing GI prophylactics over them.

We arrived at the wreckage. It was a Junkers 88 and the Arabs had cannibalized it of everything they could pry loose. No doubt they would bring their loot back to our base and sell it as souvenirs.

The dead four-man crew lay exposed to the harsh desert elements. They were completely nude. Some lucky Arabs were now wearing Kraut flying gear. The film magazine on the camera was smashed, exposing the film, so there was no use bringing it back to the trailer for developing.

The Arabs were scavengers and they were *everywhere*. We would see them scratching around in the bottom of our garbage pits. They would steal anything they could carry. We would never let one get close to our photo trailer or pup tents unless he was one of our regular egg vendors. Simply reaching for a tommygun was all we had to do to send a message—*pronto!*

Of course we kept right on flying reconnaissance missions over German territory with our F-5 Lightnings. The boys and I were turning out hundreds of recon photos and sometimes worked until dawn. The prints were taken over to the photo interpretation people. They used the prints not only to establish targets and assess bomb damage, but to learn what the Germans were up to.

For example, they detected camouflaged installations by studying photos shot at different times of the day. The painted shadows didn't move with the sun.

Sometimes, however, the photo interpretation people made embarrassing mistakes. One set of our prints had them excited. They discovered a column of German tanks on a road. Our mobile forces were sixty miles away, and were dispatched to encounter the tanks. When they arrived, they found a camel caravan.

One F-5 returned to base with an unexploded 20-millimeter cannon shell in its fuel tank. The shell was taken to an armorer to be defused. He opened it and found no explosives. Instead, it contained a rolled-up piece of paper with handwriting—"This is the best we can do for you now." We wondered—Jewish slave labor?

The Rickenbacker-Doolittle Visits

THE AMERICAN WORLD WAR I FIGHTER ACE OF ACES and aviation Hall of Famer, Eddie Rickenbacker, dropped in for a morale visit. This man had been my number one flying hero since I could read, and to meet and photograph him was a great experience. Rickenbacker looked as if he hadn't aged a lot since he stood beside his famous little Spad and posed for a photographer a generation before mine. He was especially interested in the P-38 fighters and enjoyed comparing notes with the pilots.

I remembered reading a lot about Rickenbacker when I was a kid. He was my "storybook hero." He fought in the skies over France in World War I and it was always he in his Spad against a German in his Fokker D-7. They were duelists—cool, precise, impersonal. Rickenbacker believed that he should kill or be killed, and it should be done with dignity.

How times had changed. Now it was *undignified* and impersonal —a dead tail gunner, a dead navigator and a pilot coughing up blood as he landed a crippled Fortress.

Rickenbacker was the idol of the auto-racing world when America entered World War I. He enlisted in the infantry and became Colonel "Billy" Mitchell's driver at the front. Their headquarters commander was a tall captain named George Patton.

Rickenbacker was in awe of the men who were fighting in the sky. He took flight training in France and joined the American Hat-in-the-Ring 94th Pursuit Squadron. A few months before the war ended, he was the commanding officer of the squadron and had earned the Congressional Medal of Honor.

Captain Eddie Rickenbacker was not only *my* hero, but was greatly admired by my dad. After Eddie hung up his goggles as a race-car driver, he started building automobiles. They were named after him and had features far ahead of their time. Later he bought the Indianapolis Motor Speedway and made great changes and improvements there. Still later, he became president of Eastern Airlines and built it from the ground up. Dad used to boast that he and Captain Eddie had some things in common. They had both designed and built motor vehicles and were both seventh-grade dropouts.

Before Rickenbacker arrived at our base in Biskra, he had been on an inspection tour of air bases in the Pacific Theater of Operations. He crashed at sea with a planeload of military personnel and was adrift for 23 days in shark-infested waters before being rescued.

When Rickenbacker started comparing notes with our fighter pilots and reminiscing about his World War I experience, I handed the camera to Zinkgraf and started making notes in my big English journal. It was fascinating.

"How did you get into aviation, Captain Rickenbacker?"

"Well, I was in France and wrote to my mother telling her I was going to become a pursuit pilot. She replied that it was all right with her as long as I flew slow and stayed close to the ground."

Laughter.

"Then while I was taking my flight training at Issoudun, I was airsick all the way through."

More laughter.

"You flew Spads, didn't you Captain Rickenbacker?"

"Yes, but we got them only three months before the end of the war. Before that we flew Nieuports."

"Which did you prefer?"

"Oh, the *Spad*. It had a 220-horsepower Hispano-Suiza motor and had bomb racks under the wings for small bombs. And it was a lot stronger."

"How about the performance of the Nieuports?"

"*Terrible!* Our little Nieuports had a droll habit of shedding their linen fabric when plunged too furiously through the air." We were getting a kick out of Rickenbacker's picturesque language.

"The fabric came off the wings?"

"Not only the *fabric,* sometimes the *wings.* Sometimes the top wing would suddenly detach itself. The French had abandoned the fragile Nieuports and flew the newer and stronger Spads *months* before we got them."

"Did you ever have a problem with a Nieuport?"

"Yes. In fact I was diving on a German Albatross, sending a stream of tracers into him at 200 miles per hour when my right wing collapsed. It was a miracle I survived the crash."

"What happened to the Albatross?"

"He burst into flames just as I lost my wing. We were as concerned about the sudden collapse of our machine in midair as we were for the Huns."

"We're doing a lot of bomber escorting. Did you do any?"

"No. We never flew with the bombers but we always escorted the photographing machines."

"I read that you fought the famous Red Knight of Germany."

"Yes, we fought Baron Manfred von Richthofen's Flying Circus. They flew red-nosed Fokkers. As a matter of fact, Quentin Roosevelt, the President's son, was shot down and killed by a member of the Circus."

"We're firing 1,200 rounds of ammo per minute. How does this compare with your guns?"

"We fired 65 rounds per minute."

"I read that you shot down some balloons."

"Yes. An observation balloon at the front counted as a victory as well as an airplane."

"How were your victories confirmed?"

"Well, it wasn't always easy. A shoot-down had to be confirmed by ground witnesses. We would usually land after a victory, jump into a car and drive to the front and ask around for witnesses."

"How could you do this if your victories went down behind their own lines?"

"It was usually not confirmed. I shot one down two miles inside the German lines and it was *never* confirmed. Confirmation is easier now because of the gun cameras."

"Were your machine guns as unreliable as your planes?"

"Yes, they were. On practically every flight one or both of our guns would jam. We had to reach up and clear them with a tool called a jam-hammer. By the way, boys, you are very lucky to have parachutes."

"You didn't?"

"No. The Germans did, though. They had a rope attached to the body and to a parachute in the bottom of the seat. I set one of Richthofen's red-nosed Fokkers on fire and saw the pilot go over the side and his parachute open behind him."

"Why didn't you have a parachute?"

"That's a good question. We all wondered why our country would rather have us burn to a crisp than to give us parachutes. We couldn't understand why our country didn't care as much about our safety as the Germans did for their pilots."

The P-38 fighter pilots grouped around Rickenbacker seemed as thrilled as I was to be in his presence. A lieutenant who flew a P-38 said rather timidly, "Sir, my greatest ambition is to get *half* as many Krauts as you did in World War I. I am now credited with five-and-a-half."

"Well, my boy, it only takes five to become an ace. Tell you what, I'll give you a case of scotch if you can break my record of 26. Of course some of mine were observation balloons and you won't see any of those."

"But even though I got five and shared one with another pilot, I can't really be called an ace."

"That's right. You can't be called an ace *officially* because of that 1920 policy statement by the director of the U.S. Army's Air Service. I've been trying for *years* to get that policy rescinded, but I understand it. The thought was that they should not glorify one particular branch of the air service. The work of observation and bombardment was considered equally as hazardous as that of the pursuits, or as you now call them, fighters."

Lieutenant Brock's P-38 was not far from the Rickenbacker group, so he asked the captain to look at his "nose art." Of course he had five-and-a-half German swastikas on the nose, and just beneath them printed in white letters were the words: "Air-gasm (er'gaz'em) n. to experience a high speed aerial climax while diving on a Kraut."

Rickenbacker chuckled with appreciation, then continued his talk.

"Lieutenant, your P-38 has more firepower than my whole

squadron had in 1918. One reason I wanted to survive the war was that I was so interested in comparing notes with my counterpart in the German Flying Service. Unfortunately *he* didn't survive the war. Of course I'm referring to Baron Manfred von Richthofen. I'm very fortunate, however, to have the English translation of many of his letters that he sent to his father.

"Some of the things that come to mind are listed on this note pad. Before coming here, I was in England talking to the men in the 8th and many of them asked questions about Richthofen, so I jotted down a few things that might interest you. These items were all in his letters. They aren't in any particular order, but here they are:

"He crash-landed on his first solo flight.

"He called himself an air fighter and referred to his plane as a 'chaser.' In one letter he called himself a 'chaser pilot.'

"He was an observer in the rear cockpit before becoming a pilot. He especially enjoyed 'bomb throwing' on Russian rail yards. He threw small bombs over the side of his cockpit. He worried about having an engine failure over Russian territory because the Russians massacred downed pilots.

"Before joining the flying service, he was a Cavalry officer. He said he knew nothing about airplanes and their markings, so he and his men shot at everything—the German planes marked with crosses and the English planes with circles.

"I never met Richthofen personally in the air, but heard about his tactics. These were in his letters also. He would usually depend on his first rush at an adversary rather than a prolonged dog-fight, and opened fire at a close 50 yards.

"He led his men out in packs of ten to fifteen. He flew a brilliant red 'chaser' and his men painted theirs any way they wanted to—yellow noses, blue bodies and green wings; blue underneath and black on top. Some were painted in streaks or spots.

"This is why they were called 'The Richthofen Flying Circus.' They would put on two shows a day. Another reason they called themselves a circus is because they changed their location a lot by train. They lived on the train, carried spares, mechanics, ammo and everything necessary to set up quickly and 'put on their shows.'

"Richthofen demanded that his pilots display chivalry. He had them fly over enemy lines and drop packets of letters from captured Allied pilots and the personal belongings of the dead.

"Now here's what he thought about you boys flying the photo planes. He said that a reconnoitering pilot's task was more important than fighting. He reasoned that frequently a photographic plate was more valuable than shooting down a whole squadron.

"And you men flying the B-17 Flying Fortresses—bet you didn't know that he was probably the first person to refer to a large bomber as a 'Flying Fortress.' In a letter to his father, he described a British Handley-Page as a flying fortress because it had a gun at every corner. Sound familiar?

"Of course you know that in only two years of flying, he brought down 80 enemy planes before being shot down by a Royal Canadian Air Force pilot by the name of Roy Brown. It is ironic, but he went down over the valley of the Somme, which he told his father was his 'happy hunting ground.'

"I should say that even today historians do not all agree that Roy Brown brought Richthofen down. He was over some Australian ground machine gunners and *they* claimed to have killed him. Anyway, he was given a British military funeral with all the honors, including a firing squad. Later, a British pursuit pilot flew over his airfield and dropped a photograph of his grave. He was twenty-five years old when he died.

"After his death, his second-in-command took over the squadron. He was killed and our arch enemy Herman Goering took command."

Rickenbacker started easing himself through the crowd. "Before I leave, I have something in my pocket I'd like to show you." He reached into his shirt pocket and pulled out a silver cigarette case.

"This was given to me by Ernst Udet, Germany's *second* highest scoring World War I ace. It has his signature *and* the signature of Baron Manfred von Richthofen inside."

There was a chorus of "Ooohs" and "Aaahs" as he left. I would have given *anything* to hold that cigarette case in my hands.

I was absolutely in awe of my World War I flying hero. Getting his words down in my notebook was a rare and unforgettable experience. I regretted that Duck Pond was not with us to see and hear this remarkable man. Duck had told me about the Spad model airplane he had built as a kid. He said it was Captain Eddie's Spad. Duck was off somewhere on a mission shooting at Kraut fighters.

In a way, we felt sorry for our P-38 pilot with five-and-one-half kills who wasn't officially an ace. Everybody on the base had already started calling him "Ace." He had scored the first victory against a German after we were in Biskra. He came zooming in about two hundred feet over the field and did a "victory roll." Then he pulled up his nose and shot straight up while he did three quick snaprolls in a row before losing too much flying speed. It was spectacular! Cheers went up all over the base.

For the rest of the day, we were all slapping each other on the backs and excitedly discussing his rolls. It was a great morale builder! We wondered if a B-17 gunner with five confirmed kills would be called "ace." We doubted it. Besides, who had ever seen a B-17 do a victory roll?

Two weeks following Rickenbacker's visit, there was a nice write-up about him in *Stars and Stripes*. He had spoken with disbelief and disgust when the subject of slowdowns, featherbedding, strikes and absenteeism was brought up. A direct quote was printed, "I have come to the conclusion that if you brought our combat troops back to the States, put them into our factories and sent the defense workers overseas, our production would *double* in a few weeks."

After reading this, Zinkgraf said, "Those political lounge lizards in Washington are too busy at their cocktail parties to look into this sort of thing."

On the day of Rickenbacker's visit, there was a bad F-5 accident. The pilot had flown east to photograph bomb strikes, and as he was coming in for a landing, he dropped his air speed a little too low and stalled about 20 feet above the ground. The plane slammed down hard, bouncing high and out of control. When it hit again, it collapsed a landing gear and dropped a wing, causing it to ground-loop into a Gooney-Bird (C-47). A fire started, and a mechanic who had been working on the Gooney ran over to the F-5 and pulled the pilot out of the cockpit. They were both badly burned. A "meat wagon" (ambulance) hurried them over to the medic's tent for treatment. We learned later that they were taken to a general hospital for further treatment. Both planes were totaled and had to be hauled over to the "graveyard."

Some accidents weren't serious. In fact, *one* was *humorous.* A mechanic was sitting on top of a P-38 gasoline drop tank preparing to weld a hole. Zinkgraf was watching him and described what happened.

"He had made sure there was no gasoline left in the tank. He then climbed up on top of it and straddled it like he was riding a horse. He lit the welding torch, adjusted the flame, and lowered it to the tank. Almost immediately, the thing blew up. It made a loud *boom* and the guy holding his torch was blasted up in the air and landed about ten feet away. He jumped up, dropped his torch and ran like a frightened rabbit."

Tucker told Zinkgraf to go back, locate the guy, and tell him we wanted to come over with a camera. If he would repeat his stunt, we would shoot it, send it to *Life Magazine* and make him famous.

Movie wars shot on Hollywood's back lots were *always* romantic. There was nothing romantic about a *real* war, however, when you were right in the middle of it! But it was exhilarating, and the adrenaline went crazy in your body like *nothing* in peacetime could cause it to do.

At times I thought I couldn't stand it any more. The bomb blasts were almost unbearable. Many of the men went to pieces and turned themselves in to the medics. Their pitiful condition was diagnosed as "anxiety neurosis." During World War I, it had been called "shell shock."

For some unexplained reason, we didn't have regular fuel trucks. Aviation fuel was trucked down from the harbor in Algiers in five-gallon tin cans. A Negro motor pool provided the trucks and drivers and they made the fuel run every day. Gasoline was valued at $8.00 a gallon, FOB Algiers.

One day while the fuel trucks were on the field, "Jazzbo Jim," a Negro driver who always performed a comical shuffling jig for us, was handed a cup of coffee by a mechanic who asked, "How do you like your coffee, Jazzbo, with milk and sugar?"

"No, suh! I likes my coffee like I likes my women—hot as fire and black as night!"

Each afternoon after the B-17s and P-38s were back from their missions and parked, trucks loaded with the five-gallon cans would back up to the planes and a dozen or so men would form a "bucket brigade" and pass the 32-pound cans up to a couple of men standing on a wing. The gas was poured into large funnels that were stuck into the wing tank openings. It took about 1,700 gallons of fuel to fill a B-17.   340 CANS

As each can was emptied, it was tossed to the ground behind the wing. Several Arabs would grab as many cans as they could carry and take them home with them. Some of the GIs would also rescue a few for their use.

The cans were used for a variety of things. My boys and I cut some of them in half the long way and used them for film-developing trays. We cut a couple down to skillet size and made egg omelets in them. We even found that we could bathe and shave out of them easier than using our steel helmets. Some were used for chairs, tables, stoves and lockers. I doubt that many cans ever got to the junkyard.

The Arabs gained financially because they cut up the cans and made a variety of trinkets which they brought back to the base and sold or traded for cigarettes. They knew that just about everybody wanted an Arab dagger to take home as a souvenir, so hundreds of flimsy thin blades were made from the cans. They could probably be used as letter openers but nothing else.

Once a week, a 16mm Hollywood movie would arrive in the mail. We especially enjoyed the war movies because "war heroes" like John Wayne and Ronald Reagan fought their battles on the studio backlots where it was a lot more realistic than our African battlefields.

On movie days, we would set up the projector and screen in the datepalm grove and wait until Jerry had finished dropping bombs on us and it got dark. About three hundred men would come over to the "theater," bringing their tin cans for seats. After the men were all sitting on their cans, we would start the show.

One night, right in the middle of a sickening love story, the radar guys started cranking their air raid sirens. *Pandemonium!* Three hundred men jumped up off their cans and stampeded out of the theater and headed for their slit trenches! I switched off the projector and was right in the middle of the crowd. The noise of tin cans being kicked and crushed under feet was deafening!

Jerry had surprised us by making *two* raids that evening. Duck Pond later remarked that missing the last half of a love story wasn't so bad, but if it had been a good war movie with Wayne or Reagan, he would never have forgiven the Krauts.

We received a lot of war movies through the mail. The locations and stories were different, but a second lieutenant always got the girl—never a dogface. It was disgusting! I felt very smug knowing that my wife, Wilma, had had a boyfriend in her hometown who was a "second looie" but *I* got her. I let everybody know it and showed her picture around a lot. There were usually remarks like, "She sure *looks* like an officer's girl."

By now we were as busy as autumn squirrels. The German bombings continued night after night. There was no letup.

Finally, one morning, Major General Jimmy Doolittle, the top boss of our air groups and another Aviation Hall of Famer, arrived on an inspection tour.

General Doolittle had come to North Africa with the newly formed 12th Air Force to command the Fortresses of the 97th and 301st heavy bomb groups, and the P-38s of the 1st and 14th Fighter groups. He also had the 33rd Fighter group, which was composed of P-40s.

According to our spy in the headquarters building, Doolittle was *furious* about the nightly air raids. "How could anybody here with an ounce of brains in his heathen head allow this thing to happen?" He raved on until every officer in the building was in a state of shock. He screamed like a wounded eagle. The little guy had a temper!

Our headquarters spy was Corporal "Slowfire" Jackson. He had told us about the Doolittle Explosion and was our source of all the scuttlebutt from the inner sanctum. We kept him dishonest by slipping him an exciting photograph now and then.

When asked how he had gotten the odd nickname "Slowfire," he explained that he had been sent to Chanute Field to learn to be an aircraft engine mechanic. "I was always the last student to get an engine fired up. Guess *that's* where it started."

"Obviously you didn't finish the course?"

"Naw, they sent me to typin' school. At least my fingernails ain't always dirty."

That evening at 6:15, we watched the general climb the outside stairs to the roof of headquarters to have a good view of what was happening. We noticed that not even the base commander was brave enough to go up there with him.

Jerry was on time and did his figure eights. After each series of three bombs exploded and it became momentarily quiet, we were close enough to hear old Jimmy screaming and using words he must have picked up from the sailors on the aircraft carrier that took him over for the Tokyo raid. "Where are your heathen 38s? Why aren't they up there mixing it up with the heathen Krauts?"

The Krauts made their turns and came back over us. We crouched back down in the slit trench waiting for the rain of death about to be dropped from the sky. Three bombs hit close to us, throwing up huge columns of smoke and debris into the air. Flames shot up above the trees. The sky became red. Was it our fuel dump? An airplane? Someone shouted that an enemy plane was on fire and going down in the desert.

The next afternoon, our planes returned from their mission. Some of them were pretty badly shot up and had dead and wounded on board.

Doolittle walked up to a plane from which the crew was just emerging. The upper part of the tailgun compartment had been shot away. It was a miracle the gunner had survived without a scratch.

The general asked the tailgunner, "Were you in there when this happened?"

The gunner snapped to attention and said, "Yes, Sir."

As Doolittle was walking away, the peeved gunner turned to a crewman and said in a loud voice, "Where in blazes did he *think* I was—out buying a hamburger?"

A frightened lieutenant, afraid the general might have overheard, said, "My God, man, don't you know who that was?"

"Sure I know," the irritated gunner said, "and I don't *give* a damn. That was a *stupid* question."

The next morning, Doolittle flew out of Biskra, leaving a speechless and trembling base commander to mend his fences.

All of us in the photo section were great fans of General Jimmy Doolittle. He had been one of *my* flying heroes since I was nine years old. I had been amazed at that age when he became the first pilot to fly blind from takeoff to landing. He accomplished this daring feat in the rear cockpit of a Consolidated biplane, under a canvas hood.

Then in 1942, after the Japanese had destroyed our morale at Pearl Harbor, Doolittle brought a bright moment to the Americans when he flew his improbable raid on Tokyo. His group of B-25 Mitchell medium bombers shook the enemy and gave us a much-needed "shot in the arm."

Doolittle had taken a group of volunteers to Elgin Field in Florida, and together they learned how to take off in fully-loaded B-25s from a marked distance of 750 feet in a near-stall attitude.

At this time, he was 45 years old and General "Hap" Arnold, his boss in Washington, had no intention of letting him go on such a risky mission. Lieutenant Colonel Doolittle hounded and badgered his boss until he got the job.

On April 18, 1942, at 0820 (8:20 a.m.), Doolittle, flying the lead plane, and the remaining 15 Mitchells took off from the deck of the aircraft carrier *U.S.S. Hornet*. They knew it could be a one-way mission from which they might not come back. They were over Tokyo at 12:30 p.m. after a four-hour flight. Their raid lasted only 30 seconds.

Doolittle was awarded the Congressional Medal of Honor and contrary to military tradition, he was jumped from lieutenant colonel to the rank of brigadier general.

Earlier in his military career, Doolittle had been jumped from first lieutenant to major, skipping the rank of captain.

After General Doolittle's visit, I walked over to the squadron orderly tent and spoke to our C.O., Captain Van Cleave.

"Sir, how many prints do you want made of the Doolittle visit?"

"Better make four sets, Sergeant."

Captain Van Cleave adjusted his Masonic ring, smiled and said, "It was quite a coincidence, but Doolittle's Tokyo raid occurred on the anniversary of Paul Revere's midnight ride on April 18. And another coincidence—they were both Master Masons at the time."

I tried to act impressed.

He continued, "And still *another* coincidence, Sergeant— Captain Eddie Rickenbacker was a Mason when he became our ace of aces in World War I."

Again I acted impressed.

"You want another coincidence, Sergeant Thompson?"

"Sure. Yes, Sir."

"When you reported to me following your High Wycombe visit in England, you told me you had gone to a Mozart concert."

"Yes, Sir."

"Wolfgang Mozart was a Mason when he wrote the beautiful music you heard at the concert."

"Yes, Sir. Will that be all?"

"Okay, Sergeant. I'll appreciate it if you can have the prints over here this afternoon."

I wondered why Van Cleave had gone off on the Masonic tangent. It did make me wonder how it was possible for a low-ranker like Van Cleave to be a member of such a fraternity.

I gave the film pack to Tucker to develop.

"Here, Tucker, we'll need four sets of prints. You know, Van Cleave seems more interested that Doolittle's a Mason than he is that he's our big boss."

Thoughtfully, Tucker offered, "Well, our *big* boss is General Hap Arnold in Washington, and my dad told me *he's* a Mason. My dad was always proud that George Washington was also one."

"What does it take to join them, Tucker?"

"I don't know. Even though my dad is a member, he never told me how to get in."

Stars and Stripes: Probably the biggest show of the campaign was put on this week at the La Maddaloena naval base. On April 10, Flying Fortresses of Maj. Gen. Jimmy Doolittle's Northwest African Strategic Air Force bombed the heavy Italian cruisers Trieste and Gorizia. Direct hits were made on both vessels and photo reconnaissance the next day definitely established that the Trieste was sunk.

The afternoon after Doolittle's visit, Harrington came back from headquarters with the latest scuttlebutt.

"Wa-wa-wa-we won't see Ja-ja-ja-Jerry anymore. Do-do-do-Doolittle has put a sta-sta-sta-stop to it. They're sa-sa-sa-sending up some pa-pa-pa-P-38s tonight."

Harrington's teacher in stuttering school had drilled into his head that no matter what, *"Finish your sentences!"*

That night, just after sundown, two P-38s roared out to go hunting. They headed east and disappeared. Doolittle had made it very clear that there was absolutely no excuse for letting the Krauts fly over our field and drop their trash on us.

We were preparing for our evening battle. Major General James Howard Doolittle, Sc.D. (Doctor of Science), was 250 miles away in the peaceful city of Algiers preparing for his evening "attitude adjustment" hour at the plush officer's club.

There is nothing especially funny about the moment when a man thinks he is about to die, but when "the grim reaper" reaches out and *misses*, things often become *very* funny. A good example was Harrington's stuttering.

The radar troops were set up a short distance from our photo trailer. It was a few minutes before the nightly air raid when we heard one of them shout, "Jerry's ten minutes away!" Guns were picked up and checked, the religious ones were counting their beads, and my boys and I were turning off our generator and securing the labs for the evening.

Then, the now-familiar routine—jump down into the trench and wait. Ziggie hopped over on his three legs and looked down at us to see if Duck Pond was there. Martini grabbed at him to bring him in with us, but he hurried on down the line to find his master. I believe that Zig-Zig and Duck were a comfort to each other during these awful times.

We heard the droning of the engines. In a few more seconds they started their unsynchronized yum-yum-yum. It was Jerry, all right; P-38s don't yum-yum. I was surprised that the P-38 pilots had let them slip through. We all crouched down, lowered our heads and pointed our machine guns up.

We knew the first Kraut was close enough to release his first three bombs, so we started putting finger pressure on the triggers. Just then, Harrington jumped up out of the trench, stood straight up and shouted, "Da-da-da-da-don't shoot, they're pa-pa-pa *Boom . . . Boom . . . Boom* P-38s!!

Dear stuttering teacher, if you only knew, you would be so proud!

The sun was coming up and it was time to go out and photograph the damage left from last night's raid. Three B-17s and one P-38 had collapsed where they were parked and now looked like blackened dinosaur skeletons.

Molten aluminum had dripped from a blazing Fortress, creating slim silver rivers in the sand beneath the plane. A gunner from this B-17 had raced out to his gun position last night to do what he did best—fire at enemy aircraft. This morning his crew had gathered to search for his body parts.

It was so quiet. So peaceful.

The night the two P-38s had gone out Kraut hunting, they returned after dark and collided on our blacked-out field. One had been taxiing and one was landing. The wing of one ripped off the cockpit of the other and decapitated the pilot. We made the usual damage photos the next morning. One plane was totaled and hauled over to the graveyard.

We then found where *Old Ironsides* was parked and made the necessary photos of it. Flack had hit it while it was near the target and blew the bombardier's nose almost completely away. Only one .50-caliber machine gun was left sticking out. The crewmen had watched helplessly as their bombardier, navigator, and their "office" plunged toward earth. The same flack burst had also killed the pilot.

Then I walked over to *Duffy's Place*. It was full of gaping holes from the wings all the way back to the tail. I slid the camera into the ship and hoisted myself up through the door. When I picked the camera up, the bottom was covered with a gob of blood and guts. There was no time for nausea but I had a dazed sense of numbness.

It would take a few more trips through mangled and smashed planes before it would seem no more than just a mess for the ground crews to clean up. Anyway, this fellow was probably one of the lucky ones. It was a quick death. How callused we were becoming to it. But the reality of it was still hurting.

As I was jumping down out of the plane with my engineering shots, a crewman was standing by the door waiting to go back inside and look for a personal item.

"I'm sorry about your buddy," I said.

"Yeah. There was one up front, too. It bothers me most to clean out their gear and personal stuff like pictures of their folks and things. After living with them for several months and joking with them and arguing with them, I get a sick feeling in my stomach when I have to help clean out their stuff. That's when it *really* gets to me."

Stars and Stripes: The crowning achievement of the week was scored by a group of Flying Fortresses which sank the 10,000-ton Italian cruiser, *Trieste,* and badly damaged the cruiser, *Gorizia* in the harbor of La Maddelena on the north coast of Sardinia.

Each section head was responsible for keeping track of his men. This was no problem for me because I had the smallest section in our squadron—only five of us.

One evening Hal Harrington failed to appear for the evening meal. In fact, he failed to appear for three *more* evening meals. He had "gone over the hill," absent without leave. The ground-pounders had another term for this—desertion.

I broke the rules and even faced disciplinary action when I failed to report him to the squadron commander. Surely Harrington would find his way back before we had to send out a search party.

My patience was well founded, because he came back. A Limey truck drove slowly in front of the trailer, and without stopping completely, a bedraggled and rumpled "Arab" slid off the tailgate. It was our missing photo lab technician, with bloodshot eyes and a three-day blond stubble on his chin.

As they drove away, the lorry-load of cheerful young Limeys burst out into loud guffaws, then started singing their bawdy soldier's song:

> *"Bless 'em all*
> *Bless 'em all*
> *The long and the short and the tall.*
> *Bless all the sergeants*
> *And their bloody sons . . . "*

and they were gone in a cloud of dust.

We turned to the disheveled, barefooted, blond-headed Arab standing nervously before us wearing a long brown native garment and said, "Okay, Hal, what happened?"

"Well, I wa-wa-was . . . "

"All right, that's enough. You'd better get over to the dispensary tent and have Doc check you out."

"I'd b-b-better n-n-n-not go o-o-o-over there d-dressed li-li-like this."

Zinkgraf said, "Hal, you look like you've just finished a few rounds with Joe Louis. You'd *better* see Doc."

Because of Harrington's stuttering it took him a long time to explain, but finally a most unlikely story emerged. Unlikely for anybody else, perhaps, but not for our squadron character.

Harrington had hitch-hiked a few miles up the road to a British motor pool. The Limeys, he explained, usually had some pretty good grog on hand for their visitors. They had grog, all right, and he proceeded to get well grogged. He then wandered off and found himself in an Arab settlement. There were no foreigners there, only natives.

He heard weird-sounding Arab music coming from a small, dimly lit mud building. Native men were standing around the door visiting. Harrington was the only one of our photo boys who spoke fairly good high school French, and a lot of the natives in this part of Algeria also spoke French.

In his euphoric, intoxicated condition, Harrington bravely joined the group at the door and had no trouble finding a fellow who was willing to trade his traditional native outfit for a GI uniform. The Arab came out ahead because he got a pair of shoes.

Harrington's new friend then confided to him that there was a very beautiful woman inside dancing to the music, but absolutely *no* foreigner was allowed to witness the show.

Our character barged in anyway, and was there only long enough to see the end of the strip-tease show. About 50 men were sitting on the dirt floor eagerly looking up to a platform where a fully robed woman was swaying back and forth so slowly that flies were landing on her. Only her eyes were visible. She was just starting to lower her veil so the audience could see her face—*the big climax,* when several men spotted Harrington's blond hair and grabbed him.

After a short scuffle in front of the terrified woman, he was dragged outside and severely beaten. Why they hadn't cut his throat was a mystery. How and when he finally got back to the Limey motor pool was also a mystery.

We kept Harrington's secret and he escaped punishment for his dumb trick. Two days later, however, he wasn't so lucky. The squadron bulletin board was nailed to a wooden post in front of our headquarters tent. Harrington spotted his name on the KP roster for duty in the mess tent, so he set fire to the list. The whole bulletin board went up in flames. The fire department was called. He spent the next two weeks doing all the dirty work in the pots and pans department.

Harrington didn't exactly believe in playing by the rules, even knowing the consequences, but he certainly added a lot of humor and variety to an otherwise serious war.

A guy from the radio section had been admiring some of our pictures. We knew, of course, that not only is a picture worth a thousand words, but it is also worth almost any tangible thing we wanted. Jokingly, we told him that he could have his pick of our war pictures if he would give us a shortwave radio. Much to our surprise, he came over with a large Hammerlund Professional shortwave radio. The thing *must* have been worth several hundred dollars, but what difference did *that* make? *Everything* in wartime is expendable, and he would simply "write it off" his inventory some morning after an air raid. The boys and I *knew* we were in the right business.

The British Broadcasting Company (BBC) broadcasts from London came in loud and clear on our powerful new radio. They usually played classical music and read the news. It was interesting —funny, actually, the way they always tried to minimize *their* losses and exaggerate the *German* losses . . . "We brought down 30 enemy bombers last night. Our aircraft again raided the continent. From this, and other recent operations, three of our aircraft are missing."

It would have probably been more accurate to say, "From this, and other recent operations, *sixty* of our aircraft are missing." We supposed our own people in the States were also being fed erroneous figures like this about *our* gains and losses.

One day the BBC announcer said, very seriously, "Bombs fell into Regent Park Zoo last night. Monkey Hill took a direct hit. The morale of the monkeys remains high."

Christmas day came, and we managed to catch the Yuletide spirit. We didn't want to spend this sacred occasion without the most important thing—a decorated tree. We seemed to have thought about bringing most of the important survival gear with us from the States, but Christmas tree ornaments were an over-sight of major proportions.

We again had to call on our American ingenuity. We scrounged around the junkyard for the slender metal ribbons that had been unwound from Spam and C-ration cans. We were lucky and found lots of them. We took them back to the trailer, washed them and stretched them out to form long, shiny, spiraling icicles. We hung them on a small palm tree beside the trailer and the sunlight made them look almost alive.

Duck Pond and Zig-Zig spent Christmas day with us. By now Duck was like the brother I always wanted but never had.

The Return of Thunderbird
and All American

IT WAS LATE AFTERNOON, and my photo guys and I started scanning the eastern sky in anticipation of our returning bombers. This was one of our daily routines, and as soon as they were all back and safely on the ground, we would return to our lab work in the trailer.

Nearly everybody on the field would sweat them out. We would always know how many left for the mission and the ground crews at their hard-stands would strain their eyes and start counting.

The sun went down, and very soon darkness started settling on the desert. Usually the officers who stood up on the rooftop platform counting and identifying the planes left after they were all down. Today four men were still up on the roof and had their binoculars pointed toward the eastern horizon.

We closed the lab and fixed our supper. If the Krauts made their usual visit, it would be soon. We put fresh drums of ammunition in our tommyguns and placed our steel helmets on the ground near the slit trench. Now we would stand around close to the trench and wait. Our thoughts would be thousands of miles away with our families. Would we be doing the same thing tomorrow—would we even *see* another tomorrow?

Suddenly, there was some excited shouting up on the platform. We heard the "pop" of a flare gun and a green flare arced up into the sky. At the same time, we heard the distant droning of engines. This *can't* be Jerry, we thought. We certainly wouldn't be welcoming him with a green flare! The droning got louder. This *wasn't* Jerry, because the engines were in sync. We heard some loud popping like the sound coming from engines when they are throttled back too quickly. And then nothing.

The next morning, Slowfire Johnson came over to the trailer and said, "Sergeant Thompson, the old man wants to see you in his office at headquarters." I put my shirt on, rubbed a damp cloth across my shoes, and reported to him.

"Sergeant," the general said, "I want you out at *Thunderbird's* pad—no later than nine o'clock. You'll be making some pictures."

I was there on time. A small group of men were circled around *Thunderbird's* crew in front of the plane. I recognized two of them —Ernie Pyle, the columnist, and Will Lang, the *Time Magazine* reporter. The general was just walking up to shake hands with the two famous reporters. Then he turned to me.

"Sergeant, I want a group picture of this crew standing in front of their plane; then, you can make your usual damage photos."

By now, I was learning what had happened, and why we had been sent over here for a "new conference." I lined the crew up under the nose of the plane so the name *Thunderbird* would be in the picture. I posed the officers in the center and arranged the enlisted men on either side. After making three shots—to be sure I got one with all eyes open—I had the pilot stand under the number four engine and point up to it. The engine was an ugly, blackened mess.

The spectators again ringed around the crew, and I got up close to hear what was said. Ernie and Will started asking questions, and an incredible story unfolded—a *miraculous* story!

Will Lang: "I talked with some of the crews who returned last evening, and they told me they had last seen you leaving the target in Tripoli with an engine on fire and you were going down."

Ball turret gunner: "Yeah. I'll bet it didn't take the guys long to divide up our personal stuff." Chuckles.

Ernie: "They thought you were on the ground somewhere in Libya and the Jerries were taking you with them for supper."

Engineer: "No chance. We don't like sauerkraut."

Ernie: "Lieutenant Cronkhite, what happened?"

"Cronk," the pilot, started his story: "Just as we were unloading over the target, some flack hit number four and it burst into flames immediately. *Boy*, there was flack out there by the *bushel!*"

Co-pilot: "And if *that* wasn't bad enough, number *three* started smoking and quit. I thought we'd *had* it!"

Cronk: "We dropped down below and behind the other planes and a couple of dozen Jerry fighter jocks were on us like a bunch of heathen vultures! Our P-38s stayed with us as long as they could and fought those heathen Krauts like crazy, but when they pulled out of the fight, we knew they were heading home because of their fuel problem."

Engineer: "When our little friends left, the Krauts had a *field day!* They followed us about 50 miles west of Tripoli and zoomed back and forth, pouring their ammo into us. We started looking like a sieve. All of our guys were firing at *them* and some of the Jerries were sorry they had been playing games with us."

Cronk: "They finally ran out of ammo and went home. We were still losing altitude and had flown about 20 more miles, when another Me-109 caught up with us. He was all around us—12 o'clock, three—six—nine—*everywhere! He* ran out of ammo also, and left us."

Cronk continued: "The plane was completely out of trim and cocked way over. Jim and I were using all the strength we had to keep the bird from spinning in. I thought it was time to talk to the boys in the back so I got everybody on the interphone and held a conference. I told 'em we had some problems—two engines were out, the radio was gone, we were losing gas, we were losing altitude at the rate of 500 feet per minute, and the *bad* news was, we were 400 miles from home! I said, 'Whadda ya wanna do, jump?' "

Cronk paused and looked around at his crew. He put his arms around two of them and said, "Ya know what these idiots said? They said, 'Take her home, Captain.' I was kinda hoping they would bail out of the heathen thing so I could get some fresh air myself. Well, what could I do? We kept going."

Co-pilot: "It was badly out of trim and one wing was low. This is why we were losing altitude. Cronk and I worked with it, though, and finally got it trimmed and it stopped losing altitude."

Cronk: "By then, we were down to under a thousand feet, but there were some mountains between us and home. Those heathen mountains were higher than *we* were!"

Cronk's little brown dog came through the circle of men and sat down in front of him. Cronk picked him up and hugged him. I *thought* I saw tears in his eyes. No, probably just perspiration.

Cronk again, still holding his dog: "We flew along the edge of the mountains for a long time and finally found a lift from an up-current. Suddenly we were at fifteen hundred feet, so we turned into the mountains."

Co-pilot: "I closed my eyes! Then I opened them. If our wheels had been down, we'd *still* be in those mountains. We didn't clear by more than a few inches."

Cronk again: "We didn't go *over* the mountains, we went *through* them!"

Co-pilot: "I was blowing on the windshield trying to *push* her along!"

The story kept unfolding; Cronk saying a few words, the co-pilot interrupting to throw in *his* two cents worth, and an occasional addition from one of the other crewmen.

It seemed that everything was going against them. Their gas gauges were telling them that they should "throw in the towel," they had picked up a headwind and . . .

Finally, the navigator said they were only 40 miles from home. They crept along just barely able to stay in the air.

It was hard to find the Biskra field in the darkness. They had never landed here in the dark, but they knew they were near the base. Cronk told the engineer to fire a red flare. He shot it, and it disappeared behind the plane. They all held their breaths waiting for an answer to come in the form of a *green* flare. A few seconds later, they saw the most beautiful sight they had *ever* seen—a green flare!

When the plane touched the ground, Cronk cut the switches and let it roll. He *had* to because he had no brakes. When the big bird was nearly stopped, it veered off the side of the runway and spun around two times in violent ground loops. It ended its journey by running backwards 50 feet before it stopped. Ground crews close by heard loud cheers and whistles coming from *Thunderbird*.

When they checked the gas tanks, they found most of them dry and one down to 20 gallons—enough for a couple of more minutes!

Ernie: "Lieutenant Cronkhite, I'll bet the *first* thing you did was jump down and kiss the ground."

Cronk: "The *first* thing I did was crawl out the co-pilot's window to get a look at those two dead engines. As I dropped down on the wing, I stepped on some heathen oil and my feet flew out from under me and I hit the heathen ground! The medics thought I'd been wounded and before I could stop them, they picked me up and threw me into their heathen meat wagon.

"I yelled at those heathen medics before they could drive away and told them to put me back where they found me! I was so glad to be there on the ground, that I just wanted to give a prayer of thanks to the guy who invented the heathen 17, the guys who built it, and anybody else who came to mind."

The crippled Fortress had flown for over four and one-half hours on one pair of engines on the left wing. A Boeing technical representative standing there listening to this unbelievable story shook his head in disbelief and said, "It's impossible! I'll have to report this to Seattle, but when I do, they'll *fire* me for *lying!*"

The base commander had the last word. "Men, during your agonizing homeward crawl, you managed to destroy an amazing total of six German fighters. We have confirmation." The crowd cheered!

There was another miraculous return of a Fortress from a Tunisian raid. The *All American,* driven by Ken Bragg, of the 414th Squadron, 97th Bomb Group, was attacked by an Me-109.

While the Jerry was coming in on them, the left waist gunner was pouring a stream of bullets into him. The pilot was probably killed, because his plane was out of control and sliced through the B-17 between the left waist gunner and the tail gunner. Not only did it practically cut the plane in half, it tore off the entire left horizontal stabilizer and elevator, leaving Ken's plane with only half a tail.

The frightened tail gunner tried to crawl up into the waist compartment, but couldn't. A large piece of the Me-109's wing blocked his way.

An hour and a half later, Bragg lined up on final for the Biskra field. We saw his red flare and dashed out to be close when he landed. The pilot made a nice two-wheel landing and kept the tail wheel off the ground as long as he could. When the tail settled, the entire plane buckled. "Tail-end Charlie" had to be pried out of his station. The faithful old Flying Fortress had brought its crew home again.

The crew crawled out of their B-17 and gathered around the tail wheel. Then, the pilot called out his orders "by the numbers." Every crewman urinated on the wheel. "Why?" I asked one of them.

"Good luck, fella. We always do it. Got us back again *this* time, didn't it?"

While they were performing their ritual, one crewman turned his head toward the guy standing next to him and said, "You and your sour notes. I *knew* something would happen." I asked him what he meant by that.

"Tony Barzini, here, always plays 'Home on the Range' on his mouth organ before we take off. When he doesn't hit any sour notes, we always have a smooth mission, but when he goofs, we know it's gonna be white-knuckles time."

I recorded this ritual on film and later gave each man a print.

Again, the Boeing tech-reps just shook their heads in disbelief.

Another miracle. Three days later, the *front* half of *All American* was on another mission; this time, with the *rear* half of another B-17 that had been languishing in the bone yard.

General Jimmy Doolittle was practically everybody's hero, no doubt about that, but *my* heroes were the ground crews who kept the aircraft flying under *impossible* conditions and the crews that brought home mangled and "unflyable" aircraft.

One-thousand-pound bombs were being placed on the ground near *All American*. They would be loaded on one of the nearby B-17s. A name was printed on each bomb—the name of a crewman who had been killed in action.

I walked back to the trailer. The radio was on and Axis Sally was playing something that was bringing moisture to our eyes.

Vera Lynn, the English songstress, was singing:

> *"We'll meet again,*
> *Don't know where, don't know when.*
> *But I know we'll meet again*
> *Some sunny day . . . "*

The Churchill Visit

WE STARTED A NEW DAY. The same day we had lived through so many times already. Work, heat, air raids, mail call . . . looking ahead was like looking back at yesterday.

We were fortunate to have a few *Reader's Digests* and *Saturday Evening Posts* to pass around. The articles didn't always ring true. *Reader's Digest:* " . . . These men shall not have died in vain." *Baloney!* An ad in the *Post:* "If your dealer doesn't have your favorite Life Savers flavor, please be patient. It is because the shipment he would have received has gone to the Army and the Navy." Well, maybe the *Navy* got them. *Saturday Evening Post:* "Our troops made a retrograde movement—a disengagement." Gobbledygook for, "They ran like sacred rabbits!"

"Oh, Lord," I thought, "I'm going home disillusioned and cynical. Will my folks know me?"

There must have been some "shrinks" around who were gathering data for a research paper or something. One day we were each given a questionnaire asking us to describe our physical signs of fear. The five of us in the photo section made similar responses, such as: Cold sweat. Trembling all over. Pounding heart. Feeling sick to our stomachs. One of our guys admitted to having soiled his britches. We thought that if the shrinks were really here with us, they wouldn't have had to ask *us* those questions.

After the shrinks finished with their project, the internal medicine guys had *their* shot at us. We were now to start taking Atabrine tablets every day for the prevention of malaria. These were bright yellow tablets and a rumor was started immediately that if we took them we'd turn the same color.

The rumor got so strong that the tablets were being thrown away. So to be sure we swallowed them, they were given to us at breakfast in the chow line. One of our lower-ranking officers stood there to be sure we popped them into our mouths. The skeptics either avoided breakfast or learned to "palm" them when they made a motion to their mouths. I wasn't very adept at sleight of hand so I avoided morning chow.

It was early, so I thought I would run downtown before my noon photo shoot and buy a few souvenirs.

I had enjoyed playing my little ocarina when I was a kid. It was during the depression, and I had been begging my parents for a trumpet. One day, my dad came home with a little oval clay thing with several finger holes and a projecting mouth piece in it. He said, "Here, play this. We just can't afford a trumpet, and I'll bet you can play this easier anyway."

That came to my mind as I walked past a music store in the village and glanced into the window. Several ocarinas from large to small were lined up in a row.

When I entered the music store, I heard the repetitious beat of Ravel's *Bolero* coming from a small wind-up phonograph sitting on a glass display counter. How unlikely it seemed to be hearing *Bolero* in this hot desert village.

I gestured for the French proprietor to follow me outside so I could point to the middle-sized ocarina through the window. We went back inside and he took one down from a shelf. "Combien?" I asked. "Quarante francs," he said. I thought that meant 40 francs. Maybe I can knock him down on the price, I reasoned. This was the usual procedure. So I said, "No, trop chere. *Vingt* francs." He looked at me briefly, probably thinking that the Yanks were all a cheap bunch of bums, and shook his head in refusal.

The very first French words we had learned were, "Combien" and "Trop chere." (How much" and "Too much.")

I held up the 20-franc note and indicated that it was my limit. He shrugged his shoulders and lifted his hands in that familiar gesture of despair, handed the ocarina to me, and said, "C'est la guerre!" "*Sure,* its the *war.*" That's what they *always* said.

There was no way I was going to be able to describe the guttural, outlandish sounds the Arabs made when they spoke. So I asked—with gestures—if he had any Arabic records. He had dozens of them. I tried several on his small phonograph, but couldn't find one that had just a speaking voice. Most of them were weird-sounding Arab music. Only two of them had women singing, so I bought them. Another 20-franc note was satisfactory. The records and packing fit nicely into a 16-mm film can and the ocarina was promptly misplaced and never found.

Ernie Pyle, the columnist, poked fun at the Arab language by saying, "If you were to sneeze, cough, whistle, choke and hiccup all at once, that would mean, 'I love you, baby. Meet me in front of Walgreen's right after supper and leave your veil at home.' "

When I stepped back into the street, an Arab boy ran up to me with his palm outstretched. "Hey, Joe, chok-co-lot, choo-wing-goom?" A soldier couldn't walk a block without the little beggars running up and asking for candy and gum. I had given my treats to some other kids so I waved him off with an irritated, "Allez-vous-en!"

The Arabs had a market place in their quarter of town. I walked over there and it was interesting. They squatted behind piles of oranges, tangerines and dates that were stacked on the ground. At a tiny ramada a hunk of meat was hanging, but I couldn't see its color because it was covered with flies.

I asked an Arab how much he wanted for his tangerines. He picked up a small abacus, pushed a few beads around on the wires and held it out to me to indicate the price. I couldn't figure it out and moved to the next Arab vendor.

Returning from Biskra, I found an Arab riding his camel through our squadron area. I hurriedly handed the Speed Graphic camera to Zinkgraf and asked him to photograph me on the camel. I held up a package of cigarettes and the Arab had his camel kneel down on its front knees, which nearly pitched him off, then the camel settled down on his rear haunches with his stomach on the ground. The Arab slid off and held his hand out for the cigarettes. I pointed to myself and then to the camel. The Arab understood and helped me get aboard this smelly, mangy, un-gainly-looking creature.

The camel got up, reversing his getting-down procedure, and nearly pitched *me* over his head. After he was all the way up, it felt like I was sitting on a tall stepladder. The beast swung his head around toward me, curled his lips and let out the nastiest growl-ing, snarling sound I had ever heard! He knew I was an impostor and let me understand this immediately. I yelled at Zinkgraf to hurry up and shoot, because my curiosity was satisfied. I had dis-covered that I would make a very poor desert nomad!

A group of men were standing around watching this scene, and as soon as I had run far enough away from that "ship of the desert" to escape his stench and ugly disposition, I noticed that *they* were lined up and handing cigarettes to the suddenly fortunate Arab. They yelled to me and asked for pictures.

It brought back another childhood memory. One summer be-fore the depression—probably 1926 or so—a photographer came through our neighborhood with a cute little pony. For 25 cents, he would pose a kid on the pony, and later mail the picture to his parents.

Today, if I had been using my own film, I could have charged the guys 100 francs apiece and gone home a wealthy man! Apparently the Arabs hadn't thought of it, or they would have scrounged some film and a camera somewhere, and traded their camels for Rolls Royces.

That Arab's right hand was missing. We had seen a few Arabs hanging around our area with a foot or a hand missing and just as-sumed they had been victims of the war. Not so. Arab law was swift and extremely drastic. A public hanging was the penalty for lifting the veil of another Arab's wife. When an Arab committed a crime such as stealing, the hand that stole was immediately cut off. A foot was removed if it had kicked somebody else's donkey.

And yet they could steal anything at any time from a foreigner. *That* was simply a way of life. It was a new learning experience for me.

It was 11 o'clock, and close to the time I had been ordered to stand by with the camera. Some V.I.P.s were coming, but we weren't sure who they were. The usual rumor mill had gone into high gear, and was it going to be Eisenhower, the top Algerian Arab—*President Roosevelt?*

Our little photo section was keeping busy night and day loading aerial camera magazines before the missions and removing the film from them and developing it after the missions. We were turning out hundreds of 9x9 inch prints every day which were being studied by the intelligence and photo interpretation people.

We were concentrating the bombing mostly on the big port cities in Tunisia—Tunis, Bizerte, Sousse and Sfax. The Germans were bringing all of their troops and supplies into these ports. We were giving them a very hard time, because we were eliminating a lot of their ships.

All of this activity had come to the attention of the British Prime Minister, Winston Churchill. He was vacationing in Marrakech, a city in Morocco, and had taken his artist's brushes and paints there for some relaxation and serious painting. Since it involved only a few hours flight to visit with us at our base in Biskra, he rounded up a few of his highest ranking officers and came down.

Since his visit was to be a momentous occasion for us, our base commander asked me to stand by with my Speed Graphic camera and plenty of film.

The first amphibian aircraft I had ever seen landed, taxied up close to our headquarters building, and dropped its little stairway. It was a fairly large plane with the name *Anaconda* painted on its nose.

I rushed over to be at the foot of the stairway when the great man descended. Fortunately, I had some flash bulbs with me to fill in the facial shadows cast by the blinding desert sun. These large, foil-filled bulbs had been with us since we left the States. We had not had an occasion to use them before, and I wasn't sure how good they were, but I had stuck one in the flash gun and a couple in my pockets.

I positioned myself directly at the foot of the stairs in front of the general and his welcoming committee, and waited. A portly gentleman smoking a big cigar appeared in the door of the plane and started down the steps. No mistake about it, *this* was Prime Minister Winston Churchill.

Just as Churchill's foot was making contact with the ground, I dropped to one knee, pointed the camera up at him and squeezed the trigger. The defective flash bulb exploded into a million shards of glass. It sounded like a pistol shot! I rocked back and plumped down on the ground. I thought I would be shot on the spot. "Good Lord, I've blinded the most famous and revered man on earth!"

That wonderful old man simply bent down to me and said, "Don't let that bother you, son. I've probably had more of those damn things go off in my face than you've ever seen."

Churchill had arrived just in time for lunch, and I followed him and his entourage into the mess tent. I didn't go in there to eat, however, but was still doing my job as a "news" photographer.

I watched in disbelief as England's sophisticated, genteel Prime Minister ate his lunch. He was breaking every bit of table etiquette ever taught to me at home. His table manners were *atrocious!*

He bent over his soup bowl so close, his lips were about two inches from the liquid, and slurped it until his spoon scraped the bottom. He spilled things. He picked up food with his fingers, then wiped them on the only tablecloth on the desert. He talked constantly with his mouth full. His only saving grace at *this* table was his fabulous command of the English language.

After lunch, Churchill asked to see how maintenance and repairs were being handled "in this bloody no-man's land," and he was taken to some hard-stands where the mechanics were working. He was then shown the graveyard, where hopeless wrecks were being cannibalized to repair the flyable ones. He shook his head and remarked, "You chaps have picked these machines as clean as one of your bloody Thanksgiving turkeys."

The Prime Minister had brought several of his top military officers with him. Some of *our* big brass were also in his party. It was the "Who's Who" of the English and American military. Only General Eisenhower was conspicuously absent.

The English officers were General Sir Hastings Ismay, Army Chief of Staff; Commander Thompson, Navy Chief; Sir Arthur Teddar, Air Chief Marshall; General Sir Allan Brook; Anthony

. . . and All American *flew all the way back from Tunis after being rammed by an Me-109.*

"Hurry up and make the shot, Otto. I wanna get off this smelly thing!"

After lunch, Prime Minister Winston Churchill, Anthony Eden, and General George Marshall attended a briefing.

Old Ironsides *returned without her bombardier and navigator.*

Eden, Foreign Minister; and Captain Randolph Churchill, the prime minister's son.

The American officers were General Jimmy Doolittle, Air Force; General Atkinson, General Alexander, General George Marshall, our top general; and General Carl "Tooey" Spaatz, our top Air Force man.

A list of the celebrities had been handed to me just before the *Anaconda* landed. I was to photograph each man and identify the shots as I made them.

I had photographed all but one man. The only name on my list not checked off was Sir Arthur Teddar, England's *top* airman. I walked over to a tall Limey who was wearing a leather flying jacket with no rank showing, and said, "Excuse me, Sir, can you please point out Teddar for me?"

The gentleman started grinning, bowed his head slightly, and said, "My name is Teddar."

Before the day ended, we had developed the film shot of our celebrated visitors and delivered three sets of 4x5 prints to the general. I was pleased with my work and appreciated the flattering compliments from the headquarters staff. Everybody agreed that the one of Churchill stepping down from his *Anaconda* (the flash-bulb shot) was the best. It showed a stooped, portly gentleman with a rotund, cherubic face with a cigar in his mouth, a walking stick in his right hand, a gray fedora on his head and a gold watch chain stretched across his heavy middle.

We couldn't understand why a lot of the world's top politicians and officers were gathered in one group. Later, we learned that Churchill and his top military men, and Roosevelt with his, had just finished a conference in Casablanca. They had made plans for the completion of the North African campaign and the invasion of Italy.

The Krauts were still getting through our P-38 fighter defense occasionally. They came with a vengeance one night. As usual, the boys and I were down in our slit trench by the time the Junkers 88 made their first bomb run.

The explosions were much louder than usual. They were dropping heavies. There was a terrific crash . . . the earth shook! A hot gust of air slapped our faces. Nearby palm trees splintered and spattered our trailer. The concussion pierced our eardrums. The adrenaline was racing through every vein in my body and my heart was thumping in my throat. Deafened and battered, we crouched lower in the trench. This went on for ten more minutes. It seemed like an eternity.

We crawled out of our trench haggard, grimy, and dusty. We had sand in our eyes, our noses and our teeth. I had a loud ringing in my ears. For a couple of minutes I couldn't hear the boys talking and thought I was deaf. Then my hearing returned, but the ringing persisted (and still does.)

We kept sweating out the missions every day. Some of our Forts came in firing red flares, a signal they had wounded on board. Some had dead on board. No flares. Some like *All American* were so battered it seemed impossible for them to fly, but unbelievably the crews were unscratched. Many didn't return at all.

We were always out there waiting to make our engineering shots—the damage photos. We were there when the crews crawled out of their ships. Some would be laughing and slapping each other on their backs. Others would be weeping. Many would have mixed feelings—joy mixed with guilt because they had come back after having seen their best friend's plane explode in midair or go down in flames with no parachutes visible.

I usually avoided the dead and wounded as they were brought out because it disturbed me greatly. I had never even been able to look at a dead or wounded *animal.*

The Life Magazine Photographer

THE BOYS AND I WISHED THAT SOME of our distinguished visitors had stayed for *supper* and then stuck around to see what Jerry put us through after dark. We certainly didn't blame them, however, for getting out of the area before the sun set. They all knew what was going on and couldn't have helped us if they *had* stayed.

Sometimes we had near misses. One evening a bomb hit so close to our trench that we were showered with flying dirt and small scraps of tents and blankets. Some of the men were now homeless. A date palm tree was uprooted and fell across our trench. The concussion had slammed us deeper into our trench than we thought possible. We examined the crater the next morning. Two 6x6 trucks could have been placed in it with room to spare.

This was the evening when a palm-sized piece of shrapnel tore a hole in our trailer. It became a good souvenir. We no longer bothered to pick up pieces of shrapnel to take home; they were so plentiful that we ignored them.

"Doubt that I'll ever find as good a souvenir as my brother did in the Pacific," one fellow said. "He shot a Jap and then cut his head off. When he had time, he skinned it and then cleaned it with GI lye soap and polished the skull. He had a picture made of himself holding the Jap skull and sent it to our mom. It made Mom sick so she gave it to Dad, who took it to work and became an instant hero. All I have so far are a few lousy pieces of German bomb shrapnel."

"Your brother must be some kind of a beast," a buddy remarked.

"No, he isn't. Practically everybody in his platoon did the same thing after they found that the Japs were chopping off our guys heads, hands, feet and *everything*."

Jerry always sprayed us with machine gun bullets on his bomb runs. This was called strafing, which was a German word meaning "punishment or penalty of death." The Texans, who knew about such things, said the bullet holes looked like prairie dog holes. We decided to dig our slit trench a little deeper.

The shrapnel hole in the trailer was through the end the printing dark room lab was in. Zinkgraf said, "Well, we can't use *that* lab for awhile. That hole will let the *dark* out."

We had work to do. We had to have the trailer repaired in a hurry. The sheet metal mechanics were magicians when it came to patching up the B-17s and P-38s, so I asked a fellow to bring a piece of aluminum over and fix our hole. He came. He looked. He left. An hour later he came back with some special sheet metal tools. He hadn't known that our aluminum sides were corrugated and his flat piece of metal wouldn't cover the hole. He spent quite a while corrugating his piece of aluminum. He did a fine job, so we gave him a couple of prints.

The air raids began to be less frequent, thanks to General Doolittle's "recommendation" to send up P-38s. When we *did* have raids, however, the Krauts came in larger numbers and stayed longer. They were also coming several times a night. They used to visit us around 6:30 in the evening, go home and stay there. Now, we were roused out of bed so often that we practically dozed off on the job. Just the results they wanted, we thought.

When I was a kid and saw the desert movies, I was convinced that any visitor over here would pass out with the heat. Our days got a little hot, at times, but the cold nights were almost inhuman. We always slept fully clothed—*wool* clothes—and wore overcoats, sweaters, and everything we had. We were still cold. We tried to tell our folks back home about the freezing weather here on the Sahara desert, but they were probably not convinced.

The famous *Life Magazine* photographer with a double-barreled name, Margaret Bourke-White, made the scene. She had come down to the desert to shoot some action for her magazine. One of Margaret's photographs had been used on the cover of the first issue of *Life*.

She had left her husband, author Erskine Caldwell, in London, and had wasted no time in becoming *very* friendly with our base commanding officer. She could go anywhere she wanted. She could sit in on classified briefings. Whatever Margaret wanted, Margaret got.

One morning, about an hour after the 17s had flown out for their mission, a P-38 took off. By now, we were able to instantly recognize the sound of a malfunctioning engine. The 38 was starting its climb when the worst thing that could happen *did* happen. One engine malfunctioned. The pilot nosed it over to gain flying speed, but was too low. He went down into the "Garden of Allah," a special place set aside by the Moslems for worship and meditation.

I jumped into the jeep with my camera the moment I knew he was in trouble. As I raced in the direction of the Garden, it suddenly occurred to me that we had been warned to *never* set foot in that sacred place—our throats would be slit.

The fire truck, ambulance and a lot of other jeeps were dashing toward the area, however, so I nosed into the line of traffic and drove right in with them.

By this time, black smoke was billowing up through the palm trees. I arrived right behind the fire truck. Two fire fighters jumped off the side of the truck and grabbed foam hoses. These men were wearing large, bulky asbestos suits with hoods covering their heads and shoulders. They could have been monsters from another planet.

The plane was wedged down into the trees at about a 45° angle and didn't appear to be very badly damaged. It had caught fire, however, and the pilot was trying desperately to raise the hatch and get out.

The firefighters started shooting chemical foam directly on the cockpit area to keep things cooled down while the pilot worked on the hatch. It looked like he was trying to stand up in the cockpit and push the hatch open with his back.

I had started shooting pictures the moment I got there and

wasn't aware of anything or anyone around me. Suddenly, I heard a woman standing next to me scream at the firefighters, "Hey, you! Move over here and you go over there!"

It was Margaret Bourke-White distracting the firemen and ordering them where to stand so the composition of her shots would be better. I couldn't believe what was happening! The firemen couldn't either. They looked at the general, who was standing beside Margaret, and he nodded his head in a signal to, "Do what the lady wants."

The firemen followed Margaret's orders, and while they were "posing" for her, the pilot slumped back down into his cockpit, sat there and burned alive. Flesh burned from his head and he became black and blistered; his eyes staring out of his head and his hair completely burned away.

Fifty-caliber ammo was exploding and the white and red tracer shells were zigzagging and skipping crazily all over the ground and between my legs. I held my position and continued shooting. Margaret had obviously captured her next *Life Magazine* cover and had trotted off with the general.

Her actions made me *sick*. Photographers *never* interfere with rescue personnel, and this was very unprofessional. Of course the general, with his crash experience, might have known it was too late to save the pilot. Nevertheless, I felt that Margaret had contributed to the poor fellow's death.

It was a grim fact that in this war at least one aircraft was being destroyed accidentally by a malfunction or by pilot error for every one lost to the enemy.

That afternoon, Margaret came over to our trailer and asked for me. Zinkgraf pointed me out to her. I hated this woman enough to grab my machine gun and shoot her on the spot! After all, she might have deliberately killed someone in order to get the picture she wanted.

She smiled sweetly and asked in a sultry voice if I would please be kind enough to develop three rolls of film for her. "I've just made some *marvelous* shots and I'm anxious to see them."

"Sorry, Miss Bourke-White, but we are too busy here to do work for civilians. Sometimes we work until 4 a.m."

"The general told me you would be pleased to develop *my* film."

"Well, I guess the general has forgotten how busy we are."

Her "sugar and spice" demeanor *immediately* turned to vinegar and she stomped back over to the headquarters building.

Not more than ten minutes later, a major came back with her three rolls of film.

"Sergeant, the general wants you to develop these rolls *now!*"

"Major," I said evenly, "we aren't set up to handle small rolls of film. If we tried, something might go wrong."

"I said *do it now!*"

"Yes, Sir."

I gave the rolls to Tucker and said, "Here. Soup this stuff."

After processing the film and washing it, Tucker came out of the lab with the wet negatives. He clamped them to the awning to dry.

My boys were all as disgusted about this as I was. Tucker said, "Wouldn't it be terrible if these negatives all fell down onto the sand while they are still wet?"

We'll never know how it happened, but Miss Bourke-White's negatives *did* all fall down on the ground, and before we realized it, we had walked all over them. They were no longer recognizable.

One of the great unsolved mysteries of World War II.

A few days later, Miss Bourke-White asked for and got permission from the general to go on a mission in a B-17. The wise old general, not wishing to risk the life of such a valuable and indispensable person, made sure it would be a "milk run." In other words, the mission would be an easy one where our intelligence officers had predicted there would be no enemy flak or fighters.

The "facility" on the B-17 consisted of a funnel attached to the front bulkhead of the radioman's compartment; then it connected to a hose that went through the wall into the bomb bay—a convenience we called the relief tube, and *not* designed for women.

On the morning of Margaret's mission, I reached under my cot to get my steel helmet before getting out of bed. This was the usual routine because I would fill it with hot water and use it for shaving. But *this* morning it wasn't there. The helmet liner was there, but somebody had stolen the steel shell while I slept—my life-saving headgear!

I was asking around to see if anybody had seen what had happened to it. One of the radar operators said, "Yeah, I seen one of them guys from *Little Bill* slip it out from under ya and take off with it." "Why would he do that," I wondered. "*All* of us have steel helmets, and we each have only one head."

The 17s came back very early that afternoon because they had probably just gone out a short distance and unloaded on a sauerkraut storage building or something.

About an hour after the planes had landed, parked and shut down, the crew chief from *Little Bill* walked up to me and asked, "You Thompson?"

"Yes."

"This your helmet?"

"Well, mine's missing. Where did you find it?"

Sheepishly, the crew chief said, "Well, Miss Bourke-White rode on my plane today. She thought that she might need a potty, and she specifically asked for *your* helmet."

While the planes were landing from one mission, we saw a column of smoke off in the distance, east of the field. It reached a thousand feet or more. It was *black* smoke. There was no doubt about it, one of our B-17s had crashed while trying to reach the field. It was too far away to see if there had been any parachutes.

This meant that about a dozen or so men would now own nice flight jackets and other articles that were supposedly "lost on that plane." Every time a plane was lost, dozens of other guys personal items were claimed to have gone down with it. New ones were always issued. American ingenuity.

One evening somebody got lucky with a 20mm rapid-fire cannon and hit a Ju-88 at dusk and he went down right on the field. As soon as the bombing stopped, several vehicles raced out to the scene of his crash landing. I missed the opportunity of a lifetime because our jeep was jacked up with a wheel removed.

Bourke-White and our commanding officer were out there

when the German four-man crew was crawling out of the wreckage. *Nobody* was supposed to talk to an enemy before an interrogation officer is through with him. The officer hadn't arrived.

Margaret pounced on the injured crewmen with her camera
and questions. The interrogation officer got there just as she was
leaving. The prisoners were so nervous and jumpy after Margaret's
whirlwind session that the officer couldn't get anything out of
them.

The crew chief of one of the P-38s came over to our trailer with
a film cassette from the gun-sight camera. He said the pilot
wouldn't be very proud of the results because of what the camera
had recorded.

"The lieutenant told me that he was coming back with the
bombers and decided to drop down and see what was going on below. He was flying right on the deck. He zoomed over some trees,
and there in a field straight ahead of him in his sights was a long
line of German soldiers getting their chow from the back of a
truck. He was there so fast, the Germans didn't have time to run.
He opened up on them with his 20mm cannon and saw Germans
and pieces of Germans flying all over the place."

"Well," I said, "looks like he would be proud of killing so many
Krauts on only one pass."

"No, he isn't. He wants to shoot at their airplanes, not at their
chow-line."

"Okay, we'll soup this stuff and see what he got."

"My lieutenant is still shook over what he saw a few days ago
while he was escorting the B-17s. They had turned back from the
target and were still over 'flak alley.' It was strange, but Kraut
fighters were right in there with them, flak and all, so he went in
after the Jerries. He said the 17s were blowing to bits above and
below him and he was lucky he didn't hit any debris.

"He said he saw a blasted mass of flesh swinging under a parachute but didn't know if it was out of a 17 or a Focke-Wulf. He
circled it and saw some guts hanging down and swaying back and
forth as the chute oscillated. He got so sick he threw up in his
oxygen mask."

I had been hearing far too many things like this and vowed I would *never* shock the folks back home with the gory details. I thought it would be better to let them see the "sanitized" versions of the war in movies where the hero was always wounded in his shoulder.

Of course I didn't believe the folks back home would ever read about the mutilated bodies or the men who went stark raving mad. They also wouldn't read about cowards, deserters, murderers, and looters. How could they?

Ernie Pyle told us that even *his* dispatches were heavily censored. I hoped that someday after the war somebody would have the courage to tell the uncensored truth about this "gentleman's war."

The French Foreign Legion

I WAS WALKING DOWN THE MAIN STREET in Biskra one mid-afternoon when I saw a long line of GIs leading up to the back of a big English lorry. Upon further examination, I noticed several folding cots sitting on the dusty, blazing-hot pavement beside the lorry. There was a painting of a large, ugly-looking vulture on the canvas side of the rig. It had its wings spread and its mouth open.

Men were stretched out on the cots, and two Limeys wearing white coats were going from one cot to the next, connecting and disconnecting blood withdrawal tubes.

We had heard that just before the major battles started, Limey bloodmobiles came into areas populated with thousands of Allied soldiers. They always had more volunteers than they needed because they traded a pint of English beer for a pint of blood.

Drinking warm English beer was not very high on my list of favorite things to do, but I was taking the day off, and thought this was for a good cause, so I joined the line. In a half-hour, I was flat on my back, blinking up into a hot, brilliant desert sun.

As I watched my blood dripping into a glass bottle sitting on the pavement, I wondered who would get it. It would be a foot soldier, no doubt, who had stopped a German bullet or a piece of shrapnel. So *much* blood was being lost out there. Why?

When the needle was jerked out of my arm, and I sat up on the cot, a pint of beer was placed in my hand. The fellow next to me was just getting his beer too. He was dressed in a French Foreign Legion uniform. They had a regiment in Biskra.

I asked the trooper if he liked English beer.

"Blimey Yank, 'tis the nectar of the *Gods!* Not as good as we 'ave in Ireland, but good 'nuf for *seconds.*"

"Will they give you seconds?"

"*Sure* they will. I'll get me back in line an' toss this 'un down while I move up to get me next one."

"My friend, if you give two pints of blood, and drink two pints of *that* stuff, you'll be in pretty bad shape, won't you?"

I handed my pint to the Legionnaire and said, "Here. Now you won't have to go back for seconds."

A new friendship suddenly blossomed. He said, "Would ya 'ave anythin' printed in English ya can let me 'ave? I'm the only one in this regiment who speaks and reads English. All of the newspapers and magazines in me barracks are printed in French, German, Italian and Spanish. Most of our men are Spaniards just out of the civil war up there, but we 'ave our share of the others too."

"Yes, I believe I have an old *Reader's Digest* and a couple of *Stars and Stripes* I could let you have."

He introduced himself as Legionnaire Donovan, and asked if I would like to walk over to his regimental compound and look around. I had always had a fascination for the Legion, so I readily accepted.

This was certainly the most famous fighting unit in the world. The Legion was manned by the only true mercenaries left in existence. They would fight whomever their leaders told them to. Death on a battlefield was their highest goal.

Legionnaire Donovan and I left the Limey blood wagon and started walking past a block of white two-story buildings. Stores and shops were on the sidewalk level and Donovan explained that there were rooms and apartments above them.

A small white sign had been posted above an open door off the sidewalk. Two French words were printed on it in black—"CABINE PROPHOLOCTIQUE."

On the second floor directly above this sign was a small balcony and an attractive young lady was standing there leaning on a black iron railing. She started smiling and waving at us.

"Looks like she knows you," I commented.

"She bloody well does, Yank. I'm one of 'er friends. 'Er name is Mademoiselle Juliette and she is half French and half Arab. She has *many* friends and lets us come up to see 'er whenever we want to. Later this evenin', a long queue of 'er friends will be standin' 'ere on the sidewalk waitin' to go up and visit with 'er one at a time."

We turned a corner and walked two blocks to the Legion post.

We stepped into a long narrow hall that served as their barracks. It was plain and unadorned—no curtains, no pictures, no tables and no chairs. Each bed was simply two gray blankets on the floor—one was folded in half the long way, and the other was in a tight roll and placed at the head of the bed.

There was a sign printed in French hanging on the far wall. Donovan interpreted it for me.

"You Legionnaires are soldiers made to die. I send you where you die." It was signed by their commanding officer.

Donovan explained to me that many men with fine minds, for reasons of their own, joined the Foreign Legion. He joined because he had murdered two men in Ireland, and had escaped into the "protective arms" of the Legion *just* in time.

Donovan said they were paid a few francs twice a month, and most of the troopers would spend it all on cognac and Mademoiselle Juliette and forget their problems until they sobered up.

We sat down on Donovan's blanket, and he told me some more about the French Foreign Legion. His narrative was fascinating, though a little jumbled.

Their headquarters was north-west of Biskra at Sidi-bel-Abbes. Various regiments were spread around North Africa, and the one in Biskra was the Premier (first) Regiment. As he was giving me this bit of information, he reached into a small cardboard box at the head of his bed and pulled out a regimental insignia badge with "Premier Regiment" printed on it—and handed it to me. I pinned it on my "go to hell" cap and wore it proudly for the duration.

An enlistment in the Foreign Legion was for five years. Donovan had been in for three and one-half. He said he hated it, but couldn't leave and go back to Ireland. He also said the Germans and Spaniards were the really *tough* ones and made the best Legionnaires.

I asked if there had ever been any Americans in the Legion. "Sure, we've 'ad Yanks, but I 'aven't known any meself. They say some Americans *hate* it and use diplomatic pressure ta get out—yer famous composer, Cole Porter, for example, who was a Legionnaire during World War I."

There were about 10,000 men in the Legion, and North Africa

wasn't the only place you could find them. Some of them were all the way up in Norway and Sweden. They simply went where the fighting was—and they didn't care *who* they fought! When the Americans landed in Oran, the Legion was 60 miles south of the city at their headquarters. They hurried to get up there and fight the Americans, not because they *hated* us, but because they just wanted a good *fight!*

They didn't get up to Oran in time to join the regular French army in the fighting. "One reason is that British planes bombed 'n strafed our truck 'n tank convoy before we got there. And then there was a little problem with our colonel," Donovan said.

Three days after the Allies took Oran, the Foreign Legion, along with the regular French Forces, turned their guns in the direction of the Germans. "We were anxious to start shooting the Germans," Donovan said. "Even the German troopers in our outfit were eager to shoot 'em. We '*ad* ta, our commandin' officer gave the orders."

(I later learned that the Foreign Legion was guarding the port at Casablanca when we landed there at the same time we were landing at Oran and they put up a good fight.)

Donovan placed his lips close to my ear and said, "But while our troopers were on the road to Oran, they 'ad a bit of a problem. The colonel in charge really wanted ta fight the Americans, but the troopers decided they didn't. So they disposed of the colonel and traded 'is uniform and sidearms to some French civilians for cognac and wine—*lots* of wine." "Incredible!" I thought. I knew they were a bunch of murderers, but one of their own officers?

I asked Donovan where their officers were trained.

"They are trained at Saint-Cyr, the French military academy." It sounded like West Point. "We get some *good* officers 'cuz every time a class graduates, the *smartest* student can choose 'is place of duty. And guess where most of 'em go?—to the Legion!"

An officer came through a door at the far end of the barracks and walked down the aisle past us. Donovan leaped to his feet and stood as rigid as an oak tree while he held a salute. I got up and saluted also, but our salutes were "sloppy" compared to theirs. The officer continued through the hall and left through the back door without acknowledging our salutes.

"What do they do to ya if ya don't salute?" Donovan asked.

"I've seen yer officers on the street and sometimes yer soldiers just ignore 'em."

"Well," I said, "the first thing they taught us in basic training was, salute anything that moved. If it didn't move—pick it up. If you couldn't pick it up—paint it. So when I meet an officer, I salute."

I told him about the time in basic training when I was walking through the squadron area. "I was carrying a large, heavy box. When I was passing an officer, I said, 'Consider yourself saluted, Sir.' The officer stopped and gave me the harshest lecture I'd had since my gym teacher caught me scratching my name on my locker."

"We salute our officers even when they are 'cross the street or are lookin' the other way," Donovan said. "We get a week in the stockade with our 'eads shaved if we don't salute."

We stood up, walked through a door and stopped in the courtyard. Donovan pointed. "See that little square stockade over there—the one with bars on the windows?"

"Yes," I said, "is that where they put you after they shave your head?"

Donovan laughed and replied, "Well, no, not right now. There are a few prisoners in there waitin' for execution. The Spahis brought 'em in." I asked about the Spahis and told him I had met one right after I got to the date palm oasis of Cora. I said I hadn't been sure which side he was on when he rode up on his white horse.

Donovan laughed again. "Well, when you Yanks landed on the coast, 'e was with the 'Heinies'—Vichy French, but like the rest of us in the Legion, 'e was on *your* side by the time ya met 'im."

"I'm glad he knew that when he rode up," I said, "because he had a long sharp dagger."

Donovan said that Spahis were native Algerian cavalrymen who ride white stallions, and the ones around Biskra reported to this French Foreign Legion post. "In fact," he said, "*your* Spahi and 'is partner were the ones who captured some of the prisoners over there in the stockade and brought 'em in."

The French Foreign Legion—the Spahis. "*Incredible,*" I thought. Life in the Foreign Legion must be horrible. Living to fight merely for the sake of fighting seemed inconceivable to me.

The Executions

THE LETTERS I GOT FROM HOME were always cheerful and encouraging. "Don't worry about us, everything is fine." I was lucky. Some of the fellows got upsetting letters about conscientious objectors, 4-Fs like Frank Sinatra, zoot-suiters and worst of all, the cowardly striking defense workers. These workers were as bad as our enemy and we thought of them as such.

It was rumored in some of the letters that a few defense workers had deliberately produced faulty aircraft parts to rebel against some triviality on their assembly line. They weren't concerned about the airmen they would kill or the planes that would become junk in a foreign land. We even heard that officials in a huge midwest plant were forced to provide a cover-up. We were telling each other, "I pray that I'll live through this war just so I can go back home and kill those lousy bums."

Some of the guys folks complained about conditions at home.

"We only have an 'A' windshield sticker and three gallons of gas a week doesn't take us very far."

"Your poor sister can't find Mars bars anymore."

"I can't buy a hot water bottle just because it's made of rubber."

The *worst* letters, however, were probably the "Dear Johns." These were the dreaded letters from a wife or girlfriend beginning harmlessly but exploding with the news that, "I have found someone more available."

Whenever a guy would say, "I just got a Dear John letter," we would leave him alone long enough to let him tear up all of his previous letters.

News about zoot-suiters and John L. Lewis, head of the miner's union, made us mad, too. We hated the zoot-suiters because of what we learned by reading letters from the Southern California area. Pictures of them were in a couple of photo magazines. They looked weird! Wide and pointed padded shoulders, long jackets, baggy pants tapering down to grip the ankles, wide-brimmed hats, and metal chains draping down to the knees.

It started with the Mexican and Negro kids and spread. There was even a popular tune being played in the States and, of course, by Axis Sally:

"I want a zoot-suit
With a drape shape
And a neat pleat . . . ."

We were disgusted to know this was going on back home. This is probably why Axis Sally bombarded us with it.

Then we read that the sailors and marines in the San Diego and Los Angeles area got so fed up with it that they would stop streetcars and snatch the "suiters" off and tear their clothes to shreds. We loved it.

There was a lot of anger among the troops when we heard that John L. Lewis had pulled out the miners. "They should string him up." It wasn't good enough that they were making $150 or $200 a week while we were getting bombed and shot up for a few bucks a month.

"I'd just as soon shoot that SOB Lewis as shoot a German. He's doing just as much to lose the war for us."

"Wonder what the *hell* Lewis and his gang of traitors would do if *we* went on strike over *here?*"

There was a 4-F fellow back in the States who was hated even more than John L. Lewis. His name was Frank Sinatra. News about him always sparked a lot of very unflattering remarks. One letter quoted a Marine writer who was wounded on Guadalcanal.

"I think Frank Sinatra is the most hated man by the GIs in the world—much more than Hitler." William Manchester was the Marine. Our morale officers had their hands full.

After the Germans finished their nightly bombings and went home, peace and quiet prevailed. Well, actually things were quiet, perhaps, but not always peaceful. Every night, spies and saboteurs who had been dropped in by parachute crawled out of their hiding places and went to work.

A B-17 or a P-38 would suddenly explode in the early hours of the morning. A GI sleeping in his pup tent would not live to see another day because he had died during the night with a piano wire twisted tightly around his neck. These fellows were very skillful in their chosen profession.

The job of capturing these troublemakers was handled by the Arab Spahis. They were the most feared and treacherous soldiers on the Sahara desert, riding their Arabian stallions silently around the base every night from sundown to sunup. We never saw them. We never heard them. They captured the spies and saboteurs and delivered them to the Foreign Legion prison in Biskra.

One of the spies was captured by an alert military policeman. The German spy was walking barefooted through the flight line just like dozens of Arabs did every day. He was dressed like an Arab, was deeply tanned like an Arab, but he was walking like his feet were tender and every step hurt him. This caught the attention of the MP and soon the suspect was stripped of his disguise and driven to the Foreign Legion prison.

Word spread all around the area that there would soon be a public execution near Biskra. Even the Arabs riding in from the desert on their camels and donkeys stopped in town to read the public bulletin board for the exact time and place. Tuesday was the day and noon was the time.

Our base commander asked me to attend the executions, not as an official witness, but to confiscate any cameras brought to the site by Americans. It had been announced at the base that anybody who was off duty and wanted to see the show was welcome to do so, but no cameras were allowed.

The general handed me a written order to show anybody whose camera I had to confiscate. He also said he wanted me to wear his .45-caliber automatic, "to add a little authority." I was beginning to wonder why my orders didn't always come from our squadron commander, a captain, but usually from "the old man" himself. I felt very privileged, because he often gave me access to things happening around the base that the average GI knew nothing about.

I drove the jeep to within a quarter of a mile from the place selected for the executions, parked it and removed the rotor from the distributor. If I hadn't done that, the jeep would have been stolen by another GI. Jeeps were hard to identify even with white serial numbers painted on the hoods. It was always tempting for an otherwise honest soldier to "borrow" a jeep, drive around for awhile, and then abandon it. Removing the rotor didn't always work, however, because some of the experienced thieves carried spare rotors with them.

French, Arabs and Americans were walking toward the site in great numbers. I fell in with them, and noticed they weren't acting like they were on their way to witness eleven men meet violent deaths. Everyone was laughing, chatting and acting like people crowding into a circus tent.

The site for the executions had been well chosen. It was a mile outside of Biskra. The ground sloped gently toward a long ridge of sand that was about 20 feet high, forming a perfect amphitheater for the drama.

The weather was hot with a faint breeze coming in from the desert, and the sky above was clear of the smallest cloud. A pleasant day to die.

Ten or fifteen feet in front of the ridge were four wooden stakes. They had been driven into the ground and painted a brilliant white.

Now the area was becoming flooded with the good citizens of Biskra. It was rumored that eager visitors were arriving from as far north as Constantine, where some of the prisoners were captured, and as far south as Ouled Djella, about 70 miles into the Sahara.

French gendarmes hurriedly roped off a spectators' area and struggled to push the milling crowd into place. A tarnished six-piece brass band struck up the familiar, though distorted, sound of "La Marseillaise."

Little boys tunneling through a solid forest of adult legs popped up in front of the straining ropes, only to be grabbed by the gendarmes and ushered quickly to the rear of the crowd.

As the crowd grew, voices became louder until it sounded almost like the last few moments before the first pitch in a baseball game. Some of the Arab and French boys were having a fine time running around and playing with their poor, mangy mongrels, all skin and bones and sores. The kids would pause now and then to glance down the road toward Biskra or to greet a friend.

Arab men pushed through the crowd selling dates and tangerines. Mohammed Gazda, my dart-playing neighbor, was one of
them.

Everybody in the audience turned toward the road from the village. They were coming! Five Legionnaire officers riding white
horses led the parade. They were followed by four squads of riflemen all in step and looking very stern. A flat-bed truck brought up
the rear.

We all strained to see the eleven "guests of honor" who were
standing unsteadily in the truck with their hands tied behind
them.

The parade was halted by a command from an officer. The four
armed squads marched to their positions about 15 yards in front
of the stakes.

An officer stood at the end of the truck and motioned for the
first four prisoners to jump down. They obeyed without any show
of emotion. One of the men was wearing an Arab turban.

The officer walked toward the white stakes, and the four prisoners followed in a single file with no prodding from the other officers, and still showing no emotion. It almost seemed like this had
been rehearsed.

Each prisoner stopped in front of a stake and turned toward his
firing squad. The prisoners were then ordered to kneel down on
their knees. Their hands were pulled behind the stakes and tied.
Black blindfolds were applied.

This was becoming very interesting and I didn't want to miss
any of it, but I spotted a second lieutenant trying to conceal a
35mm camera, and I had to do my duty and take it away from
him. He handed the camera to me without any questions. I hurriedly opened the back of the camera, jerked the film out, and
gave the camera back to him. He just shrugged his shoulders in
resignation and said nothing.

The show was moving pretty fast. The firing squads positioned
themselves into two rows of four men each, the back row standing
and the front row kneeling. A civilian, who was probably a clergyman of some sort, went from one blindfolded prisoner to the next.
He bent over and said something close to their ears.

The French Foreign Legion officer in charge of the executions paid us a visit.

. . . then the Arabs threw the two GIs off the highest bridge.

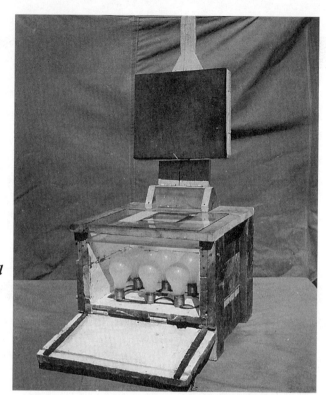

We scrounged around and found enough junk to build a contact printer.

We were probably the only guys in North Africa with an underground darkroom.

A sharp command was given and the clergyman scurried back to safety. An officer stood near each firing squad. Another officer at the end of the line raised his saber, paused for a moment while the riflemen took careful aim, then brought the saber down with a snap.

The thirty-two rifles blazed with an ear-splitting crack! The prisoners, bodies were slammed against the stakes! Splinters flew! Four clouds of dust rose lazily from the sandy ridge. The prisoners slumped forward, their heads swinging limply for a second or two.

Each of the four squad officers marched stiffly to a dead man hanging from his stake, removed a pistol from his holster, placed the muzzle near the head and delivered the "coup de grace." The Arab's turban flew off his head.

The four bodies were cut down from the bloody stakes and carried to the truck where the remaining seven prisoners stood waiting their turn.

The next four prisoners were put through the same procedure and then the last three brought the executions to a close.

The crowd behaved as though the show had been brought to town on other occasions. Laughter and merriment right up to the firing commands. Dead silence during the firing, then loud cheers and applause to show their appreciation.

I followed the crowd back to the place where I'd left the jeep, replaced the rotor, and drove to the base. After returning the general's .45, I walked back to the trailer to finish my lab work. Another day, another new experience.

A desert interlude . . . .

Stars and Stripes: Eleven Axis parachutists who were wearing civilian clothing when captured in Allied territory in French North Africa have been executed, the Algiers radio announced today.

They were among four groups of parachutists dropped east and south of Constantine, Algeria, January 21 and captured with the cooperation of Arabs, the broadcast said. Those executed were said to have included Germans and Arabs and Fascist Frenchmen who had been in France as recently as November.

Algiers

A RED FLARE WAS SHOT FROM A B-17 while it was making a straight-in approach to the field. One engine was on fire and another smoking badly. It made a wheels-up landing and skidded for a thousand feet. When it had slowed down to about 50 miles per hour, the crew members started jumping out and rolling and bouncing along behind the plane. By the time it had stopped skidding, the fire trucks were shooting chemical foam on the burning engine.

Two meat wagons hurried back down the field and retrieved the badly shaken crewmen. I was lucky to be close and got a good series of shots of the whole incident. The plane didn't burn. The crewmen escaped with only torn-up flight suits and bruises. One suffered a broken arm, but that was the most serious injury.

One of the meat wagon drivers had come from the hills of Tennessee and knew how to distill French wine into rotgut. It had the kick of an Arab donkey and was so powerful it worked well in Zippo cigarette lighters. Everything was going fine until the "Revenuers" found his still.

The lieutenant who led the raiding party sipped and savored the fiery potion until he was satisfied it was, indeed, illegal. The drunken lieutenant managed to stay on his feet barely long enough to give the order to destroy.

Some of the "die-hard drunks" would drink *anything* to get a high, even Aqua Velva, an aftershave. A couple of guys drank the fluid from the expandable rubber de-icing boots on the leading edge of a B-17 wing. It was methyl alcohol. They died. Somebody broke into the medical dispensary and stole the grain alcohol. French wine was simply not potent enough for some soldiers.

One morning the BBC from London announced that the actor Leslie Howard was killed when his plane was shot down on a flight from Lisbon to London.

A captain we had never seen before was walking around our photo trailer one morning examining it like it was parked on a used car lot. I asked him if I could help him, and he replied that he had come down from Algiers to take the trailer back with him.

I was stunned. For what possible reason? Our little photo section was keeping the trailer humming with activity constantly. The bombing and photo reconnaissance missions were increasing in size and intensity to where we had practically reached the breaking point.

Immediately, I said, "I'm sorry, Captain, but this trailer isn't going to leave this spot. It's the most overworked piece of equipment in the North African Theater of Operations. *Nobody* is doing the volume of lab work that we are right here." I knew I had been insubordinate and waited for the consequences.

"Sergeant, that may be true, but I have orders from higher up to take it."

"Please explain higher up, Sir."

"Colonel Roosevelt has had his eye on your trailer for quite some time and has decided that he needs it in Algiers."

Ah *hah,* my old nemesis, Elliott, strikes again!

Since Harrington was still a "buck" private and had nothing to lose, I asked him to escort the gentleman over to headquarters where he would be briefed by the general. Harrington took hold of the captain's arm, but the captain jerked away and stormed off in the direction of the headquarters building. In about ten minutes, the old man himself came over.

"Sergeant, you've got to let Captain Wallace take the trailer with him."

"Excuse me, General, but you know better than anybody that we can't support your groups without it."

"Colonel Roosevelt and I discussed it on the phone and as of now it's *his.*"

I knew I was getting *way* out of line. Staff sergeants don't talk to generals this way, but if I was going to lose my trailer, I might as well lose my stripes.

"But Roosevelt is only a colonel, and you are a *general.* You out-rank him."

"Sergeant, you are becoming insubordinate. Anyway, he is the son of the President of the United States. Does that make any sense to you?" And with that, the general turned and started back to headquarters.

Martini said, "Sarge, you've *had* it."

"Here we go again," I thought, "a guy with a famous dad . . . ."

Captain Wallace had been waiting at headquarters, and must have been given a quick "go ahead" because he was back in a matter of minutes with his two men and their deuce-and-a-half.

The three of them sat in their truck and watched us for the next half hour as we removed all of our personal belongings from the trailer. This gave Zinkgraf time to perform a dastardly deed.

Otto had recently received a package from his girlfriend in Plymouth, Wisconsin, the cheese capitol of the U.S. This package contained a large chuck of the smelliest cheese ever invented by man. It smelled like an unventilated room full of Kraut infantry-men who hadn't changed their socks since the war started.

What *really* made it so bad is the fact that the cheese had gone to England, and finally the post office personnel had traced Zinkgraf to North Africa. By the time the package arrived at our base, the oil in the cheese had saturated the heavy brown wrapping paper and it was *ripe!*

The highlight of my day was always morning mail call. I lived for the letters from my wife, Wilma. The day Zinkgraf got his package, the mail-call crowd thinned out until everything was gone, except for a greasy-looking parcel lying on the ground under the mail table.

We were walking back toward the trailer when the mail clerk shouted, "Hey, Zinkgraf, ya got somethin' here." Otto went back and the clerk handed him the package, saying, "You'd better hurry and open it. I think it's *dead.*"

Now for the dastardly deed. While the rest of us were cannibal-izing the trailer, Zinkgraf was busy on the back side of the trailer removing the grill from the air conditioning vent and stuffing the vile-smelling wrapper down into the shaft that brought air into the two labs.

Our faithful old trailer disappeared, and we were left standing beside the irrigation ditch with nothing left but our pup tents and a small palm tree with tin icicles hanging from it.

I was as furious as Doolittle had been the night he stood on top of our headquarters building screaming profanities. I was suffering from poverty of vocabulary, however, because even Webster couldn't come up with the words describing how I felt.

I slept under the stars that night, because the trailer awning had always been my shelter.

Still finding it hard to believe that the old man had allowed himself to be "taken in" by that jerk in Algiers, I went over to his office and again got a little out of line.

This time the general settled me down and started his "sympathetic father" routine. "Thompson, I know we've lost something we really needed, and I also happen to know that it was your pride and joy because you brought it all the way over here from the States. It's gone, my boy, it's *gone!*"

"Okay, then, how are we going to do our lab work?"

"Sergeant, you have earned a few days off. I want you to take my car and get out of here and cool down. I don't want to see you around here for a couple of weeks." I didn't argue with him.

The old man's car was *beautiful!* It was a light blue Hotchkiss convertible made in France. There was an eight-cylinder *in-line* engine under the hood. He had "liberated" it from a wealthy French merchant somewhere up the road.

I threw a camera and a few personal things on the rumble seat, gassed it up at the fuel dump and headed north all by myself. No one would have wanted to be near me anyway.

In a little over three hours I arrived at Constantine, "the city of seven bridges." The scenery had changed completely. No more flat desert . . . mountains and large trees, instead. This was an area where some of our men had come to hunt hyenas.

I parked the Hotchkiss and removed the rotor. As I was walking away, a crowd of GIs started gathering around to see this vehicular spectacle. They probably thought I was some kind of a prince or potentate in disguise. The Fifth Army Headquarters, newly arrived from the U.S., was here.

Constantine was divided by the Rhumel River and stretched over the top of a huge, deep chalk cliff and was connected by seven bridges. It had been named after Emperor Constantine by the Romans during their occupation.

I ate at local GI mess halls, but was curious about French and Arab food, so I tried to find an Arab restaurant. There were none to be found. Somebody told me the Arabs had no restaurants.

After trying the food in a French restaurant, which was nothing to write home about, I asked the waiter what kind of food the Arabs ate. He said that couscous was their favorite food and they always had some on hand in their kitchen. So, even though I had already eaten, I ordered some couscous.

This Arab "delicacy" was made from wheat that had been steamed, and it was served with some kind of meat, vegetables and a soup-like sauce. It was no better than the French food, and there was a dead fly in the sauce.

The streets and sidewalks were full of Arabs. Their main capacity seemed to be for squatting on their haunches wrapped in filthy robes, staring endlessly into space. There were few women and no girls.

The Arab boys didn't sit around with their elders. When the GIs would light cigarettes while walking on the streets and sidewalks, the boys would follow them. When the butts were tossed to the ground, the kids would pounce on them. Three or four butts would make a cigarette, and that could be traded for food at the Arab market.

The three days I spent in Constantine *did* calm me down somewhat. I was now just an American tourist sitting at the Cafe Charbons, a sidewalk cafe, sipping sweet muscatel and watching American, French and Arab people walk by. My "hotel" was the local gendarme station, now being occupied by American military police. It had running water and real beds!

One day I was sitting in front of the Petit Chat, another sidewalk cafe, talking with two soldiers who were stationed in the city. We were discussing Arab customs and culture, when one of the soldiers told me just how treacherous the natives could be.

Apparently two American GIs had been found in a ravine nine hundred feet under the highest of the seven bridges. They were both nude and their genitals had been cut off and sewn inside their mouths. They had probably been seen glancing at an Arab woman on the street. The "Welcome to North Africa" book had warned us about such things.

Tourist attractions were plentiful in the area, but I couldn't rid my mind of the fact that our photo trailer was now somewhere up in Algiers, and I wanted to find it and see what the "idiot" was doing with it. On the way out of town, I stopped at Tlergma airport to see what kind of aircraft were there.

I headed northwest toward Algiers. There were very few French people on the road, but the hundreds of Arabs and their houses were interesting. They lived in what looked like hollowed-out dung hills. They rode around on tiny donkeys, their feet almost touching the ground on either side.

The rags the Arabs dressed in were made of hundreds of scraps of cloth crudely stitched together. Most of the Arabs had horrible sores on their arms and legs. It was no wonder they begged us to trade our mattress covers to them for anything of value they had. One of our friends told us that an Arab had brought his daughter to the field with him, and offered to trade her for a mattress cover and a package of cigarettes.

After six hours I was in that famous port city on the Mediterranean, the home of the Casbah. It was also General Eisenhower's home—Supreme Allied Headquarters.

I drove southeast of town to the Maison Blanche airport to see what kind of planes were there and perhaps find Roosevelt's 5th Photo Recon. While I was making inquiries, I was told that General Eisenhower's driver might be able to help me locate Roosevelt.

"She knows all the brass," a fellow told me, "because she's been driving for the old man since they were in London." As he was talking, he pointed toward the ramp where a dull four-door olive-drab Packard staff car was backed up against the fence. It was the old man's car, all right, because a red sign with three stars was fastened to the front bumper. The woman driver was leaning against the fence with her arms folded. She was wearing an American .45.

I thanked the fellow and started walking toward Ike's driver. The guy called to me. "Want to have some fun with 'er?" I turned and looked at him. "She always wears that .45. Call 'er pistol-packin' mama, and I'll bet she'll take a swing at ya."

"Pistol Packin' Mama" was a very popular tune currently being played in the States and on radios over here. The GIs had probably been driving this poor lady crazy by identifying her with the feisty girl in the tune.

I walked over to the fence and introduced myself.

"I'm Sergeant Thompson, and I'm trying to find Colonel Roosevelt. I was told that you work for General Eisenhower."

"Yes, Sergeant, I am the General's driver, but I don't know where Colonel Roosevelt is. My name is Kay Summersby."

Kay spoke with a lilting, clipped enunciation—very refined. She was wearing a leather flight jacket, an overseas cap, a pair of men's pants and GI shoes. She had red hair and green eyes and was far better looking than the average English girl. She looked like she was about my sister Alice's age—probably a few years older than I.

Kay hadn't mentioned her rank, as I had, when we met.

"Are you a sergeant, lieutenant, or what?" I wanted to know.

"None of the above," she answered. "I'm a civilian." I thought it was odd that an English civilian was Ike's driver, but before I asked, she said, "I was a civilian volunteer ambulance driver in London, and when your generals started coming over, some of us became staff drivers—and I was assigned to General Eisenhower."

Kay was glad to have somebody to talk to—she seemed bored waiting for the general's plane to come in. Since she was English, I told her I had been stationed in England and described my trip from England to Africa. I mentioned that Ernie Pyle, the war correspondent, was on our ship and we had made it through the Strait of Gibraltar without being torpedoed.

"Oh, I met Mr. Pyle in England," she said. "He came into our office to talk to the general and that's when he was told which ship he would be on in the convoy to Africa."

"It was one of *your* ships, the *Rangatike*," I said.

"I knew that ship went over a month before we did," Kay said, "but we weren't so lucky when *we* got into the Mediterranean. We were torpedoed and our ship went to the bottom."

"You are very lucky," I said.

"Yes, my three friends and I all got into the same lifeboat together and weren't picked up until the next morning. You have probably heard of one of them, because she is a famous American photographer for *Life Magazine*—Margaret Bourke-White."

Margaret Bourke-White! I had to bite my tongue to keep from verbalizing my reaction to that hated name. While Kay was telling me what a good bridge player Margaret was, I was thinking what a *monster* she was!

"Do you have time to hear a funny tale," Miss Summersby asked, "or must you be dashing off?"

"I'm in no hurry," I replied, "my war has been put on hold for a few days. Yes, I'd like to hear it."

"One of our chaps flew over from London a few days ago, and he told us this story. The general thought it was simply *smashing*.

"The Bosch were bombing the bicycle factory in Covington one night. It probably seemed to the Bosch that they had been unable to bring us to our knees, but if they destroyed our ability to produce bicycles, we would give up immediately.

"A neighborhood air raid warden was trying to get an elderly couple out of their house and into a shelter.

"At first, the old folks said, 'That bloody old Hitler wasn't going to run them out of the house they had lived in for 50 years.' Finally, when a stray bomb hit across the street, they agreed to run to the shelter with the warden.

"They had hurried down the steps and were on the sidewalk, when the old woman turned and started running back into the house. 'Hey, where you goin'!' the husband shouted.

'I'm goin' back and get me teeth,' the wife replied.

'Hell, woman,' he said, 'they're droppin' *bombs*, not ruddy ham sandwiches!'"

I chuckled, we exchanged parting pleasantries, and I left.

I drove back into the city and stopped at the first MP station I saw, and they gave me directions to the 5th Photo Recon complex.

None of the soldiers up here looked like they had been closer to the war than the news they listened to on BBC. They were all dressed in class "A" dress uniforms, had shiny shoes and saluted everything that moved—even French mailmen. They were "canteen commandos," because they had the Red Cross, the USO and the Naafi. The Salvation Army was conspicuous in its absence, however. They were somewhere up close to the "sharp end," the front.

This made me a little envious, in a way, because these happy, well-fed, well-entertained men were the ones who kept our bombs and gasoline trickling down to the *real* war, and they would probably never hear a bomb blast or have to duck red-hot tracers streaming down at them.

When I got to Roosevelt's area, I found a building surrounded by olive trees. There were also several pyramidal tents and vehicles of various types scattered around.

The trailer was there, all right, parked between two trees. I drove up to it wondering if I was about to have a confrontation with the President's son. He wasn't there, but four fellows were busy stripping everything out of it. I said, "Hey, what are you guys doing?"

"We're throwing all of this junk out of here so we can convert it into an air-conditioned villa for Colonel Roosevelt."

Converting it into a *villa?* I couldn't believe it. Here was a piece of equipment that had been serving the war effort in a very important way and then some big shot came along and grabbed it to satisfy his own personal comfort! *Everybody* sacrifices a few personal needs during wartime, but not the *President's* son!

My thoughts at that moment were, "I'd like to punch him. I'd like to punch that S.O.P.—that Son of a President!"

I was upset all over again and thought that another few days at those sidewalk tables in Constantine would help, but feeling a little homesick, I headed south for the desert.

Chateaudun du Rhumel

I GOT BACK TO BISKRA AND STARTED DRIVING down the one-mile stretch of desert to the base at about 45 kilometers per hour, when a little Arab boy ran out in front of me. I hadn't seen him at the side of the road playing with some other kids. When I hit him, he was thrown up on the hood and rolled off. I was *horrified!*

I slammed on the brakes and jumped out to pick the boy up, but he was on his feet and running! I ran after him and grabbed his arm. He struggled to get away as I talked to him as reassuringly as I could, pulled him back to the car and pushed him in.

I drove as fast to the base as the Hotchkiss would go and rushed the kid into the medical tent. "Doc" checked him over carefully and said, "Looks like a good meal is really all he needs."

We drove over to the kitchen tent, and I asked the mess sergeant to give me a few groceries for the kid's family. We then went back to the place where I had hit him, and from there, he directed me to his house.

We got out of the car and the boy bolted through his front door and disappeared. Two other boys were standing in the doorway. I set the box of food down in front of them, and as I was rising back up, the taller boy thrust something close to my face. It startled me—I couldn't believe what I was seeing! He was holding a chicken's foot and the claw was opening and closing like it was still attached to its original owner! The kid was manipulating it by pulling the tendons.

What a way to end a vacation! I returned the general's car and thanked him.

The 17s and 38s flew out and didn't return. They had moved to Chateaudun du Rhumel, several miles northeast of Biskra.

The boys and I were afraid that when we got there we would

took our place in the caravan.

Chateaudun was a modest-sized village in a part of Algeria that
was predominately agricultural. We drove through the village and
continued east. About two miles out of town, we arrived at an airfield where we found our aircraft dispersed over a large area.

Since we had been happy living close to headquarters in Biskra,
we followed the headquarters personnel to a spot they thought might
be okay for them. They would no longer have a comfortable building
like they did in Biskra, but would have to work in large tents.

We were about ready to set up our pup tents, when a truck
drove over to us and two fellows threw a large brown bundle on
the ground. One of them said, "No more pup tents, fellas, we're going to live in pyramidal tents from now on." What luck! We could
all live in this *one* tent and could even stand up in it. Harrington,
our squadron non-conformist, thought out loud that we could
probably sell our pup tents to the Arabs.

A line of tents went up between ours and headquarters. They
were, in order: ours, the one the chaplain and base security officer
would share, the orderly tent, and finally the large headquarters
tent. They were 30 feet apart.

The chaplain's roommate wasted no time in hanging a sign in
front of their new home: "Is there life after death? Trespass here
and find out!"

We were in the high-rent district.

Stars and Stripes: Latest reports tell of a mammoth Flying Fortress
attack on Sardinia. Nearly 100 of the huge bombers took part, placing
their loads on Cagliari harbor and three airdromes. Five merchant
vessels were victims of direct hits, and two were set afire.

The next morning we woke to the drumming of rain on the
tarpaulin. It was coming down in torrents. In fact, it looked like a

solid curtain of water joining heaven and earth and some of the fellows were standing naked in the rain soaping up.

We weren't sure the mess sergeant would be open for business because nobody would want to sit out there on the bomb crates and get soaked while they ate. We had a few candy bars, so breakfast was no problem.

About mid-morning we opened the tent flap and the five of us sat shivering inside, looking out toward the road, which was about a hundred yards away. Nobody had been out, but suddenly we saw a steel-helmeted soldier wearing a raincoat splashing along the road. He was bent forward slightly trying to shield something he was carrying. We later learned he had just picked up his ration of candy and cigarettes.

There was a loud crash of thunder, and a bolt of lightning struck the fellow squarely on top of his helmet. It knocked him down and his rations flew in every direction. Seeing something like this seemed unreal. The poor guy had taken everything the Germans had thrown at him in Biskra, and now, as Zinkgraf said, "God threw a bolt at him because it was his time."

A few minutes later, we heard a tremendous roar in the direction of town. It sounded like the entire universe was exploding. We stuck our heads out to have a look and thought the whole town was on fire!

Time for action! I threw my raincoat and helmet on, grabbed the camera, jumped into the jeep and was on my way to town in a few seconds.

A British ammo train had been hit by lightning while it was sitting on a siding in the middle of town. Buildings on both sides of the track were flattened. Bits of shrapnel and pieces of the train had been thrown up and scattered all over Chateaudun. The odor of the exploded shells and ammunition was pungent and sickening. There wasn't very much left to photograph, but the Arabs were already poking around in the rubble looking for anything salvageable.

I walked along the shattered siding looking for anything that was large enough to be recognizable. The carnage was unbelievable! Not a single whole body lay along the tracks—only bits and pieces, like half a helmet with hunks of bone and hair sticking to it, legs, arms, torso pieces and a shoe with a foot still in it. Bodies had even been splashed against the shattered shells of warehouses. A shapeless black mass like thick syrup covered a twisted wheel. I poked it with a stick and a wave of nausea choked me when a shin bone appeared with shreds of flesh still sticking to it.

I turned and hurried from this sickening scene, vomiting all the way. This, I knew, could happen to anybody—even *me*.

Just a few days before, I had received a letter from my mother in Lansing, Michigan, telling me that my name had shown up in the newspaper's daily casualty list, as having been killed in action. She hoped it wasn't true, of course, and doubted that it was. She had learned from experience that the *State Journal* didn't always get the facts right, or maybe the government's information service was faulty.

When I was in the aerial photography school at Lowry Field in Denver in 1940, the same newspaper reported that I had died in an accident. She called the base commander and asked why she hadn't been notified before it came out in the paper. It was on a Sunday.

A sergeant, who was the charge of quarters that day, walked over to my bunk where I was stretched out reading. I was the only one in the barracks that Sunday morning. Everyone else had gone to town, or up into the mountains. The sergeant looked at my name on the tag at the foot of the bunk and said, "You Thompson?" I said I was. He said, "Okay, roll up your mattress and blankets and take them over to supply."

"Why?"

"Because you're dead."

"You sure you've got the right Thompson?"

"You're Robert L. Thompson, aren't you?"

"Yes, but the bunk under me belongs to Robert *E.* Thompson, and the one over there is where *William* A. Thompson sleeps."

"Well, you'd better go up to headquarters and talk to the colonel. Somebody called him this morning and he came out here to the field in his civilian clothes. He didn't look very happy."

I found the colonel, the base commander, in his office. Nobody else was in the building. He was very concerned and pleasant to talk to. After I had him convinced that the wrong Thompson's name had been printed in my hometown newspaper, he picked up his telephone and called my mother.

"Mrs. Thompson?"

"Yes."

"There is somebody here who wants to speak to you."

He handed the phone to me. "Hi, Mom. It's Bob. How are you?"

"I'm fine, Bob, but how are you? I've been a little worried about you!"

I had supposedly "bought the farm" on two occasions. I hoped that such upsetting misstatements about my health would stop bothering my dear old mother. But having seen the sudden and unexpected deaths today, it was possible the *State Journal* might finally get their facts straight. When anything as freakish as a lightning strike gets you, your number is up, regardless.

It was another Sunday. As usual my thoughts were back home with my family. One of the reasons Sunday was so special to me was that this was pancake day. From the time I was able to remember, my mother gave us pancakes for breakfast *every* Sunday morning—*never* during the week—*Sundays*. And later, my wife continued the tradition.

I asked the mess sergeant why he never served pancakes. "Cuz I ain't got no bakin' sodie." Baking soda, huh? "Well, we've managed to improvise with dozens of other serious problems," I thought, "so we had better get to work on *this* one."

"Zinkgraf," I said, "what's in that stuff they give us for tooth powder?"

"It's baking soda with just a little salt," he answered.

"That's what I thought. Can pancakes be made with it?"

"Don't see why not."

"You like pancakes?"

"Sure, and I miss 'em."

"Well, so do a lot of other guys. I've talked with them."

I started around the squadron area with my steel helmet. The guys started dumping their tooth powder into it. Filling it about a quarter full with GI tooth powder was no problem when I explained my mission.

"Rather have pancakes than clean teeth," one of the men said.

I took the powder over to the mess sergeant and said, "I've gone to a lot of trouble to get some soda for you. Now will you do a favor for me and make pancakes next Sunday morning?"

There were a lot of surprised and happy men at our pancake breakfast. They were a little flat and salty, but, as the French say, "C'est la guerre."

The first order of the day in Biskra had been to fire up the generator, plug it in and open up the trailer for business. Here, we had no generator, we had no photo trailer, we had no business.

The boys and I wandered around our new base, wondering if we might find some kind of work we liked and could volunteer for. We didn't want to wait for our squadron commander to dream something up.

During our meanderings, we bumped into a radio operator who told us that the ship that brought us to Africa from England had been sunk on the way back. We hated to think of the good old *Rangatike* being on the bottom of the ocean. Tucker said, "If a ship has to be sunk, why can't it be one loaded with Spam and kidney stew?"

We came across a large tent with a white cross on the front. This was the new base hospital. We stuck our heads through the flap to have a look and were surprised to see that it was sitting over a large hole in the ground. The hole was four feet deep and had grass mats on the floor. What a great idea! If the Krauts dropped "daisy-cutter" bombs, nobody would get hurt. Daisy-cutters exploded three feet above the ground and sent hundreds of pellets in every direction.

On the way back to our tent, we started discussing the possibility of digging a hole and building a dark room in it. We found our squadron commander and told him what we might do. He said, "Okay, give it a shot."

We scrounged some picks and shovels and went to work. Ten days later we were ready to hold open house in our new darkroom. We had dug a hole deep enough so that we had a three foot roof over our heads. This was an improvement on the hospital hole, because we would be safe from daisy-cutters and *maybe* even near misses from 500 pounders.

We had even managed to dig a curved tunnel leading to the lab, which would act as a light trap. It would not be necessary to have a door. We could be in total darkness and not have to worry about some idiot letting light in while we were in the middle of developing film.

"Okay, guys," I said, "we have a nice new darkroom with nothing in it for film developing and printing. Let's look around and see if we can find a few things to improvise and make our own equipment."

A few days later, running water was coming down to the lab through some curved piping from the hydraulic system of a B-17. A spigot from a wine barrel was on the end of the piping. Paper developing trays had been made by cutting five-gallon gas cans in half the long way. Our chemicals were stored in champagne bottles that we had stolen from the chaplain. A contact printing box had been made from fragmentation bomb cases. A safe light came from the red stop light on our jeep. The electrical wiring was in and working. It had once served a function of some kind in a bombardier's control box.

We were the proudest bunch of guys in Algeria! The whole project had taken only two weeks from idea to completion. We doubted that there had *ever* been anything like it in the world. Men can do the impossible when they have to!

In fact, some of the guys got fed up with having to leave their tents and run to fox-holes during the air raids and decided to build underground homes. The most elaborate one we saw was built by members of an ordnance crew. They named it "Shack-Up" and it was dug down four feet and measured ten by thirteen feet. The guys placed two rows of gasoline tins packed with sand around the hole to raise the ceiling another twenty inches. They claimed this would make their place bullet-proof.

Our latrines were also surrounded with sand-filled gas cans stacked eight or ten high. The interior walls were covered with wood from bomb crates and slabs from GI stew cases.

Union Jack: **Axis-occupied territory in Tunisia has now been whittled down to about one-third of what it was before the British 8th Army and the American 2nd Corps, aided by elements of the French Desert Camel Corps, began their squeeze play on German-Italian forces in southern Tunisia some three weeks ago.**

Everybody else on the base became proficient at scrounging things to solve problems. When there was a requirement for something we didn't have, American ingenuity and imagination would come to the rescue.

There was a terribly crippled Arab boy in the village who was about eight or ten years old. He couldn't walk. People in town paid no attention to him as he crawled on his stomach through the dirt and filth in the streets.

Master Sergeant Claude Coffee was one of the chief aircraft mechanics on the field. One day Coffee saw the little native kid crawling through the dirt. He went back to the field and had a couple of his men take the wheels off a battery carrier and make a little wheeled platform for the boy to lie on. He could now roll along instead of crawl.

Some of the men had made an amazing discovery soon after we arrived at Chateaudun du Rhumel. They had driven north a few miles and found a stream of hot water coming out of a mountain. After hunting hyenas with their sub-machine guns for awhile, they examined the wooden bathhouse that straddled the stream. A Frenchman owned it and was charging a few francs to use it.

Soon, 6x6 trucks loaded with off-duty men were making trips to the hot stream for baths. Of course we could have easily stuck a .45-caliber pistol in the old Frenchman's face and walked into the bathhouse without paying. We didn't do that. We simply waded into the stream a few feet from his bathhouse, with our soap and towels, and enjoyed the best baths we could *ever* have. Only *modest* people used the bathhouse anyway. And there was *no* modesty in the U.S. Army!

The Birthday Party

MY TWENTY-THIRD BIRTHDAY CAME AROUND while we were digging the hole for our lab. Harrington, our squadron problem-solver, thought we should celebrate the occasion. He said he would provide the French champagne if the rest of us would bring the "horses doovers." We wondered how a buck private could afford French champagne.

"Simple," he said. "Ta-ta-ta-take a lo-lo-look next door and ya-ya-ya-you'll notice that the si-si-side of the chaplain's te-te-tent is rolled up. Ta-ta-ta-take a closer lo-lo-look and you'll se-s-s-see several bottles of cha-cha-champagne on the ground un-un-un-under his cot."

"Sure," Martini said, "but he didn't spend a month's pay on that stuff just to give it away when somebody has a birthday."

"I have a p-p-p-plan," Harrington said.

This guy *always* had a plan. That night after dark when the chaplain was sound asleep, a bucket brigade was formed between our tent and the chaplain's tent. Actually it was a *bottle* brigade. I wanted no part in it and stayed in the tent. After all, it was *my* birthday.

Duck Pond and Ziggie came over to help celebrate my birthday, and he taught me a couple of card tricks while the boys were doing their "midnight requisitioning." Duck tried to teach me to do a "Donald Duck" routine but I was a miserable failure when it came to duck talk.

Tucker, Zinkgraf, Martini and Harrington formed the line between the two tents with Harrington on the chaplain's end of the line. He very carefully and noiselessly slipped a bottle out from under the sleeping chaplain's cot, handed it to Zinkgraf, who handed it to Martini, who handed it to Tucker, who tossed it over beside our tent.

When seven bottles had been requisitioned from under the cot, Harrington decided to leave the last one there for the chaplain. The looters came back to our tent and the party started.

I had never *seen* champagne in person, only in the movies. I seemed to recall that the movie people always had a bucket of ice under the bottle and a white napkin over it. Since we were traveling light, we did without.

Zinkgraf handed an unopened bottle to me. I read the fancy label—"Royal D'Arck" and stuck my finger into the large depression in the bottom.

"Is that good champagne, Sarge?" Tucker wondered.

"Tucker, I've asked you guys to knock off that *Sarge* business and call me Thompson or Tommy. I don't know anything about champagne. Ask me about Postum or Ovaltine."

Harrington did the honors. He popped the corks on all seven bottles and proceeded to fill our kidney-shaped aluminum canteen cups. We were afraid the popping corks might wake the chaplain, which would bring a screeching halt to our party.

There was enough for seconds and the "seasoned" drinkers "killed" the bottles. I didn't finish mine because I felt dizzy, groggy and silly all at the same time.

It was late. The party was over. I was worried that the raid would be blamed on us unless we got rid of the bottles.

Tucker said, "Martini, you're *drunk.*" Martini dropped an empty bottle on the floor and said, "Well, ya know what Prime Minister Churchill said to Lady Astor, don't ya?"

"I haven't the slightest idea."

"She told him he was drunk, and he said, 'I may be drunk, but *you're* ugly and tomorrow *I'll* be sober.' "

"That's a good Churchill-Astor story," I said. "My favorite was the one I read about the time they were feuding and Lady Astor burst out with, 'If you were my husband, I'd put poison in your coffee.' Churchill shot back, 'If you were my wife, I'd drink it.' "

"Okay, guys," I said. "Let's get rid of these bottles so the chaplain won't kill us."

I asked Harrington to volunteer to take the bottles out on the airfield and scatter them around. He left with the bottles and almost immediately we heard shots being fired. A terrified

Harrington raced back into the tent, bringing the bottles with him. He plopped down on his cot and said, "*B-B-B-Boy*, I sure didn't know there were *guards* sitting on the ground under the B-B-B-B-17s!"

Duck said, "Well, if you guys will excuse Ziggie and me, we'd better hit the sack, because I'm on a mission in the morning and some guy will be shaking me out of a sound sleep before daylight."

The next morning we heard the chaplain screaming some very un-Christian expletives. Zinkgraf had soaked the labels off the bottles and hid them in his belongings to take home for souvenirs. Soon thereafter the bottles were down in the darkroom filled with photographic chemicals. The chaplain was unaware of his generous donation to the war effort.

Stars and Stripes: U.S. Bombers Stage Greatest Air Battle in African Campaign—The greatest air battle so far of the French North African campaign was staged last week over northern Tunisia. Flying Fortresses, with an escort of P-38s, flew over La Goulette, the harbor of Tunis, and with deadly accuracy dropped their bomb loads.

Scarcely had they left their targets when a swarm of ME-109s and Italian fighters were shot down against only seven Allied planes that day. All B-17s returned, although one had hundreds of flak holes, two cannon holes as big as barrels, two engines smashed and two men wounded. It was a banner day for the 12th Air Force, which took care of 23 Axis planes while losing only one. The R.A.F. handled the others.

Our bathing facilities on the base were not as good as they were in Biskra, where we had plenty of irrigation ditches with water, but we got by. Every morning, one of us would drive the jeep around for awhile and then drain the hot radiator water into our steel helmets. We would set the helmets on the ground, remove our clothing and enjoy a pleasant "sponge" bath.

One morning while I was bathing, a corporal from our orderly tent came up to me and said, "Sarge, Captain Van Cleave wants you to come over."

After I had bathed and shaved, I reported to the captain.

"You sent for me, Sir?"

"Yes, Sergeant. Just got a call from 'Black Jack' Cooper—ah, I mean *Captain* Cooper at the Negro motor pool five miles east of town. He wants ID shots made of his men. He has close to one hundred."

"Yes, Sir. His parents had a real sense of humor when they named him, didn't they?"

"Well, we kid him about commanding a Negro outfit and he got stuck with the nickname just like General John Pershing did when *he* commanded Negroes."

Of course this was a segregated war and Negro soldiers were always based a few miles away from the white troops. I remembered hearing that no Negroes had been sent overseas for combat duty at that time, so it didn't surprise me that I'd be photographing black men in a motor pool. Although I still found it hard to believe, the brass didn't trust them for combat. Instead, they worked as drivers, dockworkers and in supply depots. All of their officers were white, however.

I threw a camera and some film into the jeep and took off. When I got to the camp, I located a place near a big tent that was in open shade. A driver brought a blanket over and we hung it on the wall for a background. We placed a wood "C" ration box in front of it for a posing stool. I put the camera on the tripod and motioned for the first man in line to sit down and face the camera.

When the 81 sittings were completed, I returned to the lab and gave the film to the boys for developing and printing.

The next morning, I returned to the camp with the small contact prints. Captain Cooper asked me to spread them out on a long table that had been set up outside his office. He then told his men to gather around the table and pick out their pictures.

Pandemonium! The men started pushing and shoving and grabbing prints from the table and away from each other. "Gimme that, you black buggah, that's *me!*" "Here, Leroy, this is you. I ain't *that* black!" "Mine ain't here, but you sho nuff took it!"

The frustrated captain shouted over the chaos and moved his men away from the table. Not *one* man had been able to identify himself.

This project had to be repeated, obviously, so the next day I returned and re-shot the sittings—with one minor change. This time each man held a sign against his chest with his serial number printed on it.

I had been told since grade school that all Negroes look alike, but this had been another learning experience for me. They all looked alike to each other!

We were certain, one night, that we had shot down a German Ju-88 during the raid. Our .45 caliber machine guns probably missed him, but we had some 20mm rapid-fire cannons spread around the field, which had a range of 6,000 feet or so. No doubt *they* got him. The next morning a jeep-load of fellows drove north of the field where the 88 had probably gone down. Soon, they returned with a piece of aluminum from the fuselage, containing German words, as proof they had found it. They said it was about ten miles from the field.

I was told to go out there with technicians from different areas, including armament, communications, and maintenance. A medic also went with us. We rode in the back of a deuce-and-a-half truck. It was my job to examine the aerial camera, remove the film magazine, and return it to our lab for developing and printing.

From the skid marks, it looked as if the pilot had been trying to make a wheels-up landing. The plane had skidded into a large tree and the front part of the fuselage was torn apart. This is where the pilot and navigator sat. Bits and pieces of the plane were scattered around, and we found the bodies of the four crewmen in the wreckage.

One man, probably the pilot, was dragged back alongside the fuselage so I could get a good shot of him lying next to his damaged plane. After I had finished photographing him, two of the men "shook him down" looking for souvenirs. One of the men straddled him, pried the Kraut's mouth open with a screwdriver, and started prodding around. Somebody said, "Hey, you ain't a heathen dentist, yer supposed to be lookin' at the heathen bomb sight."

The fellow with the screwdriver said, "Yeah, but this Kraut might have some gold teeth." I told the fellow standing next to me that I couldn't believe anybody would stoop so low as to do a thing like this.

He shrugged his shoulders and replied, "Oh, Graziano's from the Bronx."

The medic, with help from the technicians, tossed the four dead Krauts into the back of the truck, the bombsight technician from the Bronx removed *his* prize from the wreckage, and I went to work on the camera. I returned with the film magazine and a small nomenclature plate from the lens cone. *This,* I slipped into my pocket. It was a *great* souvenir.

I walked out to the ordnance area one afternoon and found Corporal Jim "Snake" Ferris, one of our armorer friends, sitting on top of a 1,000-pound bomb smoking a cigarette. I had found a can of white paint and a small brush and, like, so many others, wanted to send a greeting to Benito Mussolini, the dictator of Italy. Snake stood up, turned around, and wiped the side of the bomb to clean the dirt away. I then carefully printed the message: "To Benito from Wilma and Bob," and took a picture of it. Jack Benny had been over here and sent *his* message: "Love In Boom." ("Love In Bloom" was Jack's theme song.)

"How in the world do they make these things?" I wondered out loud.

"Ya came to the right guy," Snake replied. "I know how they do it. My brother is a spinner in a bomb factory in Pittsburgh and he wrote me about it."

"Spinner? Sounds more like he makes yarn or something."

"He spins them, all right, and said if he *didn't,* I would be out of work."

"Okay, how does he spin them?"

"Well, it's kinda complicated, but here's what happens. My brother runs a large machine called a spinner. A big piece of thick pipe comes to him with one end heated white-hot, which is hotter than red-hot, from a nearby furnace. When he has the pipe in the spinner, he clamps down the unheated end and starts it turning. Some steel rollers begin pressing down on the heated end while it is still white-hot. They keep pressing and shaping until a point is formed."

"Okay, he has a pointed piece of pipe. *Then* what happens?"

"The other end is heated and tapered to form the tail. Then it goes down the line to the men who weld lugs on it, like the ones on this bomb, so we can fasten them to the shackles up in the bomb bay. Of course it has to be fitted for a tail and painted before it goes to an army arsenal to be loaded with high explosives."

"Thanks, Snake. Hope this one falls right on Benito's head. By the way, how many thousand pounders do you load on a ship?"

"Six."

I then walked over to the P-38 repair area to make some engineering photos of large flak holes in a wing. The wing was just being removed from the left boom of the plane and lowered to a 2 ½-ton truck. As the truck was being driven away, another 2 ½ with a new wing was driving up alongside the plane.

"We'll just stick 'er on and have this bird in the air before the day's over," one of the mechanics said.

Another mechanic continued, "This counts as just minor repair out here. *Man,* at home if a plane was damaged like this, it would be sent back to the factory or scrapped. But this is an $80,000 bird and we need it up there shooting at Jerries, not sitting over there in the bone yard."

A private first class said, "Hey, ya hear about Lootenant McCall?"

"No."

"He was flyin' a 38 and got into it with a gaggle of Me-109s. They shot 'em down behind their own lines. He crash-landed and crawled outta it still wearin' his parachute. Some Ay-rabs closed in on 'im with them big sharp daggers. The lootenant wasn't armed, so he turned his back on 'em Ay-rabs and pulled the ripcord. Ya know how crazy 'em Ay-rabs is for our mattress covers—well they wuz *wild* about the parachute. While they wuz fightin' over the chute, the lootenant ran like crazy. He wuz back here on the field in three days."

Stars and Stripes: Enemy opposition in the air was "not too strong." But there wasn't much the Germans could do as A-20s spread fragmentation bombs, P-40s riddled tanks, P-38s took on comers and P-39s strafed ground troops. As an example of the tempo, one A-20 outfit performed five missions in a single day. In three days alone 24 Axis planes were knocked down and out. In one week 16,496 bombs were dropped on enemy targets.

The Chaplain and Four Jills in a Jeep

EVERY SQUADRON HAS A "MAN OF GOD." Elmer was *our* Man of God, and he was unique among Army chaplains. He joined our squadron after being called to active duty from the Oklahoma National Guard.

The good folks at Elmer's church had given him a big ice cream and cake social send-off. They were proud of their Army chaplain. His wife directed the choir.

Elmer was not his real name. Soon after we arrived in England, we started calling him Elmer Gantry after the flamboyant preacher in the Sinclair Lewis best-selling novel of the same name. He was every bit the "Gantry" character, and *then* some.

Less than a week after we had arrived in England, and settled in at the Molesworth RAF base, Elmer came staggering back to the base one evening. He had spent a couple of hours at The Black Swan where, he had picked up a young English woman.

Elmer and his painted-up frowzy-looking companion walked around the squadron area arm-in-arm. He was showing her off with the same pride of ownership that a fisherman displays when he holds up a nice catch for his companions to admire.

This went over like a "lead balloon" with his faithful followers and Sunday church attendees, so they "dropped off the vine" and left him with practically no congregation.

By the time we arrived at Chateaudun, *I* was his congregation. It wasn't that I admired his work, but just wanted to irritate him. I tried to get Duck to go with me, but he declined.

Elmer was obligated to make a Church call every Sunday morning because it was an Army regulation. He ambled between the rows of tents half-awake and muttered, "Church call . . . Church call . . . Church call . . . ." Nobody could hear him, however, because he practically *whispered* his words. After all, if nobody showed up, he could go back to his tent and hit the sack.

It was my devious plan to always be up and dressed in my finest Sunday fatigues and hide just behind the tent flap where he couldn't see me.

Just as the chaplain would arrive in front of my tent whispering his church call, I would jump out and say, with a cheerful smile, "Good morning, Chaplain. Nice morning for your service."

He would look at me with his, "Oh, not *you* again" expression and plod over to the place where he had set up some bomb crates to form a pulpit and pews.

Usually only one other man would be in attendance. Hymie Waxman, our keyboard artist, would trot over to the "Chapel" when he saw that somebody was there. Hymie would open up the foot-locker-size portable organ and wait until he was asked to play something.

Waxman took requests. I always asked for, "Jesus Loves Me, This I Know," because it was the only church tune I remembered from childhood.

The first time I asked Hymie to play it, he said he didn't think he had heard it in his synagogue and asked me to hum a few bars. Hymie had a good ear because from then on he didn't miss a note. It gave me a good feeling to start a new week by going to church on Sunday morning.

Everybody liked to make jokes about our chaplain. Our line chief, Master Sergeant Claude Coffey, who was from the *deep* South, told a story about Elmer one evening while we were sitting on our bomb crates having supper.

Coffey said, "I been tryin' to find that guy who said he ain't scared when the Krauts drop their bombs on us. Know what I'm gonna do when I find 'im? I'm gonna shake his hand—and then knock 'im down for bein' a liar!"

It never took too much coaxing to get Coffey started on one of his stories. He said, "Know what? Even the *chaplain* is scared and *he* has a private line to the *big* boss. Me 'n him was out in my work area a few nights ago havin' a drink and them old Jerries come over us before we even knowed they was there. We both run fer the nearest trench and flung our ole carcasses in."

Zinkgraf said, "And that's when you found out the chaplain's afraid?"

Coffey went on, "Yeah, one of 'em *big* ones come whistlin' down and hit so close, it might-near buried us alive! It pert nigh come right down in our hole. Pert nigh—but not *plumb!* I said, 'Chaplain, let's get the hell outa here!' We dropped our bottle and took off fer them mountains, me 'n him. Them old hills mighta been twenty mile away, but when yer runnin' fifty mile a hour, it don't take ye long to git there." Coffey swallowed some hash browns and continued.

"We slowed down to 'bout *thirty* mile a hour, but there wuz this big ol' bright moon and Jerry seen us and come down just a shoot-in'. I flung myself into a irrigation ditch plumb full of water. I said, 'Chaplain, are ye with me?' He said, '*With* ye—hell, I'm *under* ye!' "

We all loved to listen to Sergeant Coffey's deep Southern hill-billy drawl and provincialisms. One day I told him Hymie Waxman had taken Duck Pond and me into town to meet a Frenchman he had become acquainted with. The French gentleman lived in a nice house with expensive-looking furniture. It turned out that the man was also Jewish and was a merchant in town.

I described the afternoon of Hymie's piano playing and pleas-ant conversation, and then remarked that the merchant was a very nice person. Coffey, in his lazy tobacco-patch twang, asked some-thing that sounded like, "Dee dee fee gee?" I had to quickly mull this over in my mind and try to translate it within the context of what I had been saying to understand what Coffey had asked me. I finally figured it out. Coffey had inquired, "Did he feed you?"

We used to amuse ourselves when we introduced an unsuspect-ing fellow to Sergeant Coffey by asking him to tell us what he did as a kid to earn spending money.

"Ahuh jes' wen' rown up n' don them roahs skeerin' bogs offen caten plains."

Of course by this time we knew he was saying, "I just went around up and down those rows scaring bugs off cotton plants."

We walked over to the chow line for breakfast one morning. It was about 20 feet long and set up on bomb crates in front of the mess tent. We always started at the right end of the line and worked our way down to the other as watery dehydrated scrambled eggs, or S.O.S., greasy bacon and lumpy hash brown potatoes were dumped into our mess kits.

This morning something new had been added. Red Cross girls were standing at each end of the line. We were surprised, because we had seen Salvation Army people in various places in Africa, but *never* the Red Cross. They were always up north in the big cities where they had comfortable hotel rooms and good restaurants.

When we got to the first girl, she handed us a cookie and gave us a big smile. The girl at the other end of the line held out a tray into which we dropped our donations. Those who dropped a donation also got a big smile. Most of us left her without getting a smile.

This wasn't the only surprise that day. Four Hollywood movie stars made the scene to entertain the troops. They were Martha Raye, Mitzie Mayfair, Kay Francis and Carol Landis.

A long flat-bed aircraft salvage truck was brought into the personnel area to be used as a stage.

The planes returned early from a short mission and practically every man on the base gathered in front of the stage and sat on the ground to have a look at the famous beauties from Hollywood.

The performance started at 4 p.m., and some of the men in the front rows had been sitting there on the ground since noon, even though there had been a half-hour of rain and wind. Why? Because they were going to hear English words from a woman's mouth for the first time in months.

Martha Raye was first at the microphone. She told us about her experience making films with Bob Hope, Bing Crosby and others, then went into a humorous wise-cracking routine where she kidded about our naive, bumbling officers. We loved this, of course, and the officers howled with laughter.

Mitzie Mayfair was next and did her famous acrobatic dance routine. Then Kay Francis sang, "There'll Be Bluebirds Over the White Cliffs of Dover." Finally, the beautiful pinup girl, Carol

Landis, had only to stand at the microphone to be appreciated. She couldn't be heard because of the constant wolf whistles, applauding and cheering from her enthusiastic audience.

That evening, the boys and I decided to eat at the squadron mess area instead of staying in our tent and having our usual home-made egg omelet. We heard a rumor that our squadron was the lucky one selected to feed the ladies.

Near the mess tent, various-size bomb crates were lined up that we used for tables and chairs. Everybody wanted to sit near our four famous guests, and there was a lot of pushing and shoving to see who would be lucky.

A good cook can make even the dehydrated food taste good. A poor cook can ruin fresh food on the infrequent occasion when it can be found. *Our* cook made such a mess of the dehydrated food that it was almost as bad as the Limeys' kidney pie. The only thing I liked was the Klim. This is what dehydrated milk was called. Klim was a trade name and was milk spelled backwards. The S.O.S. wasn't too bad but that was served only for breakfast.

The four ladies ate the miserable chow as though they liked it and not *one* of them threw up. Of course, they were all trained actresses. Martha Raye even went back for seconds—then *thirds!* This was undoubtedly the greatest compliment our mess sergeant had ever received.

We had hurriedly developed and printed the shots I'd made of the show, and we gave a set of prints to each of the girls. Carol Landis asked for my home address, and I gave it to her. Some of the jealous guys immediately applied for jobs in the photo section.

The Circumcision

I CAME UP OUT OF OUR UNDERGROUND darkroom one morning and found the crew chief of *Air Mail-Special Delivery* waiting to see me.

"You Thompson?"

"Yes."

"Would you do a favor for *Air Mail-Special Delivery*'s crew?"

"If I can. What ya got?"

"Well, Hank Zilinski, our radio operator, was in the dispensary tent with his pants down one day while Doc looked at a boil. Doc told him he should be circumcised. Hank objected and said he'd gotten along okay for twenty-one years like he was. Doc told him it was unsanitary and he should be circumcised. Hank finally agreed and a date was set. It's today after he gets back from his mission."

"How do *I* fit in?"

"Well, we want you to come over to Doc's dispensary and photograph the operation."

"They didn't teach us medical photography in photo school."

"It's going to be a big surprise for Hank. He thinks only the Doc and a medical corpsman will be there. Our pilot got the air and ground crews together and we're *all* going to be there. Doc said he'd go along with it."

"Okay, count me in."

The mission returned and Zilinski walked over to the dispensary tent. When he was inside and the tent flap was closed, all the members of the air crew and the ground crew gathered silently near the tent so they could hear the conversation inside. Doc was telling Zilinski to remove all of his clothes. I was there with my camera and a couple of flashbulbs listening to the conversation in the tent.

Doc gave the secret words to let us know when to come in.

"Okay, sergeant, just relax. I'm going to put this mask over your nose and mouth and sprinkle some ether on it. Breathe deeply."

This was our signal to come in. The pilot threw the tent flap aside and we all rushed in and formed a ring around Hank. He was lying on a board that was supported at the head and foot with bomb crates. A white sheet was placed from his shoulders down as far as possible. A sheet spread up from his feet as far as possible. *Possible* was *exposed!*

The corporal who was assisting stood beside Hank with a tray of instruments in one hand and a rolled up *Stars and Stripes* newspaper in his other, with which he was swishing the flies away.

The sieve-like mask with a gauze pad in it was over Hank's nose and mouth. Doc was standing over it with an eye-dropper full of ether. Hank looked around, gasped a couple of times and yelled, "What are you guys doing in here?" The pilot said, "Doc is going to let me do the butchering while he gives me instructions." The drops of ether continued hitting the mask. The pilot added, "And we're going to sew some buckshot into your skin. When it heals, you'll have a dandy . . . "

"Like *hell* you are! I want y y y o o u u . . . ."

Doc didn't let us stay to watch. I saved a couple of flashbulbs and Hank didn't get a souvenir photograph to show his grandchildren someday.

The 97th was my favorite bomb group because I knew so many of its crew members, and my best friend, Duck Pond, flew with them. They had allowed me to join in on their games and conversations, probably because of the photographs I gave them. They always had stories to tell about their missions. A lot of the stories were humorous, and these were the ones I especially enjoyed, but occasionally they had frightening tales of tragic incidents.

The 97th group was in a fierce battle with several German Me-109s. One of the 97th's Fortresses flying in the middle of the formation was fatally hit and on fire. The crew bailed out but one man opened his chute as he was going out the bomb bay and the canopy was caught on the door. He was left hanging and whipping in the breeze as the burning plane flew on. He was doomed to die a horrible, fiery death. There was no way to help him. The 17s flying close to him scrambled to get away to avoid the imminent explosion that might bring them down with it.

Suddenly the battle stood still while a Jerry Me-109 flew right into the middle of the formation. Everybody was amazed that the Jerry had the nerve to do this with so many guns pointing at him. They all quit shooting and watched as the German eased his 109 up to the helpless airman and shot him. Not one shot was fired at the enemy as he peeled off and flew away.

Then the battle started again.

Later a crewman who witnessed this tragic scene said, "Instantly the paratroopers song, 'Blood Upon the Risers' came to my mind. I could even hear them chanting it to the tune of 'The Battle Hymn of the Republic:'

> *"There was blood upon the risers,*
> *There were brains upon the chute,*
> *Intestines were a-dangling from his paratrooper's boots;*
> *They picked him up still in his chute,*
> *And poured him from his boots,*
> *He ain't gonna jump no more.*
> *Gory, gory, what a helluva way to die,*
> *Gory, gory . . . ."*

Ernie Pyle

Stars and Stripes: A Mediterranean Air Base—The 301st Bombardment group flew its 200th mission in 17 months of overseas service Saturday to lead the Flying Fortress attack on Reggio Emillia, in northern Italy.

ERNIE PYLE, THE PULITZER PRIZE-WINNER author, had jumped aboard our ship, the *Rangatike,* just before she left England. War correspondents must have secret ways of locating people even when they have been swallowed up in the bowels of a huge ship. It was this ability that enabled Ernie to find Cheedle Caviness in our dungeon.

Sergeant Caviness was the nephew of Senator Carl Hatch of New Mexico, who was Pyle's friend. Ernie had probably felt obligated to find the Senator's nephew and say "Hello." We felt lucky that this had happened, because the famous writer decided to attach himself to our squadron. He lived with us for a while after the start of the African campaign.

Each day after Pyle had interviewed a few men and had the information he needed for his daily dispatch to the States, he would come over to the photo tent, sit down at our print-sorting table, set up his little black portable Underwood typewriter and start pecking away.

Ernie used his two forefingers for the keys and his right thumb for the space bar. He typed like lightning and we doubted that a good secretary could keep up with him.

His articles were being published daily in newspapers all over the U.S. In one of my letters from Wilma, she said that she turned to his article immediately every day as soon as the paper came. She was excited that her favorite war correspondent was somewhere in Africa with us. This was before I told her he was right here with our squadron.

She was overwhelmed, one day, when she received a letter from me in which Ernie had written a few lines in his own handwriting. I had told Ernie that my wife was a world-class spaghetti sauce maker and that after the war I wanted him to visit and see for himself.

In his note to Wilma, Ernie said that the photo boys were feeding him so well that he felt sorry for the folks back home. He was referring to the evening egg omelet orgies in our tent.

The stuff they put out on the chow line was so bad that we had taken evasive action. We designed our own gourmet dinners with the help of the Arabs.

A soldier's first three needs are (1) good mail service; (2) radios; (3) cigarettes and candy. Since we were in an area designated as a battle zone, cigarettes were issued free—six packs a week.

None of us in the photo section were smokers. This meant that we would accumulate 30 packs of a cheap brand of cigarettes called "Wings." They were probably sent to us because Stateside smokers couldn't stand them. The natives didn't seem to mind, though. In fact they would *fight* each other for them.

Every afternoon, the Arabs came around with baskets of eggs and onions. Our favorite vendor would trade a steel helmet full of fresh eggs for one pack of "Wings." He got one pack for *two* helmets of onions. Because of our weekly quota of cigarettes, we were eating like royalty!

A steel helmet was the standard unit of measure when we were trading with Arabs. It was used when we traded for tangerines, dates, almonds or anything we wanted in exchange for our cigarettes.

Some of the natives were nonsmokers, however, and sold their goods for cash. We found a way of getting the cash back from them. We sold our white mattress covers to them for $20.00 each. The Arabs went wild for the covers. To them, they were garments —ready-made new outfits. It was only necessary to cut a hole in one end for the head and two more for the arms. I doubted there was a mattress on the entire base with a cover.

We didn't feel guilty about selling the GI covers because we had seen an Arab coming out of our neighbor's tent with one folded under his arm. It had to have been sold to him by our base security officer or the chaplain.

Ernie Pyle was always our dinner guest. He was the nicest and most congenial person we'd ever met. It was good to have an experienced elderly fellow around. Ernie seemed to be an elderly man to us. After all, he was pushing 42!

Ernie was a very ordinary-looking little fellow. His face was pale and he was quiet as a mouse. He was always cold and wore Army coveralls, an enlisted-man's mackinaw, knit cap, and overshoes. The only way we could tell he wasn't a private was that he was too old.

Even though our days were scorching hot, Ernie usually wore his olive-drab winter wool helmet hat. Nobody else did, of course, and that style hat soon became known as "the Ernie Pyle hat." Ernie was thin and frail-looking. He told us that he was always the first guy in any group to get a cold, flu, malaria, sore throat, or anything else that was making the rounds. He said when his doctor friends couldn't diagnose an ailment, they simply called it, "Puny Pyle's Perpetual Pains."

While Ernie worked at his typewriter, Harrington would crawl under the mess tent and steal a can of cheese while the rest of us cracked the eggs, chopped the onions and prepared to construct a *huge* omelet.

We had cut a five-gallon gas can down to skillet size and would dump two dozen eggs into it, along with the onions and cheese. We used a blow torch for heat. Since the cheese was tropical, it wouldn't melt. Nevertheless, a tastier dish probably couldn't be found in the finest French restaurant up in Algiers.

Ernie enjoyed his evening feasts with us so much that he wrote an article about it. He even let us read it before he sent it back to the States.

Ernie thought we had such a unique photo operation that he wrote another article about us and described our "hole in the ground" darkroom in great detail. It was not only printed in the

. . . then Graziano rolled the Kraut pilot over so he could probe his mouth for gold teeth.

These 1,000-pounders were going to Italy, so I painted a message on one of them.

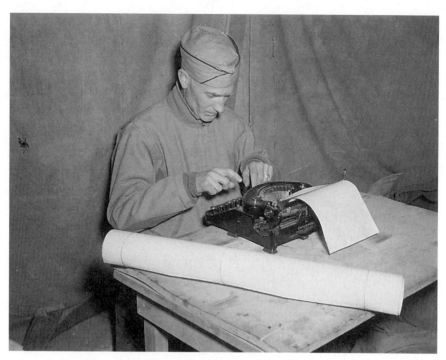

Every afternoon, Ernie Pyle would type his dispatches on our print-sorting table.

I felt lucky to have both of my legs when so many of my friends at the hospital didn't.

papers but became part of his Pulitzer-Prize winning book *Here Is
Your War.*

Ernie told us that after the war, he planned to spend a couple
of years traveling around the country visiting the men he had written about. He thought his readers would enjoy follow-up stories.
He asked how he could find me, and since I wasn't sure where I
would be I gave him my mother's address in Michigan.

One evening while we were eating our eggs, we told Ernie it
seemed to us that he had been shot at and bombed enough since
he had been with us that he deserved to spend the duration at
home. He said that half his readers had loved ones in the Pacific
Theater of Operations and he felt an obligation to go over there.

Ernie wrote about our nightly air raids. In one of his articles, he
said, " . . . It was just that on some nights the air became sick and
there was an unspoken contagion of spiritual dread, and we were
little boys again, lost in the dark . . . ."

One evening while Ernie was eating eggs with us, he asked "Do you
know the boys at *The House of Jackson?*" We told him we had met the
"skipper," Lieutenant Jackson, for whom the B-17 was named, when
we were photographing bullet holes he had brought back from a little
run-in with some "bandits" on one of the Bizerte raids.

Ernie said, "Well, I was just over there this afternoon talking to
the crew, and I just about fell on the ground laughing when they
told me *their* egg story. The day before they left Biskra to fly here
to Chateaudun, their egg man came around, and the crew 'sold'
their plane to the Arab for 20,000 eggs. I asked one of the men if
he thought the Arab would be surprised to find them gone when
he brought the eggs over. The fellow said he probably wouldn't be
half as surprised as *they* would have been if he really *had* brought
the 20,000 eggs."

We always enjoyed Ernie's visits because he got around so
much and saw so many interesting things that his stories kept us
fascinated. He asked us, "Have you seen any of the Arabs praying?" None of us had. He said that he was riding around in a jeep

with a sergeant a few days before and they passed a donkey and a two-wheeled wagon carrying a whole Arab family.

Ernie said, "The old man was down on his knees and elbows at the side of the road, facing east toward Mecca. His wife and kids were sitting in the wagon. The sergeant said he was probably making a deal for the whole family."

Otto Zinkgraf came up with "A Soldier's Soliloquy," which started making the rounds, and we all got a big laugh out of it:

I am one of the fellows who made the world safe for Democracy. What a crazy thing that was. I fought and fought, but I had to go anyway. I was called in Class A. The next time I want to be in Class B—B here when they go and be here when they come back.

I remember when I registered: I went to the desk and the man in charge was my milk man. He said, "What's your name?" I said, "You know me." "What's your name?" he barked. So I told him "August Childs." He said, "Are you alien?" I said, "No, I feel fine. He asked where I was born and I told him Pittsburgh. He said, "When did you see the light of day?" I said, "When we moved to Philadelphia." He asked me how old I was, so I told him 25 the first of Sept. He said, "The first of Sept. you'll be in France and that will be the last of August."

The next day I went to camp, and they didn't think I'd live long. The first fellow said, "Look what the wind's blowing in." I said, "Wind nothing, the DRAFT is doing it." On the 2nd morning, they put clothes on me. What an outfit! As soon as you're in it, you think you can fight anybody. They have 2 sizes—too large and too small. The pants are too tight. I think it is impossible to sit down. The shoes are too big. I turned around 3 times, and they didn't move. And what a raincoat they gave me. It strained the rain.

I passed an officer all dressed up with a funny belt and all that stuff. He said calling after me, "Didn't you notice my uniform when I passed?" I said, "Yes, but what are you kicking about? Look what they gave me.

Oh, it was nice when they called us out at five below for underwear inspection. You talk about scenery—red flannel, BVD, all kinds. The union suit I had on would fit Tony Galento. The lieutenant lined us up and told me to stand up. I said "I am up, sir, this underwear just makes you think I am sitting down. He got so mad he put us out digging a ditch. A little while later he passed and said, "Don't throw that dirt up here." I said, "Where am I going to put it?" He said "Dig another hole and put it there."

Three days later we sailed for France. Marching down the pier, I found more bad luck. I had a Sergeant who stuttered, and it took him so long to say "Halt" 37 of us marched overboard. They pulled us out and lined us up on the pier, and the captain came by and said, "Fall in." I said, "I've just been in, sir."

I was on the boat 12 seasick days, nothing going down and everything coming up. I leaned over the railing all the time. In the middle of one of my best leans, the captain rushed up and said, "What company are you in?" I said, "I'm all by myself." He asked if the Brigadier was up yet. I said, "If I swallowed it, it's up." Talk about dumb people. I said to one of the fellows, "I guess we dropped anchor." He replied, "I knew they'd lose it; it's been hanging over ever since we left New York."

Well, we landed in France; we were immediately sent to the trenches. After 3 nites in the trenches, the cannons started to roar and the shells started to pass. I was shaking with patriotism. I tried to hide behind a tree, but there weren't enough for the officers. The Captain came around and said, "Five o'clock we go over the top." I said, "Captain, I'd like to have a furlough." He said, "Haven't you any red blood in you?" I said, "Yes, but I don't want to see it." Five o'clock we went over the top. Ten thousand Austrians came at us. The way they looked at me you would think I was the one who started the war. Our Capt. yelled, "Fire at Will." But I didn't know any of their names. I guess the fellow behind me thought I was Will, for he shot me in the _____.

Kasserine Pass

THREE WEEKS LATER Captain Van Cleave called me over to his tent.

"Come in, Sergeant Thompson, and sit down. You are being sent off the base for a few days for a photo assignment, but it must be a hush-hush thing because you'll get your orders from the general and all he will tell me is to send you over to him dressed like a private. Go to supply and get a couple of shirts without stripes."

"Sir, does this mean that I've been busted?"

"No, you haven't been busted and I don't know what the general has in mind."

I reported to the general looking like a private with slick sleeves, and told him that my C.O. had sent me.

"Sergeant Thompson, we're going out and sit in my jeep away from the crowd in here because what I have to tell you is for your ears alone."

The general slipped into the driver's seat and I sat down on the passenger's side.

"Sergeant Thompson, you have a secret clearance and war photographer's credentials and that's exactly what is necessary for this little boondoggle. You are the only man on this base qualified for the job so I'm sending you. As of now you are TDY with the OSS."

"Sir, I'm on temporary duty with the Office of Strategic Services? For how long?"

"Probably for just a few days. I'm going to have you flown to Thelepte in Tunisia which is not far from Kasserine and Sidi Bouzid. There have been some problems over there and I'm afraid my bomb groups are involved."

"And I'll need to take a camera?"

"No, Sergeant, you'll go with no photo equipment. You'll report to a man who will identify himself as Skavarda after you land at Thelepte. He is your OSS contact there. That's all I can tell you."

The pilot, co-pilot and I were the only passengers aboard a C-47. After we were airborne and heading east, I went forward and leaned against the back of the pilots' seats to see if they could tell me what was going on. They were also in the dark but said that the airstrip at Thelepte had been abandoned by our aircraft and captured by the enemy during the battle there a short time ago, but was again in our hands—at least, they *hoped* so. They said that Kasserine Pass was about twenty miles north of the airstrip and Generals Patton and Rommel were now up there in the process of trying to kill each other.

When we landed, the co-pilot hurried down to the tail and dropped the aluminum steps. He patted me on the back and said, "Good luck" as I was stepping down. He then hurriedly pulled the steps back inside as the plane was starting to taxi toward the end of the runway. The engines never stopped running.

The field was deserted except for a fellow sitting in a weapons carrier. He was dressed like a private and was wearing a green arm band. He motioned for me to come over to the vehicle.

"Skavarda," he said. "May I see your credentials?"

"Yes, Sir, here they are."

He unfolded my Official War Photographer's document, which contained my picture and signature, laid it on the hood of the weapons carrier, pulled a tiny camera out of his pocket and photographed it. I had never seen a camera which was about the size of a package of chewing gum.

"Does that little thing actually take pictures?"

"Sure does. It's a German Minox spy camera. The film is wound on a spool a half-inch in diameter and the film itself is a little more than one-quarter of an inch wide."

"My lab fellows will get a kick out of hearing about that camera."

"You won't have to *tell* them about it because I'm going to *give* you one to take back. Okay, *Mister* Thompson, put this armband on your left sleeve."

Skavarda handed me a green, felt band with the words War Correspondent printed in white letters in both English and French.

"Here's a German Leica 35-millimeter camera, which is already loaded with 36 exposures—film speed 100—and here are six more rolls. And you'd better wear this steel helmet while you're here because we are close to a fluid front and you never know what might happen."

"Is Skavarda a code name?" No response.

"Is your name Skavarda?" No response.

"Are you a soldier or civilian?" No response. He was becoming irritated.

"What shall I call you, Sir?"

"Don't call me anything, and knock off that *Sir* business, okay?"

He must have been a civilian, a major or a colonel because he looked old enough to be my father and talked like a highly educated person.

"And now for the reason you are here, Mister Thompson. Your general is in big trouble. I don't know what good it will do, but he wants you to photograph this part of the Tunisian real estate—his bomb damage and so forth."

"Sir, how could my general be in trouble out here? Looks to me like the *ground-pounders* have been messing up this place."

"We're going to drive over to Sidi Bouzid a few miles from here. You're going to photograph a lot of destruction there caused by your general's bombers. On two occasions your B-17s dropped bombs on our front-line troops instead of the Germans. The Germans seized that opportunity to scatter the First Armored Division. They panicked, abandoned their weapons, including their tanks, and fled to the rear.

"Then, we're going to drive south. Your navigators couldn't find Kasserine because of clouds, so they dumped on the Arab village of Souk-el-Arba, which is *100 miles* from Kasserine. A lot of natives were killed and wounded and their village is a mess.

"The morale of our troops was bad anyway and when your bombers clobbered them, it was the last straw. Major General

Fredendall lost all respect and control of his troops. For one thing, he had used a couple hundred army engineers to blast an underground bomb shelter for him in a mountain more than sixty miles from the front. Fredendall was more concerned with his own safety than for anyone else's. General Eisenhower fired him and brought old 'Blood and Guts' Patton out here from Morocco to put things back in order."

We started driving around the area in Skavarda's weapons carrier while listening to the muffled rumbling of heavy guns several miles north of us. Those same ground-pounders had been through this area just a short time earlier and left the place looking like an enormous junk yard.

We drove past a burned-out American tank squatting awkwardly on the ground with one of its tracks off. There were several more abandoned tanks, both American and German, about 100 yards down the hill. They were shattered and burned. I wanted to stop and examine one of the Kraut tanks for souvenirs, but Skavarda told me not to go near it. "Might be booby-trapped," he said.

The terrain was scarred with anti-tank ditches. There were places along the road and near the tanks where fox-holes had been dug. There were gun emplacements, burned trucks and blasted artillery pieces. There had been quite a struggle here.

I asked Skavarda to stop the weapons carrier so I could wander around and make a few pictures. I walked up a hillside toward the beautiful late afternoon golden sky. Small stones slipped away from under my feet and thorns caught my pants-legs as I climbed. I found a flat palm-sized rock with words scratched on it. I picked it up and read the message, "Jesus Saves." Only a busy infantryman could have said so little which meant so much.

I continued photographing the blasted vehicles and huge bomb craters. I had never seen a battlefield before, except on the recon photos we had printed. The ground was littered with boot fragments, canteens, twisted trench spades, bits and pieces of uniforms, and knapsacks. These items were both American and German. No doubt the "ragheads" had already liberated everything of value for themselves.

I tried to visualize the action of two great armies pounding at each other, killing, maiming, and then moving on, leaving their useless junk behind them. Who would clean it up? It had never occurred to me to wonder what happens in a case like this. I thought that surely *somebody* would clean it up before another war came this way. People back home were salvaging tin cans and every scrap of metal they could get their hands on for the war effort. *Here* is where it was going! And for what purpose? Who would gain? It was hard to believe that such a beautiful place had recently been the scene of great destruction and death.

While I was walking back down the hill, Skavarda waved and pointed toward fifteen freshly mounded graves lined up with German wooden crosses fashioned from tree limbs at the heads. There were no names or dog tags on the crosses. On two of them, empty schnapps bottles had been stuck upside-down into the graves. I knelt down to examine the bottles. Scraps of paper were inside, probably the names of the soldiers. At first I didn't want to violate the graves by pulling the bottles out. Then I thought the papers would make great souvenirs. As I was reaching for a bottle, Skavarda yelled, "Booby traps!" I stood up, backed away and made a couple of shots with the Leica.

The mounds were under several large trees whose black trunks felt hard as stone. Sharp pieces of shell fragments jutted out menacingly from the crevices and corrugations of their rough bark.

The deafening noise of a desperate and bloody struggle had turned to the peaceful sounds of a gentle breeze rustling the leaves on the splintered trees.

I still didn't really know why I was supposed to photograph anything of interest I saw out here but continued shooting anyway so the general could see what the ground troops had been up to. There were a few tiny native huts scattered around the hills and I photographed one of them. At first it looked deserted, but then I saw a donkey stick its head out the door and out of the corner of my eye, I detected a slight movement behind one of the glassless windows. It was too dark for more pictures, so I returned to Skavarda, who had been sitting in his weapons carrier.

We drove south a short distance until we arrived at a quartermaster's grave registration unit where we spent the night. They didn't have any spare cots so we slept on piles of body bags.

About a half-dozen made a good mattress. I was almost afraid to close my eyes because we were still hearing the rumbling of the big guns up ahead and knowing that the body bag beneath me would soon be assigned to someone else worried me a bit.

The next morning, Skavarda said, "We're going to spend a couple more days in this area so you can see for yourself, from ground level, how your B-17s are bombing the front. Of course, we're going to drive up as close to the Kasserine Pass as the officers there will allow us. You might have a chance to get shots of the exploding bombs from your B-17s."

This was the most frightening time I'd ever experienced. It was even worse than the German bombing attacks at our base in Biskra.

During the next two days, high-flying formations of B-17s came over, released their bombs and turned west. The bomb blasts were too far ahead of us to tell if they had fallen on our troops or the Germans.

On the morning of our third day in this area, Skavarda announced that we were going to the village of Souk-el-Arba, which was about a two-hour drive.

The village was a mess! Our bombs had leveled about half of it. We saw no French people, but hundreds of Arabs were poking around in the rubble of their homes and trying to clear the streets. Even though Skavarda had mounted a white flag on the front bumper of his weapons carrier, I was very uncomfortable because of the angry way the Arabs stared at us as we were creeping along through their streets. For the first time I realized why I had been disguised as a civilian correspondent.

I had climbed down into a large bomb crater, which was probably from a 500-pounder, and when I looked up, I saw a ring of Arabs around it staring down at me. Skavarda was standing at the edge of the crater with them jabbering away in fluent Arabic. Later he told me that he was assuring the Arabs that we were going to pay them a large amount of money for the damage we had caused. He said if he hadn't promised the money, the Arabs would have killed us.

We drove back toward Kasserine Pass and got close enough to hear the noises of battle. Again we bedded down on the body bags with the graves registration people.

The next morning, Skavarda drove me back to the Thelepte air-strip where the C-47 was scheduled to pick me up. I removed the exposed film from the Leica and handed the camera to Skavarda. He reached into his pocket and handed me a tiny Minox spy camera. "Here," he said, "take this home with you. It won't be government property because nobody else knows you have it. Sorry there's no film in it and you won't be able to get any unless you find some Germans like we do."

It was daylight but the sun had not appeared over the hills when the C-47 set down on the Thelepte airstrip where we were waiting. It taxied up to us, swung around and sat there for a moment with its engines turning over while I hurried aboard.

As we were climbing out of Thelepte, and banking toward the west, I took one last look at the ground, which was dotted and punctured with the blasts of heavy guns and wished I still had the Leica so I could record this mess. I was sure the scars of war were temporary and would probably be healed by time and the wind. The scars would disappear like a cut on a finger.

We lost no time getting away from the area and flew no higher than 1,000 feet as we headed west for our field at Chateaudun in Algeria.

I immediately reported to the general and handed him the 35mm film cassettes. I asked the general if he wanted me to develop the film and reminded him that we didn't have a way of making prints because we had no enlarger. He replied that it wouldn't be necessary because he was going to take the film up to Algiers where there was equipment that could blow them up into 8x10s.

I walked back to our tent and found Zinkgraf, Tucker, Martini and Harrington standing around our print sorting table. It looked like they had been busy making prints while I was away—probably photographs of the area where I had recently been a ground observer. They all started asking questions about where I had been, why I had no chevrons on my sleeves and why I had left without a camera. I just grinned.

I took off the shirt with the slick sleeves and slipped into *my own* shirt. Once again I was a staff sergeant.

A month later we read an account of the battle at Kasserine

Pass in *Stars and Stripes*. After the battle General Patton had stood on one of the hill crests with another officer surveying the American and German tanks still burning in the valley below. It was now peaceful and relatively quiet. Patton said to his companion, "I fought here 2,000 years ago and won *that* battle also."

Who, in his right mind, I wondered, would believe a statement like that? On the other hand, who in his right mind would believe that *I* had found an English police station in total darkness with a pea-soup fog and *knew* it was there, and directed the way? I'd thought about that and had convinced myself that I *had* been there in a previous existence.

The Hospital

ONE DISMAL RAINY MORNING, the ordnance guys were unloading 500-pound bombs that were still packed in their wooden crates. There were four bombs in each 6x6 truck. Usually, the bombs arrived uncrated without their fins attached, lying side-by-side in the truck.

The drivers had a quick way of unloading them. They would back the trucks up fast and when they were at the unloading area, they would slam on the brakes and the bombs would all roll out at once. They were not fused, of course.

There was no photo work that day, so we busied ourselves by helping with the unloading operation. I was one of four "catchers" standing on the ground at the tailgate of the truck. Four men up in the truck were the "pushers."

Just as a crated bomb was teetering at the end of the tailgate, we got a big surprise from Jerry. He had never been over during daylight for a visit, but this bleak day he jumped us before we knew he was in our neighborhood.

Jerry zoomed over us and released his bombs. My three "catcher" buddies forgot what they were doing and bolted away to the nearest slit trench. The 500-pound bomb slid down and pinned me to the ground. I was unable to move while the rain and bombs continued pouring down.

After Jerry left the area, my buddies ran back to the truck, and with difficulty, managed to remove the heavy weight from my body.

Martini bent down and started to help me but somebody shouted, "Don't move him, his back might be broken!" A mad dash was made to the hospital tent to get help. Doc ran back and knelt down to look into my eyes and started punching around a little. He asked me to move my legs. I couldn't.

The meat wagon drove up and I was put on a stretcher and slid inside. Doc got in the back with me, and we started down the road away from the base. I asked Doc where he was taking me, and he said he didn't have an X-ray machine, but the big general hospital north of us at Bou Saada did.

I didn't know what the hospital complex had been before the war, but it now appeared to be a large well-equipped place where any problem could be handled. Several smaller buildings surrounded the main facility.

They took me inside and placed me on a high table with bright lights above it. The only other time I'd been in a hospital operating room was when I was born.

Several people wearing white coats gathered around both sides of the table and started mumbling things I couldn't understand. Next came the X-ray room. Then, they wheeled me into a long ward and placed me on a bed.

This was a terrible place. It was *horrible!* There were guys with no arms, no legs, half-faces—some were wrapped like mummies. The worst I'd seen until now was the detail that walked around our personnel areas in Biskra every morning after the air raids picking up body parts and dropping them into bags.

The two orderlies who had put me in bed took my clothes and gave me a tag in return. They gave me a pair of flannel pajamas and a red corduroy bathrobe, and placed my shoes under the bed.

The orderlies left, and I started wondering what my boys were doing and if the water from the rain might get down into our underground darkroom. I really didn't feel any pain and wondered what all this fuss was about.

The last time I'd been in a hospital was when I enlisted in the Army Air Corps at Chanute Field in August of 1939. I reflected back on that unforgettable experience. I was one of eleven recruits who were ordered to report to the base hospital for physicals. A raspy-voiced heavy-set buck sergeant, wearing chevrons on the sleeves of his white lab coat, met us at the door.

"Okay, you $21-a-month heroes, follow me . . . now go in there and strip down." During the next two hours we were all naked as a nest full of day-old chickadees.

We lined up and walked down a long row of tables from one doctor to the next. As each doctor examined a part of us, he put a mark there with a soft red crayon. By the time we reached the end of the tables, we were tattooed from head to toe.

A bald-headed doctor wearing thick coke-bottle glasses, squatting on a short white stool, told me to bend over and spread my cheeks. I thought this was a rather strange request, but did as I was ordered. I bent over and spread my cheeks as far as I could, exposing all of my teeth. He snarled at me to stop clowning around. I discovered I had *two* sets of cheeks.

The last doctor had me sit in a strange-looking chair. He blindfolded me and spun the chair around until I felt drunk, then whipped the blindfold off and told me to walk toward a water fountain against the far wall.

What a strange exam. We were all told that we had just completed a "six-four," the flying cadet's physical.

"But I don't *want* to be a flying cadet," I whined, "I want to be an aerial photographer."

"Same thing, Private. Put your clothes on."

Two doctors came to my bed and discussed their options. One doctor looked like a skinny teenager. He did more listening than talking.

The orderlies came back with a bed-sized plywood board and managed to slip it under me. The two doctors returned and tried to tickle the bottoms of my feet. I wasn't tickled. The doctors left.

The GI in the bed on my left said, "Hiya, buddy. Where'd *you* get it?" I explained. He said that his right leg had been blown off near hill 510, and he would be going home soon. He said he was very lucky because the two men who were near him when the shell hit had disappeared without a trace.

The fellow seemed glad to have a new guy to talk to. He told me what had happened when they brought him in.

"Just before they put me up on the operating table, they started to remove my pistol belt. I grabbed it and told them I wanted to keep it on. I had replaced the grips on my .45 with some ivory ones I made myself. I wasn't *about* to part with it. They took it anyway and said they would return it later. And I had three German watches on each arm and two German finger rings on my dog tag chain. They were supposed to give *those* back also." He sighed deeply and said, "They didn't."

I rolled my head to the right just as a nurse was removing a large turban-like bandage from the head of the fellow on that side. I felt sick to my stomach. Most of his face was gone.

A week went by—then another. I still couldn't move anything but my head and arms. The poor faceless fellow on my right was fading away. The nurse put a large square of gauze over his face. He could breathe through it, but we couldn't see his face. A chaplain bent down and said a short prayer, and then hurried down the ward to minister to someone else. The dying man was left alone. We lay there quietly, watching him slip away.

An Irish soldier nearby looked at the dying fellow and said, "May ye be in heaven, Laddy, a half-hour before the Devil knows yer dead."

In a few minutes, the nurse returned, placed a stethoscope to his chest, then pulled the sheet over his head. Two ward boys had come back with the nurse because they had to quickly remove the body and prepare the bed for the next patient.

Why hadn't *somebody* been there to squeeze his hand and let him know he wasn't alone?

The fellow with the missing leg was sent home and a new man was placed in the same bed. This fellow was anxious to tell us about his operation. The surgeons had picked out more than a hundred pieces of shrapnel from him. There was hardly a place from head to toe that wasn't touched. None of the fragments had hit a vital part, and he was already thinking about "healing up" and returning to his outfit. He said, "You oughta see the blisters all over my body that were made by the red hot pieces of metal."

Many of the patients enjoyed telling about their close calls. One private first class thanked a German "screamin' meemie" for saving his life. The shell blew him out of a four-foot hole and while coming down, an aerial bomb exploded in the hole, killing his buddy. This fellow had lost both hands and he resented it when the other patients acted like they felt sorry for him. "I'm lucky," he would say, "I've got my elbows and when I get home they're gonna put some claws on me. But that kid over *there*," and he pointed a heavily bandaged stump, "he's got *no* elbows and he'll be helpless. Go on over and feel sorry for *him*."

The dead faceless fellow hadn't been removed for more than ten minutes when another soldier was placed in the bed. This guy was a lot more fun. He was here for the same reason I was.

Soldiers from all of the Allied Armies were being treated here. The new man was with the British army and was Irish. I told him about the Irish fellow I had found in a French Foreign Legion uniform. He laughed and said that you could get away with murder if you were swift enough to race to a Legion recruiting office.

He introduced himself as Paddy—no last name, just Paddy. He was light-complexioned and snaggle-toothed. He had bright red hair and a magnificent drooping mustache. I immediately started calling him "Corporal Green" because of his red hair.

Paddy had a shamrock circled by thorns on his left forearm. I asked about the thorns.

"I was in Liverpool and got fallin' down drunk with some bloody sailors. We decided to go upstairs over the pub 'n 'ave the tattoo artist decorate us. I remember goin' up there, but not much else. I didn't even tell the artist what to draw on me arm—one of those bloody blighters musta. Anyway, when I sobered up 'n found this beautiful shamrock with ugly thorns around it, I *prayed* I'd find those bloody blokes again so I could kill 'em. Only a bloody *Protestant* sailor would pull a dastardly deed like that!"

Paddy had a great sense of humor. I thought he delivered his jokes like a professional comedian. No wonder—he had been a comic-magician in Belfast. For the next several weeks he taught me some very good card tricks.

Another man with a missing leg complained that it was itching. We asked him how that could be possible when it was gone. It bothered him so much that he yelled at a nurse and told her it was driving him crazy.

After the nurse finished what she was doing, she came over and sat on the edge of his bed. She started talking to him in the quiet and understanding way that she had probably learned in "Compassion 101."

A fellow a couple of beds away said that his amputated leg had itched, but after it was cremated, the itching stopped.

The miserable guy said, "How the hell can they cremate *my* leg? I left it out there in pieces where I was hit!"

More weeks passed and the medics were now beginning to "level" with me. "As things stand right now, you are a paraplegic, but we're still working on it."

That was a new word for me and it took some explaining. I didn't want to go home like this. A thousand thoughts ran through my mind. How could I do away with myself? Hadn't old Socrates been put to sleep painlessly with something called hemlock? Would my favorite "bed-pan commando" orderly bring some for me?

One day when the doctors were making their rounds, they came to my bed and introduced an English doctor. I liked this gentleman instantly because he reminded me of Winston Churchill. This doctor had studied my X-rays and wanted to see what *he* could do. "Now we're getting someplace," I thought.

The English medic went to work on me. Then the therapy started. It was very painful, but at least I had feeling where none had been before. We worked long and hard on some contraptions in the English doctor's "torture room," but I still couldn't walk— or *wouldn't* because of the pain. One morning the bed-pan commando and another fellow came to my bedside and announced that they had been ordered to withhold the pan. When I had to go, I was to use the latrine at the end of the ward.

"I can't get down there. Give me a pan!"

"Sorry, chum. You're *going* to walk or disgrace yourself."

They had me swing my feet over the side of the bed and eased me down to the floor. One of the men shoved my feet into some slippers and told me to stand up.

"I *can't* stand up!"

"Buddy, ya ain't goin' ta get no pan, ya'd better come with us."

They half-dragged me through the ward. I refused to put much weight on my legs but managed to take a few light steps while they held me up.

Slowly I graduated to standing up beside the bed and with its support, taking a few steps. Every morning after breakfast, my two "helpers" appeared and walk-dragged me to the physical therapy room where the Limey doc was waiting to place me on his torture racks. I progressed to a pair of crutches, then two canes. I walked slowly up and down the ward noticing mutilated soldiers fighting for their lives. I was ashamed. How could *I* complain?

The same English doctor had also been working on my Irish friend. We were *both* making headway. I wondered if the fact that the Irish fellow was in the British Army and occupied the bed next to mine had anything to do with that particular doctor taking care of *both* of us. I started to lose faith in the American medics. Why had they given up? I asked a nurse about this and she carefully avoided "bad mouthing" our doctors, but said the Limey was an osteopath and had become famous in London for putting his patients back on their feet.

Flies were pretty thick in North Africa, and we had our share in the hospital wards. They were attracted to the food at bedsides and the open wounds.

Paddy was good at killing flies. He had a rolled-up *Stars and Stripes* newspaper and made a score every time he whacked at one. I asked him to tell me the secret of his success.

"Well, I've spent many years of me life in pubs, which usually 'ave their share of the bloody little blighters, and I learned that Irish flies always take off backwards. So if you aim about two inches behind 'em, you always get the bloody things. Their little African cousins take off the same way."

Ever since I had finished primary flight training while attending Michigan State College, I had been interested in *anything* with wings. I remembered reading that the Wright Brothers studied birds to see how they controlled their bodies in flight.

Since there wasn't anything better to do while lying in bed, I watched the flies buzzing around and wondered how *their* control surfaces worked.

Paddy and I were now able to sit up in bed and have some fun with the flies. We didn't have the Wright Brother's birds, but we *did* have a good supply of flies to experiment with.

African flies were Texas size, but slower and we could grab them quite easily without making them too mad. Our favorite bedpan commando had given us a pair of surgical scissors, and we started trimming the fly's wings.

At first, the altered flies would just walk around on our beds and jump off almost foolishly suicidal. It occurred to us that we were probably cutting too much off the wings and the heavy flies couldn't get airborne again.

Practice makes perfect. After putting dozens of flies out of circulation, we finally trimmed one correctly, and it took off and headed for the ceiling. *Eureka!* Now we're getting somewhere! It was making wide right turns as it approached the ceiling.

During the next few days, we got so good at altering the wings that we had the flies doing right and left hand traffic patterns. We tried very hard, but couldn't get them to do loops.

A British fighter pilot in a bed across the ward had also become interested in flies. He thought it was important to learn how, when landing on the ceiling, a fly made his approach. Was it with one-half of an inside loop or a half roll? He never found out. The flies were slow, but not *that* slow.

I suppose nowadays, fly lovers would call this cruelty to animals, or something. But it was therapy for us and probably kept a few of the little rascals off somebody's dehydrated eggs.

Both Paddy and I were progressing right on schedule. We were now able to stand upright and even walk a short distance without falling on our empennage.

One morning, soon after our wake-up call, a major and a corporal walked through our ward, examining names on the signs hanging at the foot of the beds. They stopped at my bed and the major said, "Sergeant Thompson, you have been awarded the Purple Heart, and I'd like to present it to you."

I had been watching them slowly working their way down the long ward, stopping to award the Purple Hearts. Some of the men got out of bed and stood at attention when the major spoke to them. Some were so badly wounded and near death that they were unaware of anything going on about them. This really touched me. They would probably die not knowing that they had "earned" the medal. I slid out of bed, came to the best "attention" I could manage and said, "I don't believe you have the right man, Sir."

"Well, you're on my list, Sergeant."

"Sir, when I got here, I was all in one piece. I've been here for quite a while and have seen men come and go with various parts of their bodies missing. I just don't think I deserve it."

"Sergeant, your name wouldn't be on my list if your injury wasn't enemy related. The order says it's a direct result of hostile enemy action. I'm not going to argue with you. It's on the record and you can have it any time you change your mind."

An interesting operation was performed in this hospital. An American fighter pilot had reported to his field dispensary after returning from a little quarrel with a German FW-190. He had a stomach-ache and had noticed a little blood under his parachute harness. He had also found a few holes in his cockpit and left wing.

The medics had an X-ray machine on his base, so they made a snapshot of his stomach area. What they saw on the film nearly caused the dispensary personnel to head for cover. There was an unexploded 20-millimeter cannon shell in his stomach!

The medics probably didn't want the pilot hanging around there, so a couple of volunteers put their steel helmets on, slid him into the meat wagon, and drove slowly, avoiding bumps, to the big hospital here at Bou Saada.

The pilot walked into the hospital corridor carrying his X-ray film and handed it to the first doctor he saw. This was probably the only live shell that had ever been brought into this quiet place, and they were anxious to get rid of it.

Sand bags were hurriedly piled up around an operating table and a surgical team volunteered to remove the thing. A Limey demolition expert was located a few miles from the hospital, and was asked to put on a surgical gown and stand beside the operating table while the surgeons worked on the pilot. It didn't take long to remove the offensive piece of Kraut hardware from the pilot's stomach and the chief surgeon turned to the Limey and placed it gently into the little wooden box he was holding.

Someone ran ahead of the fellow carrying the box and opened the doors for him. "He walked calmly to a place in a field next to the hospital where another demolition man had prepared a place to work on the shell. About ten minutes later, and with a little coaxing, the shell exploded.

Paddy and I were now able to travel the entire length of the long ward and back without a wobble. The nurse, who had been encouraging us, asked if we wanted to walk a block down the street to the mess hall. We wanted to.

On our way to chow, we passed a small building with a store-front window. The dirty shelf inside the window was bare except for one item standing gloriously right in the center—a bottle of Coca-Cola with a pink ribbon around it! A hand-printed sign was lying in front of it, "To be raffled off. Selling chances for 25¢ each. See Sergeant Kardos in Ward 6." Nobody had seen a Coke for months so it was a highly prized item that would make the new owner the envy of his friends.

As we were leaving the Coke display, a fellow wearing his bath-robe and slippers walked up to the window. Half of his face and jaw had been shot away, and he looked like a grimacing gargoyle with a twisted smile. We looked the other way. "This," I thought, "will be the reaction of everybody he passes on the street for the rest of his life."

Later, we learned that this poor fellow had been hit by a piece of shrapnel that pierced his face just below his left eye, tore out his cheekbone and jaw, then went out through his neck. Again I thought about how lucky I had been—at least up to that time.

The last building before we got to the mess hall was long and narrow. A sign on the front identified it as, "Ward 10—Psychological." Loud pathetic cries and screams coming from this building caused us to quicken our pace.

A few steps later, we arrived at the mess hall. Inside the building we saw a good old-fashioned mess line with a large round metal wash tub of iced tea on the end of the line. Ice was floating in it. *Real ice.* How long had it been since we'd seen such a welcome sight?

I eagerly dipped my canteen cup into the tea and moved down the line. Paddy did the same, but thought he was getting punch. He had never seen iced tea.

We sat down and I started sipping the delicious cold beverage. Paddy swallowed a mouthful, looked a little startled for a moment, then slammed his cup down on the table so hard the tea splashed on both of us and shouted, *"Blimey! They've sabotaged the bloody tea!"*

Union Jack: Allies Race Up Tunisian Coast—What were yesterday front-line towns in Tunisia were pushed far to the rear as the triumphant Allied armies swept northward and eastward in pursuit of the rapidly withdrawing enemy. The French populations of Sfax and Sousse went delirious with joy as they greeted, with upraised fingers forming the 'V' for victory signs, the advancing Allies. The French tricolor, symbol of the liberty and equality of the Republic, again flew over a good two-thirds of the Tunisian coastline.

Tunis

I HAD BEEN AWAY FROM MY SQUADRON for nearly three months, which seemed like an eternity. There was always so much going on at the air base . . . long work days, visits from the Krauts, Harrington's troubles, egg-omelet suppers and surprises. I missed it. In the hospital, it was the same old dull routine with no excitement.

One afternoon, an orderly came to my bed with my clothes and shipping orders. The orders said I was to report back to my squadron in Tunis. *Tunis?* I had no idea the city had actually been occupied by American forces. We followed the news on the radio, but the last we heard, the ground-pounders were just starting to make their final push into the city.

My transportation arrived. Three other discharged patients and I clambered into a jeep, the driver shifted into gear and we were on our way.

It was about 375 miles from the hospital in Bou Saada to Tunis and sometimes the going was slow. We drove through and around numerous battlefields still littered with the remains of the struggles. We had seen war damage on hundreds of recon photos but the scenes from 30,000 feet did not bring reality to the war the way driving through it did.

We were a little more than half-way to Tunis when it started getting dark. We found an American tank repair depot and ate their chow and slept on their blankets until morning. After topping the gas tank at their fuel dump, we continued our journey to Tunis.

We drove past a lot of farmland on the way. In one field, an Arab was guiding his wooden plow being pulled by a camel. We saw a field with large trees standing in rows. Later we learned they were cork oak trees and every ten years the outer part of the bark was cut away and this yielded the cork.

At the outskirts of the city, the driver made a detour to show us the mess our B-17s had made of the marshalling yards and dock area. It was interesting to see this in person, because I had seen the same thing on the recon and bomb strike photos we had developed and printed in our underground darkroom in Chateaudun.

Crews of Army engineers with French and Arab helpers were cleaning up the overturned locomotives and railroad cars in the yards, and removing the twisted tracks and laying new ones. One locomotive was sprawled on its side across a sidewalk. The large roundhouse had been laid wide open.

Along the dock area, there were huge broken blocks of reinforced concrete. Twisted steel beams reaching toward the sky like qrotesque fingers were silhouetted against the sun. There were curled sheets of blackened corrugated tin, tangled rolls of steel matting and collapsed buildings. Craters were everywhere with the black scars of smoke and fire circling them. We saw several small Arab boys wading in a large water-filled bomb crater. The rubble in most places rose high above our jeep. There was a foul and nauseating stench of rotting flesh—bodies still buried somewhere under the rubble. I thought that since General Patton enjoyed destroying things so much, he should think about becoming a bombardier on a B-17!

On our way into the center of Tunis, we noticed that there was almost no damage left by our air raids—only ground fighting damage. Good marksmanship!

The three men in the back seat were dropped off at an infantry compound, then we stopped at the military police station downtown to get directions to my squadron. The downtown area was bustling with American troops. Some of them looked dirty and tired. They were the ones who had entered the city the hard way

—with the Germans making things unpleasant for them. Other men were walking around wearing neckties and shiny shoes. Of course the Arab boys were still running up to the GIs saying, "Hey Joe, chok-a-lot, choo-wing goom?" and they were rebuffed with, "Allez! Imshay! Get away!" But sometimes when a little beggar was given a treat, the kid would breathlessly say, "Baraka," and dash off.

The jeep driver dropped me off at our camp, which was located in an olive grove. I found a tent, unpacked my bag, and was very disappointed to discover that some souvenirs and photographs, including my favorite exploding flash-bulb shot of Winston Churchill, had been liberated at the hospital. Then I found Otto Zinkgraf wandering around through the trees, and invited him into my tent.

"Otto, bring me up to date on what happened to you and the rest of the photo guys while I was in the hospital."

"After you left for the hospital, Tucker and I did the camera work—the engineering shots and so forth. I wasn't allowed to take a break between assignments, though. They had me on KP, guard duty and even the gas detail fueling the planes. The only bright spot during this period was the announcement that our 37th Service Group had been given a commendation for superior support. We were the best service group in England and Africa.

"We enlarged the underground lab and Harrington found an old tin shack to place over it. We then had an upstairs-downstairs facility. We even added a German print dryer to our otherwise homemade lab equipment. Sure speeded up our print drying.

"Captain Robinson became our new squadron commanding officer right after you left. Our other C.O., Captain Van Cleave, was killed during the raid when you were hurt. Another German spy was caught in our area dressed like an Arab selling eggs. He was betrayed by his tender feet.

"We packed up, pulled stakes, and settled at Ain Beida. After a short time, we moved to Chateau Chaud, about 35 miles south of here. You should have seen this place. It was a French health resort and had been occupied by the Germans before we ran them off. It even had a swimming pool.

"Then, we moved up into this olive grove where you have finally caught up with us."

I learned that something new and unique had just been added. We now had a bunch of Italian prisoners of war in our midst.

A prison complex for Italians had recently been set up a half hour's drive from the olive grove. Italian prisoners were being taken by the thousands, now that the Germans had fled to Italy without them. As far as the Germans were concerned, the Italian troops were just in the way and they could now "shift for themselves." The Italians had surrendered in groups of *hundreds*, sometimes, to a single startled American GI.

The prison camps were bursting at the seams and something had to be done—and *fast*. Our top brass decided to start "issuing" Italian prisoners to American officers and high-ranking non-commissioned officers.

I had been assigned to a pyramidal tent that was already occupied by another staff sergeant and his Italian prisoner. I had been in the tent for just a few minutes, when our squadron first sergeant walked in with a fellow dressed exactly like an American private.

"Here is your prisoner, Thompson. Davis will tell you what to do with him."

Sergeant Davis told me that all of the prisoners assigned to our squadron were so happy to be here with us, living like human beings, that all we had to do was let them follow us around all day and act as our servants.

The first sergeant hadn't told me the name of my new "servant." This was no problem, however, because my man spoke a little broken English and introduced himself.

"I am Dino Gali. I am also a pilot like you."

Well, this guy knew how to start off on the right foot—by *flattery*. While Dino was making up his bed, he told us a little about himself.

He was a flying sergeant and had been shot down in his Folgore fighter soon after he had taken off from Pantelleria, a tiny island between Tunis and Sicily. A Brit had brought him down. He didn't know what kind of plane the Brit was flying, because the chap had caught him while his back was turned.

Dino finished with his cot and sat down on it to continue with his story. He was proud of his little Folgore. It looked a lot like the British Spitfire. It had a German in-line Daimler-Benz engine and could do a little over 300 miles per hour. It was a Macchi-Castoldi 202. "Folgore" meant lightning.

I asked Dino if he had ever shot at an American plane, and he was quick to say he hadn't. In fact, he hadn't had an enemy in his sights. He explained why.

He and his buddies would fly up along side a formation of Allied bombers, making sure they stayed out of range of the gunners. They would then put on a little air show for their adversaries as they flew along with them.

"We would do loops, snap rolls and *everything* we learned in fighter pilot training. We fired our guns aimlessly to use up the ammunition."

These air shows were put on for two reasons. First, when they returned to their airfield in Pantelleria, it had to appear that they had used their fuel and ammo fighting with the enemy. Secondly, they really didn't hate anybody but the Germans and were not motivated enough to try to hurt someone. And, of course, they didn't want anybody shooting at *them.*

There were four of us in our tent: Sergeant Davis, his "servant," Dino, and I. It would concern us a little when the two Italians would start jabbering rapidly in their language. Were they planning to kill us? Were they planning an escape?

The prisoner assigned to Davis had been a ground-pounder and had raised his white flag when the British Eighth Army got him cornered. We needn't have worried about the loyalty of our prisoners, however, because they had it so good with us you couldn't *run* them off.

So Dino became my own personal "dog robber." In the Army, a dog robber was a fellow who cleaned the officers' quarters, shined their shoes, ran errands, drove their jeeps and did all kinds of menial tasks. It made me feel important to have my own dog robber.

Every morning after Dino had satisfied himself that he had done a good job shining my shoes and making up my bed, he would go outside with a cigar box and pick up cigarette butts. The guys knew he enjoyed doing this so instead of "field stripping" their cigarettes, they threw them on the ground. In an hour or so, Dino would bring the box of butts back to the tent and slide it under his cot.

When Dino's box was full, he would say, "Sarge, let's go to the camp." He was referring to the prisoner of war camp where he had been squeezed in with a mob of fellows behind wire fences.

The camp was about twenty miles south of our olive grove. The prisoners were given enough food to keep them alive and healthy, but they were not given cigarettes. This is why Dino spent so much time gathering butts.

I no longer had my own jeep, but could easily borrow one. Dino and I would drive out of our area with him at the wheel and me in the passenger seat holding a tommygun. Orders dictated that anybody leaving the area with a prisoner must have him guarded.

I would rather drive, so as soon as we were out of sight, I'd ask him to stop the jeep and we would trade places. I'd take the wheel, and Dino would hold the gun.

Just before we reached the prison camp, I would stop the jeep and we would trade places again. We would drive right up to the wire fence and park. I would stay in the jeep while Dino took his cigar box of butts over to the fence.

The prisoners, dressed in ill-fitting greenish uniforms, would be jammed against the fence so tightly you couldn't see daylight between them. They always knew that when the little jeep arrived, their old pal, Dino, had a real treat for them. Dino would walk slowly along the fence and poke the butts through the wire to eager hands. This was the enemy, but I couldn't help feeling sorry for them.

Our six weeks' "vacation" in the olive grove, while we waited for the ground-pounders to clear out a place for us in southern Italy, was spent getting acquainted with the interesting city of Tunis.

Sitting at sidewalk cafe tables watching the world go by was my favorite way of killing time. I was fortunate to be a "first three

I stood on the hood of the jeep and watched Dino pass out the cigarette butts to his buddies.

I set the shutter on time exposure and caught the Kraut flares and Limey ack-ack on a Bari dock. (see page 241).

Zinkgraf and I were awestruck when we discovered Djemela in the middle of a poppy field.

This Djemela scene later won the Third Air Force Art Contest at Coffeyville, Kansas. Title: "Lost Empire."

grader" because we weren't given any duties. The lower-ranking men were put to work in supply depots, on the docks, and in warehouses.

The Allied soldiers strolled along leisurely, window shopping. There wasn't much left to buy from the merchants, but they always seemed to have enough small bottles of perfume to go around. They were probably making this stuff as fast as they could because *everybody* wanted to impress his best girl back home by sending her a bottle of genuine French perfume.

The olives in our grove were black and beautiful. I saw a fellow pick one off a tree and pop it into his mouth. He bit down on it and blew it right back out. He twisted up his face and started the most violent spitting I had ever seen. I tried one very cautiously, and found it to have a bitter, puckering taste. We later learned that olives have to be treated in brine before they are fit to eat.

An Arab camp was just up the road from our olive grove. When we were down-wind from it, we *knew* it was there.

One morning, Zinkgraf and I decided to drive out into the countryside and shoot a few scenes with our K-20 aerial camera. This was the one I had taken apart on my desk in England and had been messed with by Elliott Roosevelt.

The K-20 was a 4x5 inch fixed-focus aerial camera not made for ground use because it was set on infinity and there was no way to change it. This meant that everything from the lens to about thirty feet in front of the camera would not be in focus. When we wanted to get the *maximum* depth of field with a *ground* camera, we would focus on the hyperfocal distance for the lens we were using.

We drove east of Tunis for about 40 miles and came across a field of red poppies. They stretched all the way to the hills on the horizon. They were so red and vivid that their beauty was strangely saddening. Both of us couldn't help being touched by their ironic loveliness.

Right in the middle of this beautiful scene was a partially excavated Roman ruin, which we later learned was the ancient city of Djemela. French archaeologists had been working there for twenty years but had stopped when the war started.

We parked the jeep, picked up the K-20 and waded through the waist-high poppies toward the magnificent stone columns and buildings that had been a thriving Roman community 2,000 years ago.

It was so quiet—so peaceful. Seeing the ghostly remains of a lost empire and listening to the gentle breeze blowing through the poppies gave us a strange, eerie feeling.

A beautiful scene filled the view-finder everywhere we pointed the K-20. There was a fifty-exposure roll of film in the camera, and we didn't stop shooting until it was all gone.

We were walking on the same stone streets where the sandals of people 2,000 years ago had raised the same dust. We tried to visualize the ancient scene in our minds.

After making the last shot, we turned around to head back to the jeep and practically bumped into an Arab who had quietly joined us. He seemed to have come out of nowhere. There wasn't a sign of life as far as the eye could see, but there he was with his arm outstretched and his palm up.

This was one of the smiling natives, so we felt safe. We looked at his palm to see what he wanted to show us. He was holding several partially eroded Roman coins and wanted to trade them for cigarettes. We had no cigarettes, but offered him a couple of dollars. The trade was made, he said, "Baraka," and disappeared.

Zinkgraf and I drove back to our olive grove and arrived just as the evening meal was being served. We no longer had to sit on bomb crates   folding tables and chairs had been found somewhere. There were a lot of excited conversations about a radio address President Roosevelt had just made. He said, "Now that the Tunisian campaign is over, and the Germans are up in Italy, the mothers and wives of the men in North Africa are in for a big surprise."

Roosevelt hadn't elaborated on that remark, but the guys all thought he meant we would be going home soon.

The Italians had "thrown in the towel" and would no longer support their leader, Mussolini. He had been hated by a great many of his countrymen ever since he gave Hitler his support. The leaders of the "Stop Mussolini Movement" wrote a crude message to their people. They asked us to drop thousands of their leaflets from our planes to show their joy for the Allied invasion. The spelling and syntax were bad, but the message was loud and clear:

> *"Brothers!*
>
> *After thirty-nine months of war, pains and grieves, after twenty years of tyranny and inhumanity, after have the innocent victims of the most perverse gang at the Government; today, September 8, 1943, we can cry at full voice our joys our enthusiasm for your coming.*
>
> *We can't express with words our pleasure, but only we kneel ourselves to the ground to thank God, who have permit us to see this day.*
>
> *With you we have divided the sorrow of the war, with you we wish to divide the day of the big victory.*
>
> *We wish to march with you, until the last days against the enemy number one.*
>
> *We will be worth of your expectation, we will be your allied of twenty five years ago.*
>
> *Hurrah the allied. Hurrah the free Italy."*
>
> THE COMMITTEE OF ANTI-FASCIST
EX-FIGHTERS OF THE BIG WAR

One of our cooks had been given a leaflet from a friend in a bomb group. The cook was an Italian-American from Brooklyn, and he translated it verbatim. As I was reading the translation, and copying it down to show the folks at home, I glanced over at Dino, who was sitting on his cot holding his box of cigarette butts. "Dino," I thought, "Your war is *really* over but I'll bet you don't even know it. No wonder you guys were turned out of your prison to live in 'almost freedom' with us."

We were getting Axis Sally as loud and clear in Tunis as we had in England. She was still playing the latest tunes from the States and this is the only way we could hear them.

She played a record made by a fellow we all despised. One of the guys said, "If Sally plays that cowardly draft-dodging dago one more time, I'll never listen to her again."

Another fellow said, "Yeah, and they say the dumb broads back home are *swooning* over him."

Dino still walked around the squadron area every morning doing his cigarette-butt routine. He always sang songs like "O Sole Mio." He took requests but this was the song most of the fellows liked because he would belt it out in robust melodious tones. We thought he was good enough to be an opera tenor.

Everybody liked my man, Dino, not only for his singing, but for his political beliefs. He referred to Mussolini as, "The Top Wop." He knew this pleased the GIs when he used the demeaning term 'Wop.'

We were well-supplied with the GIs favorite newspaper, *Stars and Stripes*. Those of us who had become friends with Ernie Pyle especially enjoyed an article about him in the paper.

General Omar Bradley was interviewed and said, "My men always fight better when Ernie is around." A cartoon by Bill Mauldin was printed where a soldier was crying and another was explaining to a buddy, "Ernie Pyle misspelled his name." It was reported that many men said they would rather see their names in Ernie's column than get a medal.

Sally was still trying to cram her false propaganda down our throats. One late evening she said, "Our gallant airmen have successfully bombed Algiers tonight, and when last seen, the city and harbor were in flames. Shipping was destroyed and facilities crippled. You can't win. Heil Hitler." Then she signed off with her usual, "Pleasant dreams, Allied soldiers."

Several days later we learned the truth. German Stukas had dive-bombed a convent, killing 15 nuns and dozens of children. They hadn't hit anything else.

Then rumors by the dozen started popping up out of thin air again and swept through the squadron like a forest fire.

Sicily was sanitized and the ground forces invaded southern Italy. The rumor sparked by the President's address had been "shot down." After the ground forces had driven the Germans up just north of Naples, we packed everything and got ready to relocate to southern Italy. The Adriatic port city of Bari is where we would be moving, and the 15th Air Force headquarters would be established there.

It was necessary to send our prisoner-servants back to the Italian prison camp. Dino burst into alligator tears and pleaded with us to take him along. There wasn't anything we could do about it. We knew that as soon as an Italian prisoner's feet hit the ground on his native soil, he would disappear into thin air.

Just before Dino left for his prison camp, I asked him to teach me a few Italian words. He said he would recite a soldier's toast about the four basic necessities of life and that it was short and it rhymed, so I would pick it up in a hurry. It had just a few words, so I repeated it to him, even using his Neapolitan accent.

The Washington Post: Stimson Disclosed Costly Bari Attack—Allied shipping in the harbor at Bari, Italy, was heavily damaged in a raid by German bombers at dawn on December 2, Secretary of War Henry L. Stimson revealed yesterday in releasing details of the attack.

Two ammunition ships were hit and the resulting explosion caused fires which damaged port facilities and destroyed a number of Allied ships, including five American merchantmen.

Fortunately most of the cargo had been discharged prior to the attack, the Secretary added. "Consequently, the loss of supplies was not great."

Stimson said he did not know the total number of ships hit or destroyed. His statement followed a report from a source described as "unquestioned" which said that 17 Allied ships had been sunk in the raid, carried out by 30 bombers which flew in very low and fast and attacked a newly arrived convoy. There were 1,000 casualties.

PART THREE

Italy

We joined in a circle of planes orbiting Vesuvius and got a good shot on the upwind side (see page 248).

Bari

WE HAD LEFT COMFORTABLE PYRAMIDAL TENTS with "servants" in a pleasant olive grove near Tunis and now found ourselves back in pup tents. No olive grove *this* time.

We pitched our tents and set up our squadron operation in a field on the southern outskirts of Bari. This was a fairly large port city on the Adriatic Sea on the southern coast of Italy. It had recently been the scene of "the second Pearl Harbor." During the invasion of southern Italy, troop and supply ships were crowded into the harbor when Luftwaffe bombers came over and sank and destroyed more ships than had suffered under the Japanese attack at Pearl Harbor.

The docks were jammed with a great variety of material, most of it highly explosive or flammable: gasoline, bombs, ammunition, weapons and rations. The whole waterfront was sent up in a roaring fire.

Thirty German bombers had flown in low and fast to attack the newly arrived convoy. We were caught by surprise—just like the attack on Pearl Harbor. Seventeen Allied ships were sunk and there were 1,000 casualties.

Within hours of our arrival at this field, it started raining. It *poured* for two days and two nights. We shivered in the sudden cold. Slowly but surely the ground began to turn into mud. We slogged around the squadron area between our tents, the mess tent and the latrine until our boots were so thick with mud that it was an effort to place one foot in front of the other. We simply couldn't cope with the thick, black Italian goo. I thought that the first travel agent I saw when I got home who had a picture of sunny Italy in his window was going to have a large rock through the glass.

After filling my mess kit at the kitchen tent, I slogged my way back through the mud to my little pup tent, crawled inside and sat on the dank ground to eat my lunch. My mind was made up. I wouldn't put up with *this* anymore, I'd see our C.O. again to try to find out when we would move to a dry place and get back into the photo business. If I "struck out" with him I would hitch a ride into Bari and find suitable employment elsewhere.

Our squadron commanding officer wasn't able to tell me if or when we would be able to start up our photo operation. He seemed to be too preoccupied about something else to waste his time on a small problem like a photo section. I was disgusted with his attitude, and decided to go ahead with my plan.

I caught a ride into town and soon located the new 15th Air Force headquarters building, which was sitting on a hill overlooking the bay. It had been an Italian Air Force headquarters building a short time earlier, and before that, a school.

I walked across the spacious lobby with a shining marble floor, and stopped the first man I saw with stripes on his sleeves.

"Sergeant, can you tell me where the photo section is?"

"Well," he replied, "I don't know about a photo section, but I did see an officer pushing a dolly down the hall yesterday. It had cameras and stuff on it."

"Which way did he go?"

"Down the front hall over there."

I started knocking on doors and finally hit pay dirt. When I knocked on the last door, someone said, "Come in." I opened the door and found a small room full of motion picture cameras mounted on tripods and stacks of 35mm motion picture film cans on the floor.

An officer sitting at a desk at the end of the room looked up and said, "Come in, Sergeant." I walked over to his desk, saluted and introduced myself. He introduced himself as James Craig, without preceding his name with his rank and without returning my salute.

I recognized his name instantly, because I knew that a James Craig had invented the "Craig film splicer" in common use in the movie industry and also a tool we had used in photo school. I also knew that a James Craig had written and produced a film called, "Danger Is My Business," about his experience as an underwater and aerial photographer.

I asked him if *he*, by any chance, was *that* Craig. "Yes," he admitted, "I'm afraid I'm the guilty party." I liked him at once because of his relaxed un-military way. I gave Craig a brief oral resume about my photography training in the States, elaborating on the still and motion picture *aerial* photography. I even told him we had used his film splicer in class. He smiled.

"Sir," I said, "I'll gladly trade my pig pen for anything you have available."

"Strange you should walk in here just after I moved in and started making plans to form a new unit," he said. At this point, he stood up and dragged a chair over to his desk.

"Sit down, Sergeant. We have things to talk about."

This man worked fast. He was not a career military officer and knew how to skip the red tape and get right to the core of things.

"The replacements are on their way over here from Hollywood," he explained. He picked up a list of names and scanned it. "There isn't one man in this bunch who has your particular qualifications to be the NCOIC (Non-commissioned Officer in Charge)."

"Who is your C.O.?" he asked.

I gave him the information he needed to contact my squadron. I sat there in disbelief. Craig wasn't going through military channels—he was a Hollywood producer who knew how to get things he wanted *now!*

Craig picked up the phone and started tracking down the people he wanted to talk to. While he was on the phone I had a chance to study him. He seemed very tired. He appeared to be about 40, and although his features looked young enough, his eyes were bloodshot. Through his phone conversations, I also learned he was a major.

After completing several calls to the proper officers, Major Craig pushed the phone aside, stood up, stuck out his hand and said, "Welcome to the 9th Combat Camera Unit, Technical Sergeant Thompson."

"Thank you," I said, "but I'm only a *staff* sergeant."

"You were a minute ago, Sergeant, but when you leave the office you better go over to supply and pick up a few tech sergeant stripes."

This had happened so fast it nearly left me breathless!

Craig started telling me the long sad story of why I had found him sitting alone in a room full of film cans and cameras.

The 9th Combat Camera Unit, consisting of three officers and twelve enlisted men, had come overseas from Hollywood to serve in the EAME. This was a quick way of saying European, African and Middle Eastern Theater of Operations. A fellow at the old Culver City Hal Roach Studio had trained the enlisted men for this work. His name was Captain Ronald Reagan.

Craig continued, "When our combat camera unit was assembled and ready to go overseas, we were sent to the Middle East and flew out of a base in Palestine, not far from Haifa and in Benghazi, Libya. The 9th Bomber Command had just been formed and that's how we became the 9th Combat Camera Unit.

"Targets in Italy were among the first we went after. It's ironic, but the Bargo Airfield here in Bari is one we bombed. We destroyed over fifty planes on the ground that day. We also bombed the Littoria marshaling yards in Rome. I told my two Catholic men that they could 'stand down' from this mission if they wanted to. They went anyway.

"In the pre-raid briefing, it was made very clear that all religious shrines and the Vatican were to be spared and those areas were marked in red on the charts. Not one bomb fell in those areas."

"So, Sergeant, there you have it. Do you still want to leave your pig sty?"

"Yes, Sir."

"Well, my friend, I've got all of my personal things ready in my room, and I'm on my way home. You'll do just fine until the replacements get here. They should be at the 'reppledepple' (replacement depot) soon." And he was gone.

I now had my own jeep again, and drove back to the mud-hole to pick up my personal belongings. I wasn't able to find the photo boys, but knew they would survive. They had made it through a lot worse than this.

While Craig and I had been talking, I mentioned my disappointment that I had missed Captain's Reagan's training. He laughed and said that according to my verbal resume, I could teach *Reagan* a few things about cameras. I would have liked to "brag this up" to the photo guys, but made the entry in my big English notebook for future reference.

Major Craig hadn't elaborated on the Ploesti disaster. He probably found it hard to talk about the worst blood-bath in military aviation history. A short time later, however, I learned some of the details.

General Lewis Brereton headed the 9th Air Force. The "swivel chair air force" in Washington made the Ploesti decision, and Brereton had to follow their orders to make a low-level attack on the Ploesti, Romania oil refineries. The swivel-chair gang grounded General Brereton, so he sent another general to lead the raid.

They took off from Benghazi, Tripoli for the 1,500 mile flight across the Mediterranean Sea and the German occupied Balkans. They had to fight all the way. First the Luftwaffe attacked them, and then they were over the heaviest flak concentration in Europe. Of the original 178 planes that made the raid, only 33 came through fit to fly again.

We continued learning more about the low-level attack on the Ploesti, Romania refineries. Before the mission, in the briefing, Brereton told his crews to expect 50% losses. He went on to say that even if we lost *every* plane, it would be worth it. Brereton did not go on the mission. He said that his boss in Washington, General Arnold, had grounded him. He sent Brigadier General Uzel Ent in his place.

I continued learning even more about the Ploesti raid as days went by. Not all of our camera men were lost over the target. Some of them died before they had a chance to get there.

One of our cameramen was in the lead group to leave the field. His plane had an engine failure on take-off and the pilot nosed over to get back to the runway. He hit a concrete telephone pole, spinning the plane around. It burst into flames and there were two badly burned survivors. Unfortunately our cameramen was killed.

Another plane carrying a 9th Combat cameraman suddenly went out of control for some unexplained reason, flipped over on its back, and plunged straight down several thousand feet into the sea. No parachutes were observed.

The third cameraman to die before reaching Ploesti was on a plane that took a wrong turn at the IP (Initial Point) and headed toward Bucharest instead of Ploesti. Some heavy flak concentrations in the area got them.

The heavily-loaded bombers went over the Ploesti refineries at smoke-stack level and some of them flew within twenty feet of the ground. A few flew right into the huge storage tanks. Their bombs were exploding and knocking their own planes out of the sky. They crashed into each other in the dense black smoke. Flak got a lot of them over the refineries and German fighters picked off many more as they left the target area.

Major Craig was aboard *Chug-a-Lug*, which got back, but full of flak and bullet holes. Craig hadn't gone into these gory details when he talked to me. This mission was so big and so important that *every* member of the unit went along. They spread themselves out in the large B-24 formation to be sure *somebody* would come back with some film footage.

Craig and one of his sergeants survived; everyone else in the unit died. The sergeant was immediately taken to the hospital, because he was a mental basket case. He was then sent home because he couldn't be treated properly here.

Now for my first and most important undertaking as the "new man in charge." Find a place for the replacements to live.

The Brits of the 5th Army Corps had purchased Bari with their blood and guts. They owned the town and were now ready to go into the rental business. I located their billeting office, and went in.

There were three doors. A name was on one of them—one of those double-barreled names that probably meant he was from the right side of the tracks in England. I walked in and introduced myself to Major C. Leighton-Smyth and told him what I was looking for.

C. Leighton-Smyth flipped through some papers on his desk

and gave me a run-down of some "very lovely fields" where we could pitch our tents. While he was describing the very lovely fields, I noticed a 35mm Leica camera lying on his desk.

"Got plenty of film, Major?"

"No, by Jove, I haven't and can't find any."

"Well, I had something in mind a little more comfortable to live in than a lovely field. Bet we could work out a trade."

"Go on, Sergeant. What do you have in mind?"

"Well, Major, you have some hotel rooms and probably some houses, and I have tons of film. Let's make a deal."

This got his attention. He was almost drooling.

"Major, if you can give me a decent place for my boys to live and a place to build a laboratory, I'll see to it that you won't run out of film for the duration."

Major C. Leighton-Smyth grabbed his cap from the top of a filing cabinet, and we were in his staff car parked out front in a pair of seconds.

We headed south on the Via Capurso road and as we were approaching the city limits near by old squadron's mud field, we stopped in front of a tall, ornate iron gate. The major got out, opened it with a key, and we drove into something that looked like God Himself had designed.

A long, palm-tree-lined driveway headed straight to a white two-story concrete building that was sitting in the middle of an orchard of blossoming orange and tangerine trees.

We drove up to the house, passing beautifully maintained strawberry beds along the way. Two marble statues stood at the front entrance to the house. The name of the place had been carved in stone directly below the flat roof—"Villa Angela."

"Let's go inside, Sergeant. I think you will jolly well agree that it isn't too shabby."

We walked through an archway into a square courtyard. "Not too *shabby*," I thought. "Holy *mackerel!*" The villa was built completely around the courtyard. Several doors led to the interior on all four sides. A wrought-iron stairway rose to a balcony that ran all the way around the second floor. Some small trees and a statue of a little nude boy were in the center of the courtyard. This, I *couldn't* believe.

"Come upstairs with me, Sergeant, and I'll show you something that is very nice indeed."

We climbed the wrought-iron stairs, walked about half-way down the balcony, and entered a bedroom. A spectacular religious mural had been painted on the dome-shaped ceiling. Angels were flying around in white clouds. All the other bedrooms also had murals on the ceilings.

"Good *Lord*," I thought. "All this for a lousy little 100-foot can of 35mm film? This guy gets a *thousand* feet!" The terms were right. We made the swap. Major C. Leighton-Smyth got enough film to last him the rest of his life, and I got a million-dollar palace.

"We aren't through yet, Sergeant. I want to introduce you to your staff."

"What do you mean by staff, Major?"

"A family has been living on the grounds for many years, and they take care of the villa."

"Major, I'm curious. Why hasn't this place been reserved for generals?"

The major disappointed me by evading the question. I was sure that he had probably been caught at a weak moment when his camera was lying on his desk with no film in it. Or, as the French say, "C'est la guerre."

Behind the Villa Angela, down a winding path and through the citrus orchard, we came to a small, modest house that couldn't be seen from the main building. A stout lady was sitting in the door-way holding a ball of dough in her left hand and pinching off shell-shaped pieces with her right thumb and dropping them into a pan.

She looked up at the major, and he said, "Mama, this is Sergeant Thompson. He and his men will be living in the villa." She probably didn't understand, but smiled broadly.

Mama stood up, placed the pan of dough in her chair and said something in her language that I didn't understand. The only Italian words that I had learned and still remembered were from my favorite Italian opera, "Rigoletto." They were, "La donna e mobile, qual pluma vento."

I had the urge to show off by repeating those words, but didn't think Mama would appreciate it. Those musical words meant, "Woman is as fickle as a feather in the wind." Anyway, it didn't seem like it would apply here.

C. Leighton-Smyth explained that Mama had things well-organized at the villa. She would wash our clothes and do the cooking; her two teen-aged daughters would clean the house and Nonno, Mama's father, would care for the yard and orchard. Mama's son, Angelo, had no official duties, but we could probably find some work for him if we wanted to.

Major Leighton-Smyth placed the front gate key in my hand after he had locked it, and we drove back to town.

We walked into the major's office so I could sign for the villa. Of course it wouldn't be entirely official until our new commanding officer arrived and applied *his* signature.

Another major was sitting in the office reading a copy of *Union Jack*. He looked up and said, "Where have you been, old chap? Thought we were to make an appearance at the club."

Major Leighton-Smyth smiled broadly and said, "Just got lucky, my good man. I now have film for my camera. The Sergeant here has traded some for one of my billets."

"Well like I said, Smitty, you old rogue, you are *always* able to trade your bloody property for anything you want, but what can *I* trade? I'm only a bloody *medical* officer and...," he turned to me and continued, "Sergeant, I'll be happy to whip off a bit of foreskin for you if you will give me some film."

This nearly broke me up. The chap was *serious,* as only the *British* can be, and he had not meant it as humor.

"Major," I said, "when I deliver Major Leighton-Smyth's film, you'll find a small 100-foot can of 35mm for yourself. Drop over to the villa anytime you want after we get our lab set up. Bring your empty film cassettes and film with you and we'll fill them up. Who knows—maybe one of the new replacements will take you up on your foreskin offer."

It was hard to stay away from Villa Angela, so I drove back in the jeep I had inherited from Major Craig. This time I paused in front of the gate to study the wall that completely enclosed the villa property.

It was stone and about eight feet high. Pointed pieces of broken glass had been set in the top layer of concrete before it had set, and were sticking straight up. The place was a fortress! A very important person had lived here. Leighton-Smyth told me that the British troops had "liberated" the villa from one of southern Italy's wealthiest families.

When I entered the courtyard this time, an elderly man with snow-white hair was snipping and shaping the little trees to make them look like giant lollipops. Later, Mama told me he was her father.

I found Mama in her little house out back, and she hurried her children out to meet me. Gesturing time again. It never failed.

Mama introduced her 12-year-old son, Angelo, and her two teenage daughters. The pretty, outgoing one was Nina and the shyer one was Franca. Her husband, Signor Signorelli, was downtown working in a factory. I never found out what he did, but Angelo's gestures indicated that he made wheelbarrows.

I had the urge to go back to the nearby muddy field where my old squadron was camped and tell the photo guys what I had fallen into, but thought I'd probably run into them later anyway.

The new 9th Combat Camera Unit arrived with Major Ivo Barovik*, the commanding officer; a captain, a lieutenant and twelve eager and enthusiastic enlisted men. It occurred to me they probably hadn't been told what had happened to the members of the *first* 9th Combat Camera Unit or they wouldn't be so gung-ho.

They were a polite bunch of guys. Each man introduced himself and mentioned what he had done in Hollywood. The major had produced "sing-alongs." I remembered seeing them in the States before the war. They were intermission films where lyrics to popular songs were put on the screen and a little white bouncing ball landed on top of each word to keep the audience singing together. They were fun.

---

* Name has been changed.

Barovik didn't try to impress us by saying he had become a major in the reserves, in fact he made fun of himself. "I went in to see a general who had come to Hollywood to recruit some talent for army motion picture units. He glanced at my resume and noticed that I had produced and directed some things and said, 'Ya wanna be a major?' I said 'Sure, guess so.' An hour later I was a major in the Army Air Force. No training-*nothing*."

Major Barovik was a big, heavy-set man, stooping slightly and a little bald with a corrugated forehead. He wasn't very good looking. He had a heavy foreign sort of face, probably Slav, with eyes slightly turning down at the corners. His accent was eastern European. He talked with a large saxophone-shaped pipe clenched between his teeth in the corner of his mouth, which he nervously lit and relit. The rest of the men ranged from ordinary looking to the tall, dark and handsome Staff Sergeant Dakin.

The captain and lieutenant had worked in RKO Studio offices. The twelve enlisted men had worked in various skilled jobs, such as boom operators, sound mixers and lighting technicians at various studios. They all made a good first impression, but as time went on it became obvious they were a hodgepodge of the bold and the shy, naive and sophisticated, crude and refined, bums and gentlemen.

They all had one thing in common, however. The flight surgeons had found them to be in excellent physical and mental condition and not likely to become screaming claustrophobics when they were crowded into a slim aluminum tube at 25,000 feet under enemy fire.

The fellows hadn't known much about cameras, so they attended a class in Culver City on loading film, the use of the various lenses and a few very basic things they would need to know before they started shooting the action. Captain Ronald Reagan was their instructor. Their training took place in the old Hal Roach Studio which had been taken over by the army and was now referred to as "Fort Roach."

Since Reagan was one of my favorite actors, I asked the guys to tell me a little about him. They said he was a captain, but rank meant nothing to him. He got into trouble with his military superiors who were career officers—they made him roll his sleeves down and wear his silver bars. They also made him stop calling the enlisted men by their first names.

Another thing the men remembered about Reagan—he was "blind as a bat." When he was in front of a camera without his "Coke bottle" glasses, he had to look for the large white markers that had been placed on the floor to show him his movements.

Captain Reagan was good at acting in training films, so he was kept in Culver City for the duration. The guys all liked him and said he was very smart.

Before he got into the Army Air Force, Reagan was at the peak of his movie popularity. He made $1,650 a week and his fan-mail was second only to his friend Errol Flynn's. He had just made a film called, "International Squadron." It was about American pilots in the RAF.

Since I had brought up the subject of actors, the fellows told me that Clark Gable was an aerial gunnery instructor and Jimmy Stewart was flying a B-17 or B-24 in the Eighth Air Force in England.

Our new officers had hotel rooms only three blocks from the office. I overheard the lieutenant say, "It's a shame that Thompson found a place way out in the boondocks, probably an abandoned chicken coop, for the enlisted men." He hadn't seen Villa Angela!

The new boys and I drove out to the "boondocks" to see the "chicken coop" where we would be living. They were amazed. By this time I had selected a downstairs room, and left it up to the rest of the boys to go upstairs and fight over who would get the angel ceiling, who would sleep under the horses and meadow, and so forth.

After settling in, it was time to do a little sightseeing in town.

The highest-ranking enlisted man in the new unit was Staff Sergeant Larry Dakin. He seemed like a nice guy, but would later show his resentment because I outranked him. Today, however, he just wanted me to drive him downtown so he could buy a few postcards.

The two of us drove up Via Capurso into town. Dakin was Catholic and wanted to visit the big church he had seen near the headquarters building. We parked the jeep beside the church, removed the rotor from the engine's distributor so the jeep couldn't be taken, and went inside.

It was a large and impressive building with a lot of ornate gold-trimmed statues inside. My first thought was, why hadn't the Italians sold all this gold stuff and fed the hungry people we had passed on the sidewalk?

Dakin knew exactly what to do. Visiting Catholic churches was probably the same all over the world. First, he stuck a couple of fingers into a stone bowl of water just inside the door and touched his forehead and crossed himself. He then walked slowly in reverential silence down a side aisle toward the front, stopping briefly to pay homage to several life-sized statues standing against the wall.

I followed him all the way down to the altar where he knelt on one knee and again crossed himself. He stood up and pointed to a closed door to the right of the altar. We walked over to it and Dakin knocked. There was a reply from behind the door.

"Avanti."

Dakin looked at me, "Ya suppose he said come in or scram?"

A bit flustered, I replied, "You're the Catholic, so the decision is yours."

Dakin opened the door slowly and peeked inside, then we entered a small room. A short, chubby Franciscan wearing a brown habit with a white cord around his waist was seated behind an antique desk. He looked up at us over the top of his small, round gold-rimmed glasses.

The Franciscan stood up and said, "Now I can use my limited English. Not long ago I was using my limited German."

For the next ten or fifteen minutes, we were given a brief history of the church. This was Saint Nicholas Cathedral, named in honor of the revered clergyman.

"We keep some of the Saint's bones in a glass box under the altar," he explained. "Every year at the start of the commercial fishing season, we take his bones a short distance out into the Adriatic Sea in a rowboat and dip them into the water. This calms the sea for the safety of the fishermen."

We asked if we could see the bones. The Franciscan took us out to the altar and asked us to get down on our hands and knees and crawl under it. Here, in a depression in the floor, was a glass box about 18 inches long and a foot wide, containing a couple of bones that appeared to be from a leg.

The Franciscan walked back up the aisle with us, and just before we left, he handed each of us a tiny Saint Nicholas medal and asked for a package of cigarettes. Dakin gave him the rest of his Old Golds.

I drove. Dakin sat in the right seat and did a lot of rubbernecking. This was his first time in a foreign country, and he was making remarks about a lot of things I was already taking for granted.

We were driving down a narrow street slowly when Dakin shouted, "Stop!" He got out and walked across the street and entered a flower shop. I stayed in the jeep and watched as the proprietor parted some drapes and reached into the display window to remove a large bunch of yellow tulips.

Dakin walked back to the jeep with his tulips, got in and sat there silently looking at them. Tears started running down his cheeks and then he began sobbing uncontrollably.

I just sat there a little embarrassed and wondered what would happen next. In a few minutes, he wiped the tears from his face with his sleeve and tossed the tulips onto the back seat.

These few minutes were puzzling to me, wondering what in his conscious or subconscious mind had sparked this display of emotion. I thought I understood, because every time I heard the song, "I'll Get By as Long as I Have You," I felt a little choked up, because my beloved wife ended every letter she wrote me with those words.

We drove around for awhile, and by the time we got back to the villa, the tulips had wilted and remained in the back seat. Apparently they had served their purpose.

Since the Germans had caught so many ships in Bari harbor, our intelligence people predicted that if several more ships docked at the same time, "the curtain would go up on the second act." I visited the docks every day when I drove in to our office to see how many ships were there. If there was going to be a "second act," I wanted to capture it on film.

For a couple of weeks it was impossible for more than two ships to come in at the same time. Several ships had settled to the bottom of the bay and superstructures were sticking up from the water. Soon, most of this was cleared out.

Whenever there were four or more ships in port, I'd take a 4x5 Speed Graphic camera out to the end of a dock, set it up on a tripod and sit there until well after dark.

It was beginning to look like this was a waste of time, when one night, about 9 o'clock, I heard the distant droning of German engines. Then, suddenly, a brilliant white flare popped in the sky—then another—and another. They glowed brighter and brighter until the black sky turned bright. Everything around me was clearly visible—the ships, the docks and the city. It made me feel naked and exposed. It felt like Jerry was thousands of feet above, but was looking directly at *me*.

I set the shutter on time exposure, opened the shutter, stopped the diaphragm down to f-16 and pointed the camera down the dock toward the city. I knew the film wouldn't be completely exposed until the fiery action started.

Limey searchlights were stabbing the sky in an effort to catch a bandit flying above the flares, and then their ack-ack opened up, sending thousands of fiery tracers into the night above. It was an awesome sight. I was glad I'd had the foresight to bring my steel helmet.

I was afraid a bomb would hit the dock where I was standing and jiggle the camera during the time exposure. This, of course, would ruin the shot. Later, after it was all over, it occurred to me that a hit on the dock would have probably ruined *me!*

Cherry-red flames were still burning steadily in the row of wooden buildings at dockside when I put the camera back in the case and returned to the villa.

The next morning, I developed the film and made several prints. I knew I had some good trading material now, because long ago in Africa, I had learned that with a good action photograph, I could trade for just about *anything*. I remembered trading good prints for the big Hammerlund Professional short-wave radio.

My patient waiting on the dock had paid off!

Major Barovik called all of us into his office in the 15th Air Force headquarters building one morning, and after a few minutes of small talk, cleared his throat, laid his pipe down and said, "Men, we've started going on missions and already some of you have come back with horror stories. According to the statistics, if you go on more than 15 missions you're either going to be dead, wounded or a POW (Prisoner of War)...whichever comes first. I hate to be so blunt. Now that you understand your prospects for survival, you can ask for and get a reassignment to other duties and *no* questions will be asked and *no* reason will be entered on your record. The missions are strictly voluntary." He glanced up and scanned the solemn faces in the room. There was dead silence. Nobody spoke up.

As we were leaving the office and walking down the hall, "Spunky" Spunkmaster broke the silence.

"Well, *somebody* has to do it or this heathen war'll *never* end."

"Barovik doesn't have to worry. Betcha *he'll* never go on a mission."

"Yeah, he'll send *us* out and let *us* be sitting ducks day after day for the Germans who tried but failed to kill us just the day before."

"Whadda ya want to do, go on permanent KP?"

"I knew this would be tough before we came over here, but *damned* if I knew it would be *this* rough."

The Food Depot Raid

I HAD DISCOVERED A HIDDEN TALENT that got us the villa—bargaining. It bought us a great place to live, and now it was time to stock the pantry.

We always passed a gigantic warehouse on Via Capurso on our way into town. This was one of the places where food was stored and distributed to the American and British troops in Italy. It was located at this particular place because of its proximity to the seaport and railroad terminal.

I had done a little reconnaissance there and found the whole place was being run by a major and a master sergeant in the Quartermaster Corps. Each had his own office, complete with young English-speaking Italian secretaries.

A raid was planned. I asked A.A. "A-Square" Mooneyham, the sound-mixing technician, to help me with the camera, sound mixer, tripod and cables. This was real Hollywood stuff and would be impressive. A-Square was a trained sound mixer from United Artists Studio and could make our little deception look like the real thing. We called him A-Square because he wouldn't tell what his initials stood for. He was a tall, skinny kid with buck teeth, red hair, freckles and a bobbing Adam's apple. He didn't fit my image of a Hollywood movie technician *or* a combat cameraman.

We drove to the food depot, went inside the building and located the sergeant's office. He would probably be an easier target than the major. He was sitting at a big desk with his cute little brunette Italian secretary at another desk behind her typewriter.

"Sergeant," I said, "I'm Sergeant Thompson from Hollywood, and I'm here in Italy to shoot some stories that the folks back home will find interesting. You are responsible for the most important thing a soldier can have—food. I want to shoot your story so it can be shown in every theater in the U.S."

The sergeant sat up straight and glanced at his secretary to see if she had heard the Hollywood man's flattering remarks.

The sergeant said, "I'll be glad to help you any way I can."

"Good," I said, "but before we get started, I want to give this photo to you. It shows some of the action that took place in the harbor a few nights ago. It'll be fun to show your folks back home."

I saw the smile of gratitude in his face as he stood up and placed the print down in front of his secretary. This laid the groundwork. He was now convinced he was dealing with real "pros."

A-Square and I brought the equipment into the office and mounted the big 35mm Mitchell on the tripod, connected the cable to the sound mixer, plugged in the microphone and pointed the camera at the sergeant.

I was also wearing my "director's hat," so I posed the sergeant behind his desk, moved a chair up close to him and asked his secretary to sit down with her steno pad and pencil. Then I held the microphone between the sergeant and his secretary and asked them each to count to ten while A-Square twisted his dials. A-Square pointed to his headphones and gave us a thumbs-up sign. The sergeant adjusted his necktie, cleared his throat and put on his best "executive" expression. He was ready for his big scene when I said, "We're rolling!"

After the filmless interview, the "star" took us out into his cavernous warehouse and told us to load up with anything we wanted. We browsed around for awhile and had a warehouse worker, an Italian, help us load as many boxes and cans of food as we could carry into the jeep.

When we arrived back at the villa, "Porky" Pigg unloaded the groceries and took them into the kitchen.

Joe "Porky" Pigg was a short, lean fellow, had a pale melon-like face and looked like a burlesque comedian. When he introduced himself to anybody, he would always say, "It's spelled with *two* G's." I later learned that in spelling his name on any of the reports I had to submit, if his name was spelled with only *one* G, he would explode in a trembling fit. He was a small fellow but one not to be angered.

Right up to the time we gave the villa back to Major C. Leighton-Smyth, we were never without 55-pound boxes of frozen steaks, pork chops, chicken breasts and gallon cans of fruit and vegetables.

It was the best of all worlds.

The only thing we couldn't get from the warehouse was *fresh* food. Everything was either frozen or in cans. I had made friends with a lieutenant at the Bari Bargo Airfield who flew B-17s and C-47s. He had flown me around the area several times when General Twining wanted oblique aerial shots of various types of aircraft in flight. When I learned that he made a weekly run to Tunis with mail, I asked him if he brought fresh food back.

"No, we just stay at the airfield and shoot the bull until we get bored, and then come back."

"My outfit lived in Tunis long enough to make contacts with vegetable and egg merchants—mostly Arabs," I said.

"Then why don't you go down there with us and we'll do some grocery shopping?"

"I'll see if the major will authorize it," I said.

Major Barovik thought some fresh eggs and vegetables would be a real treat, so he gave me written permission to carry a .45 "for protection from the Arabs," and suggested I make a few trips.

About every two weeks thereafter, the lieutenant, his co-pilot and I would make the mail (and now food) run to Tunis. We would use a B-17 or a C-47.

As we prepared for one flight, I told the pilot that before the war I had soloed a 65-horsepower Aeronca.

"Wanna see if you can handle a slightly heavier piece of equipment like this B-17?"

"Sure do."

"Okay. Joe, the guy who rides the right seat (co-pilot) usually has a hangover when we take off, and I'm sure he'll be glad to drop back into the radio compartment and flop down on the floor and sleep it off."

I sat down in the co-pilot's seat feeling very important and didn't take my eyes off the pilot as he went through the pre-flight and take-off procedures. Joe was already flat on the radio compartment floor.

When we were at altitude, he said, "Okay, let's see what you can do with 4,800 horsepower." He removed his hands from the half-wheel and lifted his feet from the rudder pedals and said, "She's all yours."

I had never been so excited in my life! It didn't take long to become familiar with the navigational instruments and a few other little switches and knobs I could twist and push without placing us in an uncomfortable situation.

We were heading for a bank of very dark, stormy clouds. This worried me a little, so I asked the pilot if he wanted to go around them. He said it wouldn't be necessary because he had "read" the clouds and there was nothing to be concerned about.

When we got into the clouds, it seemed almost like night. Faint rings of fire started dancing around the propellers and wing tips.

"What's that, Lieutenant?"

"Saint Elmo's fire."

"Something that will set us on fire?"

"No," he laughed, "it happens sometimes when we're flying through a relatively strong electric field, and when it's dark enough, you can see Saint Elmo's fire. Hundreds of years ago, sailors saw this phenomenon when they were sailing through storms and didn't know what caused it. For lack of something better, they named it after Saint Elmo."

I felt better.

During these long over-water flights, I asked many questions about the airplane. One interesting thing I learned was how the aircraft was turned over to the bombardier on the bomb runs.

"When we arrive at the IP (initial point where the run starts), we switch the auto-pilot on. It is connected to the Norden bomb sight, so the bombardier controls the plane through his sight until he finishes his work and says 'Bombs away.' We then switch the auto-pilot off and take over again."

This made me wonder if he might have the bird on auto-pilot and was letting me *think* I was controlling the thing. I pushed the control column forward slightly and we started a shallow dive—pulled back, and we climbed. He looked at me and grinned.

"Piece of cake, ain't it Sergeant?"

I had asked Sergeant Dakin for a GI prophylactic before we started these over-water flights. I stretched it over my little Bible and tied the end in a hard knot. If we should have to "ditch," everything would get wet but my Bible.

We flew from Bari to Tunis, mostly over water, in a little over three hours. We would leave Bari early in the morning, right after daylight, so we would have enough grocery shopping time in Tunis before having to start back and arrive in Bari before dark.

Every time we landed in Tunis at the La Goulette Airfield, I would borrow a jeep from the motor pool.

"How can you get a jeep, Sergeant? We can't do that."

A few good war photos handed to the right person in the motor pool would always get us a jeep with a full tank of gas.

On one trip, the three of us drove out to the olive grove where our squadron had lived. It was now occupied by a Negro outfit that drove trucks and worked on the docks and in the marshaling yards.

The fresh fruit, vegetables, eggs and booze we brought back always brightened the day for a lot of our friends. Major Barovik especially enjoyed the cognac.

Rigoletto, Carne Gatto and Vesuvius

WE NEVER HAD TO WORRY ABOUT FOOD preparation. Mama was our cook. We had no refrigerator, so a lot of meat would spoil if we couldn't find something to do with it. Mama knew *exactly* what to do with it. She must have had the best-fed family in the Italian Theater of Operations.

Mama's daughters kept the villa clean. Angelo was my side-kick, and he was at my side constantly. He called me, "Sergeant Chief," and I loved him for it.

Most of the Italian people, except for *our* family, were very low-class looking. They were poorly dressed and looked like they had been for a long time. They were expressionless, lethargic and sloth-ful. The only time we saw any animation at all was when they got into an argument with each other in the street—then there were screaming outbursts and flailing arms.

The opera was a different thing altogether. Pack an opera house with men, women and kids and they would come alive.

It was opera season, and the world-famous opera company "San Carlo" had escaped from Naples, which at that time was still occu-pied by the Germans, and fled to Bari, now in Allied hands. It was probably safer in Bari.

I had been brought up in a home with plenty of opera records that we played on our wind-up Victrola. I loved the operas so much that I started learning the Italian lyrics at a very early age. One day, Angelo and I went downtown to attend "Rigoletto."

The opera house was packed. Men, women and children of all ages were there. The women had wicker baskets of food and wine on their laps, which they dug into during intermissions. The whole opera house smelled like garlic.

The Italians were a very loud and emotional crowd. They knew the libretto intimately. When the Duke sang his "La Donna e Mobile," nearly everybody sang along with him. When Gilda went into her "Caro Nome che il mio cor," they sighed loudly.

In front of us, a fat signora toasted every high point with a large guzzle from a wine bottle and wiped her mouth with the back of her hand. She kept ripping chunks of white bread from a long loaf and stuffing them into her mouth.

Five minutes from the end, amid sobbing and sniffling by the much-affected audience, a fight broke out behind us because somebody had decided to leave early. Instantly, everybody around us turned and started hissing and shaking their fists, totally forgetting poor old Rigoletto standing alone on the stage with a sack containing his dead daughter. Then the sobbing became so loud that we couldn't hear the beautiful aria that brought the curtain down.

This had been my first "in person" opera, and I felt so good about it, that I suggested to Angelo that we find a nice restaurant and live it up.

Angelo said he wasn't hungry and wanted to go back to the villa. I had never eaten in an Italian restaurant, not even in the States, so I dragged Angelo with me as we entered a nearby restaurant.

The place was small but clean, and a tall bottle of Chianti sat in the center of each table. Since we were the only customers, we selected the best table in the house—the one by the window, and sat down.

Angelo said, "Sergeant Chief, let's go home." The waiter brought a menu, and I asked Angelo to interpret it for me. "Sergeant Chief, let's go *home!*"

I held up the menu, ran my finger down the list of items, stopped on one and told the waiter this was my choice. In ten minutes he returned with a plate of pasta and some kind of meat saturated with olive oil. The waiter set the plate in front of me and said, "Buon appetit! Mangia!"

I wasn't very impressed with my first real Italian meal, but ate it anyway. Angelo sat there glumly without saying a word. I started thinking that I would rather be eating kidney pie. I cleaned my plate, however, and washed it down with the sour Chianti.

On the way back to the jeep, I asked Angelo what I had eaten. "Carne Gatto," he replied. Well, I knew what carne was, because I had learned in high school Spanish that carne meant meat. But *gatto?*

It was charade time again. I mooed like a cow. "No." Clucked like a chicken. "No." Gobbled like a turkey. "No." It had been meat, but what kind? It was surprising that the restaurant offered meat of *any* kind, because there was very little left in Italy.

We parked in front of Villa Angela and got out. Angelo's big black cat came over to him with his tail sticking straight up and started rubbing against his legs. Angelo picked him up, hugged him and said, "Gatto mio."

Good Lord! I had just eaten somebody's cat!!

It had been raining all morning and by noon the sky was black. I heard Mama out front yelling her head off, and I ran out to see what was wrong. She was running around in circles with her arms raised to the sky screaming, "Madonna mia, *Vesuvio, Vesuvio!*"

It wasn't raining *water,* it was raining *black mud!* The ground, the jeep, the statues—*everything* was black! It was the weirdest sight I had ever seen. My mind started racing. Mama was screaming Vesuvio and that meant Vesuvius, but how could *that* be? Mount Vesuvius was 150 miles from Bari, all the way across Italy on the west coast.

A cool head prevailed, and I was able to put two and two together. Vesuvius hadn't erupted *this* badly in generations, but it was erupting now, and the strong west wind was bringing black volcanic dust all the way across Italy. The mixture of dust and rain was causing a "mud fall!"

I ran back into the villa, grabbed a Bell and Howell movie camera, and a Speed Graphic still camera, threw a blanket over them and dashed out to the jeep. I couldn't see through the windshield, so I slammed it down against the hood and took off.

I got to the airfield in record time. Two B-25s were being given quick pre-flights. I ran over to the closest one, held up the two cameras for the pilot to see and quickly explained that I needed to get over to the volcano to make some official photographs.

In a little over an hour we were there. The pilot worked his way into the long line of aircraft that was circling the volcano in a counter-clockwise traffic pattern. There must have been 10 planes full of sight-seers.

There was a B-17, a P-38, a C-47 and several B-25s. As we flew around the down-wind side of Vesuvius, we were in the blackest void in Hades. When we circled around to the upwind side, the pouring rain washed the opaque windshield, and we were able to see if we had been holding our position on the aerial carousel.

I was getting good shots of Vesuvius but wanted to get closer on the up wind side as we circled so I crawled forward and shouted to the pilot to get over to the edge. He started moving over but what we hadn't counted on was that near the crater there was a difference in the air currents caused by the high temperature and we started a frightening drop! The pilot hit the throttles and made a diving turn away from the inferno! *Anything* for a good shot.

It is a *miracle* that there were no mid-air collisions in the black inferno east of the volcano.

We got some good movie footage and still shots of the amazing show put on by Mother Nature. We later learned that several Allied planes at nearby Pomigliano airfield and a few at Capadichino airfield were damaged by fragments of rock hurled from Vesuvius.

One morning before getting out of bed, I heard a loud fight going on somewhere in the villa. I left my ground-floor room and went into the courtyard. "Mouse" Morris and "Dutch" Vandervoort were out on the second floor balcony punching and slugging away at each other. I yelled at them, but they paid no attention.

I went back into my room and picked up my .45. I fired it into the ground and the fighting stopped. Mouse and Dutch were completely exhausted and slumped on the iron railing as they looked down at me.

"What are you guys doing—what's the matter?" I yelled.

Mouse said, "This dumb jerk said that Falstaff beer bottles are *green* and I *know* they are *brown.*"

Mouse got his nickname because he had worked in the ink-and-paint department of the Disney Studios.

They were still recovering from an especially rough mission they had both been on the day before. I understood, but the folks back home would have a hard time comprehending the strange ways a combat soldier releases tension that has reached the "boiling point."

Nina's Wedding

MY BEDROOM WAS BETWEEN THE KITCHEN and the photo laboratory. There was also a large storage room on the ground floor where we kept cameras, cans of film and lab supplies. We also kept our flying gear and parachutes hanging in this room. The rest of the men had bedrooms upstairs. This segregation was the way I had planned it. They were a wild, vino-drinking bunch, and I didn't fit in.

The boys were upstairs engaging in their nightly revelry, and I was downstairs sound asleep. Suddenly, I was startled by several gun shots.

I jumped out of bed and ran out into the courtyard where the shots seemed to have come from. A few of the men were standing there looking down at something on the ground.

Some of the men scampered up the stairway when they saw me coming. Larry Dakin and a couple of others stayed there, probably too drunk to move that fast. Dakin was called "Crazy Larry Dakin, the Village Idiot," by the enlisted men in our unit.

When I got close to them. I found that Dakin had his .45-caliber automatic in his hand and was looking down at a parachute.

I took the pistol away from him and then saw what he had done. He had unloaded his weapon into my parachute. *My* parachute! By now, I knew he had a mean streak, but this was far and beyond meanness. He knew that my back pack had a silk canopy, and I was proud of it because all the others were made of the newer material called nylon.

When I was in our office at the 15th Air Force headquarters building the next morning, I explained why we would have to "surplus" a parachute. Major Barovik got on the phone and called the villa. He read the "riot act" to Staff Sergeant Dakin and finished by telling him he was now a "buck" sergeant. Crazy Larry had lost a stripe.

Nina, the younger of Mama's daughters, was engaged to marry her fiancé in two weeks. He had been shot up by the Limeys while he was serving as an Italian soldier but was now a civilian.

Mama knew that she could use our surplus food for the banquet following the wedding, but she was faced with one problem. Nina would not have a wedding gown.

I thought we might be able to do something about this. I asked Mama to come into my office-bedroom and pointed to the ruined parachute on the floor.

"Mama," I said, "I think we can solve the wedding gown problem." With that, I pulled the rip cord, and the spring-loaded pilot chute nearly hit the ceiling! I then opened the flaps on the canvas container and showed her the beautiful white silk canopy.

"Can you do it with this?" I asked. Mama knelt down on the floor and scooped up some of the silk. She looked up at me with tears in her eyes and jumped to her feet.

"*Si, Si,* Sergeant Chief!" she exclaimed. I removed the silk canopy from the container, unfastened the connector links and cut out a gore for myself. The rest, I piled into her arms.

A folded note had shot out with the pilot. It had been written by the hand of a female, probably meant for a parachute rigger. It wished the finder good luck and a safe and speedy return home. It was not signed.

Mama lost no time in her wedding gown design and construction. She spent every day on the project. The boys and I told her she didn't have to come up to the villa and cook for us while she worked on the gown. We would handle the food preparation ourselves.

Within a week, Nina was fitted. The gown was a beautiful silk creation that could easily have come from the shop of a fancy Italian designer. I gave Angelo the parachute harness and container to play with, and I was stuck with a nylon back pack.

Mama had plenty of silk left, so I had her make a nightgown for my wife, Wilma. I had found some black net and lace downtown and she used this for the top of the gown. It was a "see-through" creation seldom seen in catalogues, and *never* in the Southern Bible Belt!

Now that the food and gown problems were out of the way, only one thing remained to make the wedding perfect—wedding photographs. Well, the Signorelli family was certainly in the right place at the right time.

It was morning of the great day when Nina's husband-to-be came up to the villa with Angelo. Angelo introduced him.

"Sergeant Chief, this is Giuseppe, and he will be my brother today."

I shook hands with the tall, slender young man and wondered if he felt any animosity toward me. He shouldn't, I thought, because the Limeys were the ones who had taken him out of the war.

Giuseppe was wearing an ill-fitting dark suit that looked like one he had outgrown. He and his bachelor friends had partied all night and saw the sun come up before they got any sleep. He did look quite dissipated.

Mama had gone downtown with several dishes of food created from our ample supplies. It's a good thing that our leftovers could feed a very large family, because about 30 of her friends and relatives showed up for a feast like they probably thought they'd never see again.

This was the first time I had ever covered a wedding as a photographer. It was held in none other than the church where Crazy Larry Dakin and I had seen the bones. I used a 4x5 Speed Graphic camera for the formal wedding pictures, and later I delivered an album of 8x10 sepia-toned prints to the family.

The banquet hall was on the second floor of a building three blocks from the church. Angelo and I drove there in the jeep, parked it and removed the rotor.

The guests had beat the wedding party to the hall and were

standing around laughing and gesturing wildly. It was evident that they had worn their "Sunday best" even though patches and threadbare places were visible.

The wedding party arrived and took their place at the head of the long table. Angelo sat beside me at the middle of the table.

There were about 15 people on each side of the table and everybody started savoring "Sergeant Chief's" food. Many appreciative glances were cast my way.

Following the happy meal, the gentlemen started rising, one by one, to toast the bride and groom. As the last gentleman was finishing his toast, it suddenly occurred to me that my prisoner-servant, Dino Gali, had taught me a soldier's toast in his language before we parted company in Tunis but hadn't bothered to translate it for me.

Dino's toast was short and it rhymed, so I had memorized it. Why I had remembered it and was now able to repeat it word for word at this reception was surprising.

I stood up, smiled at the happy couple, raised my glass and started. "Aqua fresca, vino puro..."

Angelo grabbed my sleeve and yanked so hard, it spilled wine on the fat toothless lady sitting next to me. I stopped the toast abruptly and glanced down at him. He was standing up and pulling me toward a door at the side of the room.

"Holy mackerel," I wondered, "have I violated an ancient protocol of some kind?" Angelo led me through the door and over to a window. He then tried to explain what I didn't know about the soldier's toast.

"Aqua fresca, vino puro" was easy. I knew that meant "Fresh water, pure wine," but the rest was lost to me. I was too embarrassed to go back into that room full of people so we could use the stairway. I opened the window, grabbed the downspout, made a rapid slide to the sidewalk with Angelo right behind me, jumped into the jeep and made my escape!

I made a vow then and there that I would go back to Tunisia, break into that Italian prisoner of war camp, and punch out Dino Gali for not translating the toast!

Angelo and I drove back to the villa and changed into our work clothes. He had said that after the wedding we would go out behind his house and pick the mulberry fruit that had ripened. We made gluttons of ourselves on the juicy berries, but our hands turned purple.

When Mama came home, she saw our purple hands and burst out laughing. She went into her house and brought out some sulfur. She lit it and gestured to us to rub our hands over the fumes. We did. No more stains.

Before daylight one morning, two of our cameramen, Mike Silva and Brad Foster, had driven up to Foggia for a mission. That evening the jeep returned without Mike. He had been assigned to fly in the coffin corner group. Brad was flying in a group ahead of and higher than Mike's coffin corner and didn't see what happened, but was told about the incident by another crewman who was flying on Mike's right wing.

"I was in the ball turret and turned directly toward Mike's plane. Flak hit the right inboard engine and it broke off and fell. Almost immediately, the right wing tore away and started fluttering downward with flames streaking behind it. Then the ship turned belly up and slowly rolled back, nosed over and started spinning wildly until it was out of sight. No chutes."

I hadn't known Mike long enough to have a great affection for him, and no reason to dislike him.

Mike's personal belongings were quickly gathered and sat out on the balcony. His bed was stripped and the pillow and blankets were also taken from his room. We sat down to the supper Mama had prepared for us, and the conversation began.

"Well, what can you expect when you fly in coffin corner? It's the low, rear group and the Jerries pick you off like sitting ducks."

"You know very well why they want to put us in coffin corner, that's where the *action* is."

"Yeah, Lieutenant Grover and Don Howe were both in the corner when *they* bought the farm."

"This is Hollywood, man, anything for good action shots. So what else is new?"

Brad, who had flown with Mike today, changed the subject.

"You'll never believe what I saw. I happen to know the radio operator and he came back in the waist while we were at 25,000 feet and 40° below zero. He took his left glove off and stuck his hand out the window long enough to freeze his fingers stiff. I knew he had been scared out of his mind and was trying to figure a way to be grounded."

"Did it work?"

"Dunno yet. Saw him goin' over to a medic after we landed."

"Well, he didn't have to freeze his hand to get grounded. All he had to do was put some GI lye soap in his armpits and he'd break out and get a high temperature. And if he kept on doing it, he would be grounded for good."

"Bet he'll get a Purple Heart for it."

Later that evening the usual vino party started upstairs. It was longer and louder than usual. Four of the drunks lined up on the balcony outside Mike's room, raised their .45s to the sky, and squeezed off a few rounds. Then the party continued with loud laughter and more frivolity. Rumors must have been spread of my excessive sobriety because I wasn't invited to the wake. Tomorrow there would be no more mention of Sergeant Mike Silva. He would have just been a stranger who passed this way.

We were all fatalists. Fatalism was paltry protection against such tragedies as this, however. The only consolation was that Mike had been killed with a camera in his hands doing what he wanted to do.

Combat men came to look with a callous indifference upon the sudden death of their friends. This necessity, to my mind, was one of the greatest horrors of war.

I overheard Crazy Larry telling somebody, "He shot him in the head."

"Who shot who in the head, Larry?"

"A crewman shot his pilot in the head."

"Why?"

"Don't know all the details but they crash-landed and the plane was in a mess. All the fellows but the pilot got out and ran because the plane was on fire. The pilot was pinned in his cockpit and couldn't move. He was screaming for help and said his legs were crushed under the instrument panel. The plane was caved in and the cockpit window was open and only about five or six feet from the ground.

"The crew got as close as they could and yelled that the fire trucks were on their way. It was hopeless, though, and the poor guy was burning alive. The pilot screamed for somebody to shoot him. The crew stood there frozen for a few seconds, then one of them got as close to the pilot's window as he could, aimed his .45 carefully and shot the pilot in the head. The pilot's head pitched forward and the crewman fired again into his head."

"Surely they won't punish the guy who shot him, will they?"

"Who knows? Hope we find out."

Three nights after Brad Foster had returned from the mission that had killed his friend, Mike Silva, we heard a gunshot in his room. Two of the men rushed in and found Brad stretched out on his cot. He had blown his brains out.

The Purple Hands

WHEN LARRY DAKIN CAME OVER FROM HOLLYWOOD with the replacements, he was a staff sergeant, the highest-ranking enlisted man in the group. It seemed logical to him, therefore, that he would become the NCOIC—non-commissioned officer in charge—as soon as they got to Bari.

Wrong. When the group walked into the combat camera office, he spotted technical sergeant stripes on my sleeves, one stripe more than *he* had. Instantly, I became his nemesis for the duration of our service together.

Dakin was a real, genuine Hollywood "leading man" type. He was tall, dark, handsome and he swaggered around acting like he was about to be called back on the set to finish shooting his scene.

He had never been in front of the cameras. He had been behind them—*way* behind them. His job at Metro had been riding around from one sound stage to another on his bicycle delivering scripts and messages.

Larry was an extroverted, cocky swashbuckler who enjoyed striking poses while he held his Old Gold cigarette at a jaunty angle between his lips.

Our ladies' man was delighted, one day, to learn that Colonel Oveta Culp Hobby had brought her little group of WACs to Bari to release a few good men from their typewriters. The WACs were the first military women to be sent over here. As luck would have it, for Dakin at least, they landed in our 15th Air Force headquarters building.

The WACs were upstairs at their typewriters one afternoon when our Lothario swaggered in. The clatter of typewriters stopped. All heads turned. "Hey, Gertrude, there's that handsome movie actor from the Hollywood office downstairs."

It seemed that our messenger boy had spread a few interesting rumors about himself. From this moment on, the ladies lined up for their turn to sit with him at his favorite sidewalk cafe and listen to fascinating secrets about Hollywood stars.

Colonel Hobby had a rule that her girls could be "signed out" of their hotel for an evening, but they had to be returned by 11 p.m. Dakin's radar had zeroed in on the most attractive of the bunch, and he would be around at six to "check her out."

Everything had to be perfect. The "actor" had to be "made up" for his next scene. Dakin had been upstairs in his room with the Angel ceiling for two hours getting himself together, combing his hair repeatedly and shining his shoes.

Finally he came down to the lab where I was mixing chemicals. "Look at my fingernails, Thompson, they are as brown as walnuts."

"That's because you keep your hands in the developer tray so long that the mono-methylparaminophenol sulfate in the solution stains them," I explained. I was having some fun with these big chemical words—just showing off. Larry hadn't been to photo school and hadn't added impressive-sounding chemical words to his vocabulary.

"Okay, Tommy, don't be a wise-guy! What made my fingernails turn brown?"

"The metol."

Dakin was getting a little panicky about his appearance. He *had* to look perfect. He thought that since I was the unit chemist, I would have a solution. I did.

"Okay, Dakin," I said, "put some of this potassium permanganate in a tray of water and soak your hands in it for about ten minutes. This chemical will remove the metol stains from your fingernails."

After soaking his hands for ten minutes, he held them under the faucet to rinse them, and discovered that his hands had been dyed a deep, dark purple.

"Hey, look what happened. My hands are purple!"

"That's okay," I said. "That's just the first step. Now you'll soak your hands in a solution of sodium bisulfite for a few minutes, and it will remove the purple stain, then your hands and fingernails will be back to normal."

I was reaching for the bottle of sodium bisulfite when a diabolical idea flashed through my mind. I would retaliate for the parachute shooting incident! Dakin wouldn't know what I was doing because all our chemicals came in bulk powder and granular form and had to be carefully weighed and mixed into solutions. This was all alien to Larry.

"I'm sorry, Dakin, I thought we had some sodium bisulfite on the shelf, but guess we haven't." Dakin mumbled something about my ancestors and stormed out of the lab.

That evening at six, a dashing young "Hollywood actor" with purple hands checked out his fair lady.

Some of the dogfaces were jealous of the ones who were strutting around town wearing ribbons on their blouses. These resourceful fellows solved the problem very easily. They bought colorful scraps of fabric from local stores and made their own.

The fabric came in many bright colors and patterns and by cutting off an inch and folding the material over, they made some authentic-looking medal ribbons.

The less talented guys had a tailor make them. This was the same tailor who had customized my blouse. He made it look more like an officer's uniform, but it was just short of being illegal.

When I came back to the tailor's shop to pick it up, he showed me a dozen "ribbons" he had made and suggested that they would go very nicely with my newly customized outfit. It was tempting, but I decided to earn my own decorations the hard way. Besides, there was nobody in town I wanted to impress.

Some of the men were proudly wearing a chest full of "ribbons" and impressing the Italian ladies for awhile before being spotted by officials who were unable to identify them. It was American ingenuity at its very best.

The First Combat Mission

SOON AFTER THE 9TH COMBAT CAMERA UNIT replacements arrived in Bari, we started flying combat missions. I had been flying non-combat photo missions out of Bargo Airfield in Bari. Several airfields were spread around the Foggia area about 70 miles northeast of town and the big warplanes used these fields.

The 97th and 301st heavy bomb groups had flown their B-17s up from Africa and had brought their "little friends" with them. The little friends, of course, were the P-38s that flew top cover for them. The planes of the 460th heavy bomb group were there also. This was a B-24 outfit newly arrived from the States.

We lived in Bari and our combat photographers drove the 70 miles to Foggia when they went to work. Major General Nathan F. Twining had taken over the 15th Air Force from General Doolittle, who had just established the headquarters in Bari. Doolittle was transferred to the 8th Air Force in England. Twining had come from the 13th Air Force in the Solomons—the Pacific Theater of Operations.

I felt that top brass tended to be prickly and arrogant. Not General Twining. His friendly, unassuming and considerate ways were very exceptional. I didn't see in him any of the incredible inefficiency of Army bureaucracy and wasn't alone in this evaluation. And he was *not* a profane person like so many others were.

At first I wasn't flying out of Foggia with the rest of the guys. I was sticking around my office in the villa keeping the home fires burning. There was always something to do: write reports, mix chemicals, develop and print, and do the grocery shopping.

It was more uncomplicated for the others. All they had to do was fly their missions by day, and party by night. Their evening vino binges accomplished two things: first, it "brought them down" from their last mission; and second, it got them into the right frame of mind for their next one.

Another job kept me busy around town. General Twining had a large floor-to-ceiling mission status board or "tote board" as he called it, on a wall in his inner-sanctum. It reminded me of Colonel Zartman's confusing chart in Oran.

Twining's mission board contained the number and crew names of every bomber and fighter under his command. This was a top-secret room, and very few people were cleared to go in there.

I had been doing a lot of personal photo work for the general, and he knew I was the best-qualified lab man in our unit. He had admired some of my bomber and fighter pictures, especially the ones shot in the air, and had me blow some of them up to 20x24 inches so he could display them in his office and private quarters.

The general had also asked me to keep his 35mm camera loaded, then process and print his shots. Some of them were of a highly personal nature, and nobody was to be in the lab while I was working on them.

General Twining asked me to build a darkroom in a small closet in his mission status room so I could photograph the wall chart every evening and deliver an 8x10-inch print to him without having to leave the room. He wanted a photo record of every day's activity.

Every evening, when all of the planes had returned from their missions—and many of them didn't—the general would gather reports from each bomb and fighter group. An assistant would then record the data on the big chart. Twining would dismiss his assistant and sink down into his big leather chair facing the wall to study the whole picture. His shoulders would sometimes slump and his ramrod West Point stature would seem to crumble. He would study the wall for an hour, making occasional notes in the blue leather folder he held in his lap. Here was a man with the life and death of thousands of men at the tip of his pencil.

This was probably the quietest room in Italy while Twining was studying. Nobody said anything. It was obvious that he was agonizing over his losses. The Germans were probably doing the same thing. I wouldn't have traded jobs with him.

This is when I would set the Speed Graphic on the tripod and photograph the wall. When the film had been developed and *one* print made, I would bring it over to him along with the test strip.

One evening after General Twining had my 8x10 print in his hands, I asked for permission to leave. He looked up, smiled and said, "Thank you Sergeant Thompson, that will be all."

A warrant officer was sitting behind his desk in an outer office and I stopped to mention how much I liked the general.

"We're lucky to have him. He almost didn't get here. When he was the C.G. of the 13th Air Force in the Pacific, he and fourteen companions left on a flight from Guadalcanal to Esperito Santo. They had a problem and ditched near New Hebrides and floated around for six days in life rafts before being picked up by a couple of PBYs."

"I didn't know that," I said, "but one of my heroes, Eddie Rickenbacker, had a narrow escape in that same part of the world. This happened in 1942. The plane he was on ditched and they floated around for *twenty-four* days before being located and rescued. They had to drink their own urine to stay alive."

"I'd heard about that but don't know the details," the warrant officer said. "Fill me in."

"I only know what was printed in the *Stars and Stripes*. Rickenbacker and seven air corps fellows were flying from Hawaii to Canton Island 1,800 miles southwest of Hawaii in a B-17. They got lost, ran out of fuel and ditched about 500 miles from their destination. They had three liferafts. They only had a few oranges with them and those didn't last long. They were near starvation when a seagull landed on Eddie's head. He grabbed it and the eight men had a banquet. The ordeal was rough. One man died and the rest of them were near death when the Navy spotted them and picked them up. Rickenbacker had lost fifty-four pounds, which brought him down to 126."

It finally occurred to me that I might never have a chance to visit Germany if I didn't do it now. Major Barovik had told me that as the non-commissioned officer in charge, I could pick and choose my missions, be a supernumerary or not go on any at all. I decided to fly missions, which would also make me eligible for the air medal.

I had become fatalistic enough by now to think that "it could only happen to the *other* fellow." And I still had about half of my nine lives left.

I had flown in a few B-17s on non-combat missions, but never where the Krauts would be occupying the same air space at the same time. It sounded challenging.

As soon as the fellows who had been on a few missions learned that I was going to fly, they immediately started trying to worry me.

"You'll have fun shooting the Kraut fighters, but that *flak* is something you'd better stay *away* from. When the flak starts, take a close look at the ground and sometimes you'll see the flashes from the guns way down there."

"When the flak hits the ship it sounds like somebody had thrown a handful of gravel up on a tin roof. Sometimes you don't hear it at all, you just suddenly see some holes."

"The ship ahead of me got flakked real bad and blew up. Pieces of it slammed into our ship, and either a body or a piece of metal or something went through one of our props."

"The flak'll start when you're on the bomb run. It usually starts low and in front of you. Then the Kraut gunners raise it up gradually until you think the next one has your name on it."

"Ya better hope the Krauts are listenin' to Strauss Waltzes because that makes 'em happy and friendly, but ya better look out if they are tuned into a military band with the oompah-oompahs— that makes 'em want to *fight!*"

This conversation got my attention. I started to wonder if I would really enjoy flying missions.

The other fellows had said they would never forget the details of their first mission, so I probably wouldn't, either. As usual, I would make pencil notations in the pocket Bible and the big notebook to show my grandchildren someday (I hoped).

Somebody in our office called the motor pool and told them they would have one passenger for the Foggia run tomorrow. The driver was to pick me up at 3 a.m. He was given directions to the villa and told to wake me if I wasn't already up.

The evening before the mission, I checked my flying suit and parachute to be sure they were okay. Then I made sure my dog tags, a picture of Wilma and my New Testament were ready to pick up. I placed my billfold, letters and a few other small items into a metal .50-caliber ammo box to be handy for the guys to send home in case I didn't get back.

I had trouble going to sleep. I kept thinking that by this time tomorrow I might have burned to death. The average life of a crewman was somewhere between six and eight missions and the brass figured this in their planning. Would I draw a ride on one that will be chalked up on General Twining's tote board as MIA?

I had sat in on a briefing by a flight surgeon before the guys started flying. He told us to always take a good bath and put on clean underwear before a mission to reduce the danger of infection from flak and bullet wounds that we might encounter. He also suggested we be clean-shaven to reduce chafing from the oxygen masks. So this I took care of. I scrubbed down real good in the metal washtub we had. Then I checked the CO_2 bottles on my Mae West to be sure the pins hadn't accidentally punctured them and opened the inspection flap on my parachute to make sure the rip-cord seal hadn't been broken.

I nearly worried myself out of going up to Foggia. It wasn't too late. I could change my mind and nothing would be said about it. But could I sit at the supper table with the rest of the guys and imagine what they were thinking? I couldn't. Besides, the pay was good and the photo opportunities were unlimited.

I was up and dressed at 3 a.m. This was the first time I had worn an electrically heated suit. It reminded me of the long johns I wore as a kid when I played in the snow. These brown long johns, however, had electric wires running through them. I put my wool shirt and pants over them and decided to get into the heavy sheepskin-lined leather flying suit just before boarding the plane.

I heard the jeep in the driveway, stepped outside, and asked the driver to wait so I could run back to the kitchen and get a gallon can of peach halves to eat on the way up to Foggia.

After turning on Via Capurso road out of the driveway, the

driver made a wrong turn and we wound up on a wide dirt path. The headlights illuminated a broken down old two-wheeled wagon with a mangy-looking nag pulling it. A white-haired Italian fellow dressed like a farmer was sitting up on a perch holding the reins.

"Hey, you dumb idiots!" he screamed, "Get that thing out of my way!" He then stood up, waved his arms and shook his fist and gave us a detailed profane lecture that was straight out of Brooklyn. We excused ourselves and left.

I turned to the driver and said, "Boy, that guy doesn't know how *lucky* he was. If 'Frenchy' Larocque had been riding with you, he would have pulled out his .45 and blasted that farmer right off his perch." Frenchy lived in the angel-ceilinged room with Larry Dakin. For some reason, he hated Italians with Brooklyn accents.

Frenchy saw himself as a runt and had the biggest "runt complex" of any little fellow I'd ever met. He was actually almost average height—about 5'6"—but weighed no more than 125 pounds—soaking *wet*. When we first met, I thought, "Hitler, you're in *trouble!*" Most runts are like Napoleon and have to attack the big boys to satisfy their perceived poverty of stature. I soon learned to avoid him as much as possible.

We found the right road and were soon on our way north to Foggia. "Well," I thought, "that farmer proved that Italian life was still going on and he had some early morning chores to take care of."

We sped along the road not having anything to say to each other, but I was talking to myself. "Why am I doing this? Why am I tearing down a deserted road at 70 miles per hour, heading for a rendezvous with several hundred other men with sleep in their eyes? Why can't we slow down and wait for the first light of day to bring life and form to the vineyards and olive groves?"

Surely we would shatter the stillness and startle into life the sleeping farmers in their sheltered houses along the road. They would probably sit up in bed and wonder what madmen were up and about at this ungodly hour of the morning.

But now, the unknown lay ahead. Everything was yet to be proved and accomplished on today's mission. What would *I* prove? What would *I* accomplish? It would be tough. The mission would be tough. A combat cameraman was never invited to enjoy the easy milkruns but was taken along to record the fiercest of the fighting. I wasn't scared. A little nervous, but not really scared.

All that talk at our dinner-table, however, and the thoughts of the struggle ahead were magnified in my mind. "Is this what thousands of combat airmen are thinking before a mission?"

Dawn was breaking. It was time for breakfast. I reached over to the back seat and picked up my peaches. As I was opening the can, the driver said, "Why ya doin' that? We always have chow in the mess tent when we get there."

"Well," I answered, "nobody told me about that. This is my first trip to Foggia and I thought I had to furnish my own breakfast."

"Where ya get them peaches?"

"It's a long story."

I started eating. I wasn't sure I could eat the whole gallon, but surely *somebody* could help me—maybe a little Italian kid standing somewhere beside the road.

I thought about my wife, Wilma, and about my mother. About Jake, my pet squirrel, living in my mother's basement. About Butch, the huge White Wyandott rooster, I had raised from a day old chick. I wondered if Butch was still running dogs off our property with his wings flapping and his long sharp spurs thrusting out in anger.

I was anxious to go on my first combat mission, yet I wanted the driver to stop the jeep, turn around and take me back to the safety of my little bedroom-office in Villa Angela. I tried to convince myself it would be fun flying in a B-17 again. But my mind was saying, "I never want to *see* another B-17!

"When I get back to Bari, Angelo and I will go to another opera. I probably *won't* get back. I can just see those guys now. They'll descend upon my personal belongings like vultures. They'll cannibalize my box of souvenirs. Wonder who'll get my prize German helmet? The first thing I want to do when I get back is see if I can mail the stuff in that ammo box home to Wilma."

I had heard of mixed emotions, but mine were out of control! "Wonder if everybody goes through this the first time they are preparing for aerial combat?" I would have been too embarrassed to ask.

There were ten airfields in the Foggia area. They were being used by both bombers and fighters. Someone had told me there was a Negro fighter group in the area but, of course, they were segregated on their own field. The driver took me straight to the mess tent, but since I'd eaten nearly a half-gallon of peaches, I wasn't hungry. I sat in the jeep while the driver and crews ate and then followed them to the big briefing tent.

We sat down on bomb and fin crates and watched a briefing officer step up on the wooden stage and pull the drapes aside. He turned on the flood lights and we saw the big map. There were groans and "Oh, *no's*" in the audience when we saw the length of red yarn stretching from a pin sticking in Foggia to the pin at the Messerschmidt factory at Weiner-Neustadt, near Vienna, Austria. Someone cried out, "Mama, take me home!" Another fellow yelled, "Is this trip really necessary?" Then there was laughter, groans and catcalls.

Next, the briefing officers went into great detail describing the weather outlook at the target, the proper approach to it and the amount of flak and fighters we could expect.

An intelligence officer stood up and said, "If you bail out over enemy territory, try to evade the Nazi SS at *all* costs. They are ruthless, vicious murderers. They will not hesitate to murder every man, woman and child in a village where someone is suspected of sabotage. The French village of Oradour is an example."

We were then given our position in the formation. More bad news. An upset officer on our crew turned to me and exclaimed, "Coffin corner again, thanks to you!"

Forgetting he was an officer, I shot back, "Friend, you didn't draw coffin corner because of me, *I* drew it because of *you!*" Some of the guys referred to our position in the formation as, "Purple Heart corner."

I hadn't known an easy target from a hard one, but I gathered that *this* one was *hard!* The fellows were squirming around nervously and some were crossing themselves. I had learned from Dakin that this is what Catholics do as they are having a quick word with the Deity. The thought came to my mind that perhaps I should do the same thing, but I quickly decided I'd better not try something I wasn't familiar with because it might backfire. It seemed to be working for Crazy Larry Dakin, however, so I thought I'd better check it out with him later.

Several of us on our crew plus the driver piled all over the jeep precariously clinging to each other. We looked like a human hay-stack as we rolled down the line to the hardstand where our plane, *Tondelayo*, was parked.

I really shouldn't have been at this briefing. It was for the offi-cers—the pilots and navigator. Since I was posing as a news pho-tographer, however, nobody said anything.

The gunners had gone ahead to the armament shack where they were chatting with the armorers. When I joined them they were all trying to make happy small talk to settle their nerves.

"Hey Bud, do ya get dysentery or constipation when one of them Jerries comes after ya?"

"I'm not wearin' my monkey suit (electric long johns) today be-cause it makes me sweat so much I'm afraid I'll short the damn thing out and burn some lines on my tail."

"Hey Joe, I get dubs on your shot of whiskey today if ya still don't want it."

The co-pilot passed out the small escape kits. They were less than an inch thick and fit easily into the zippered pocket on the right leg of my leather flying suit. The kit contained fifty dollars worth of foreign currency in small denominations, water-purifying tablets and high-energy tablets of Benzedrine. There were maps printed on silk, a tiny compass, fish hooks, some nylon cord, a miniature razor and some small blocks of concentrated chocolate.

The four officers on this crew, like all the other flying officers, were casual in appearance. They had removed the wire stiffeners from their garrison caps, which made them limp, enabling them to place their headphones over their caps. This casual and dashing headgear was referred to as "the 50-mission crush."

A chaplain drove up under the wing in his jeep where we were standing and called out some kind of nondenominational blessing, then hurriedly drove to the next plane.

We all slipped into our heavy flying gear and I put on some silk gloves and the thick leather gloves. The silk gloves were necessary to keep my fingers from freezing to the camera in case I had to remove the leather ones and clear a jam or reload the film magazine. I knew that a 100-foot spool of film running at 24 frames a second would last only two minutes and thirty-five seconds so I would probably *have* to remove the leather gloves and reload. The experienced fellows had told me to reload in a hurry because at 40 degrees below zero my hands would be frostbitten after about two minutes. They had also cautioned me to keep the camera against my chest or it would freeze up in a few minutes.

First Lieutenant Dave Kibbe had "owned" *Tondelayo* and a scantily-clad Polynesian girl representing her had been painted on the nose of his plane. Scanty, all right—only bracelets! She was riding a big fat bomb like a wild steed. Her long, black hair was streaming out behind her, and she was grinning like a Cheshire cat. She was bringing him luck.

Kibbe had just seen the new movie, "White Cargo" before he named his plane. Hedy Lamarr played the part of a half-caste temptress named Tondelayo who lived on a rubber plantation. Walter Pidgeon and Frank Morgan were also in the film. Somebody in the 8th Air Force in England had also named a B-17 after Tondelayo.

I had two cameras with me—a Bell and Howell Eyemo 35mm motion picture camera and a K-20 still camera. I couldn't resist making a quick shot of *Tondelayo,* so I handed the Eyemo to another crewman and made the shot, hoping it would be sharp because there was no way of focusing the K-20.

A ground crewman saw me making the picture of *Tondelayo* and said, "It's a good thing you made your picture now, because General Twining looked at her yesterday while he was here on inspection and said, 'Better put some clothes on her. She gets cold at 30,000.' That's the way he is. He doesn't always just order you to do something, but makes suggestions in a friendly way and then you had better *do* it. So we'll have to find the guy who painted her and see if he has her clothes."

I walked to the open door in the waist section, shoved both cameras inside and crawled in. "Tail-end Charlie" crawled back

Colonel Oveta Culp Hobby asked for a photo of her inspection of the WACs' kitchen.

"Mouse" Morris got a good shot of me before my first mission.

"Ya better hurry and get a shot of her because we've been told to put some clothes on her."

Even my buddies agreed that my wife, Wilma, was a better "Pin-up" than Betty Grable.

into his tailgun position, and the two waist gunners, the ball-turret gunner and I got settled in the waist. I had been told that the cameramen had the run of the ship, from nose to tail, but the waist gun windows were the largest in the house, so this is where I would stay.

Kibbe would not be going on this mission because he had gone home on rotation. Another pilot, whose name I didn't know, would be the aircraft commander.

The fire crew took up their positions and the medics got into their meat wagons. I felt nervous, curious and anxious at the same time, wondering how I would react in the face of danger. The gunners were laughing and joking. I wondered what they were *really* thinking down deep.

One of the gunners slapped his buddy on the back and said, "We'd better make every .50 caliber count, Sam. Remember they cost our taxpayers 24 cents each and we'll need every one when the Jerry airborne firing squads line up on us."

Out on the right wing an inertia-starter whined. The prop on number three spun and the engine caught, sending back a cloud of smoke. Then, one after the other, the remaining engines barked into life. A ground crewman jerked the chocks away from the wheel and we started taxiing slowly to the runway amid the squealing of brakes and the gunning of engines. As we were doing this, the gunners checked the flow of the ten-yard-long .50 caliber ammo belts running from their aluminum boxes to the breeches of the guns.

We plugged into the intercom outlets to hear the chatter between the pilot and the control tower. I spotted a panel at the upper right corner of the left waist gun window. This looked like the place where I could plug in my electrically heated long johns.

"There isn't a way for both of us to plug in," I observed to the gunner.

"Plug in if you want to, because these electric suits seldom work anyway and I'm not going to fool with it."

"Okay, I won't either, because I'm sure I'll want to roam around with my camera."

I had been told where to find walk-around oxygen bottles, so I unsnapped one from its rack and set it down on the floor under the window. There were thirteen bottles on board with up to twelve minutes supply of oxygen in each and I had been briefed to go to the top turret—the engineer's position—and recharge a bottle through a valve up there in case it was necessary.

Before we boarded the plane the pilot said that we would have to climb through eight thousand feet of overcast before rendezvous. I had heard that sweating this out was worse than the rest of the mission because there were a lot of collisions while circling through the "soup" to get altitude. "Oh, *great!*" I thought, "*Double jeopardy!*"

While we waited for the take off, some of the crew members went into the bomb bay and chalked messages to the Germans on the bombs, then they took their stations. About 6,860 rounds of .50 caliber ammo had also been brought aboard. The weight of 2780 gallons of gasoline added to the weight of the bombs and ammo made our take off very critical.

The pilot turned from the taxiway onto the end of the runway, gunned the engines and we accelerated forward. The two waist gunners squeezed around the ball turret and sat down on the floor with their backs against the radio room bulkhead. The ball and tail gunners entered the radio room and sat with their backs against the front bulkhead. We had been briefed that this was the procedure for take-offs and landings. I wanted to see what was happening so I stood at the left window and held onto the gun to keep from falling.

As the plane took off I watched the field slip back beneath us. A farmer had stopped his horse-drawn wagon and was looking up and waving at us.

"Well," I thought, "he's not shaking his fist and cursing like the farmer near our villa did this morning."

The smallest member of the crew was the ball turret gunner. He had to be small to curl up inside his station. He hand-cranked his turret around so that his two .50 caliber guns pointed down, opened the entry door and slipped inside. One of the waist gunners closed the door and pounded the ball twice. The gunner then had electric control of his compartment, and rotated the ball so the guns pointed horizontally.

I wouldn't have traded jobs with the ball turret gunner or the tail gunner. These men were the only ones isolated from the rest of the crew and in an emergency it would take more time to get to them.

We had taken off with difficulty—a long take-off run. We were about 3,000 pounds over the designed limit of the B-17. Too much gas and too many bombs. We were taking off in 30-second intervals and from what I could see, everybody was making it.

We were in a gentle climb, so I used this opportunity to explore the rest of the ship to find some good camera positions. The aircraft looked large on the outside, but was very cramped inside.

I squeezed around the top of the ball turret and the large oxygen tank mounted on a post above it and stepped up into the radio operator's compartment. He was seated in his aluminum bucket seat on the left side of the fuselage and had a large black radio and a Morse code key on the table in front of him. I had spent *hours* in this compartment in various planes loading, unloading and adjusting the K-17 vertical cameras mounted in the camera well. This B-17 was not carrying a bomb strike camera, and the trap door was closed, becoming part of the floor.

After a couple of steps forward, I found a closed aluminum door. I opened it and stepped over a bulkhead and down onto a very narrow catwalk, no wider than my boots, running through the bomb bay. The inside bomb racks were fastened to the catwalk and formed a narrow "V" as they rose to the ceiling. It was a tight squeeze going forward on this walk and my back pack parachute rubbed against the two racks. Ten 500-pound gray bombs were shackled to the racks.

There were two chains about waist high, one on the left and one on the right, running the length of the bomb bay. If it hadn't been for these chains to hold onto, it would have been impossible to walk through the area without falling between the bombs and landing in the bottom of the plane.

There was another door at the front end of the bomb bay that opened into the "front office," or cockpit. I had to step over a knee-high aluminum bulkhead to enter the cockpit area. The main oxygen tanks, several of them, were fastened behind the two pilot's seats. Just behind the pilots and on the top of the airplane was the engineer's gun turret.

I stopped there because I didn't want to distract the busy pilot. He had an awesome responsibility—a quarter of a million dollars worth of four-engine bomber and eleven lives in his hands. There was an opening on the floor between the pilots that allowed the bombardier and navigator to drop down and crawl forward to their positions in the nose. Of course I wouldn't be welcome up there, so I returned to the waist of the plane.

I had decided to keep my chute on. The rest of the crew was wearing parachute harnesses with two large snaps on the front. Their parachutes were small quick-connect "chest" types and were fastened to the walls near their positions or lying on the floor within easy reach.

I had heard stories of men being blown out of airplanes with their chutes in their hands and managing to snap them to their harnesses while falling through space but I wasn't going to take that chance. Flak was usually the cause. Flak was the German acronym for Flieger-Abwehr-Kanonen.

Combat cameramen wore seat and back-type chutes. We could wear them as we moved about the plane and they didn't interfere with our camera operation.

There was a burst of static on the intercom. The bombardier came on and said, "Okay, men, let's have our oxygen check. Come in, tail gunner."

"Okay, tail."

"Come in, ball turret."

"Okay, ball."

The bombardier, who was in charge of oxygen, fire control and first aid, continued his calls until everybody had checked in. He had either forgotten me or didn't care because I didn't hear, "Come in, camera."

When we were over enemy territory, the bombardier came on the intercom again. "Bombardier to crew, test-fire your guns." I felt the floor vibrate under my feet as the ball turret gunner opened up. The two waist guns were chattering and their shell casings and clips were flying out of the breeches and shooting out the window and some were rattling down on the floor.

The explosive blasts from the guns stopped and we continued climbing. I sat on the floor and started thinking about some of the experiences the other guys in our unit had shared with me during our suppers at the villa.

They were unanimous in their feelings that they were always flying into a zone where every moment carried with it the possibility of death.

"We spend half a day at war with every second potentially our last. We know we face extinction, or at best, the possibility of being maimed."

"Yeah, we sure do. And then we return from our mission with our friends badly burned or lying dead in blood-filled turrets. Then we spend our evenings upstairs here in the villa drinking and fighting and gettin' falling down drunk."

"And we watch our bombs plunge down lazily from the yawning bays of hundreds of bombers, and bloom in devilish fury—flames leaping high."

"Oh, knock it off, Jack," Poundstone grumbled, "You're always trying to talk like those writers upstairs at the studio. You're nothing but a heathen gaffer. You'll never do anything more than just push scenery around a sound stage. A photographer, you're *not*."

"Jesus H. Christ, Poundstone! And how about the time that 17 came back with bombs still on board and bellied in? And what did *you* do while I shot the thing blowing up on the runway? You *stood* there with your camera hanging down at your knees and watched like a gawking tourist!"

"Hey, guys, here's a bad one. We were coming back from Austria the other day, and a Fortress was crippled and couldn't hold altitude. The pilot was trying to stretch it so he could at least get back south into our area, so he ordered everything not necessary to sustain flight thrown overboard. When the Jerries stopped attacking, they threw their guns out, the ammo belts, extra radio coils—everything! They ripped out everything that could be taken without the use of tools. In fact, the ball-turret gunner had rolled his ball around so his entry door was up. He crawled out into the waist, pulled the safety pins and jettisoned his ball. All that was left was a big hole in the floor. The ball-turret was the heaviest piece of equipment they got rid of because of the guns, ammo, and of course, the ball itself.

"The co-pilot came back to see if anything else could possibly be thrown out, and saw that even the ball turret had been dropped, but he found a dead waist gunner on the floor. He told the other gunner to toss him out. The fellow refused because it was his best friend's body. The lieutenant raised such a fuss that the body was finally tossed out. I've thought a lot about that. What would you have done?"

Mouse Morris had another story. "This is almost as bad. A 17 limped in behind us. I didn't actually see this, but a lot of guys did. The pilot couldn't get his wheels down and had to make a belly landing. The ball turret gunner's electrical system was out and neither he or the crewmen in the waist could hand crank him around. He was trapped. The ship slammed down on the ball turret. Of course there was nothing left of it when the ship stopped skidding."

"Think that's gruesome?" said Crazy Larry. "I just heard that a piece of flak slammed into a cockpit and decapitated the pilot. His head fell into the co-pilot's lap. Then, covered with blood and with the eyes of the pilot staring up at him from his lap, he had to take control of the plane."

"Geezus H. Kay-*rist*, Dakin, we're eating our supper. Knock it off!"

"Tommy," said A-Square, "you told us about meeting General Doolittle on the desert in Africa. Just heard a funny story about him. He's at the 8th Air Force headquarters at High Wycombe, you know. Well, two English women came into his office, a mother and daughter. The daughter did all the talking. She asked Doolittle about a certain sergeant who flew missions as a gunner. The general had an immediate check made and found that the guy had been sent back to the States.

" 'We wondered why we hadn't seen him,' the daughter said. 'I work in the daytime and my mother works nights and the sergeant was kind enough to spend time with us between flying his missions. We live two miles from his base and he found it hard to visit us as often as we all would like, so we loaned him our bicycle. He was then able to spend more time with us. We are both pregnant because of his visits and we came to see why he had stopped seeing us. But now we understand the reason—he has been sent home.'

"Doolittle started to explain some of the rights they had under the law.

"The daughter broke in with, 'Oh, no, no, no—don't misunderstand. We don't want to cause the sergeant any trouble, we would just like to get our bicycle back.' "

Then Jake, our unit "poet," spoke up again. "We fly at 30,000 feet, the territory that is an uninhabitable land roamed by wild animals."

"All right, Jake, for God's sake *cut!*" groaned Poundstone.

That was Frenchy Larocque's cue to cut in and change the conversation to a more pleasant subject—one that he liked to boast about.

"Did you know that when I worked in Warner Brothers' publicity department, Errol Flynn invited me out on his yacht, the *Sirocco?* And while I was there he had a screaming and clawing fight with Lili Damita?"

"No, tell us all about it, Frenchy."

"Well, he..."

"Shut up, Frenchy! Fade to black! That dialogue is out of place here."

"Did you hear that Frank Capra is in England with the 8th Air Force and is shooting a documentary in color?" said Crazy Larry. "He went to high school with Doolittle."

Capra had produced and directed some of the greatest films at Columbia Studio and had won some academy awards. He was a lieutenant colonel.

"Know what we were told at a briefing the other day?" said Frenchy. "Word has come back that downed airmen are being strung up by wire from telephone poles by German civilians. And that's not all. Injured men lying wounded and helpless after landing with their parachutes have had gasoline poured over them and ignited."

"Well, that's why we're gettin' good pay. Everybody gets 20% extra for bein' overseas, and by goin' into combat flyin', we get *another* 50%. That gives us 70% above Stateside pay. I'm goin' to buy a nice orange grove with all that dough when I get back to California."

"Ya suppose the ground-pounders get hazardous duty pay?"

"Dunno. They oughta."

"Have any of you guys flown with a fringe merchant?" asked Poundstone. "I got lucky on my last mission and drew one."

"Fringe merchant" was the term the guys used to describe a pilot who got scared and ordered his bombs dropped near the fringe of a target rather than unload them over the more dangerous center of the target.

That's the way it went at our supper table "postmortems." A few colorful stories, news from the studios and always a little bickering.

It seemed to me that the guys were falling into two distinct categories. Some of them thought about what it would be like when they got there. They thought about the danger, the flak, the fighters. The rest thought only about getting to the target. They had visions of photographing whole cities going up in smoke and flames. A Hollywood spectacular! A real Cecil B. De Mille!

I thought that when the time came, I would probably be in the first category.

After we were in a tight formation, the plane bounced occasionally. I yelled to the gunner, "Air pockets?"

"No, prop wash from the plane ahead of us."

We headed toward the Italian Alps. When we were about halfway there, we met a formation of German JU-88s heading south to bomb something. Maybe Foggia? We passed a few miles apart and simply ignored each other. Our little friends were still with us, but would have to turn back before we got all the way to the target.

Bombardier to crew, "Okay, men, time to start breathing California air."

"What does he mean?" I shouted to a waist gunner.

"He means it's time to put your oxygen mask on."

"How odd," I thought. "Here we are flying over Italy and breathing air bottled in the U.S.A."

Then it struck me. "We're getting close! This is the *real* thing. This is where men are *killing* each other!"

Every 15 minutes after we were at 10,000 feet and above, the bombardier called for a crew check to see if everybody was okay and that nobody had passed out because of a malfunction in the oxygen system.

This oxygen check reminded me of the Eddie Rickenbacker visit down on the Algerian desert. He had told of flying at 20,000 feet for long periods of time in 1918 and I now wondered how that had been possible without oxygen. I must have misunderstood him.

Visibility was unlimited. The sky was a dark blue, growing paler toward the horizon. Below, Italy slowly unfolded like a carpet with its dark masses of forests, the multi-colored checkerboard of fields and meadows and an occasional toy-like village.

We were getting higher. The cold was starting to penetrate my leather and silk gloves, numbing my fingers. My toes felt like they had gone to sleep in a snow-bank. I believe I heard the pilot tell us that we were at 20,000 feet at minus 40 degrees. For the last half-hour we had been watching the beautiful white vapor trails streaming out behind the hot engines. They had appeared at about 18,000 feet.

My oxygen mask was uncomfortable and it felt like a sweaty hand was gripping the lower part of my face. It irritated my chin, nose and cheeks. I kept pulling it away from my face for a few seconds at a time thinking that anything longer might be too long to breathe without it. This bloody thing had probably been designed by a minimum-wage employee to fit the face of a baboon.

The moisture in my breath froze and formed ice in the oxygen hose where it connected to the mask. I had been warned this might happen and squeezed the hose to break the ice. This un-clogged it for awhile and then it had to be repeated.

I tested my throat mike switch and then made sure I under-stood how to replenish a walk-around oxygen bottle from the main supply.

We were flying in a carefully calculated pattern, designed to take advantage of the combined fire-power of the entire group. Each of our B-17s had a given role in the fire plan. I took comfort in the fact that we would present a formidable target for any German aircraft. Coffin corner, however, was the most vulnerable position to enemy fighters because it was the outside, left rear slot in the low squadron.

Soon we would be very busy. Right now, however, I was in awe of the tranquil beauty of the upper sky and the graceful white lines of the con-trails following our little friends boring through the crystal blue sky.

We were on our way to an aerial battlefield, but I couldn't get my mind off the scene. Here we were in the lovely beauty of the sky high above the mud and bedlam of the surface armies far be-low. It was so clean. Up here even death is clean and swift, sur-rounded by beautiful white clouds and blue sky. We droned on and on, the sound of our Wright Cyclone engines so solid and comforting.

My reverie was suddenly shattered when I saw tiny black specks on the horizon—a swarm of poisonous wasps—Krauts! In seconds those tiny wasps became large screaming eagles! Luckily our little friends were still above us when all hell broke loose. We saw two squadrons of 24 Messerschmitt-109s climbing parallel to us. The first squadron reached our level and was pulling ahead to turn on us. At this moment, the life expectancy of *Tondelayo* seemed quite limited.

The Me-109s came at us from 12 to 10 o'clock in pairs. The main show was on! I knew I was going to die, and so were a lot of others. The fear was disagreeable, but bearable.

I pulled my oxygen plug from the wall and grabbed the walk-around bottle. I could go anywhere on the plane; it depended on where the action was. And right now, the action was just outside the left waist gunner's window!

It was unreal! A Jerry came straight at us pouring a stream of fiery tracers into our plane while our tracers were ripping into his. This Jerry came to within 100 yards of us and shot up and over. We saw the big black crosses on the pale blue under-surface of his wings. His buddy was right behind him and got so close, we could see the pilot's face and the red scarf he was wearing! He pushed his stick forward and zoomed down under us.

Our little friends dropped down to engage the Jerries and that took the heat off for a short time. Then more Jerries were swarming around us. A *lot* more! They were sending in dozens of reinforcements and tracers were streaming in every direction. German bullets were burying themselves into fuselages of the 17s. Some were ricocheting and spinning out into space. Each Messerschmitt was spitting death from four wing guns.

My earphones crackled with an incomprehensible chatter of shouts, screams and curses mingled with the staccato of machine-gun fire. Without realizing it, I had held my breath through the whole attack and my heart was pounding wildly. I wasn't scared, though, because I was so intent on getting some good shots that I *forgot* to be afraid.

I was at the waist gun window with the viewfinder glued to my eye, and was so consumed with what I was doing, that I wasn't aware of anything that was happening outside the radius of my lens. I was seeing a movie—not the real thing.

The sky was brilliant so I flipped the dark lens down over my goggles and pointed the camera at a bandit just as he was completing his turn toward us. Our tracers were stabbing into him but he straightened out and flew directly toward us. He came so close, we could see the expression on his face. It looked as if he was going to *ram* us! His plane zoomed suddenly upward and a jolt of air slammed against our window. That guy was *crazy!* How close had he come to missing us? Twenty feet? Probably less than that. I didn't take time to think about it. I had never seen anything in a movie theater as exciting as this! Our intercom was full of excited chatter.

"Bandits at 3 o'clock!"

"More at 6 low!"

"Got him!"

We were in a desperate struggle for our lives!

Another Kraut went after the plane on our left, but they got him! He started down in a wing over—out of control! A sheet of flame trailed out behind him. His plane became a shooting comet of fire! He rolled over and exploded in a blinding flash. It was only a matter of seconds.

The two waist gunners kept firing in five or six second bursts with their guns chattering like jack hammers—the eye-smarting smoke that came from the spent shell casings and breeches was pungent and stifling.

I thought about my bride, Wilma. "What is she doing at this moment? Will I survive, or will Wilma's name be added to that 'instant widows' list?"

A whole squadron of Me-109s came diving down in a long diagonal slant right through our formation! Another squadron was right behind them and peeled off for their attack. Chaos was raging all around!

I was getting *great* close-ups of Jerry with the telephoto lens. Switching to the wide angle lens gave me a view of the entire aerial battlefield! What footage!

Still no let-up! The strain of being a clay pigeon at the wrong end of a skeet range was almost intolerable. *Tondelayo* shook steadily with the fire from her .50-caliber guns. "*God*," I muttered, "if you're putting me to the test, you're pulling no punches!"

Off in the distance through our formation, I thought I saw two of our planes collide. There was a huge ball of fire that lasted only a second or two, leaving a black puff of smoke in its place. Small fragments started falling to the earth, not one of them large enough to recognize. The faster falling specks must have been the engines.

Ten seconds later, another B-17 got a direct hit in the bomb bay area and exploded. Pieces flew in every direction. Small dark objects, which must have been the crew, started down. No parachutes were observed. The explosion had probably killed them.

The right waist gunner reached around and pounded my back with his fist to get my attention. The plane on our right was in trouble! He had dropped his landing gear and flaps to tell the Krauts he was out of the battle and was surrendering.

I stepped over to the right window and found that the sun was in my eyes. I quickly flipped down the dark shades over my goggles and held my thumb out to block the sun.

Even though several Krauts were swarming around him, they held their fire. There was chivalry in the sky during W.W.I, when aerial combat first became a "gentlemen's" sport. They fought like knights in single combat, but I hadn't known it was part of *this* war. I shouted this thought to the right waist gunner, and he said, "Chivalry *hell*, they just want to get one of our ships down in one piece so they can have a good look at it!"

The guns in the waist hadn't stopped. The air inside was now thick with sickening smoke and choking cordite fumes that seeped right through my oxygen mask.

A Messerschmitt was caught in a core of fire from the guns of four 17s and flew apart like balsa wood with bits and pieces fluttering down.

By now our toll was so heavy that there was a line of yellow blazes like bonfires strung along the tilled checkerboards and dark hills 20,000 feet below us—burning Fortresses that had gone down from the groups ahead of us.

The Messerschmitt jockeys backed off so the ack-ack boys could have a crack at us. Then, suddenly, we were surrounded by anti-aircraft bursts. The sky was dotted with a murderous concentration of black puffs, each sending a flying hail of metal into our aluminum skins. They were bursting into fragments in a rectangular block of air a mile long, a mile wide and a half-mile in depth. Some of the B-17s started burning, exploding and spiraling down toward earth. Parachutes were blossoming all over the sky. We saw one parachute stringing out, apparently ripped.

The shrapnel kept ping-ping-pinging into the aluminum skin

around us. *Tondelayo* kept jumping up and down, leaving me standing in the air while I held to the window sill. Our pilot was trying to avoid the flak by his violent evasive action. When he saw a burst on the left side, he would jerk the plane to the right. When there was a burst on the right, back we would go again.

The flak bursts were frightening but fascinating to watch. The close ones could be seen to burst into small puffs of black smoke with flames in the centers that spread rapidly to about ten feet in diameter and then dissipated.

We arrived at the I.P. (the initial point) to start the bomb run, and turned toward the target. The pilot switched on the auto-pilot, which controlled the attitude and direction of the plane. In about six minutes *Tondelayo* would be over the target.

We were still over farmlands just south of our objective and saw hundreds of bomb craters in them. It looked like a previous mission had come this way and made a major assault on Austrian farming. The target must have been socked in that day, or the fringe merchants had been here.

The bombardier opened the bomb bay doors and there was a spooky-sounding rumble as they swung outward. He then took over control of the plane by twisting the two knobs on his Norden bombsight, which were connected to the auto-pilot.

The bombardier called, "Bombs away!" The bombs left their shackles and we felt a decided lift. The open doors were still making the rumbling sound above the roar of the engines until they were closed.

The pilot immediately switched off the auto-pilot and made a diving turn to the right to get to the rally point. Then we headed home.

The intercom came alive with whoops and whistles and happy talk. This was the first time I had watched tons of death and destruction leave a bomber and head for the surface far below. It was hard to believe that thousands of terrified people down there were praying they wouldn't be blown to bits by the bombs we saw arching down from our formation. Looking down at the earth from this great height, people ceased to exist. Time crept along.

We really clobbered the Fock-Wulf plant at Marienburg.

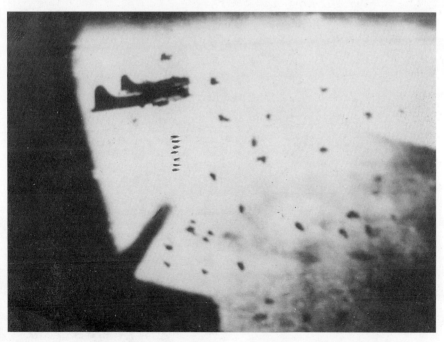

. . . and dropped our bombs into a sky filled with flak bursts.

Our little friends, the P-38s, stayed with us as long as they could.

The famous Norden bombsight, displayed at the Pima Air Museum in Tucson, Ariz.

There was little movement up here. We looked back and saw the bombs bursting in large mushrooms on the aiming point (target).

Two of our planes had gone down in flames right over the target. No chutes were observed. The bodies of some of our buddies were now scattered among the Germans we had killed but not seen.

The pilot punched his mike switch and said, "Get off the intercom, there are Jerry fighters out there!" The right waist gunner called, "Bandit at 3 o'clock!" He held his fire until the Me-109 was about 500 yards away, and then started firing continuously into the Kraut. The Kraut kept coming, and the gunner kept firing, but his line of fiery tracers were streaking down under the bandit. He lifted his gun slightly, like raising a garden hose, and his stream of fire struck the bandit.

With all this action at the *right* window, I wheeled around and stuck my camera out and glued my eye to the viewfinder. There were pieces of cowling shredding from the nose of the 109. The Jerry stopped firing, did a snap roll and darted under our plane. It was close!

I stepped back to the left window and continued filming the 109, and now it was trailing smoke and flame. He was getting a little out of range, so I lowered the camera just as a voice on the intercom yelled, "He hit the silk!" I had just missed a good shot.

The intercom filled with excited chatter again. "Bandits 3 o'clock low!"

"Me-109 6 o'clock low!"

The machine-gun fire nearly drowned out the voices. "Ball turret to pilot. A 109 came through. Picked him up at 600 yards. Gave him a short burst."

"Left waist, he went under our left wing! I gave him 20 rounds and he's smoking!"

"Yeah, I saw him. He's had it!"

"Tail to pilot. A 17 in the low squadron is on fire!"

"Pilot to tail—who is it?"

"Dunno."

"Roger."

"Fighters at 9 level!" The gunfire drowned out the voices.

"Ball to pilot. We've been hit!"

"Where?"

"Pieces flyin' off our right horizontal stabilizer!"

"Pilot to ball—you okay?"

"Roger. Think so."

"Top turret to pilot. Half my turret gone!"

"You okay?"

"Guess so. Don't see no blood."

"Roger. Thank you, top turret."

This excitement lasted no longer than ten seconds.

I turned around to go back to the right window—and tripped over the right waist gunner. He was flat on his back and trying to pull his helmet off. "My God, I was just there," I thought. The left gunner saw him at the same time.

We pulled out a first-aid kit and hurriedly searched for the morphine. There was none! We were shocked to find that we had to open five more kits before we found one containing the strong pain killer.

The left waist gunner went to work on his buddy's head wound, and I stuck my camera back out the left window to look for more Jerries.

By this time the bombardier had arrived with his big first-aid kit and went to work on the gunner. After the gunner had been treated, he lay on the floor briefly, then stood up, grabbed his two gun handles and started blasting away.

About three minutes later, the tail gunner's unexcited and calm voice came through the intercom. "Sir, I'm sorry, I've been hit." The bombardier came through the waist with his medical bag and crawled back to see "tail-end Charlie."

Charlie had been hit in his right leg. It wasn't deep but it was bleeding badly. The bombardier shot him with morphine and sprinkled sulfanilamide powder on his wound, then bandaged him well enough to get him back to Foggia. The gunner stayed back there on his knees and kept the Jerries off our tail.

Right in the middle of this chaos, the tail gunner's strong voice came back on the intercom. "Boy, I'm glad there's a doc around here who makes house calls."

A B-17 was turning gradually out of the formation to the right, maintaining altitude. I stepped over to the right window and pointed the camera out just in time to shoot a brilliant explosion! It disintegrated into a cloud of debris and simply disappeared in a ball of fire and smoke! It was there one moment and gone the next!

B-17s were dropping out in every stage of distress. Engines on fire, controls shot away and some were spiraling lazily toward the earth. Friendly and enemy parachutes were dotting the sky. Sometimes they were so close to each other hanging under their canopies that they could shout back and forth. There were so many chutes in the air that it looked like an airborne invasion! The German chutes were darker than ours.

We were obviously getting ack-ack fire now, but I hadn't seen any bursts. Nevertheless, the Jerries were leaving, so I knew we were entering the anti-aircraft flak field.

The flak bursts were thicker now. Through the formation on the left, there was a large puff of smoke and a Fortress broke in half and started its five-mile plunge to earth. Only two parachutes could be seen. The remaining eight crewmen were being dragged down in their blazing aluminum coffin. In about three minutes the flak stopped.

Almost immediately the sky again erupted with battling aircraft. The B-17s came under *severe* attacks from swarms of Me-109s! Our fortress shuddered with the rapid explosions of the .50 calibers. The fighting became a great confusion of spinning aircraft, hammering guns, fiery tracers, planes shedding fragments, and dead gunners slumped behind silent weapons—

And there was one frightened cameraman!

The radio operator knew there were a lot of nervous men on board so when we were away from the flak and fighters, he found some German classical music on his radio. He got the pilot's permission to patch it in so the rest of us could enjoy it. It was either Beethoven or Wagner. Whatever it was made me realize that people down there were enjoying the same kind of music I liked. I wondered, "How can people who write and listen to music like that be so cruel?"

We finally arrived at the Foggia air field with all of the engines turning, but with two wounded men. The engineer fired a red flare and we were given a "straight in." The meat wagon was waiting for us and as they lowered the wounded waist gunner from the plane on a stretcher, he managed to show a weak smile and give a feeble thumbs-up. He had lost a lot of blood.

The left waist gunner said excitedly, "Dave was hit and kept right on fighting." The chaplain bent down and asked the guy on the stretcher, "You were hit and kept right on fighting?"

He replied, "Sure, why not?" I knew I had just met a hero.

As we crawled out of the Fortress, we were each handed a shot of whiskey to help us unwind. I had never tasted whiskey and wanted to retain my teetotaling status, so I handed my shot to the chaplain, who quickly tossed it down.

I walked forward to the nose hatch, which was just being opened. When the aircraft commander dropped down through the opening I said, "Sir, do you want us to gather around the tail wheel and relieve ourselves?"

He looked at me with an incredulous expression and said, "Why should we do a stupid thing like that, Sergeant?"

"Just wondered, Sir."

"Come on. We're going to debriefing."

"Yes, Sir."

The "relieving" ritual had certainly brought good luck to the crew of the B-17 *All American* in North Africa and I saw no reason why it wouldn't work here.

A crowd had gathered around the plane parked next to ours. I walked over to check it out and nearly lost my peaches when I saw the sickening gut-wrenching scene. The ball turret had been hit by flak so badly that what remained of the gunner was being washed out of his shattered turret with a hose. There was nothing left but mixed elements of viscera, bones and blood mashed into shapeless globules. I was a little ashamed of my ghoulishness. Then as I turned away I felt a cold sweat break out all over my body and the distasteful misery of nausea well up from my stomach. Then I glanced at another plane just as a leg was being handed down through the nose-hatch. There was a boot still on the foot. I wished I hadn't given my whiskey to the chaplain.

We were called together for a debriefing by the group intelligence officer who was seated behind an interrogation table. He asked each of us for our impressions and reactions to what we'd seen. I wondered what good this did because everybody seemed to have seen things differently. It was almost like none of us had been on the same ship.

When it was *my* turn, I realized the reason for the variance in observations. It was hard for me to remember exactly *what* I'd seen because I'd been on oxygen for seven hours and was still half-frozen and stiff and jumpy from the flak and fighters.

I arrived back at the villa and felt like going upstairs and celebrating the completion of my first combat mission with the boys. Instead, I sat down on the edge of my cot, picked up a picture of Wilma, looked at it for awhile, and still holding it, flopped down and dozed off.

It would seem, since I had gone to sleep with Wilma's picture in my hand, that she would be in my dreams. Instead, I saw myself surrounded by dancing spirits, sorcerers and monsters watching me dig my own grave.

I was so mentally and physically exhausted that I was still wearing my heavy flying boots when the sun came up.

My father, speaking of W.W.I had said, "There were no atheists in the foxholes."

Speaking of W.W.II, I would tell my children, "There were no atheists in the ceaseless hostility of the sky."

Speaking of W.W.III, if it ever happens, my descendants will probably tell their children....

The next morning Bill "Swede" Larsen came into the lab. "How'd it go, Tommy?"

"Piece of cake," I lied.

After "souping" some film and hanging it up to dry, I went back to my bedroom to make notes of the mission in my notebook. My thoughts were much clearer now than they had been at our debriefing.

I had a couple of days off, and spent a lot of time in the lab making prints. Angelo was always my "hypo splasher" and even got brown fingernails from the developer.

Angelo knocked a metal trash can over on the tile floor of the darkroom. The sudden sharp crash made me jump, shudder and turn pale. I wondered how long sudden noises would affect me like this.

The Fourth Combat Mission

THE GLORY-HUNGRY 8TH AIR FORCE IN ENGLAND seemed to be confirming every kill reported by their B-17 and B-24 gunners. Our gunners in the 15th reasoned that they might have *thought* they were getting the kills because when an FW-190 came diving through the formation firing and then rolled over on its back and darted away, a black puff of smoke would stream out behind it. This was probably caused by the fuel-injection system and the Jerry might not have had problems from the gunners.

Competition jealousy resentment. This was probably healthy and might have been engineered by the top brass.

I thought I never wanted to go on another mission—I really didn't have to, but on the second day after my first raid I went in to see Major Barovik and told him that he had better send me out again so I wouldn't be ashamed to sit around the dinner table with the rest of the guys.

"Okay, Sergeant Thompson, you know you can pick and choose your missions. Want to go on one with Sergeant Dakin tomorrow?"

"Yes, Sir."

"Okay, you've got it."

"Major, as I told you in my post-mission report, I got a lot of good shots of the Me-109s. They were beautiful but awesome."

"And they have been Germany's best fighter for a long time," the major said. "The Messerschmitt 109 was first used and improved from 1936 to 1939 in the Spanish Civil war. We did a documentary on this at RKO. Hitler sent 6,000 Luftwaffe airmen to assist Spanish insurgent leader Francisco Franco, who was fighting the loyalist Republicans.

"By the time the Spanish war was over, German engineers had

drawn on the lessons in aerial combat to develop this remarkable bird. You will be seeing a lot of it."

"This reminds me of my last year in high school Spanish," I said. "Our teacher, Effie Erickson, was in Spain during the war and probably saw the 109s. Anyway, she was so mad about it, that all we had to do to avoid getting into our lesson was to say something about the war. Effie would pace up and down in front of us and really let Franco *have* it."

"Well, go on back to your villa, Sergeant, and dig out your electric longjohns. And get some more good 109 footage."

"Yes, Sir, I'll try."

It was the day of my second mission. This time Crazy Larry went along as the major said he would. This was becoming old stuff for him because this was to be his seventh time in enemy skies. We didn't see each other again because we were widely separated in the formation when we took off.

I was assigned to *Mailed Fist*. A huge mailed fist, right out of King Arthur's Court, was painted on the nose. We could look around and see a lot of beautiful art work on the noses of the ships as they taxied out to the runway.

Again I took my favorite position at the left waist gun window. The two waist gunners were busy checking the flow of their ammo belts threading from the large aluminum supply boxes to their guns. They couldn't have been more than teenagers. At age 23, I felt like I should be helping them build model airplanes.

I wondered what motivated these kids to be nonchalantly preparing their weapons to kill someone. It was probably not for God, flag or mother's apple pie that made a guy volunteer to lose his life in an obscure adventure. It was for the kid standing *next* to him; he *couldn't* let *him* down. They *needed* each other. We *all* needed each other, and felt stronger for each other's support.

Most people in the States would never know the powerful brotherhood that existed between these two gunners. How could they? The folks at home would simply read the casualty reports in their daily newspapers, but it would be nothing more than a list of names.

When we got the "go" from the tower, our overloaded ship began to slowly creep ahead and finally accelerated so that objects along the runway started whipping past in blurred images. I wondered if the pilot would get the bird over the olive trees at the end of the runway or would our survivors begin to refer to us in the past tense.

We cleared the trees so low that they bent with our prop-wash. Then we climbed to our position in the formation and sailed along with nothing to do but enjoy the beautiful white clouds. I let out a sigh of relief because we had successfully struggled into the air with a load that the technical manual said couldn't be lifted on such a short runway.

For awhile it looked like we might be enjoying a milk run, but flak and fighters were probably waiting for us down the road. We weren't disappointed. They came at us from six o'clock high, firing as they closed on us. Then they came up from three o'clock low—more tracers.

The hurricane of flaming bullets from the fighters was awesome. The bullets we couldn't see until they ripped holes in our plane's fuselage were even worse.

"Ball turret to pilot. Skipper, there's holes in the bottom of the right wing."

"Thanks, ball. Any leaking?"

"Yeah, seen some gas comin' out of them holes I think."

"Pilot to crew. No smoking. *No more* smoking!"

"Roger."

"Roger."

"Roger."

"Tail to pilot. Jerry coming up three o'clock low!"

"Roger."

"Tail to pilot, he turned away."

"Roger."

"Ball to pilot. Fortress going down at nine o'clock!"

"Tail to pilot—he's out of control and burning!"

"Don't yell on that intercom!"

"Come *on* you guys-get out of there!"

"There go two chutes!"

"There goes one more!"

"See any more?"

"Negative. No more. Oh, *God!*"

As usual, the fighters left and the frightening black flak bursts peppered the sky around us. It seemed that those ack-ack gunners down there had us pretty well zeroed in because a chunk slashed through our engineer's compartment and cut the oxygen lines to four stations. I was getting good shots of incoming flak.

Some flak came up through the floor between the waist guns and the radio room and cut the elevator control cables that ran along the ceiling from the cockpit to the tail and the pilot was having trouble controlling the plane. None of us in the waist had noticed the severed cables but we saw the large hole in the ceiling.

The engineer came back and spotted the cable trouble immediately. He went forward and came back with the radio operator. The engineer was carrying a brown canvas bag containing a few tools and some odds and ends. He opened the bag and fumbled around in it for a few seconds and came up with a small coil of cable and some cable clamps. He and the radio operator had the cables spliced in short order. I was amazed at this in-flight repair.

"Right waist to pilot. Flak on our right."

"Thanks, waist. It's out of range."

"Bombardier to pilot. We got a hole in the nose."

"You okay?"

"Roger."

"Bombardier to pilot. Bomb bay door motors not working. I'll have to go back there and crank them by hand."

"Roger, bombardier. Be careful."

"Ball turret to pilot—ship ahead going down."

"Roger, ball, I see it."

There was a bump and I thought we'd been hit but the pilot called the crew: "Relax, men. That was just the prop wash from the ship falling into the space ahead of us."

At that time, prop wash was always blamed when a plane taking off or flying close ahead caused the plane behind to jump or bump. Actually it was the vortices—the whirlpool cones of air with vacuum centers formed by the wing-tips of the leading plane.

Flak was bad news anywhere but it was terrifying when we were on the bomb run because we had to fly straight and level for several minutes. The German gunners down below knew where we would be at any given moment and would throw up a "box barrage." This kept the area full of bursting shells and there was no way of avoiding it. Sometimes the black bursts were so concentrated that it looked like we were in a thunder cloud. Some of the fellows called it "iron cumulus." There was only one defense. It started, "Our Father, who art in Heaven . . . ."

Nobody on our plane was hurt on this mission—it was a miracle!—but we took a lot of punishment. The radio operator's Morse code key had been shot away, so he sent a message to the base by touching two exposed wires in the smashed radio. The intercom was also out, which gave us a strange feeling of loneliness.

After we had landed, taxied to our hardstand and shut the engines down, the ground crew began counting bullet holes. They started at the tail and got to 180 before getting tired of counting. The disgusted ground crew chief complained, "You left with my *airplane* and came back with a *sieve.*"

The third mission was one of the *prayed* for milk runs. We were left pretty much alone by the fighters and encountered only moderate flak over the target. I felt I had earned the right to have an easy mission.

I crawled aboard another 17. Just as we had taken off, we flew through a flock of pigeons. It shattered the Plexiglas nose and wounded the navigator. The pilot immediately aborted the flight and returned to the field.

My jeep was waiting for me, but before returning to Bari, I wanted to check out the Wellington bomber a British pilot had flown to our field. There was just one and I couldn't find out why he was here by himself. Making a few pictures of it seemed like a good idea, so I walked over to it.

The construction materials were straight out of the Wright Brother's 1903 Dayton shop—wood and fabric! This was the RAF's big, main bomber, and it hadn't occurred to me that it would be made from such ancient materials. Once inside, however, it started making sense.

The fuselage was of a geodesic design. It reminded me of my mother's wooden rose trellis—large squares made by fastening flat narrow strips of wood together. *This* design looked more like diamonds because instead of the wood strips running up and down, they ran diagonally around the fuselage like a basket weave. I knew from my model airplane building days that this would give the plane great strength. I also noticed that patching bullet holes was a lot easier with fabric squares than with aluminum.

I hadn't expected a bomb sight like the one in the nose. This little gadget had been made by the Singer Sewing Machine Company and consisted of an 18-inch length of aluminum, two inches wide and about a quarter of an inch think. There was a narrow slot running from top to bottom through the middle with calibrations marked on each edge of the sight. It *had* to have cost all of $3.00 to produce!

There wasn't a Limey around to explain this, but it made sense, because they only went on night raids where they just had to know roughly where their target was. Pinpoint accuracy, of course, could only be possible with an expensive, complicated sight like our Norden.

It was at this moment, by association of thoughts, that an incident in 1939 came back to me. I was reminded of the time I came very close to driving a British machine like this.

A few months after graduating from high school, my classmates and closest friends, "Buster" Rhoades and Glen Wonnacott and I learned that the Royal Canadian Air Force was desperately searching for pilot trainees. They were practically accepting Americans whose seeing-eye dogs were not flat-footed!

"Hey, Buster, let's get Glen and go to Canada," I said.

The next morning, the three of us stood beside the highway on the eastern edge of Lansing and stuck our thumbs out. Piece of cake! A salesman driving a brand new four-door De Soto picked us up and took us all the way to the foot of Woodward Avenue in Detroit. That was the place where we boarded a city bus that took us through the Holland Tunnel, under the Detroit River and into the Canadian city of Windsor.

A large colorful poster at the bus stop told us how to get to the recruiting office—only one block away.

There were about 50 men milling around a long metal table waiting to be helped by the four military men sitting there. One of the Canadians stood up and announced, "You'll need written permission from a parent or guardian if you are a Canadian under age 18 or an American under age 21. Here are the forms."

The three of us each took a couple of forms, and dejectedly walked back to the bus stop. That evening we confronted our parents. I thought my father was the smartest fellow in the world. I even took his *hints* seriously because he always seemed to be right.

"Bobby, I know you've just finished basic flying school and want to be a professional pilot. But you're also pretty involved with photography. I'll bet you can combine them in some way and becoming a *flying* photographer."

"But at the RCAF office, they promised we would be trained to fly Spitfire fighters or bombers and then stay in Canada to instruct others."

"Well, the way Germany's acting, England will be fighting them in a month or two so they might send you over there."

"I called Buster and Glen a while ago and their parents signed right away."

"Bobby, we're going to be in a war sooner or later, and wouldn't you rather be in an American uniform?"

That did it! There was never a moment's hesitation when I knew I could do something to make my dad proud of me.

Angelo and I went to another opera. This time it was "Lucia di Lammermoor." Same crowd, same pungent odor of garlic and the same outburst of emotions.

I was spending a few days away from the war to do a little sightseeing around town and to consider my "druthers." Would I druther just stay in Bari and take care of my duties on the ground, or go back up and shoot some more Krauts? I was lucky to have a choice.

It is very strange that my decision came at this particular time and place, but Angelo and I were at the docks watching a fisherman's wife down on her knees pounding octopus tentacles with a fist-sized rock when it came to me.

"Sure. Why not? It can't happen to me, just to the other guy!" A man has to feel that way or he'll go *crazy*. I didn't like it, though. This was certainly not a heroic, glamorous business—it was a nasty, sordid, murderous means to an end.

My last mission was supposed to be number four. It had been aborted, however, and didn't count, so I was scheduled to drive up to Foggia with Sergeant "Rocky" Poundstone to try again. This would be Rocky's ninth mission.

We arrived at the base just in time for breakfast. They were short of ground personnel, and because flying crews were the "elite" of the Air Force, they didn't have to pull KP. We were surprised, however, to pass down the chow line and have a *major* hit our mess kits with a large ladle of dehydrated eggs.

In the briefing tent, an officer said, "Don't get the notion that your job is glorious and glamorous. You've got dirty work to do, and you might as well face the facts. You're baby killers and woman killers."

The brass continued hardening us for these civilian killing missions and it was taking effect. One fellow's justification for killing women was that they feed their husbands and those husbands go to work building weapons that kill *us*. It was known that air crews parachuting into Germany were lynched and pitchforked to death by the women.

The fellows sitting next to me started mumbling. "I don't think

We were flying in Coffin Corner . . .

Our fragmentation cluster bombs were dangerous to carry and devastating to enemy ground troops.

Our crew cheered when we looked back and saw our bombs bursting on target center.

about the people. From five miles up, it looks like they live in toy cities, and I think of the people as toy dolls."

"They're *Krauts* and the women are producing more Krauts!

Of course we had mixed emotions. Killing Germans wasn't *fun,* but we lost very little sleep over it. Just how many of *our* lives were saved from the bombings, we'd never know.

On this, my fourth mission, we flew with the 97th Bomb Group—four squadrons of 12 planes each, or 48 Flying Fortresses. I was assigned to Lieutenant Frost's *Dirty Girty.* Frost said he only had her name on the nose, because he didn't know what she looked like—"Probably ugly anyway."

This was my first trip with somebody I knew. Frost was the "driver" and was well-known and respected in Africa as being a pilot who could "bring 'em back." Bob "Duck" Pond was a gunner and it was great to have a chance to fly with him. I hadn't seen Duck since I was sent to the hospital in Algeria.

"Duck, old buddy, thought you'd be back in the States by now."

"Should have been, but I took sort of a respite from flying and still don't have my 50 missions."

"Where's Ziggie?"

"Couldn't take him up here with me and gave him to another guy to take care of."

"Well Duck, we shared a slit trench while the Krauts dropped their hardware on us and now we'll be sharing a machine that'll drop some goodies on *them.*"

Duck carried on an entire conversation like Donald Duck as we walked out to the plane. The radio man said Duck always did this before starting on a mission because it loosened up the other guys, and they left for the battlefield with a chuckle.

We would *need* all the chuckles we could get today because our assigned position in the formation was Coffin Corner again!

I knew that some of us would die, yet I was anxious for the battle to begin. I had learned that seeing action through a viewfinder was almost like seeing a movie. It didn't seem to be as dangerous as "eyeballing" it. We heard the high-pitched whine of the warm-up generators, then the explosive roar of the engines.

We were over the Adriatic Sea at 15,000 feet and flying straight up into Austria. This time we were going to hit the Linz marshaling yards. We would be at 31,000 feet when we got to the I.P. to start the bombing run.

At 25,000 to 35,000 feet, where we made most of the runs, our bodies didn't get so cold—it was our hands and feet. Sometimes they got so cold they would be numb. We never got cold while we were fighting. Sometimes we would even sweat, but when it was all over, the moisture on the backs of our electric long johns would make us even colder.

At that altitude the hundreds of contrails made our deadly air machines acquire a stirring beauty against the blue sky. We always made still pictures of this dramatic sight with the K-20 still camera. The white trails were spectacular but deadly. German anti-aircraft gunners knew exactly where each plane was.

Duck had placed two empty wooden .50-caliber ammo boxes on the floor under his waist gun window. I asked why he had done this.

"They are my own personal bombs. I'll throw them out over the target," he said.

As usual, Jerry was sitting out there waiting for us, this time with Focke-Wulf 190s. There was no mistake about it, they looked exactly like the silhouettes we had studied. They had short wings, radial engines, long transparent hoods and square-cut tails. And *these* birds had yellow noses—the elite. The pride of the Luftwaffe. This meant trouble!

In seconds we were caught in the middle of a whirlwind of yellow noses and black crosses painted on ochre and green fuselages.

Something new had been added. They were attempting some air to air bombing by dropping time-fuse sticks from above us. We wondered if that was some more of fat, pompous old Hermann Goering's fiendish ingenuity.

The Focke-Wulfs were deadly. Their pilots must have been among the best in the Luftwaffe because they were scattering our burning planes and shattered bodies all through Austria.

When the 190s left us, we knew we were approaching the flak fields. Only the bravest or dumbest Jerries would fly through their own flak. It had been reported, however, that in the heat of battle, they had been seen doing it. Probably some young kids who were trying hard to win the coveted Blue Max medal.

Hundreds of black puffs of smoke suddenly appeared all around us. It was thick. It was this concentration of fire-power that prompted some of the fellow to say, "The flak was so thick, you could get out and walk on it."

It was these hot, jagged fragments that tore wings off planes, sent bombardier's "offices" plunging to the earth and even caused blinding explosions when a frag would make a direct hit in the bomb bay. This day you could walk on it.

The German ack-ack batteries were deadly accurate and their score was becoming impressive. The 17s were exploding and coming apart all around us.

We were in constant danger by debris from our own planes: doors, engines, bodies, partially opened parachutes and all kinds of assorted fragments. A tail wheel ricocheted off one of our wings. A shiny silver rectangle of metal sailed over our left wing. It was a main exit door.

Then a black lump came somersaulting through the formation barely missing our propellers. It was a man hugging his knees to the chest. He shot by us so close that I saw one of his boots come off. He was probably making a delayed jump to get out of this chaos in a hurry. All of this action was recorded on my Bell and Howell Eyemo 35mm movie camera, most of it with the telephoto lens. There was no let-up. There was neither rest nor mercy.

We estimated that there were more than 50 white dots in the air at one time—parachutes! A 17 on our left was burning. The co-pilot left through his side-window because there had probably been damage behind him that prevented him from going out through the bomb bay. A question flashed through my mind—followed by a possible answer. "How was it possible for him to squeeze through that small opening?" It *seemed* impossible.

The co-pilot hit the horizontal stabilizer and was probably killed on impact, or fell to his death. He wasn't wearing his para-chute. In fact, he *couldn't* have been wearing it when he squeezed through his window.

We lost 21 bombers on our way to the target, but kept closing up to maintain a tight formation.

I had spent nearly all of my time at Duck Pond's left waist gun window, because I was getting such great shots there that moving to another location would not have been an improvement.

I liked Duck's station anyway, because he had pasted a full-length pose of Betty Grable above his window. Betty was standing with her back turned toward us and was wearing a one-piece backless swimsuit. She had her hands on her hips and had turned her head around to smile at us over her right shoulder. Duck noticed me looking at her. "Inspiration," he said.

Duck was excited because a Kraut fighter had exploded while it was flying straight at him, and he was positive his .50-caliber gun had done it. Confirmation came later.

Sometimes, during prolonged battles, the guns got so hot they had to be force-cooled. The gunners would point the guns forward and pull back the bolts so air could blow through the inside of the barrels. All guns on board could be cooled this way except the tail guns and the radio operator's gun.

I remembered that at high altitude the Eyemo camera would freeze up in a few minutes so I held it close to my chest while looking for my next shot. I had lost track of time with all the action outside the window, used up my film and had to reload.

I had just moved to the nose of the ship and back to the window and because I was carrying the camera and parachute and breathing pure oxygen, it felt like I had run a couple of miles non-stop.

We arrived at the I.P. and turned into our bomb run for the Linz Marshalling yards. The bombardier was now flying the aircraft through his Norden bomb sight. In a few minutes we released our bombs and there was a slight lift. The bombardiers ahead of us released theirs at the same time. We could see long stacks of bombs exiting the bomb bays. They wobbled for a few seconds, then gained stability as they nosed over and started their dive toward death and destruction. We knew that thousands of eyes were looking up at us.

It would be peaceful and quiet down there for a few more moments. The bombs were on their way and nothing in our power could stop what we had done. If there was life where those bombs hit, we would take it. The bombs were still falling but were now out of sight. People down there were still breathing.

Then, just as we started turning back, we saw hundreds of exploding circles and columns of smoke. The target was covered with flames. It looked like some gigantic hand was tearing up the earth in huge handfuls. I witnessed this awesome sight through the camera's viewfinder while standing in the bomb bay without an oxygen hookup. The bombardier usually closed the doors immediately after bomb release, but he had promised he would keep them open for me until we saw the explosions.

Life down there no longer existed. Enemy or not, this bothered me. The flak didn't let up even when we were over the target. The bomb bay doors closed and I went back to Duck's window. Duck's empty ammo boxes were gone.

The gunner on the other side said he was waving at a friend in the waist window of the 17 flying along with us, when suddenly it disappeared right before his eyes. There was nothing left but a puff of black smoke where the plane had been.

The intercom came alive announcing other flak hits. A piece was torn out of the top turret, and one came very close to where Duck and I were standing. It ripped a jagged hole between tail-end Charlie, the tail gunner, and the tail wheel that had been retracted up into the fuselage. The tire was blown out.

I looked at the shattered tire and wondered how the pilot would handle this problem when we landed. He had only two options, of course: Land with the tail wheel up and drag the tail-end of the plane, or lower it, if he could, and take a chance of tire debris flying up and damaging the plane. Duck called the pilot on the intercom and reported the damage.

The flak bursts were huge, meaning they were close. This was almost unbearable, and I thought I couldn't take it. And then I said to myself, "Look here, you idiot, you *can't* quit now—and if you *could*, where would you go? Now pull yourself together!"

Having given myself that command, I carried it out.

The black puffs of exploding flak stopped and suddenly a squadron of Focke-Wulfs came screaming out of the sun, boring into our formation. Their wings were lit up by fiery flashes from their 20mm cannons. A Fortress was hit and burst into flames. It nosed up sharply, a wing sheared off, and it burst into flame as it nosed over and spun earthward, leaving a huge question mark of black smoke in the sky.

One of the FW-109s burst into flames, and rolled over and we saw the pilot push himself out into the hostile air.

The 20mm cannons being fired from the FW-190s wouldn't just go *through* something, they would explode on impact. One came right through the formation with his yellow nose pointed straight at us. Duck's gun kept up an endless chatter that sounded like a jack-hammer pounding in my head. It was a *duel!* Duck was pouring a steady stream of .50-caliber bullets at him and he was firing straight at us. His 20mm cannon shells were flashing around us as they exploded.

I stood beside Duck as he kept hammering away at the 190. We saw his tracers rip into the radial engine. Suddenly the Focke-Wulf exploded in a blinding flash like a hand grenade. Duck yelled into his intercom, "I got one! I *got* one! I *got* one of the devils!"

The engine plunged down and the tail started spinning and fluttering. It was only a matter of seconds. It was an awesome sight. My legs shook with a nervous tremor and my teeth chattered. Another 190 came straight at our window and opened up with his 20mm cannons. I was standing shoulder-to-shoulder with Duck, shooting at the 190 with my telephoto lens, when suddenly Duck's head exploded and his warm brains splattered all over my frozen face and camera. His head was completely gone! He was slammed down to the floor!

In less than a second, I reached around to the front of the camera and twisted the turret lens assembly from telephoto to normal and stood there shooting Duck flopping around on the floor. I really hadn't had time to think what I was doing. It was simply a spontaneous reaction—a conditional response from training.

The intercom connector box near the window had been blown away. I heard the crash of static in my earphones—then a steady hiss. I started up front to tell the pilot what had happened. The waist section was riddled with holes from one end to the other. As I passed through the radio compartment, I was amazed at the battle damage. There were gaping holes everywhere! The radio room door had a huge hole near the bottom. The radio operator was sitting on the floor with blood pouring down his face and the oxygen hose to his mask was shredded. I glanced at his oxygen flow indicator and saw that it was not moving. I hurried through the bomb bay and reported the trouble to the engineer. He grabbed a walk-around bottle and a spare mask and hurried back through the bomb bay to the radio room.

I then continued forward to talk to the pilot. He had his hands full, because he had lost one engine, and another was sputtering and smoking.

I came back to Duck's window, sat on the floor with my head in my hands, my elbows on my knees and stared at Duck's headless body. I bent over and straightened his blood-soaked sheepskin collar. Then a sudden wave of grief took my breath away.

I removed my headgear and wiped Duck's blood and brains from my oxygen mask and helmet. Tiny bits of metal were embedded in them. A jawbone with teeth still in it was sticking in the aluminum skin above Duck's window. Betty Grable's right leg was gone.

I was overpowered by a shocking sense of irreplaceable loss. I was numbed and dazed with horror and no longer heard the frightening noises of battle.

I reached over and took Duck's left hand in both of mine. "I'm sorry, Duck," I managed, then I burst into tears.

When we were out of the flak and fighter areas, the co-pilot came back and examined the damaged tail wheel. He tried to hand-crank it down, but couldn't. He went back up front and the pilot called us and said he would have to land with the tail wheel up. He ordered the gunners and me to come forward into the radio operator's compartment and close the door.

We all took our previously assigned positions, sat down on the floor and braced ourselves for the landing.

By the time we were on final for the Foggia airfield, Lieutenant Frost was flying on two engines. The engineer fired a red flare into the sky to indicate that we had wounded on board and we were cleared for an immediate landing.

The tires barked as they touched the runway and the pilot did a skillful job of holding the tail up until we were at stalling speed. When the tail finally settled and touched, we heard a loud scraping noise that didn't diminish until we stopped rolling.

I jumped down from the parked plane and stood watching as Duck's headless body was lowered to the medics who were standing at the open doors of the meat wagon. I was still sobbing unashamedly.

Operation Pointblank

A REPLACEMENT CAME OVER TO FILL the vacancy left by Mike Silva, who had been killed on a mission, and the Hollywood guys lost no time in worrying the poor fellow. They suddenly developed fearful twitches and nervous habits while eating and sitting around shooting the bull, trying to shatter the calm of the new fellow. They looked down on him anyway because he wasn't a studio man —he had worked as a camera repairman in downtown Los Angeles. I knew how he felt.

We had to give up our beautiful Villa Angela and say good-by to Mama and Angelo. Mama cried and wailed like she was losing part of her family and in a way, she was. Angelo didn't show up as we were driving out the gate. The last we saw of him, he was running down the path to his house crying his eyes out.

We moved to Bastia, on the eastern coast of the island of Corsica and set up housekeeping in a delightful old one-story stone building overlooking the sea. Napoleon Bonaparte had been born on this island in the town of Ajaccio, on the southwestern coast.

Why, we wondered, did the brass decide to move us so far north of the enemy lines? We were north of Rome, and the Germans were *still* in that area. Another thing that didn't make a lot of sense to us—we could no longer jump into a jeep and drive to work in Foggia, but would have to catch a C-45 shuttle plane and fly south along the coasts of Corsica and Sardinia until we were out of German ack-ack range, then head east to Foggia.

Corsica was located about 35 to 40 miles west of the tiny island of Elba. Napoleon was held prisoner there after he was forced to abdicate his reign as Emperor of France. The Germans were now occupying Elba, so we were again becoming accustomed to frequent, almost routine nightly bombardments. The Krauts weren't using airplanes this time, but fast boats armed with fairly large guns.

In Africa, we usually knew about what time to expect the Krauts. Here, we didn't. Their swift hit and run raids would take place anytime during the hours of darkness. We hadn't dug any slit trenches here; we simply went to bed and slept until we heard the first explosions.

The shelling was usually down in the dock area. One night I took my small mattress and blanket down near the dock on a hillside hoping to have a bird's-eye view of the action at a safe distance. Feeling very confident I had chosen the right spot between some boulders, I soon went to sleep on the ground. In Bari I had photographed the action while standing on the docks, but I didn't intend to make any shots here.

It was a cool and pleasant night. The moon, not yet fully up, lit a path across the barely perceptible ripples in the harbor. It seemed like the queen of the night had more stars than she could handle.

Then, about three in the morning, the shelling started. They were hitting *very* close and I could feel the detonation waves in my body. I wasted no time crawling over behind a large boulder and watched in fascination as streams of heavy tracers strung out from shore like fiery ropes. The Krauts must have been close!

The tracers weren't coming in my direction, so I stood up to get a better look. There was an explosion! I was knocked off my feet by the hot blast that tore the air from my lungs and left me gasping and choking for breath like an asthmatic.

I started running back up the hill to jump behind a large rock when another explosion sent a clod of earth into the back of my head slamming me to the ground. I quickly ran my hand around my head and neck to see if I was bleeding. Good news—there were no brains or blood on my palm.

It's strange, the kind of thoughts that pass through a man's mind in such a situation. "Am I dead? Am I going to die? Do I have any parts missing? Can I see? Can I talk? And hear?" There were mental flashback pictures of horrible wounds I'd seen before. All this took place in seconds. Then I said, "Thanks, God. You were certainly in the right place at the right time."

I crouched down behind the boulder and cursed myself for being so stupid—leaving the relative security of our quarters up the hill for *this!* Then for a dozen terrible seconds the explosions continued all around me—then stopped.

I had been driven by curiosity! "Mom," I thought, "you had always warned me that 'Curiosity killed the cat.' " Well, it hadn't killed the cat *this* time, but it was close! It occurred to me that I might be killed here, and I worried about how my wife and mother would take it when they got the, "We regret to inform you . . . " telegram.

I wanted to get back up the hill to our house, but not while this shelling was going on. Some of the shells falling in the harbor raised brief spouts of water. Others falling in the water seemed to explode on impact with the bottom, raising great fountains of spray.

Then the concrete buildings along the dock started exploding, sending up a thin rain of cement dust. Eruptions of flying sand and pebbles shot into the air from large streaming brown craters. Suddenly, I had a great respect for the infantry ground-pounders who lived with this every day.

Then there was a loud explosion and a red ball of fire appeared in the road just down the rocky slope. Jagged shell fragments screeched through the rocks. I was temporarily deafened by the explosion and shaken by the blast. There had been a direct hit on a staff car. Nothing remained but its four wheels and the steel axles that held them together.

Suddenly it was quiet. Jerry had made his nightly hit and run. I walked down the slope to examine the remains of the car. Acrid black smoke was still swirling around the rubble.

Across the road, and in a depression, a man was lying face-up. He had been split open like an overripe watermelon dropped to the ground and his guts were oozing out like gray pulsating snakes. His arms were outstretched and his eyes and mouth were open as if asking, "God, why *me?*"

Another night, in the early morning hours, I was sound asleep in my room when the bombardment started. This was a surprise because instead of hearing the explosions two blocks away at the dock, they were *right on us!* I rolled out of bed and was flat on the floor in a second, not even bothering to throw my blanket off! Stones from our front wall were heaved into the air and crashed down through the roof, shattering the bathroom fixtures in the next room.

Nobody in the house had been hurt, but we grumbled and whined a little, and called the Krauts some very bad names. One of the guys, Sergeant Clarence "Buck" Dollar, was terribly upset because his girlfriend had sent him a large box of homemade chocolate fudge, and now it was all over the walls and ceiling. We all agreed with Buck that it was far worse than losing our john.

One morning at a meeting in major Barovik's office, he banged out the tobacco ashes of his pipe on the heel of his hand and said, "See this pipe? It came from the briar grown right here near Bastia. The world's best briar pipes are made of it." None of us were especially interested in the major's pipe, but we had to listen patiently as he gave us a brief history of briar. He told us that it was actually spelled "bruyere," but the French called it "briere" and we had simplified it to "briar." Big deal . . . .

We were quite excited as we walked out of the large camouflaged briefing tent. Operation "Pointblank" had just been explained to us. We were taking our B-24s into Germany to hit the Junkers factory in Bernberg. This was where the hated JU-88s were built.

"Pointblank" was the code name for the combined 8th and 15th Air Force bomber offensive against German aircraft factories, ball-bearing works, oil refineries, rubber plants and maintenance facilities.

The generals had decided that we, in the 15th Air Force, would be helping the 8th Air Force write a glorious page in the military history books.

Generals in their swivel chairs did not necessarily share the same war with sergeants freezing at 30,000 feet in a bomber. Generals, the chess masters, saw the *big* picture—the entire chessboard from their lofty positions at the rear of the board. We ordinary dogfaces, however, saw the war from the narrow waist of an aerial fighting machine and judged the progress of the war by its effects on ourselves and our buddies. Of course, the guys in the waist section were only pawns on the front ranks of the chessboard. So it was the old army motto, " . . . for us to do or die." More than likely do *and* die.

The excitement was built around the fact that we would be working with the 8th Air Force flying out of England. It would be a *biggie!*

The 8th Air Force was getting a lot of publicity by the news media. We, in the 15th Air Force, were beginning to think we had been forgotten. We resented it.

The new movie "Casablanca" had a theme song that everybody was humming, "As Time Goes By." This was being parodied by the guys in Foggia . . .

> *"It's still the same old story,*
> *the Eighth gets all the glory,*
> *while we go out to die . . .*
> *The fundamental things apply,*
> *as flak goes by."*

As usual we had heard why we shouldn't be too concerned about killing civilians. This meant we would be unloading in a civilian-populated area. "If we can eradicate the enemy's means of making war, he will stop fighting." We all knew this but what *really* got our attention was the remark about how our "bailed out" aircrews were treated by the civilians, men *and* women, if they weren't lucky enough to be picked up by the German military.

"The women will come running over to where you land and jab pitchforks into you until the men arrive. Then if you are still alive, they will lynch you." We had heard this before.

I hadn't been too happy when I was ordered to report to the 460th Bomb Group, because they were flying B-24s. The B-17 had become *my* ship, because I had learned from experience that a 17 could come home when it seemed impossible. The 24s were newer, however, and they had more powerful engines and could carry a slightly heavier bomb load.

There had been a lot of "bad mouthing" about the B-24s. They were designed and engineered by Consolidated, a very good and famous aircraft builder. Consolidated couldn't come *close* to rolling them out of their factory fast enough to supply air corps requirements, however, so Henry Ford, the production line genius, put up a building nearly a mile long and a quarter of a mile wide in Willow Run, Michigan.

From this facility, the mass production automobile experts got into the aircraft building business. It wasn't quite like driving cars out the end of the factory but the auto makers and inspectors had *one* primary goal—*roll them out!* They were shipped and flown overseas and our mechanics were finding a lot of very shoddy workmanship in them.

Rivets missing. Skin crooked. Control cables rubbing and binding against each other. A ground chief could take one look at a B-24 and say, "This damn thing came out of Ford's plant. *Consolidated* wouldn't have let it pass." I wasn't very excited about becoming a passenger in one.

We found a bulkhead that wasn't riveted all the way around. Somebody said, "Guess some poor dumb defense worker had been on the job for eight hours already that day, and had to work overtime at time-and-a-half, and was just plain worn out."

Another guy replied, "Yeah, and the poor goof probably had to drive two whole miles after work to get to his favorite cocktail lounge. I sure feel sorry for those poor heathen defense workers."

"Well, at least that brave feather merchant wasn't out on strike," another voice chimed in.

I wondered why I was trusting my life to such a shoddy aircraft since I didn't have to. The only reason that came to my mind was —*insanity!* "What are you doing here, stupid?"

A rivalry had developed between the crews of the B-17 Fortresses and the B-24 Liberators. The B-24 crewmen bragged that at 225 mph, they were 14 miles per hour faster than the Forts and could carry a heavier bomb load. The Fort guys boasted that they could fly higher, hold a better formation and take a lot more punishment from fighters and flak. The comparison that *really* upset the Liberator crews was, "You B-24 people are flying the big ugly crates that our B-17s were shipped in."

Today it didn't really matter *how* I got to the target. This was my fifth mission, and with it would come the coveted Air Medal. "Let's get on with it!"

There was no cartoon on the nose—only the name, *Princess Maritza*. This big bird was a "nose-dragger" and sat upright on its three wheels with its twin vertical stabilizers and rudders high off the ground.

Then I spotted 12 little white bombs painted on the nose. One of the ground crew members was standing next to me holding a fire extinguisher.

"Is that right, your plane has been on 12 missions?"

"Yeah, 12."

"So this one is number 13?"

"No, its number 12-A. And the one after this will be number 14."

I felt better.

There was no formality when I met the crew. Nobody even said hello. I followed them to the plane, crawled in and started looking for good places to stand and operate the camera. It wasn't too different from the interior arrangement of the B-17. The waist gun windows were even a little larger than the 17s and the gun pedestals weren't mounted to the floor directly in front of the windows but off to the side, making an emergency exit easier.

Unlike the B-17, this aircraft had waist gun window doors. The gunners could unlatch them, hinge them inward and up to the ceiling, and secure them. The guns, on pedestals, could be swung away from the windows, leaving large unobstructed openings.

It's amazing how a man's place of work, *anywhere,* becomes his all important world. It's even more than that. It's his shelter and home, enclosing and protecting, giving a sense of security no matter how precarious it is—even blasting through the air toward an uncertain future.

I had seen Sergeant Poundstone crawl aboard the plane that would be flying on our left wing and wondered why. Combat cameramen were supposed to be spread out in the formation.

We heard the whine of starters and the first cold sputters of the engines coughing themselves into even roars. Then, we felt the rush of air and exhaust smoke past the window. A fire guard was standing below the number two engine. Another man standing near the wheel jerked the chocks out and they both ran to the sidelines. Our plane began creeping along and nosing into the long line queuing up on the taxiway.

We left Foggia and headed straight west while we formed up over the Tyrrhenian Sea. Then we passed Sardinia and were finally over the Mediterranean, where we turned north toward the south coast of France. Our flight plan showed we would arrive at the coast near Marseilles.

I opened the door covering the window slightly and saw big puffy white clouds in the sky. I looked downward and saw a large ship floating in a violet mist. I didn't know if it was ours or theirs, but it gave me a distinct sense of comfort by its presence.

The steady droning of the engines made me feel safe and relaxed. I sat on the floor with my knees drawn up and my head bent down, closed my eyes and talked to Duck. Duck didn't answer. He was safely dead and out of the war.

Vivid memories of Duck lying headless on the cold floor haunted my mind. I felt a choking in my throat and fought back the tears. This was my first mission since the tragedy, but I knew it was necessary to try to forget the recent past and get ready to go back to work. There was nothing to do yet but sit on the floor and think. All kinds of thoughts ran through my mind.

I was starting to realize that the odds of getting through a mission alive were seen by different guys in different ways. Crazy Larry Dakin, for example, never carried a good luck charm. He never mentioned his family or showed us any pictures. He *must* have been thinking about somebody back home though, because of the way he acted after he bought the yellow tulips.

Mouse Morris was just the opposite. He would drive us crazy by repeatedly reading aloud the news from home and showing us a picture of his sister holding his little dog. Mouse was a devout Catholic and would pray a lot and go to Mass in Bari as often as he could. He would bow his head for a few seconds of silent prayer before eating. He also had his rosary around his neck on every mission. Mouse was a highly moral person who reminded me of Otto Zinkgraf from the photo trailer days in Africa.

Everybody but Larry had a good luck charm of some kind. Sometimes it was just a lucky shoestring from a high school gym shoe or a small twig from a tree on the old homestead. I wasn't especially superstitious or religious, but took no chances. I wore the tiny Saint Nicholas medal on my dog tag chain which was given to me by the priest in Bari, and, of course, had Wilma's comforting little Bible in my left shirt pocket. After all I'd been through, I was sure it was a *lucky* Bible.

We were also different in the way we faked our feelings. Dutch Vandervoort would say, "Well, I got through *that* one so it stands to reason they'll *never* get me." Frenchie would say, "Going to Germany tomorrow, so I'll be waiting for the rest of you guys in a German Stalag Luft."

I believe that *all* of us secretly knocked on wood and prayed— each in our own words, and each in our own way. I really didn't know the proper protocol for talking to God, but when things got rough I'd catch myself whispering, "God, hurry and get me out of this mess—you *gotta* get me out of this!"

I never promised God anything in return like, "I'll start going to church as soon as my feet hit the ground" or "I'll never start drinking whiskey." In my confused way of reasoning I felt like if God was *really* God, He'd have everything written down in his big "people manual" and would deal with me when He got to *my* chapter.

At 10,000 feet, the bombardier called on the intercom and told us to open the gun doors and put on our oxygen masks. The waist gunners swung their doors inward and up to the ceiling where they were secured. We now had a panoramic view of the formation. It was already becoming routine.

My self-induced brain washing was paying off. "They have been throwing *everything* at me. I don't think I'll *ever* die. Well, at least not today."

We were still climbing at 12,000 feet, a little over half the altitude necessary to join the 8th from England, when our number two engine started streaming white smoke. There was no news on the intercom from the front office, so we assumed this was something the pilot would take care of without worrying the rest of us.

The smoke didn't stop right away and had turned from white to black. We wondered why the pilot hadn't hit the fire button to activate the CO-2 extinguisher in that engine. Soon, the worst possible thing happened. We could see fire at the rear of the engine. Then the fire spread all the way back across the wing to the trailing edge behind the number two engine, then along the fuselage to the bomb bay doors.

A piece of engine cowling blew off and knocked a large hole in the left horizontal stabilizer about ten feet behind where I was standing.

This got the pilot's attention, because he was now on the intercom telling us that he had a problem, and it looked serious. The fire was now *under* the wing and making its way along the fuselage beneath the window.

The skipper called the crew and held a conference.

"Do you want to jump, or stay with it while I take her down and ditch?"

I had been watching this problem developing from the left waist window, and didn't see how he could keep the bird from burning up before he got to the water. I jerked the oxygen mask away from my face and shouted at the gunner, "*Bail out! Hit the silk! This is it!*" He stood there frozen!

My mind was racing! "God, I'm sure you have your hands *full* right now, but I need your advice *fast!*" I didn't wait for it or maybe He *had* told me because I swung the gun aside, went out

head-first and started somersaulting—water—sky—water—sky—
"What had that parachute instructor told us to do before pulling
the rip cord?"

"Wave your arms above your head. This will straighten you out
so that you'll fall feet first. If you pull your ripcord while you are
tumbling, you might roll up in the canopy while the chute is
opening and you'll go down like a big cocoon."

I waved my arms and *pulled!* There was a sudden whoomp and
a sharp jerk snapped me into a hanging position. When the chute
popped open, it settled me so deeply into the harness that the
chest strap jerked up and rested under my chin, which prevented
me from looking straight down. If the leg straps had been loosened
a couple of more inches, the chest strap and buckle would have
probably broken my neck.

I had noticed that it was hard moving around in the aircraft
with the leg straps of the parachute harness pulled tight, so I had
loosened them. This nearly caused a disaster.

Some blood started trickling down into my eyes. I had been hit
across the jaw and temple by a metal riser connector link when the
chute was deploying.

I grabbed the risers, threw my head back and looked up.
Beautiful! "God bless the silk worm." I even noticed blue words and
numbers printed around the skirt of the canopy.

This was something new. I had never been in a predicament
like *this* before. I was all alone with nobody to help me and had to
do it all by myself. I was scared. I wondered how hard I would hit
the water. Most of all, I was afraid I would drown. I had heard another guy say that his whole life flashed through his mind when he
"hit the silk." Mine didn't.

I started twisting myself around in the parachute harness to
find the ships that were supposed to be down there. There *were*
none. There was nothing but blue water and pink streaks in the
sky on the horizon.

"Those lying imbeciles," I thought. They had told us in the
briefing tent that the British Navy worked this part of the
Mediterranean Sea because it was an active "ditching" area for *both*
sides.

I knew the Krauts worked this area also so it might well be a toss-up whether I'd be eating kidney pie or sauerkraut for supper. My racing mind said, "Believe I'd rather have the kraut."

"If *nobody's* navy is down there, I'll have to swim, but in which direction?" I was completely disoriented. There was no land in sight in a 360° sweep of the horizon.

I started trying to recall what we had been instructed about water landings, but was still too high to worry about it yet. It was impossible to know how far above the water I was. Nothing on the horizon gave me any clues, and there weren't any waves on the water.

The loud drone of 400 engines grew fainter—then there was a very loud silence. My buddies were going into battle. I had deserted.

We had been given no more than two minutes of instruction on the use of the parachute. Most of it related to water landings.

"Unbuckle the right leg strap. Settle back in the harness. Unbuckle the left leg strap. Put your feet and knees together. When you are close to the water, unbuckle the chest strap and fold your arms across your chest to keep from falling out. As soon as your feet touch the water, throw your arms up and slip out of the harness. This way, the canopy will go into the water behind you instead of coming down over you and causing you to drown."

This little speech had been read by a bored parachute rigger and had been dry and mechanical. It paid off, however, because I was now running it through my mind and was sure I had it right.

I had lost track of time and had no idea how long I'd been dangling under the canopy. I thought it might be a good idea to start the unbuckling procedure, though. I was worried that I might do something wrong, fall out and "buy the farm."

I got all the way down to the arm folding step, but the sea was so smooth, I couldn't see anything on the surface to use as a reference.

I thought, "Well, I'm there," so up went my arms. I was freefalling! *"God help me!"* There is no way of knowing how far I fell before hitting the water or how far down I went into the beautiful, calm Mediterranean. It *had* to have been 50 feet *both* ways!

I went down—*deep* down, and started groping around for the pull cords attached to the two CO-2 inflation bottles fastened to my Mae West. I couldn't find them so I started paddling and kicking until I finally reached the surface. By this time I had swallowed so much water that I thought I'd choke.

I grabbed a deep breath and sank down again. I could feel the two steel bottles but not the pull cords. Even though I was becoming frantic, the thought flashed through my mind that I couldn't feel the cords through my heavy leather gloves so I pulled them off. I struggled back to the surface while working with the gloves and was there just long enough to suck in some more air.

The third time down I deliberately opened my eyes and found the cord on the left bottle and jerked it. The CO-2 bottle popped and I shot back to the surface. I now had time to find the cord on the right side which had become lodged behind the bottle. I pulled it and finally had a nice Mae West circling my head.

My first thought was, "Well stupid, you could have removed your gloves while you were dangling up there under your canopy with nothing else to do." Then a frightening thought entered my mind—"Oh God, *please,* no *sharks!*"

Water lapped into my mouth through my clenched teeth. I swallowed a lot and thought about all those fish around me going to the bathroom. My stomach ached. Then my head ached. My mind was a jumble and seemed to float away from my body.

My life hadn't flashed through my mind when I bailed out of the burning B-24. That would have probably been written into a Hollywood script, but it was really flashing now. *Stupid* little things. Had I dumped out the exhausted hypo in our new dark-room and replaced it with fresh? Would the new residents of Villa Angela take care of Mama, Angelo—"my family?"

Then strange memories from my childhood. "Bobby, now don't go far because supper's nearly ready."

"Put down six and carry two, la-de-da, la-de-da. That is very hard to do, la-de-da, la-de-da." *Crazy!*

I wondered if the Supreme Architect of the Universe clutters our minds with weird things to keep us from going bananas? It *must* work because at this moment the exhausted hypo was more important than the sharks.

After an eternity of floating in the water in a standing position, and trying to hold perfectly still so the big fish wouldn't notice me, I heard the faint sound of an engine. It was coming from behind me so I splashed around and saw the white bow spray of a speeding boat coming straight for my head! It was on my eye-level! "Do they see me? Oh *no*—they'll run *over* me!"

Two thoughts flashed through my mind at once: "Thank God, I've been found! Is it a Limey or Kraut boat?"

The small boat slowed down and started circling. They eased up closer and I saw four men making preparations to haul me in. "Thank God"—they're *Limeys* because they have cigarettes dangling from the center of their lips like *all* Limeys do."

I had forgotten my manners, and instead of thanking them, I said, "What in blazes took you guys so long? I've been out here for *hours!*"

"I'm sure it seemed like it, Yank," one of them said, "but actually we got 'ere in 20 minutes. Besides, wot's the bloody 'urry?"

After a half hour ride, we pulled up to a large gray ship with a stairway running diagonally up the tall steel side. My four rescuers and I climbed the stairs. I went first.

As soon as I set foot on the deck, someone thrust a white porcelain mug of hot tea into my hands and said, "Welcome aboard, Yank. Have a spot of tea."

I warmed my trembling hands around the mug of tea, which had been generously laced with rum, and eagerly buried my cold nose into the delightful warm steam. There was no rush. This was obviously a ritual the sailors who had grouped around me had often practiced. Then I gulped a mouthful, which burned down to my stomach and warmed me like a hot water bottle.

I was curious about not having seen them from the air and was told they had been there all along, but men are usually so frightened and excited that they rarely see anything.

I was taken below decks to a white room that looked like a small hospital. A sailor asked me to strip my soaked flying suit and clothes off and lie down on a padded table. When I removed my wool pants, I found that the two Milky Way candy bars in the pockets were ruined. For a second or two this seemed to be my greatest loss. Luckily, the New Testament in my shirt pocket had been well protected and was dry.

The sailor then started rubbing me with a large coarse towel. He rubbed and rubbed both sides of me until I felt raw. He handed me a pair of long underwear, thick white socks and blue trousers. Another sailor came over with a blue turtleneck sweater and a pair of rubber-soled white tennis shoes and I put them on.

A fellow who appeared to be a doctor came in and had me sit down on the table and asked if I wanted some more medicine. I told him that I hadn't *had* any medicine.

"Sure, you have, Yank, it was in the tea you had topside."

"Oh, the rum," I said. "Okay, I think I need some more medicine. Join me?"

The grinning doctor and I sat there and toasted my rescue. I felt good. And the *rum* felt good. I said, "The last time I had a toast with an Englishman was in Cambridge and we toasted your King and my President."

Without saying another word, the young doctor filled our cups again and the thoughts of my recent ordeal and the longest day of my life began to fade.

Back on deck I asked some of the sailors about their rescue experiences. One said, "The last Yank we pulled out of the drink didn't get off as easy as you did. He had dropped down out of a fighter formation with a dead engine. We watched him without our binoculars because he was going to try to ditch close to us. He rolled over about 300 feet above the water and fell out. His chute started coming out but just streamered and didn't blossom. He was so low it didn't have time to deploy fully."

Another sailor jumped in, "That chap did the most perfect swan dive I've ever seen. The chute kept him from going in too deep, but he really hit hard. While we were dragging him up the ladder to the deck, his eyes swelled shut and he kept yelling that he was blind. It took our medico two or three hours working on his eyes before the chap realized he wasn't blind."

Another sailor said, "He was bruised all over his body. I'll wager that *you* will be black and blue by tomorrow. We were watching you with our field glasses and saw you fall out of your chute pretty high above the water."

"Yes," I said, "I misjudged the distance and let go."

The next day my body started turning black and blue from the impact with the water and I ached all over. The Limey captain invited me into a small room just aft of the bridge. We both started asking questions about the incident. He wanted to know what started the fire with no enemy action. I wanted to know where the rest of the crew was.

I gave him my story, although at that time I had no real answers. Then he gave me the bad news. Our plane had gone down in flames 30 miles north of where I had splashed in. Another air-sea rescue ship had been in that vicinity and was still searching the area without finding anything.

I was shocked! I knew that most crew members I'd talked to about this said they would rather take their chances riding one down than to fling their bodies out into space. "Ridiculous," I thought.

We floated around for four days without picking anyone else out of the water, and then headed east toward Naples. Every day we saw formations of planes high over our heads flying north and south. At night we heard the German planes.

It was the beginning of our last day at sea. I stood at the rail considering my miseries and watching for land. The sun was rising over the water, a brilliant yellow ball through the haze on the horizon. I squinted to avoid the blaze of sun on the water.

Finally, there was a pale smudge on the horizon and the first dim line of land pushed up over the water. Italy! The docking procedure at Naples took too long because I was anxious to plant my feet firmly on something that wasn't bouncing around.

A staff car was waiting for me at the foot of the gangplank. I threw my heavy sheepskin flying suit and boots into the back seat and got in. I felt like an arriving general and wondered why they were wasting a staff car just for *me*.

We drove to the airfield and a C-47 was waiting to fly to my outfit in Bastia. Again I wondered why I was being pampered like this because there were no other passengers except for the crew.

The Inquest

WHEN WE ARRIVED IN BASTIA I immediately reported to our office at headquarters. Our captain was sitting at Major Barovik's desk. "I've come to report to the major, Sir," I said.

"The major isn't here, Sergeant, he's gone," replied the captain. Like a good soldier, I didn't ask why, and no explanations were offered. The captain told me to take a few days' leave.

After I had settled down for about a week, our captain called me back in. I had always felt the captain was a religious scholar; he often quoted or made references to the Bible when he was addressing us and this time was no exception. A Bible was lying on his desk. The captain ordered me to report to the 15th Air Force headquarters building in Bari. He said they had some questions to ask me. Then he began to lightly drum his fingertips on the Bible, and after a pause said, "And I only escaped alone to tell thee."

"Is that something from the Bible, Sir?" I asked.

"Yes, Sergeant, it's from the book of Job. Now go and tell all."

"Yes, Sir," I said, and left.

I thought *I* had the questions. *Their* questions turned out to be a full-blown *inquest!* Under ordinary circumstances, a little questioning would have probably closed the case. Not *this* one, however. Perhaps sabotage or some kind of "hanky-panky" had been involved.

A lot of other men had been ordered to attend the inquest. The *entire crew* of the B-24 that had been flying on our left wing when the incident occurred was there. The ground crew of *our* plane had been called in. Various other men were in the room, totaling about 30 people present.

A military policeman in the hallway stepped inside the door

and called us to attention. Three majors and one lieutenant colonel walked rapidly to the front of the room and seated themselves behind a long table, facing us. The colonel said, "At ease."

We sat down. I could see the apprehension and anxiety on every face in the room. My heart was pounding harder than it had been when I bailed out of the burning B-24. Stern-faced officers had always frightened me!

The only person in the room I knew personally was Sergeant Rocky Poundstone. It was a couple of hours before I realized why *he* was at the inquest. Another sergeant looked vaguely familiar, but I couldn't place him until I heard his name.

We were all wearing our class "A" dress uniforms, and it was always easier to recognize someone when he was wearing his work clothes. This guy was Staff Sergeant Brad "Piggy" Bankhead, the ground-crew chief of the lost plane. I had noticed him briefly, when he was in the cockpit talking with our pilot shortly before we took off.

This was the *second* time I had been surprised that our commanding officer, Major Barovik, was not around. I was again reminded of the old army motto, "It is not for us to question why . . . ."

One of the majors behind the table picked up a list of names and called the roll. All of the invited guests were present. Then it was quiet again, for a minute or so, while the four officers put their heads together and did some whispering. Things they didn't want us to hear, I supposed.

Tension grew. We started squirming around in our chairs, impatiently waiting for something to happen. The colonel shoved his chair back slightly, cleared his throat, took a deep breath and said, "Men, you all know why we're here. We now know what happened, and *why* it happened, but for the record, we want a detailed account of everything each of you had to do with the airplane, and anything else you can tell us to help close this file. The corporal sitting up here will take everything down in shorthand."

We all started looking at each other, wondering how so many could have *possibly* been involved.

The colonel continued. "We're here to wrap up an in-depth investigation of _____." (He gave the complete identification of the lost B-24.) He then read the names of the ten crewmen, starting with the pilot, who was the highest ranking man, and finishing with the lowest ranking enlisted man. This is the first time I had heard any of their names. I recalled nobody had introduced himself or even said hello when I boarded the plane with them. This was not unusual, it was simply the old cold-shoulder treatment we had come to expect from most of them. They thought it was bad luck to fly with a combat cameraman. *This* time they were *right!* Word spreads fast. I'm surprised that *anybody* from the 9th Combat Camera Unit ever again saw the inside of an airplane.

The session lasted from 1 p.m. to almost 4 p.m. The first two hours were very boring and repetitious. Each man was told to stand, give his name, rank and serial number, and explain his involvement with the aircraft. Even the members of the ground crew, who did nothing more than clean up the mess inside the plane after each mission, had to explain their jobs. There were a few chuckles and groans in the room when one of the men said, "I just sweep out the shell casing and clips and sometimes mop up the blood." There were obviously several men present who had never seen the blood as it was oozing out of a man's body. I, for one, didn't find the comment very funny.

I wondered what all this had to do with the problem. Was this how it goes in a court of law? I was anxious to get on with it!

Finally, it was my turn. I stood, gave my name, rank and serial number and said I had been the cameraman on the ship. I then started telling about being at the window when the smoke first appeared. A major, a small, sarcastic one, stopped me and said, "Sergeant Thompson, I want you to start your story when you got on the plane, and then go into every detail, no matter how unimportant you might think it is."

As I was telling my story, the little major kept interrupting me with questions I thought were immaterial and sometimes a little childish. I thought, "Well, this is probably how this big shot lawyer makes a living. Besides, he probably has a Napoleonic complex and *has* to act big."

Rocky Poundstone and Piggy Bankhead were last. This was the *big climax*. They both gave such incredible and astonishing stories, that I couldn't believe what I was hearing!

Rocky told the tribunal that Major Barovik, the commanding officer of the 9th Combat Camera Unit, had taken him into his confidence and said he wanted one of his cameramen to fly on Thompson's left wing.

"The major told me that somewhere on the way to the target, I'd see some harmless smoke coming out of Thompson's plane. He wanted me to watch for the smoke, and then shoot it with all three lenses. He ordered me to keep it to myself and *by no means* tell anybody else."

"When did you first see the smoke, Sergeant Poundstone?"

"Well, Sir, we must have been close to ten grand, but weren't on oxygen yet. I hadn't taken my eyes off Thompson's ship from the time we finished forming up. I stood at the right waist window waiting for the smoke. I thought the smoke would be black, but it was white for a few seconds and then turned black."

"And when you saw the smoke, what did you do?"

"I followed Major Barovik's orders and started shooting with the wide angle lens. First I pointed the camera toward the head of the formation to fill the viewfinder with a lot of planes, then made a slow pan back to Thompson's plane. I twisted the turret to the normal lens and squeezed off six or seven seconds, and then went to the telephoto. I sure got some good shots of the smoking engine."

"Could you see any of the crew members in that plane?"

"Yes, Sir. In fact, I could see at least two guys at the left waist window. There might have been three."

"Did you recognize the men?"

"No, Sir, but I know now that Sergeant Thompson was one of them."

"Did you actually see the fire start?"

"Yes, Sir. I didn't think that was supposed to happen, and it really shook me."

"Did you film the fire?"

"Yes, Sir. I kept the telephoto on it until I ran out of film. You use up the 100 feet of film in less than three minutes. We shoot in short bursts, so it's usually enough."

I wasn't at all pleased to be aboard a B-24 on the Point Blank mission.

Angelo looked very serious as he posed in my flying gear.

*After the inquest,
I returned from
Bari to Bastia as
the sole passenger
in a C-47.*

Duck Pond

"Did you see Sergeant Thompson jump?"

"No, Sir. While I was sitting on the floor reloading the camera, one of the guys yelled that they were starting to jump. When I finished loading the camera and stood back up, I didn't see anybody else leaving the plane, but *man,* it was really on fire!"

"Did you continue filming the aircraft?"

"Yes, Sir. It nosed over into a steep dive. Guess the pilot was trying to blow the fire out."

"Did you film the plane as it went down?"

"Yes, Sir, as long as I could, but it dropped way back and down and was out of sight pretty fast."

"Okay, Sergeant Poundstone. That's all. You may be seated."

I knew then that Major Barovik, the old Hollywood movie producer, would go to any extreme to add realism to a scene, and then "fake" the story around it. We all knew that Barovik was always trying to "scoop" the 8th Combat Camera Unit, which flew out of England because he wanted to send better footage back to the States than they did.

Why he thought he had to fake something *now* was inconceivable, because *all* of us were getting good footage of dog fights, German fighters zooming in on us firing their tracers, bombers exploding, and guys hanging under their canopies. None of us had ever shot a *close-up* of a bail-out, however. I wondered if Barovik was secretly hoping I would be his "stunt man" and give him a few seconds of action. Major Barovik didn't have the guts to go on a mission himself like Major Craig, the first C.O. of the unit had, or he could have cut Poundstone out of the loop and shot his own footage.

Piggy Bankhead was the last to testify. He went into detail about how his aircraft commander, the pilot, had talked to him in confidence. Not even the rest of the air crew members or the ground crew were to know anything about the "plan."

Piggy said, "The lieutenant told me he was going to cooperate with some Hollywood movie people and needed my help. They wanted to film some smoke coming out of our ship. They wanted me to rig up a smoke bomb in the number two engine and fix it so the pilot could set it off."

"Smoke bomb, Sergeant Bankhead?"

"Yes, Sir. They were going to photograph it from another ship. The lieutenant told me there would be a photographer on our ship also, but this guy wouldn't know about it until he saw the smoke, and then *he* would no doubt make pictures."

"Where did you find a smoke bomb, Sergeant?"

"I couldn't find a smoke bomb, Sir."

"Then how did you create the smoke, Sergeant?"

"I had to rig up something all by myself, Sir, because nobody else was supposed to know anything about it, just our pilot and that Hollywood major. And it was the *major's* fault, Sir, not my pilot's!"

"Calm down, Sergeant. How did you create the smoke?"

"Well, Sir, I kinda made up a 'Rube Goldberg' device that would squirt motor oil into the hot exhaust of number two, and it would come out as white smoke. I ran a line up into the cockpit and put a little valve on it. All the lieutenant had to do was turn the valve when he wanted the smoke to start. I gave him a final briefing just before takeoff."

Piggy choked up and couldn't continue for a few seconds. Tears were streaming down his cheeks. He stared at the floor for awhile and spoke up again, painfully and with great difficulty.

"Sir, I was told to do this by the aircraft commander. It wasn't *my* idea. I was just following his orders."

"Didn't you realize, Sergeant Bankhead, that this was a very unusual request, and one that could lead to disaster?"

"Yes, Sir, I thought it might be a little risky, but the lieutenant assured me that it would be okay to go ahead with it and everything would work out okay. That was *my* airplane, Sir, and I had kept it in the air for twelve missions. I wouldn't have done *anything* to hurt my bird! *It wasn't my fault!*"

Piggy again lost his composure and could no longer speak because of his uncontrollable sobbing. My heart went out to him. It was obvious that even though it wasn't his fault, he felt responsible for the loss of ten good friends and his beloved bird.

He was told to sit down. There were no sounds in the room except for Piggy's sobbing. It was like a funeral.

The inquest lasted for a few more minutes. There was some more discussion about how the oil tank, rigged by Bankhead, had probably caught fire, causing the fuel pipe to explode. Then they went into routine closing procedures, but I didn't hear much of it. My mind was spinning with what I had been hearing. I felt weak and sick to my stomach.

Some printed agreements had been prepared and were distributed to everybody in the room. We were ordered to sign them and hand them to an officer at the front of the room before we left.

The agreement stipulated that we could not discuss this situation for 50 years. If we violated the agreement, we were subject to a $10,000 fine and/or a ten year prison sentence. The colonel then assured us that if we violated the agreement we would never live to see beyond the walls of Leavenworth.

We were brought to attention, and two of the majors and the lieutenant colonel walked out. The remaining major at the front of the room said, "Dismissed," and everybody else left quickly. I sat back down, still shaking and hyperventilating.

The major started stuffing papers into his briefcase. He looked up at me and said, "I said *dismissed*."

I stood and walked up to him to say something or ask some questions, I don't remember which, but just stood in front of him for several seconds, removed the wings from my blouse, and laid them down on the table in front of him. He glanced up, briefly, and continued stuffing his papers as though I wasn't even there.

I left the room. The door guard was gone and the hallway was empty. The beautiful sounds of "A Nightingale Sang in Berkeley Square" were coming from one of the offices. I felt so completely alone.

Apparently a rapid investigation had been taking place while I was floating around on the Limey ship that picked me up. Sergeants Poundstone and Bankhead had "spilled the beans", and Major Barovik, our "fearless leader", had been taken into custody and moved into a small tent out in the boondocks at the far edge of the Bastia Airfield.

Guards were posted 24 hours a day in front of his tent and no visitors were allowed. Food and water were brought to him by a guy from a mess tent who drove a jeep. The major wasn't even allowed to visit the latrine without a guard.

I asked Rocky if he knew where Barovik was. He said he did, and drove me around the perimeter of the field until we arrived at his tent. A guard was sitting there in his jeep, and waved us off. If the guard hadn't been there I *might* have committed a *crime!*

In retrospect I remember sitting in Major Barovik's office one day after he had called all of us in for a meeting. The discussion got around to bailing out of disabled planes. The consensus was that as long as the ship was still flying, even though it was crippled, it was better to stay with it.

I had wanted to make a parachute jump since Clem Sohn became my hero. Clem was in my sister Alice's high school graduating class in 1933. He later became world famous for his "Batman" routine. Clem had become a jumper at air shows and to add a little excitement to his act, he developed a pair of folding black fabric bat wings and strapped them to his arms and legs.

Clem was soon in demand all over the country. He would exit a plane at about three thousand feet, spread his arms and legs to form the wings, and then make wide swooping turns as he plunged toward his breathless audience.

Clem was killed doing his parachute routine at an air show in Paris, France, in the summer of 1938.

I graduated from the same high school in January 1939. Our class had a bronze plaque made to honor Clem, and it was mounted on a wall in the hallway near the administration office.

With all this in my mind, I spoke up in Barovik's office and said, "Not *me*. You won't find *me* staying with a broken airplane. I'm getting out without hesitation!"

Was Barovik hoping that I would leave the plane when I saw the smoke, and that Poundstone would be able to get a good close-up of a bailout? Was he ready to sacrifice *me* to get a "scoop?" Hollywood stuntmen risk their lives all the time satisfying a director who then goes into a safe, comfortable screening room to enjoy *his* idea.

This was all purely conjecture, of course, but if it *was* true, then I'm glad Poundstone was sitting on the floor reloading when I dove out that window.

After the inquest, I was told to go up to General Twining's office. A warrant officer sitting at a desk outside his door was expecting me. "Sergeant Thompson," he said, "please sign this form, and after you do, General Twining will come out here and pin some gold bars on your shoulders. The general knows you personally and wants to make you a second lieutenant."

I wanted to read the fine print first, and the warrant officer asked me to sit down and study it. The fine print contained something I didn't like. It said I would be replacing our lieutenant who had been killed, and I would not be going home in the near future.

I also considered the fact that I had 131 rotation points. It took only 85 to be eligible to go home. The points were based on months in service, months overseas, battle stars and decorations. And I was wearing four "Hershey bars"—overseas stripes.

"No thanks," I said, "but I would like to see the general for a minute and tell him goodbye." The warrant officer stuck his head in Twining's door, then told me to go in.

General Twining and I had become good friends—as good as a general and a sergeant *could* be.

I walked into his office, stood at attention before his desk and gave him my snappiest salute. I told him I appreciated his offer to give me a commission, but right now, I just wanted to go home. Twining said he respected my decision and wished me well.

As I was leaving his office, the general said, "Sergeant Thompson, I know you missed getting the air medal by just a few hours, but you'll be going home with the EAME medal with four battle stars and another one you haven't heard about—the Presidential Unit Citation."

"Well," I said, "wonder if Colonel Roosevelt's dad will give *him* one?"

Twining chuckled, but made no comment. In one of our private moments I had told him about the photo trailer Roosevelt had taken from us.

It seemed like my escape from the B-24, with all the others lost, was miraculous. But it was *tame* compared to Jim Raley's experience that was being told around headquarters.

Jim was the tailgunner on a 17 that left Foggia to bomb a target in Austria. Just as they were approaching the target, Jim heard on the intercom that they were at 19,000 feet. A second or two later there was an explosion and Jim was thrown around inside his gun position and there was a loud ripping sound. He looked through his rear window and saw another B-17 on fire and heading toward the ground. Jim thought that since they had been in a close formation and in some clouds, they had probably collided with that plane.

"Jim was trapped inside his compartment," I was told. "His plane started spinning down. He said it was scary! They were not only spinning, but rolling and tossing around. The engines must have all quit, because it was relatively quiet. He was pinned in because of the gravitational forces and was sure he would die 19,000 feet later.

"The plane leveled out and Jim heard the sounds of a sliding impact. He closed his eyes, not wanting to witness his own death. Then he was no longer crashing, so he opened his eyes and saw pine trees all around. 'Thank God,' he thought, 'we made it.'

"Then," Jim said, "I banged and pushed on my door to get into the waist section of the plane. There *was* no waist! There was no *airplane!*"

At the interrogation at the end of the mission, it was learned that Sergeant Raley's plane had collided with another, and his plane had been cut in two between the waist gunners and his compartment *exactly* where the tail wheel had been retracted up into the fuselage.

The Boeing tech reps explained that Jim Raley's part of the airplane, the empennage, or tail section, had become an imperfect glider with the horizontal stabilizers for wings. It wasn't an *efficient* glider, but served him well enough to bring him down in a pine forest with no injuries.

There was a happy and sad ending to Raley's experience. He walked through enemy territory and into the Italian mountains for three weeks and rejoined his outfit. None of the other nine crewmen were ever heard from again.

As I was leaving General Twining's outer office, I asked the warrant officer if I could copy the "Combat Airman's Prayer" which I had seen many times hanging on the wall and he was glad to oblige. Evidently other men had wanted copies, so he had made some and had them in his desk drawer. He handed one to me.

> *Please, dear God, let me soar*
> *O'er green and yellow fields once more,*
> *Where there'll be no dirty clouds of black,*
> *bringing forth that anguished cry of "Flak!"*
> *Where sight of speck out in the blue*
> *will not mean "Watch it—fighter at two!"*
> *Where no screaming demon from out of the sun*
> *makes every man jump, and with flaming gun*
> *Endeavor to pay another life*
> *to the devil who started this world wide strife·*
> *If you don't think this too much of a boon,*
> *well, please dear God, please make it soon.*
>
> *— Anon*

Back at our villa in Bastia, the captain told me to relax and wait. He said that in a couple of weeks I would be in Naples at reppledepple—the replacement depot, being processed for shipment back to the States. He was now the head man of the combat camera unit and would probably be promoted to the rank of major. Major Barovik, still isolated in a small tent at the airfield under constant surveillance, would also shortly be going home.

I wished I could have used this down-time to do some sightseeing. The Michelangelo ceiling at the Vatican, for example. I couldn't. The Germans were there. The statue of David in Florence. I couldn't. The Germans were there. Venice? Germans! Why had the Italians put all the good stuff up north with the Krauts?

At least I could visit Pompeii and the Blue Grotto near Naples. I was being treated like a visiting senator from Washington. Why? Probably to keep me happy so I wouldn't go out to the airfield and kill a major.

This had been the biggest "snafu" I had ever seen. The Army term snafu means "Situational normal—all fouled up." Photo guys call it "Subject normal—all film underexposed."

I would not have to worry about underexposing any more film in the European, African or Middle Eastern Theater of Operations.

I couldn't help feeling bad about leaving my unit, even hating the whole killing business the way I did. But I had became a part of it. It felt like I was "running out" on my buddies before we were through with our job.

Everything I stuffed into my musette bag and barracks bags brought back recent memories. The German helmet—Biskra. The souvenirs I had bought from the Arabs—Chateaudun. The dozens of photographs I had made in England, Africa and Italy. The class "A" dress uniform I'd had customized by a tailor in Bari. Letters I had saved from my wife and mother. I could hardly lift the bags, but at least I wouldn't have to drag that tommygun back to the States.

Some of my buddies were in the room watching me pack. They were all envious. They wouldn't be going home for a while. Most of them didn't go back at all.

"Hey, Tommy, you won't have any use for that ugly German flag. Why don't you give it to me for safekeeping?"

"You don't want to take that old German helmet back, do you?"

"Here, drop this letter in the mail box when you hit the States. I want my girlfriend to think I'm home so she'll run her current boyfriend off."

I was still being treated like a celebrity. A C-47 was waiting at the airfield to fly me to the reppledepple. In Naples, a staff car drove me to the replacement depot.

None of us at the depot knew how long we would have to wait, and of course, it was a secret. After a couple of days, a convoy of meat wagons drove through the area. Then the litters started going from the meat wagons to the dock, a long brown line with basket cases stretched out on them. Some were going home to hospitals. Some were going home to die. This was the first indication that we were about to board the ship.

I started recalling comments made at the villa in Bastia just before I left.

"Hope that heathen Barovik is shot!"

"Wish I could sit in on his court-martial."

"Oh, he'll probably beat all of us back to Hollywood and be fouling something else up."

I had kept my dark thoughts to myself. Ten innocent young men were dead. A beautiful airplane taken out of action by "friendly fire." Bad dreams and mental anguish for the friends of the dead crewmen. Families of the deceased who would never be told the truth. No bodies to be buried in family plots.

I was just glad it was over. I was going home . . . .

PART FOUR

Home

Home

WE HAD ALL BEEN A LITTLE JITTERY and apprehensive when we were coming into the Mediterranean from the Atlantic because of the German submarine threat.

Now we were going *from* the Mediterranean into the Atlantic. The Germans weren't torpedoing most ships heading west because many of them were carrying prisoners of war to the U.S., so there was very little chance we would be bothered. *We* were carrying war casualties. We were a floating nightmare of torn flesh and screaming lunatics.

We had no problem going through the Strait. Many more lights were now visible at the Rock and in Morocco. It was good to see the lights being turned on again. This time we were leaving the "smooth highway" and getting back on the "country road."

On June 4, 1944 while we were sailing toward the States shortly after leaving the Strait of Gibraltar, the loudspeakers blared the news that Rome had been taken.

Rome! How I had wanted to go up there as a tourist and see Michelangelo's priceless work at the Vatican. I began to wish my trip back to the States had been delayed for a couple of weeks.

Then, two days later, we learned the Allies were attacking the continent. The invasion was on! It had started at 6:30 a.m. Following this report, whenever there was fresh news about the invasion the ship's loudspeakers would blast it out in a metallic blare.

This wasn't the only way we got our news. Although it was always a day late, the *Heave Ho*, our ship's morning newspaper, usually went into more detail. The *Heave Ho* was a two-page 8x13-inch typewritten rag, mimeographed on pulp paper. 500 copies were circulated among the 3,000 troops on board.

The first edition, dated Sunday June 4, 1944, mentioned the name of the ship—*Fred Lykes*. The name wasn't printed on the bow and the crew had not been allowed to tell us. *Fred Lykes* was a merchant ship commanded by a 32-year-old Master, Milford Hoffman. Other statistics mentioned in the first edition were that the *Lykes* was a C-3 freighter completed at Kearney, New Jersey in 1940 and converted into a troop transport in 1943. It carried 3,000 passengers and had a crew of 126 merchant marines. Our converted liner, the *Argentina,* which had taken us to Scotland, carried 5,000 men.

The first edition also warned us not to toss *Heave Ho* overboard because the uncensored paper would contain facts the Jerries would like to have. There was also an advertisement for a cartoonist, which stated, "If there is a cartoonist on board it would be appreciated if he would volunteer his services to decorate our rag."

The second issue had a couple of sketches and by the time the last issue appeared on June 12, there were some very fine "pinup" drawings that looked like Betty Grable posing without her famous one-piece swimsuit.

The editor thanked everybody who contributed items to the paper and gave his heartfelt thanks to Chaplain Kinard for his untiring efforts toward making life more pleasant for the patients and for those of us who were ambulatory.

Poop From the Bridge: Distance last 24 hours—418 miles. Average speed—17 knots. Wind—Southwesterly. Sea—Moderate. Weather—Overcast, occasional rain squalls . . . .

Many of us thought our ship would turn around and take us back to the war. The Catholic priest calmed our fears, however, when he told us that our bow was pointing west and there was no plan to do a 180° turn. "You men have had enough, and the war is going to remain behind you," he told us.

It would take awhile to make the transition from the noise of conflict to the quiet of home. A lot of us were looking back at our overseas tour of duty and wondering why our friends were dead and denied the excitement we were now feeling of going home.

The last glow of the sun streaked the cloud-banked horizon, making it a vivid red and strikingly beautiful. Then a full moon started rising out of the ocean. The stars got bright. I had never seen the Milky Way so clearly. Maybe it was because of the total blackout on board. I watched the breathtaking scene, but couldn't get the fighting on the beaches of France out of my mind. It was nighttime, but the struggle would go on through the night and into another day.

How many more days? How many more men would have to die before the politicians of the world were satisfied? Of course, killing the other man is the way we "civilized" people settle arguments. And I knew the Combat Camera Units would be covering the invasion. Then in the darkness someone started strumming a Jew's harp.

Heave Ho: Attempts of a large number of German parachutists to capture Marshal Tito's headquarters here have been frustrated, a Tito spokesman said today. All of them were either killed or captured. He added that there is heavy fighting going on in the vicinity of Bosnia.

I tried transferring my thoughts to more pleasant things. The washing of the water against the side of the ship sounded like the fountain in Potter Park in which I had waded as a child—that wonderful park with its zoo and playground.

I knew the transition back to normal days would be difficult for me, and I wondered if I would ever be able to accomplish it. I wasn't the same person who had been sent over here. I was someone I didn't know. I used to be gregarious, friendly, outgoing, sociable. Now I just wanted to be left alone. I didn't want anybody disturbing my thoughts of Duck Pond.

"Duck, you were standing so close to me—and then you were gone. Why you? Why not me?" I didn't expect I'd ever be free of that clinging ghastly memory. And the others. They had died before they had a chance to live, their memories treasured only by a handful of friends and relatives back home.

Why did they have to die? What did it prove? They simply *died* and we *lived*, that's all, and nobody knew why it was so. I had heard that time heals all wounds. How much time would it take? Would I survive the wait?

I wondered if I should try to contact Duck Pond's mother in Kansas and . . . how *could* I speak for her dead son? I had jotted down a few lines from a poem in a current *Reader's Digest*—

> *When you go home*
> *Tell them of us and say*
> *For their tomorrow*
> *We gave our today.*

The chaplain also passed out a mimeographed prayer that I folded and stuck between the pages of my little Bible—

> *Let them in Peter, they are very tired;*
> *Give them the couches where the angels sleep.*
> *Let them wake whole again to new dawns fired*
> *with sun, not war. And may their peace be deep.*
> *Remember where the broken bodies lie—*
> *God knows how young they were to have to die!*

I sat on the deck alone. Small groups of men were leaning against the rail and strolling leisurely along the deck. Several men were sitting in a circle on the deck playing cards. One of them said, "Shorty, what's the *second* thing you're going to do when you get home?"

"I'm goin' to pitch me a light-weight drunk," he replied, "What's the second thing *you're* goin' to do?"

"Well, bein' from Georgia, I'm gonna fill the table with hot buttered cornbread and milk and eat and drink 'till I have to be helped up from the chair."

Everybody looked at the quiet fellow who was studying his cards. "And you, Buzz?"

Without looking up, he said, "Take off my parachute."

I had nothing to share with them. I just wanted to be left alone with my private thoughts and reflections.

I thought about Zinkgraf, Harrington, Martini, and Tucker, my photo guys in Africa. Why hadn't I tried harder to find them when we got to Italy? I wondered if we would ever see each other again. I hoped so because a lasting and peculiar friendship is created between boys who fight together. No other fraternity on earth is like it.

It was hard for me to realize that *I* was still alive. I started counting up the nine lives I had cashed in. The first one was probably used just before the war when my squadron was sent to the Philippines.

My mother had come from Michigan to Savannah on a Greyhound bus to see me off. Wilma and my mother said good-by in our apartment, and I returned to the base. At this time we didn't know where we were going. A long truck convoy was parked on the base and men by the hundreds were climbing up into the rear of the 6x6s with their barracks bags.

The trucks just sat there. We wondered why. We were all anxious to be on our way to whatever kind of adventure awaited us because we had already gone through the hard part of saying good-by to our loved ones.

A master sergeant looked up into our truck and called out some names. I was one of the names called. "Jump down," he said, "you're staying here."

"Why am I going to have to stay here?"

"Because you are part of a cadre to train new men."

I dragged my barracks bag over to the photo section and walked in. It was empty except for Master Sergeant Shockley, the NCOIC of the section.

"Well, I'm back, Shock," I said. "What's going on?"

"You are going to stay behind this time and help me form and train a new photo section."

"Why?"

"Because you and I are the only ones on the base with the training and experience to do it. I can't do it by myself because I don't have your aerial photography training."

The trucks left the base and headed for the railroad station, and I went back to the apartment.

I walked in the front door, plopped my barracks bag down on the floor in front of my two crying women and said, "What's for lunch?"

Wilma and my mother gasped, wiped their eyes and said in unison, "What happened?" They were acting like they had seen a ghost. Their tears hadn't stopped flowing since we had spoken our good-bys a couple of hours earlier.

After they had regained their composure, they listened to the cadre story. Wilma said, "There's a reason—*everything* happens for the best."

For me, it *did* happen for the best. My squadron arrived at Clark Field in the Philippines on Saturday, December 6, 1941. The next day the Japs struck Pearl Harbor and Clark Field simultaneously.

At Clark Field, the Japanese caught a squadron of P-40 fighters being fueled and two B-17 squadrons lined up wing-tip to wing-tip. We couldn't have made things more convenient for them. It was a "Little Pearl Harbor." Sixteen of the 18 Fortresses were destroyed and 55 P-40s and 30 other planes were left burning. Half of the men of my squadron were killed during the bombing, and most of the rest died on the Bataan Death March. I was told I was probably the sole survivor of my squadron.

The rest of my nine lives were used up so fast that I lost track of them. It was a lot more than *nine*, though. This theory applies to cats, but people must have a mysterious way of prolonging the inevitable.

My reminiscing continued. Sitting peacefully on the deck staring out at the horizon made it easy.

I had left my four photo guys in an Italian mud hole. Again I wondered what happened to them. We had been through so much together. Some of the combat camera guys were not coming back from their missions. Wonder if *any* of them would survive? These fellows had a very short life expectancy.

We were all trying to forget the terrible slaughter we were leaving behind and concentrate on the peaceful life that was waiting for us at home.

And bets were being made as to who on board would be the first to see the Statue of Liberty.

Two more days passed. Somebody shouted, "We're here! We're in New York! I just saw something through the fog!"

Slowly and silently we came out of the fog into clear sunshine. "There she is!" somebody shouted. And there she was, still standing majestically, holding her torch aloft with her right hand and cradling a tablet in her left arm. I felt a little choked up because it seemed she was shouting, "Welcome home boys, we're still here safe and sound. We're still free. I'll protect you now."

We were given our orders before debarkation in the New York harbor. I was given ten days leave and told to report to the Hotel Patrician in Miami Beach after I went home to see my wife. By coincidence, I arrived in Savannah on Father's Day, Sunday, June 18, 1944. I had met Wilma on Mother's Day, 1941.

Getting used to the peace and quiet of Savannah was not as difficult as I had thought it would be. Terrible nightmares were awakening me, however.

We were allowed to take our wives with us to Miami Beach for R and R—rest and recuperation. After a pleasant train ride to Miami, we checked into the plush Patrician Hotel. It was right on the beach and was the most luxurious place either of us had ever seen. It was completely full of Air Force men who had returned from both major theaters of operation. In fact, most of the hotels on the beach were now occupied with GIs and their wives. It was a time for celebration—never had I seen so many happy faces! What a contrast to just a month before.

For the next ten days we were given the red carpet treatment by both military personnel and civilians. Uncle Sam seemed to be going all out to reward us for our time spent overseas.

Every morning we had to report to various military officers for debriefings, physical exams, sessions with the shrinks and so forth. One of the debriefing officers asked those of us who had flown combat missions if we had seen any German aircraft flying with no propellers. We all thought he was nuts! It wasn't until later in the air war that German jet aircraft were observed attacking our planes. Then it was off for fun and games—boat trips to the keys, picnics, food, live entertainment, movies, and more food! And no kidneys or armoured pig. It was incredible!

One afternoon I spotted a familiar face in the crowded street. It looked like Al Cooper from my old squadron—the one that was wiped out in the Philippines. But it *couldn't* be Cooper because I had been told that *I* was the only survivor of that squadron. The fellow saw me at the same time and exclaimed, "Tommy, is that really you?"

"Al?"

"Yes, it's *me!*"

"But I was told you were dead—*everybody* was dead."

"Let's sit down over here and I'll tell you about it. Those of us who lived through the bombing on Clark Field were marched to a Jap prisoner of war camp. Lots of the guys died on the way. Life in the camp was terrible. We were all trying to survive on grasshoppers and a handful of rice once in a while.

"We were forced to dig coal in a mine and the Japs whipped us when we stopped to rest. They shot a lot of guys for no apparent reason. Naturally we all had only one thing on our minds—escape!

"One by one our buddies were being shot going over the fence or trying to crawl under it. 'Pop' Durham was my best friend and he couldn't take it any longer, so he jumped on the fence in broad daylight knowing what would happen. He was mowed down by a machine gun."

I gasped. My heart was pounding! Pop was the fellow who had taken me over to Wilma's house in Savannah that Mother's Day. Tears streamed down my cheeks.

Waking up each morning without a loaded tommygun at arms reach and without having to sweat out another mission through a German flak-infested inferno was becoming a simple luxury.

We picked up our new orders. We were to report to the photo section at Coffeyville Army Air Field in Kansas. All we knew about Coffeyville was that back in the "wild west" days, the Dalton boys had shot up the place and were killed in a gun fight. And now there was an Army air field there. Wilma and I headed for Coffeyville on a train.

Coffeyville Army Air Field turned out to be a training base for F-5 photo recon pilots. After finding a small apartment in town, I reported to the base photo lab. I was surprised and almost speechless when I found Otto Zinkgraf and Hal Harrington in the building. If I had spent more time searching instead of worrying about them in the Bari mud hole perhaps they could have been located. I was delighted to see them!

Otto and his new wife, Roma, moved into our apartment building. Otto's wife called him Toby, so that's what we called him from then on. Toby explained he had had that nickname since high school. We also met fellow neighbors Bill and Lib Crisp. Bill was a staff sergeant and had been in Africa and Italy during the time I was there, but I hadn't met him.

Bill was wearing some very impressive ribbons on his uniform. Among others, he had 12 Air Medals, two Presidential Citations, the EAME ribbon with six battle stars and one that caught my attention—the DFC—Distinguished Flying Cross. Bill was the first fellow I had met in person with this high decoration. He was very modest about all of this and would point to a lesser ribbon and jokingly say, "This ribbon represents my Good Conduct Medal. It's my favorite one. I got it for being a good boy."

Crisp had been assigned to the 416th Squadron of the 99th Bomb Group, which was composed of B-17s. He had completed his aerial photography and camera repair training at Lowry Field in Denver as I had, but he became a photographer-observer.

I asked Bill to tell me about his experiences over there.

"We landed in Oran and then settled at Navarin between Chateaudun and Constantine for awhile. We were at Navarin for a short time, then formed a truck convoy and moved to Tunis.

"On the way, we stopped the convoy for a ten-minute break beside an enormous grape vineyard. The grapes were ripe. Every man in the convoy had started filling his steel helmet with grapes when a French farmer appeared carrying an antique double-barreled shotgun. He threatened to shoot us if we didn't stop stealing his grapes.

"The Frenchman was faced with 75 or 100 .50-caliber machine guns capable of firing 1200 rounds a minute, but he had the drop on us so we backed down and left.

"We arrived in Tunis and were told to dig our foxholes immediately because the Germans came over every night with their JU-88s and dropped 500-pound bombs. The ground was so hard that I dug mine only deep enough so I could squat down and bend my head over in a fetal position just below ground level.

"The Krauts came over at 9 p.m. the first night. A 500-pounder exploded close to my shallow trench and blew me right out of it. As soon as my feet hit the ground I was digging again. By daylight I had a hole so deep I could stand up in it, all six feet-five inches of me, and just barely peer out over the top standing on my toes.

"The technical sergeant in charge of our photo section flew four missions and decided he'd had enough, so I volunteered to take his place as an aerial photographer-observer. The squadron commander told me I'd have to go over to the dispensary and ask the flight surgeon to give me a physical before going on the next morning's mission. The doctor was a major and he wasn't there. I was sent to his tent where I found him busy preparing for a party. Doc was anxious to get to the party so he didn't waste too much time with the exam.

'Sergeant, how tall are you?'
'Six feet, five inches, Sir.'
'That's one inch too tall.'
'Sorry, Sir.'

'Have you ever flown?'

'Yes, Sir, as a passenger in a Piper Cub.'

'Hell, anybody who looks as healthy as you *can't* have anything wrong with him. Gimme those papers and I'll sign them. I've got a party waiting.'

"I was elated! I went to the supply tent, drew my flight suit, parachute and a .45 with shoulder holster and went to bed.

"Tommy, you asked which missions stand out in my mind. Well, there's a story in every one of the 52 missions, but a couple of them really got my attention.

"Our B-17s joined some B-24s for the second Ploesti oil field raid. We went in at tree-top level. The first wave over the target started fires that blazed higher than we were flying in the second wave. The thought passed through my mind that this is how hell looks when it's running at full capacity. I got a lot of good shots with the K-20 hand-held camera. We lost a bunch of planes.

"Another unforgettable raid was to the Messerschmitt aircraft plant near Weiner-Neustadt, Austria. We were flying out of Tunis, so we couldn't make it all the way there and back. We landed at a field near Palermo in Sicily that had been taken from the Germans only a few days earlier.

"We topped the tanks and proceeded to Austria. We had terrible fights getting to the target and back. There were bits and pieces of planes being blown all over the sky. Burning aircraft were spinning down. The sky was dotted with parachutes. This turned out to be the roughest of my 52 missions. We lost 70 bombers—40% of our force!

"Our ship got back to Sicily with two dead on board and 117 bullet holes in the waist section of the fuselage. The vertical stabilizer was shot in half.

"Then we left for a target in Italy and were circling over the bay of Tunis when the electrical wiring on the front wall of the bomb bay caught fire. The pilot gave orders to abandon ship and most of the crew lost no time getting out.

"Four of us were left—the pilot, co-pilot, engineer and me. I was standing at the door with my hands on the frame looking down wondering if I should jump when the engineer came up behind me and planted his size-12 boot in my rear. I fumbled for the rip cord, found it, and gave it a hard jerk. Boy, that whoosh and pop above my head sounded good.

"I landed flat on my back in a barley field and by the time I was up on my knees, several Arabs were surrounding me jabbering and pointing. They each had a long knife and I wasn't sure what they had in mind, so I pulled my .45 out of the shoulder holster and slid the top back to pop a shell into the chamber. They scattered. Later I learned they just wanted to buy my nylon parachute. I didn't know that at the time or I would have sold it to them.

"My job as an aerial photographer-observer was to spot potential future targets and photograph them. I also made verticals of the bomb blasts. When I was making shots with the K-17 camera in the floor of the radio room and the German fighters were pestering us, I'd jump up, grab the radio operator's gun, and start blasting them. Of course I didn't take it away from the radio operator, but when he wasn't using it, I had more fun than I had down on the farm shooting doves. I was always a good dove shooter, and I lucked out with Me-109s also. I was credited with two kills with this gun.

"We were going after a target in Greece on Easter Sunday. We were high and could pick up radio stations beamed toward us from thousands of miles away. I was fooling around with the radio dial when I picked up 'Swing and Sway with Sammy Kay' from New York City. Loud and clear! The whole crew listened to Sammy through the intercom while the bombardier did his countdown to bomb-release over the target. It was quite a contrast from sweet music to the death and destruction below."

"Bill," I asked, "please explain how you earned your DFC."

"Well, it was by accident. I heard that most decorations are earned because men make an effort to get them. I don't believe that's true because in the heat of battle you act by instinct.

"We had fragmentation bombs on board. We hated to haul them because they were so dangerous. They came in clusters of five and when the bomb bay doors are open and the little nose propellers spin off, they are armed and will go off when they hit something.

"The guys were moving back from the radio room getting ready to bail out. I didn't know why they were doing that because my intercom was out and I couldn't hear what they were shouting. They were all pointing back toward the bomb bay. I thought they wanted me to go in there for some reason. I stepped onto the narrow catwalk in the bomb bay and looked around. The bay doors were open and I saw one cluster of frags dangling on a wire under the plane. With this thing swinging and blowing around it might hit the plane and we would all be nothing but bits and pieces in the sky.

"In a second or two it occurred to me that I'd better do *something,* so I picked up a spare machine gun barrel and started beating on the wire holding the bombs. It finally broke and the bomb fell beneath the plane. I don't remember how the DFC citation reads, but it had something to do with saving a plane and possibly ten lives."

While Toby Zinkgraf, Hal Harrington and I were reminiscing about our two years overseas, I learned that they had lost track of Tucker and Martini shortly after they set up their photo lab in the 15th Air Force headquarters building in Bari.

This was an *incredible* coincidence! They were running a lab on the *second* floor of the same building where the 9th Combat Camera Unit had an office on the *ground* floor. And we had never run into each other!

Toby and I were looking through the shots we made at Djemela, the Roman ruin near Tunis, and I selected my favorite negative and made a bromoil.

Clarence Koch, a corporal working in the lab, was a photo artist who made bromoils. He was one of very few Americans who understood the process. A lot of people in France still made them because it was a French art form.

Koch still had bromoil materials he had bought before the war. Everything had to be bought from a French supplier. The ink, brushes, paper and everything necessary to make a print couldn't be found anywhere else.

Under Koch's close supervision, I tackled my first bromoil. No wonder it hadn't caught on in the States. Americans were probably too impatient because it was time consuming and difficult. I had never heard of this art form, but found out that prints could be bought in art salons in New York City.

After we finished the bromoil print, the tall, stately Roman columns no longer looked like an enlarged photograph, but now had the appearance of a detailed charcoal drawing.

I gave the print a title—"Lost Empire," and entered it in the 3rd Air Force annual art contest. After the judging was over, I was called into the base commander's office to receive a handshake and the prize money for *first place!*

Three weeks later, on May 7, 1945, the war in Europe ended. Then on August 6 the *Enola Gay,* a B-29 piloted by Colonel Paul W. Tibbets Jr., dropped an atomic bomb on Hiroshima, Japan. When Japan failed to answer President Truman's demands for surrender, a second bomb was dropped on Nagasaki.

It was over. We said our good-bys to Bill Crisp, Toby Zinkgraf and Hal Harrington and went our separate ways into civilian life.

Where Are They Now?

WE OFTEN THINK OF THE WAR YEARS and about some of our unforgettable friends. A lot of them didn't make it. The American airmen casualty statistics are awesome—24,288 were killed, 18,804 were wounded, 31,436 were taken prisoner and 18,696 are still missing and presumed dead. This is a total of 93,224. Only the infantry suffered more casualties. It was a hard-won victory.

Today I look at my children, grandchildren and great-grandchildren and realize that only fractions of inches between me and a bullet or a piece of shrapnel decided whether or not they would be here on this earth. They are living by a stroke of fate.

When we see an old movie with Martha Raye, it brings back happy thoughts. The four girls, Martha, Kay Francis, Carol Landis and Mitzie Mayfair returned to Hollywood after having driven around North Africa putting on their show for thousands of GIs. Carol Landis sent a hand-written letter to my wife, Wilma, telling her that she had met me and everything seemed to be going well. The girls made a movie called *Four Jills in a Jeep,* based on their travels in Africa entertaining the troops.

Ernie Pyle's book, *Here Is Your War,* is still in our bookcase and we have fond thoughts about him every time we see it.

Ernie went to the Pacific to cover the war from that side of the world. He was on the tiny island of Ie Shima with the Marines. Ernie was in a jeep that came under Japanese machine gun fire and took cover in a ditch beside the road. When he raised his head to look for a companion, he died instantly with a bullet through his left temple.

His body was recovered under fire by some of the Marines, who found in his pocket a rough draft of a column he had intended to release immediately after the war. In it, Ernie urged the living, in their joy, not to forget that the price of victory had been earned by the dead. Some of his handwritten lines were:

" . . . the unnatural sight of cold dead men scattered over the hillsides and in the ditches along the high rows of hedge throughout the world.

"Dead men by mass production—in one country after another —month after month and year after year. Dead men in winter and dead men in summer.

"Dead men in such familiar promiscuity that they become monotonous.

"Dead men in such monstrous infinity that you come almost to hate them . . . ."

The National Memorial Cemetery of the Pacific in Punchbowl Crater on Oahu is Ernie's final resting place. It is on a high hill overlooking Honolulu.

In 1982, Wilma, and I rented a car and drove around the beautiful grounds until we found where he is buried. There is a simple, small, flat stone at the head of his grave. His name and dates of birth and death are chiseled into the stone.

I wanted to make a snapshot of the marker, but knew the lettering would not stand out in relief because it was cloudy and the deep lettering would not have shadows to contrast with the surface.

Wilma had wanted to meet Ernie after the war because I had told her so much about him, but this was a very sad way of doing it. I started talking to him mentally and told him I was still in the photo business, but couldn't make a good shot of his headstone because of the clouds. I even mentioned this out loud to Wilma.

Suddenly a shaft of sunlight broke through the overcast and spotlighted his grave. It didn't shine on the graves on either side of his—only *his!* A cold chill went down my spine. Wilma felt it also. I made two quick shots of the stone—and the shaft of light disappeared . . .

"Well, Ernie, this lets me know you heard me. Sleep well, sweet prince. See ya later."

Colonel Beirne Lay Jr. died in 1982 at age 73.

Kay Summersby, dear old Pistol Packin' Mama, still shows up in TV documentaries occasionally.

Kay and General Ike Eisenhower became very close friends. After Germany surrendered and Ike was getting ready to return to the States, he wrote a letter to his boss, General George Marshall. In this letter, he said he was going to divorce his wife, Mamie, and marry an English woman. (Kay was actually Irish.)

General Marshall was *furious!* He told Ike that if he did a stupid thing like that, he would throw him out of the Army and make his life miserable.

Kay Summersby's book, *Past Forgetting—My Love Affair with Dwight D. Eisenhower,* was written after Ike died, and not released —at her request—until after *she* died. She had told the publisher that her kidney cancer would claim her shortly and she wanted the *book* to do the speaking for her.

Kay died. The book was published. It spoke for her. Ike's wife, Mamie, learned a few things Ike had probably neglected to mention about his campaigns.

Pistol Packin' Mama—you were quite a gal . . . .

"Buster" Rhoades enlisted in the Royal Canadian Air Force the same day Glen Wonnacatt enlisted. Buster was sent to northern Ontario to Manning Depot, a flight-training field. He was too tall to fit in the cockpit of a Spitfire, so he was put into the rear seat of an observation plane. They couldn't close the hatch—too tall. He then found the right place—tailgunner.

Buster died in 1994.

Glen Wonnacott was also sent to Manning Depot for training. After qualifying in the Spitfire, he was sent to England just in time to become involved in the "Battle of Britain."

He fought daily over the English Channel and was finally shot down by an Me-109. He spent over six months in a hospital being put back together. He then transferred to the U.S. Navy and ferried planes from a factory in California to England. On one of these trips, he crashed and spent some more time in a hospital.

Glen was an air traffic controller after the war in Sault Saint Marie, Michigan, when he died in 1982.

Toby Zinkgraf is retired and living in his hometown of Plymouth, Wisconsin.

Bill Crisp is retired and living in Roanoke, Virginia.

Hal Harrington is deceased.

Nobody knows where Martini and Tucker are.

Major Ivo Barovik of the 9th Combat Camera Unit could not be located. It is presumed that all the rest of the men of the 9th were killed in action.

In the spring of 1984, Wilma and I traveled to England and Italy. We wanted to retrace my steps in North Africa, but were advised against it by our State Department because the Arabs were still killing Americans exploring around our old battlegrounds.

London, of course, did not resemble the London of 1942—not *one* battlescar was visible.

Little 12-year-old Angelo, from Villa Angela, is still fresh in our minds. Wilma had heard so much about him while he was my opera companion in Bari, that we decided to try to find him.

We traveled to Italy and found that a high-rise apartment building had completely obliterated the magnificent Villa Angela and the lovely grounds on which it sat. The neighborhood was no longer recognizable. Quaint old Via Capurso had become a modern four-lane highway.

A search of the Bari telephone directory turned up 33 Siniorellis, but only *one* Angelo. He wasn't the one. None of the Siniorellis knew *my* Angelo. The Magistrato di Polizia (police) were of no help.

Addio, Angelo. Arrivederci . . . .

In Italy, we stood on the island of Capri and looked out over the Tyrrhenian Sea towards France. I had a mental picture of the incident that caused me to plunge into the nearby Mediterranean a half-century ago. I could see the plane going down in flames— the memory was as vivid as if it had happened yesterday.

Out there somewhere, I thought, are my 10 companions whose names I did not know, entombed in a four-engine aluminum coffin at the bottom of the sea, along with probably hundreds of other men resting inside their four-engine tombs.

Envoi

WE WERE GONE A VERY LONG TIME. We saw and did and felt things the folks we left at home will never know or comprehend. But my *buddies* will understand:

Listen, my friends—you whose hearts still beat after a half century; listen on a still day while you are standing at the edge of a quiet airfield, with only the faint cool breeze blowing, and once again you will hear the thunder of the engines. You will hear the excited cries in your headphones—*"Bandits at 3 o'clock!"* You will hear the explosive chatter of the guns. You will hear the groans of your buddy as he bleeds on the frozen floor. You will hear the welcome screech of tires touching the runway . . . it will all be there.

Listen . . . .

Acknowledgements

This book would not have seen the light of day without the enthusiasm, expertise and friendship of my manuscript editor and typist, Heather Lynn Chaboya.

For their invaluable assistance in validating and proofreading the rough draft, I am grateful to Sue Rainey, Eric Stracco, and Harriet Smith.

Mason Rutherford was always at my side in the darkroom while I was working on the photographs. Wish he had been in my photo unit overseas.

My friend, Max Conyer, flew in several times to encourage me to plod along and complete the manuscript.

A special thanks goes to Francis A. "Pete" Lyon, the Oscar-winning editor/director who reviewed the manuscript and offered many valuable suggestions.

And finally, my wife, Wilma, cheerfully read the manuscript and refused to let me get away with anything but my best effort.

Stars and Swastikas: the Survivors

by Robert "Bob" Thompson

*For all the airmen whose stories
appear in this book, and to the
memory of Colonel Beirne Lay, Jr.
who did not live to read his story.*

Stars and Swastikas: the Survivors
is published as a supplement to
Flying in Coffin Corner
Library of Congress Catalog Card No. 95-60453
ISBN 0-9639519-1-2
Published by McAlister Press, Sahuarita, Arizona
Copyright © 1995 by Robert L. Thompson
All rights reserved.
Manufactured in the United States of America

Special thanks to Frida Jung, Hans Timmerman, Otto Buehler, and
Klaus Heinermann for assistance with the German translations.

The Survivors

*The cream of the Allies' and of Germany's young manhood meet in a
battle the like of which has never been seen before and never will
again. It is the last broad blaze of a glory that has vanished from
war . . . incredibly swift, a deadly game played out five miles above
the earth with no boundaries but the limitless blue horizons.*

—WINSTON S. CHURCHILL

FOR HALF A CENTURY the stories of their accomplishments had
gradually turned to dust—their names swept into the shadows of the
dead. But some were still alive. Where were they? Would they talk
about their painful experiences?

Retirement had made it possible for me to roam through the States
and visit Germany to locate them; the pilots who flew with stars on
their wings—the men who flew aircraft decorated with swastikas. It
would be interesting to hear *both* sides. A few gentlemen were found
and their stories were so fascinating and revealing that it seemed important to share them with others . . . this book was the only way.

STARS

Colonel Beirne Lay, Jr.

The search started in Los Angeles, California. Beirne Lay, Jr., whom I had met while we were both stationed in England during the war, and wrote about in my book *Flying In Coffin Corner,* was now a screenwriter and I thought he'd probably have a good story.

While visiting the publicity office at the 20th Century-Fox Studio, I was told how to find Beirne. He lived in Brentwood, a stylish community in West Los Angeles, not far from the studio.

Beirne's wife, Philippa, answered the door chimes and after learning of my reason for the visit, asked me to come in. She quickly prepared me for the distressing appearance of the man I hadn't seen for half a century.

At first, Beirne didn't recognize or remember me. I wouldn't have known him either because he was suffering from cancer and hardly resembled the dashing young major I remembered from so many years ago. And of course, age had taken its toll. When I reminded him of the project we worked on together—the history of the Eighth Air Force—and the Mozart concert we attended in London, a smile spread across his face and the reminiscing started.

"Beirne, I was very pleased when you got the Motion Picture Academy Award nomination for Best Screenplay for *Twelve O'Clock High.* I boasted to all my friends that I knew you."

"Thank you. It won the Oscar for Best Picture of 1949 and my friend Gregory Peck picked up an Oscar for Best Male Actor."

"You have written several screen plays that I like, such as *Jet Pilot, Strategic Air Command* and *Command Decision.*"

"Yes, most of my stories have involved airplanes and pilots. *Jet Pilot,* though, was a *disaster* in my opinion. Jules Furthman, the producer, got his hands on my script and ran over to Howard Hughes with it. It was Hughes' company and the two of them *murdered* the thing. Because of their constant changes it took *seven years* to complete the film. I thought the finished product was dull and tedious and was happy when Jules decided to take credit as the head writer. John Wayne and Janet Leigh are good actors but they couldn't clean up the mess Hughes made."

"I'm always interested in how a man learns his craft."

"Well, I suppose it started at Saint Paul's School in Concord, New Hampshire and later at Yale."

"Do you still listen to Mozart?"

"Oh yes, and my *favorite* composer, Rachmaninoff."

Mrs. Lay sat some cookies and coffee on the end table between us and Beirne said, "Thank you, Luddy."

"Beirne, I heard that you were shot down on 'D' Day and were presumed dead."

"Well, not exactly. It wasn't 'D' Day and as you can see, I'm still very much alive."

"If you don't mind I'd like to turn my recorder on and hear your story."

"First of all, I was brought down by flak over Chateaudun in France on May 11, 1944, 26 days *before* 'D' Day, while I was leading my 487th Bomb Group of B-24s. The 487th had been given to me a short time earlier, and we had been operating only five days before my incident."

"Being a group commander, you had probably been promoted from the rank of major, hadn't you?"

"Yes, I was a lieutenant colonel, and it was an awesome responsibility. There were 47 activities and 2,700 men in may command."

"Activities?"

"Yes, such as the hospital, photo lab, bomb dumps, aircraft and engine maintenance, armament, mess hall and so forth. It was about like running a fairly large corporation."

"It's a coincidence but the plane I bailed out of was also a B-24. Tell me about your jump."

"We were on our way to bomb the marshaling yards at Chaumont, France. According to our intelligence officer we could expect plenty of flak over Chaumont, but probably few, if any, German fighters. We were each carrying five 1,000-pound general purpose bombs. The flak warning was bad news because our base altitude was only 12,000 feet, which was very low for heavy bombers and it seemed almost like suicide.

"I was in the co-pilots seat and the co-pilot was riding the tail-gun position as a rear observer. We were three hours into the mission when the flak started blasting us from the batteries at Chateaudun. We were riddled pretty badly. Two engines were out, an aileron had been shot away and the bombardier in the nose had been injured. I ordered 'abandon ship' and was the last one out—went through the nose hatch.

"The chute opened just in time but the ship had beat me to the ground and was blazing and sending up a column of black smoke. For a few seconds it looked like I would become a part of the bonfire but luckily I landed a short distance away and ran like hell! The bombs hadn't gone off because they weren't armed, but would explode as soon as they were hot enough to detonate.

"I was a safe distance from the wreck and flat on my stomach when the bombs went off. I thought that I was probably the only guy who had heard his own bombs go off on enemy soil.

"The co-pilot from the tail had landed close to me, and we hid our chutes and headed for the nearest barn for refuge. A couple of Frenchmen had seen us dash into the barn and came in to help us. They gave us some food and water. I spoke a little French and asked them to help us contact the underground. They were too frightened to help us because the Germans had been shooting anyone who helped the allies in any way.

"We wandered for days trying to find the Maquis, sleeping in barns and being refused help. We were given some civilian clothes, however, and kept on trying in vain to contact the underground. About two weeks after being shot down, we found an English-speaking lady living in a huge chateau. She was actually an English woman and wanted to help us but feared for her life. We understood and continued our wanderings.

"Shortly thereafter, we made contact with the underground and they took us to a farm where we became field workers. The longer we worked there, the more we looked like French laborers. It wasn't bad. We had plenty of fresh fruit right off the trees and always very good meals.

"We kept asking to be sent on our way back to England, but were told that it was impossible for the time being. Finally we heard the news about 'D' Day on the radio and wondered how much longer we would have to labor for fourteen hours a day. By then, we had become part of the French farm family.

"Finally, on August 13, 1944, three months after being shot down, the Maquis came to the farm and loaded us into one of their rickety trucks and drove like crazy to the U.S. lines and turned us over to one of Patton's armored infantry divisions. It didn't take us long to get back to England on a Gooney-bird—C-47—and from there to the States."

"Did you ever have a chance to see your French farm family again?"

"Yes. I had promised the family that I would come back someday. I owed them a lot, because they had daily risked their lives to hide me. If the Germans had found me they would have shot the family.

"In 1956, twelve years after I had left their farm, I came back and we had a tearful, hugging reunion."

Beirne seemed to be getting tired and looked uncomfortable so I said goodbye and walked to the door with his wife.

"I didn't want to tire him any more, Mrs. Lay, but I'd like to know if he was awarded any decorations."

"Yes, he has an Air Medal, a Purple Heart and the Distinguished Flying Cross."

Since I was in the motion picture studio area, it seemed like a good idea to try to locate members of my old outfit—the 9th Combat Camera Unit. The men had all worked in various studios before the war. It took a few days to make the rounds, but since I had a list of names and the studios where they had worked, I felt that somebody would point me in the right direction to run them down.

It was almost a lost cause because of the passage of time and only one lead was uncovered. A retired gentleman from the Disney Studio had known Donald "Mouse" Morris before he left for military service. Mouse was one of the twelve enlisted men in our combat camera unit and had worked in the ink and paint department at Disney. The gentleman told me that Mouse had not returned and was presumed dead. He also remarked that from what he had heard, none of the other men had survived the war.

STARS

Captain Jack Miller

Back in Green Valley, Arizona, where we had just retired, we entered the Green Valley Baptist Church one morning and I noticed that "Reverend Jack Miller, Pastor," was printed on the program.

All during the service I kept thinking that he was somebody I'd met—at least his name was familiar. This bothered me for awhile until I finally asked him where we had run into each other.

"I don't know where it could have been, Bob," he said.

"Did I meet you in Africa or Italy?"

"No, I've never been there."

One day Jack dropped a remark that led me to believe he might have been an Air Force pilot. When I asked him about it, he said that he had served in World War II and the Korean War. He then changed the subject.

Okay, I thought, he doesn't want to elaborate so I won't bother him.

Later when I asked his wife, Tomi, about it, she told me, "Well, it's possible the articles about him in *Life Magazine* and *Reader's Digest* are in the back of your mind."

"Yeah! That's it!" I exclaimed. "Now I remember his name and the incredible story about him. Do you have copies of those magazines?"

"I suppose so. They are probably down in the bottom of an old cardboard box."

Jack was still not willing to dwell on the subject, but Tomi cooperated and found what I wanted. They were the December 17, 1951 issue of *Life* and the March, 1952 copy of *Reader's Digest*.

This was quite a coincidence. The pastor of our church had become one of my heroes years ago when his daring exploit in Korea was made public.

Life Magazine headline: "*Two jets Carry a Third at 30,000 Feet*"
Reader's Digest headline: "*Piggy-back Rescue at 30,000 Feet*"
Police Gazette, August 1961, headline: "*Cheating Death at Six Miles Up*"

These magazines and other periodicals and newspapers gave astonished readers Jack Miller's incredible story. One writer summed up his article . . . "snatched back from the brink of death by the finest exhibition of precision flying in the annals of either war or peacetime aviation." Another . . . "an incredible maneuver unprecedented in aviation history . . . ."

Captain Jack Miller and his two close buddies were racing their F-84 Thunderjets back through MIG Alley after having made good hits on North Korean railroad yards. They were doing over 500 mph at 32,000 feet when the flight leader passed out from oxygen deficiency.

Jack saw his friend go into a steep dive to the left and thought he was practicing evasive action or something. He kept diving for several thousand feet then did a pitch-up, which meant he had gone through the speed of sound.

"That was characteristic of the plane," Jack said. "Then he climbed back to about 30,000 feet and leveled out. I pulled up beside him and noticed that his head was resting against his canopy, then suddenly he slumped forward. I knew right away what was wrong. Oxygen deficiency."

Remembering how he used to nudge hung-up bombs under P-47 wings with his own wing tip to shake them loose during W.W.II, Jack radioed the other wingman and told him to tuck his wing under the distressed pilot's left wing and he would do the same with the right wing.

It worked! Invisible air cushions from the two wings kept the rescued plane flying straight and level until they had gently eased him down to about 13,500 feet where the unconscious pilot could breathe "good air."

"Jack, was this miraculous save the reason you decided to go into the ministry?"

"No, I'm afraid not. That decision was made sometime later."

Reverend Jack Miller now has the number one spot on my list of aviation heroes. Lindbergh, Rickenbacker and Doolittle are the others.

It took another 15 years before the good Reverend would open up about his World War II experiences, but when he did, some *more* incredible stories saw the light.

Jack began, "We came over to England in the spring of 1944 on the French liner *Normandie,* which was damaged by fire in a New York harbor after the war. I'll cut it a little short and just describe some of the missions I'll never forget.

"We flew our P-47s out of England and over to Paris just to look around for targets of opportunity. We couldn't see anything but the top of the Eiffel Tower sticking up through the fog and smog. After making a wide circle over Paris, I looked out of my window and there sat four Jerries flying 109s. I turned into them but got into a high-speed stall that I couldn't get out of. The Jerries went down and under me and got our flight commander. They all dropped into the soup and disappeared.

"On June 6, 1944, at the start of the D-day invasion, we took off at 4 o'clock in the morning. It was dark and there was a complete overcast. The ceiling was probably 500 feet.

"We got over to the Normandy beachhead and patrolled back and forth expecting to encounter German fighters. We sat over the beachhead and witnessed the most amazing 4th of July fireworks display you can imagine. The Navy was throwing huge shells up into enemy positions. We learned later that many of the shells fell short and killed a lot of our own infantry.

"We patrolled the beach at a very low altitude to support the infantry as they hit the beach-heads, but it was nearly impossible to shoot because we were afraid of hitting our own men.

"You fellows in the heavy bomb groups had been in 'Operation Pointblank,' which wiped out the German's ability to get anything into the air. In fact, General Eisenhower told the troops just before they started across the channel that they wouldn't see any German aircraft over them during their landing. He said, 'Any planes you see will be ours.' We weren't certain of that, but sure enough, there were no Krauts.

"But the destruction and carnage along the beach was incredible! We flew back and forth on the deck and saw more ships than any human being had ever seen at one glance. German and American shells were exploding on the beach. There was a gigantic litter of wreckage for miles along the shoreline. Countless bodies were floating face down in the water. Bodies of soldiers were lying in long rows covered with blankets. The uncollected bodies were still sprawled in grotesque shapes half-buried in the sand. I couldn't begin to describe the vast and startling wreckage of man and material.

"We returned to England and went back later in the afternoon to fly another cover mission. We had just been given permission to use the HVAR (High Velocity Air Rocket) and they were awesome!

"Twenty-four hours after the beach-head was secured, the engineers threw down a steel landing mat just beyond the Normandy beach, and eight of us, in two flights, landed there. We were then transferred from England to France and began our European tour.

"There were a lot of 'bugs' in the Republic Thunderbolts before I got one. Pilots had called them 'Repulsive Scatterbolts' and all kinds of nasty names. Finally everything was ironed out and then *everybody* liked them. And why not—they carried a big load of armament. They had eight .50 caliber machine guns in the wings, they could carry four 5-inch HVAR rockets, a couple of 500-pound bombs and belly or wing tanks. And they could take a *lot* of punishment! They weighed seven tons, *twice* as much as a Spitfire. The 'Jugs,' as we called them, had enormous 2,300 horsepower Pratt and Whitney engines.

"We were now living in pup-tents and eating C-rations, which was quite a come-down from what we had in England. We lived this way for several months as we flew support for General Patton and his tank units.

"Every time Patton would move up, the engineers would throw down steel landing mats and we would move up right behind him. We were constantly on the move. We existed solely to support Patton.

"His forward controller would radio back to us and say they had a road-block of tanks, 88s, or whatever, and give us the coordinates. Then we would go out and clear a path for Patton with our rockets, machine guns and 500-pound bombs.

"We flew one and sometimes three missions a day and never got over 1,000 feet in altitude. We would take off and head for the target.

The forward controller would spot the target for us and we would go in and bomb and strafe.

"The Germans had pressed into service every means of transportation they could get their hands on to move supplies and ammo to the front. They confiscated horses and wagons from French farmers. We saw them on the road and it became pure slaughter of horsemeat. Even at 1,000 feet, we could smell the stench of rotting horseflesh.

"We all hated to shoot the horses, so finally we got pretty good at shooting the wagon tongues and reins off near the front of the wagons in order to cut the horses loose. We succeeded sometimes, and sometimes we didn't.

"When Patton didn't have us out on a special job, we would go after targets of opportunity. When we spotted a pocket of German tanks in front of Patton, we would clear them out. We had the most fun with railroad trains. Probably the biggest sport in all the war was shooting engines. We fired our machine guns into the boilers and watched the steam spout out of them like Old Faithful in Yellowstone Park.

"We became involved in some very dangerous work. When an armed bomb would hang up under a wing, it would be suicide to try to land with it on the bumpy steel mat. We conceived the idea of tipping the bomb off by flying close enough to pry it loose with our wing tip."

I asked, "And this is where you got the idea to stick your wing under your unconscious buddy's wing in Korea and lift him down?"

"Yes, exactly. I had learned that flying that close with wings overlapping was possible. Sometimes you'll do *anything* to save a buddy."

"Well, Jack, I'm beginning to see why a book about you is being planned, which has a tentative title, *What Ever Happened to Captain Jack?* It's about time to give people a chance to learn about some of your incredible experiences."

Jack went on, "Getting back to Patton. Where *he* went, *we* went. I was lucky to become Patton's leading tank killer as we moved up. I remember an incident very clearly. Patton sent us to a small village where the Krauts had eight or ten of their big Tiger tanks. The general couldn't move because he was out-gunned with their 88s. The 88 mm guns were mounted on tanks and fired an incredibly powerful 3 ½-inch projectile.

"I got one of the best hits I ever had on this mission with a rocket. One Tiger was sitting in the town square. I took aim on him and hit him in the exact center with an HVAR rocket. The Tiger exploded, broke in half and the front half went forward and the rear half went backward. It gave me a great deal of satisfaction killing that tank, but not the eight men inside.

"Nevertheless, we had been ordered to kill as many Krauts as we could, so I went after several tank men running across an open field. By now, my gun barrels were so hot the tracers were spiraling out, so I pulled up, looked down on them and said, 'You just got a life, friend.' "

"Jack, it took *years* to get you to open up, and now that you're on a roll, please go on."

"By now, our losses were exceptionally heavy. Out of the original 26 pilots who came over, there were only three of us left. The others had been killed, taken prisoner or shot down.

"We kept on moving up right behind Patton. I had never been a drinker, but by now, all of us were drinking everything we could get our hands on. General Patton, to show his appreciation, would send us cases of cognac and champagne. He 'liberated' them from wineries by the truckload.

"One morning I was awakened before dawn by someone shaking me. I had a terrible hangover and when I finally got my eyes open, I saw our chaplain standing over me. The chaplain was the biggest drinker of the bunch. He said, 'I've got a surprise for you. You're going home.' By this time I had flown 90 missions in seven or eight months. I spent Christmas of 1944 at home in the States.

"The Battle of the Bulge was underway. I went back overseas and picked up my group in Belgium, because they had left Patton when he went into the Bulge. From this point on, we started moving toward Germany.

"I took a 20mm in the engine of my P-47 one day, but managed to land in England. As I pulled up to the stand to park the plane, the engine froze. Incidentally, I went through five airplanes that were completely destroyed by flak and shells. They were all totaled and had to be hauled to the junkyard.

"Here's another close call I'll never forget. We had just left Rotterdam and dropped down low enough so we could remove our oxygen masks and light up our cigarettes. An 88 mm shell burst through the canopy, passed right by my nose, and knocked the cigarette out of my mouth. Fortunately it didn't tear up the plane badly enough for me to have to ditch it.

"I had been promoted to captain by this time, and was leading my own flight up and down the Rhine River looking for targets of opportunity. We spotted some tanks along the river so I called the rest of my flight and told them there was no use for them to go down there and get shot up, so I very foolishly went down by myself. This dumb trick got me the Silver Star.

"After completing 17 missions on this second tour, the war was over. This gave me a total of 107 missions."

"Jack, don't stop here. There's another story I want you to tell. We've talked about the difference between how we, in our heavy bomb groups, couldn't even see individual homes at 20 to 30,000 feet. You, on the other hand, were practically down to an eye-to-eye level with the Germans. Please tell us about your experience with that lonely German soldier in the center of a village."

"Okay, well, one day my buddy and I were checking villages looking for tanks. This was when we were working for Patton. As I was flying down one street, a German soldier jumped around the corner of a building and fired a hand-held machine gun at me. It was something like our tommyguns. Then he ducked back around the corner of the building into the other street before I could open up on him.

"I made two more passes at him and he did the same thing, so I called my buddy and said, 'Hey, Cobbie, there's a guy down there irritating the devil out of me. Tell you what, you go down the side-street where he disappears and run him back around the corner. I'll give you five seconds lead for a little separation so we won't have a collision over the street corner, and then I'll take him out when he ducks back around the building.' It worked! My eight guns hit him and he literally blew up! This was the war version of the game, 'Hide and Seek.'

"Our 406th Fighter Group got a Presidential Unit Citation for a very unusual action. We had the distinction of being the only outfit in the U.S. Army Air Force to have an entire German army surrender to it.

"General Patton had cut off a German army on his right flank while he was moving up to cross the Loire River. The Krauts were in a column about 15 miles long on a road and Patton sent us over there to wipe them out. We hit them with our P-47s three times that day— morning, noon and evening. There was nothing left but burning vehicles and dead and wounded soldiers.

"A lot of their vehicles were horse-drawn and we hated to shoot the horses, but of course we *had* to. During the evening mission we stopped shooting the Krauts and started shooting the horses to put them out of their misery.

"That day we killed and wounded several thousand German soldiers. We could see them clearly on the ground as we swept in on the deck and massacred them. It wasn't a very pretty sight. Some of our guys got sick to their stomachs while they were strafing.

"The German commander sent word to Patton that he would be willing to surrender, but only to *our* group commander, Colonel

Grossetta. General Vandenburg, who was commander of the 19th Tactical Air Command and our colonel went down to a bridge over the Loire River where the surrender was to take place and waited.

"The German general was the first to come across the bridge and he handed his pistol to Colonel Grossetta. The rest of the troops then came across and tossed their guns into a big pile."

Jack is a very modest fellow and I had to learn most of the following from his wife, Tomi. During W.W.II he was awarded 20 Air Medals, two Distinguished Flying Crosses, a Silver Star and the French Croix de Guerre with Palms. This medal was awarded by General Charles de Gaulle.

STARS

Lieutenant Don Carrithers

Don Carrithers was the co-pilot on a B-17 in the 301st Bomb Group in Italy. He flew out of Foggia where several bomb groups were located.

Don was another fellow who seemed reluctant to hash over his war days, but he was finally persuaded.

"Please tell us your story, Don."

"We flew only 11 missions before the war ended and lost at least *one* engine each time. In fact, on our 11th mission we lost all four!

"We flew our 14 B-17s from the States to Marrakech, Morocco. We were warned not to go into the city because the Arabs were killing Americans. Then, we went to Tunis and saw considerable war damage there. We landed at Gioia, Italy and were assigned to the 352nd Squadron of the 301st Bomb Group. We were proud to be in such a famous and distinguished flying group because we had heard about their record in England, Africa and Italy.

"Our permanent station was Foggia. On our first mission out of Foggia, we left in the dark, in clouds and flew by compass. We couldn't find the formation, so we turned back. We were supposed to jettison our bombs in the Adriatic Sea before landing, but nobody had told us, so we brought them back. It could have been a *disaster!*

"On our second flight—first mission—we arrived at the IP at 30,000 feet. There were no German fighters but all hell broke loose with ack-ack. We got some flak in an outboard engine, feathered the prop, continued the bomb run, dropped, then turned and headed home. The whole crew was proud of our accomplishment and it was something we would remember the rest of our lives.

"On the second mission, we discovered that our electrically-heated flying suits didn't always work. By this time, not every ship had a bombardier. It was decided that with such tight formations, everybody could drop on the lead plane, which had a bombardier. The rest of the ships had a guy called a togglier who released the bombs.

"Before taking off on this mission, I was sitting down in the co-pilot's seat and noticed a big sheet of heavy metal welded to the fuselage on the right of my seat. I asked why. 'Because the last pilot who sat there is on his way back to the States paralyzed because a piece of flak came through there and hit him.' 'Oh, well,' I thought, 'lightening never strikes in the same place twice.'

"At 31,000 feet on the bomb run, we got flak in an outboard engine and feathered it. We continued the bomb run, dropped, broke off to the right and started home. Flak got another engine on the other side and we dropped down gradually all the way home and landed okay.

"After that we lost at least one engine to flak on every mission. On one trip, during the bomb run through heavy flak, there was a sudden jolt in the ship. Everybody felt it. The crew chief checked with the rest of the crew but nobody had seen any flak damage. Again we lost an engine on the bomb run, but got home okay. We made a smooth landing and taxied to our parking area.

"The engineering officer came around in his jeep and counted 180 flak holes. He came in under the bomb bay—the doors were open— looked up and said, 'Did you fellows know that was there?' We looked up and saw a large gaping hole through the main strut that ran along the top of the fuselage from nose to tail. It was the backbone of the plane and held everything together. An ack-ack shell set to explode at a higher altitude than we were flying had torn through this strut and exploded somewhere above us.

"The jolt we felt had been caused by this ack-ack shell. The crew chief had walked through the bomb bay on his inspection but didn't look up because he was walking on the narrow catwalk and holding on to the chains to keep from falling.

"The engineering officer said, 'If you had known that was there, you should have *never* landed the plane.' Even though it was after the fact, the engineering officer continued, 'You should have flown over the Adriatic Sea, put it on auto-pilot and bailed out.' As he was lecturing to us, a tug hooked on to the tail and started pulling the plane away. In about ten feet, the plane buckled and dropped in half on the ground. The whole crew stood there not knowing what to say. We all felt like dropping to our knees and thanking God for the smooth landing and the fact that the airplane hadn't come apart in flight or when we landed.

"We landed with no brakes, one time, and went off the end of the runway into a deep irrigation ditch. It tore off the landing gear, one wing dipped, an engine was torn off and we finally stopped. While all this was going on, I was turning off the switches to prevent an explosion. The crew left that wreck faster than anybody would have felt possible!

"We were sent to Northern Italy to bomb enemy troops with frag bombs. These would go off 50 feet in the air and shower a whole area with steel fragments. It was almost inhumane, but we hadn't seen anything humane about this war anyway, so we dropped them.

"Our troops were so close to the enemy position that even with very precise planning for the dropping of these frag bombs, we heard later that many of our own allied ground troops were killed or injured by them. This could have been poor timing, wind directions or our own troops advancing beyond the drop point."

"Don, didn't you tell me you had lost more than two engines on your missions?"

"Yes, as a matter of fact, it was Easter Sunday, 1945 and we were on our third mission. We lost two on the bomb run and on the way back, the third started running rough. We dropped out of the formation and landed in Yugoslavia. On our 11th mission, we were coming in on two engines when the third went out two or three miles from the runway. We fired a red flare and were given permission to make a straight-in landing. The *fourth* engine went out about 100 yards from touch-down. We became a four-engine glider. No problem."

STARS

Colonel John James

John James had retired from the Air Force with the rank of Colonel. It was interesting talking with him because he had been an F-5 photo recon pilot and I was very familiar with that plane.

"Go ahead, John."

"I flew a P-38 fighter, which had been converted to an F-5 photo-recon plane. No guns at all—only cameras. We did have some pilots riding shotgun for us, though.

"We had two fighter groups consisting of P-38 Lightnings and P-51

Mustangs. They were flown by black pilots who had been trained at Tuskeegee in Alabama and they were the *best*. When they escorted photo-recon planes, they stayed with us all the way to the target, turned with us and came back with us. They never broke and ran like some of the white pilots did."

"This surprises me, John, because I'd heard the brass didn't trust blacks in combat areas and they were always segregated."

"Oh, they were segregated, all right, and had their own airfield near us. Their group commander was a West-Pointer named Colonel Benjamin O. Davis. Davis later became a three-star—lieutenant general—after the war.

"These black fellows would stick to us like glue. Sometimes the white pilots would claim they were short of fuel before we got to the turning point, and would go home. Some would leave us and drop down to look for targets of opportunity because there wasn't much action escorting recon people. We always felt good having the black pilots with us."

"Were you based at one of those fields north of Foggia?"

"Yes, it was at San Severo, just a few miles north from Foggia where you were operating. I'll never forget how we got there from Naples where we had docked from the States. We were loaded on a 40 and 8 boxcar in the middle of winter and it was as cold as a well-diggers elbows. No heat in the boxcar at all. I was one of the lucky ones because I had a sleeping bag to stay bundled up in.

"I was assigned to the 37th Photo Recon Squadron, which belonged to the 5th Photo Group. Group headquarters was in Bari where you lived. The 32nd Squadron, all of the pilots and maintenance people, were on a ship that was sunk in the Mediterranean. There were no survivors.

"My 37th Squadron was assigned to photograph areas extending up to Linz, Austria. We were briefed to keep our heads rotating to spot enemy aircraft, but at 30,000 feet, there wasn't a whole lot of traffic.

"Anytime we went north of Innsbruck, we were provided fighter escort because of the danger of running into the German Me-262 twin-engine jet fighters that operated around there. It was just as dangerous passing a formation of our own bombers and fighters, however. They were 'trigger happy' and would shoot at anything in the sky. We would detour and keep our distance from them.

"We recon pilots probably had the dullest job in the Air Force. We were always at 30,000 feet photographing bomb damage or locating new targets for bombing and there wasn't much excitement in that.

"The converted P-38s made good photo planes, but were limited otherwise. We would climb normally at 160 mph. The P-51 pilots complained that they were falling out of the sky at that speed because they needed 190 mph. Even at altitude they could out-maneuver us. They could make tight turns up there, but *we* would fall when we tried it."

"John, when we got back to the States and were stationed at a recon pilot's training base, we heard of something called 'droop-snoots.' What was that?"

"Yes, we had some droop-snoots at San Severo. This was an F-5 with an elongated nose. A radar operator sat up there in total darkness with his radar camera. He couldn't see anything for the eight-hour missions we went on. Talk about boredom!

"Bob, did you know that Major Antoine De Saint-Exupery, the world-famous author, flew a P-38 recon plane?"

"No."

"He got his P-38 photo-recon training in North Africa in Elliott Roosevelt's outfit. He then wound up at an airfield in Corsica where you lived."

"He must have been a little old to be flying a P-38, because he flew in World War I."

"Yes, he was 44 when he failed to return from a photo-recon flight over Annecy in Southern France. Our regulations had set 35 as the maximum age of a P-38 pilot, but he pulled some strings in Washington and got a waiver. He was also a close friend of the Lindberghs.

"Well, that's it for me. The war ended on my 26th birthday and I had just made captain."

Author's Notes

More than 9,900 P-38s were built during the war, many of which were converted to F-5 photo-reconnaissance planes. Military historians say that the F-5 won more battles and saved more allied lives than any other piece of military hardware.

John mentioned being shot at by our own gunners. The American public has never been informed about countless blunders and mistakes made by Americans killing Americans. My own 50-year "gag-order" was but one of hundreds. Some of the blunders that our military attempted to cover up are finally being exposed. One of the worst was the 82nd Airborne fiasco.

Before the invasion of Sicily, American Navy and ground force gunners knew that C-47 aircraft towing gliders full of airborne troops would be flying over them during the invasion. When the armada flew over them, they panicked and blasted away, shooting down 23 planes. Two-hundred-twenty-nine men of the 82nd Airborne Division were needlessly killed. Our friend Ernie Pyle was a witness to this tragedy but was not permitted to report it.

The relatives of these dead soldiers were informed by our war department that their sons and husbands had died in action. A lot of people were threatened with court-martials if they talked.

The Germans made blunders also. But ours were *monumental* compared with theirs. After all, *our* soldiers were reporting to amateurs and bureaucrats.

Negro pilots destroyed or damaged 409 enemy aircraft. They accounted for the last four victories of the Army Air Corps in the Mediterranean Theater of Operations. They flew 1,578 missions, including 200 escorting heavy bombers during which time none of the heavies were lost to enemy fighter opposition.

Four-hundred-fifty Negro pilots of the 332nd Fighter Group distinguished themselves with many decorations and won a Presidential Unit Citation.

Edward Gleed, who is a black retired Air Force colonel, made this interesting observation: "The U.S. military had definitely established the theory that a Negro was inferior. They thought he had a smaller brain than the Caucasian. He couldn't socialize with whites. *Certainly* he couldn't learn to fly. So we set up a clamor—'Why *can't* we fly? If we're going to have to go to war, we want to fly—not walk.'

"One of our black pilots went to a recruiting office with some whites to enlist in the Air corps. The recruiting officer said, 'What are you doing here, boy? The Air Force doesn't need any night fighters.'

"That 'boy' became an ace."

STARS

Captain Jack Black

Jack Black was a B-24 pilot who flew out of England with the 8th Air Force. Jack described his unforgettable experience.

"We had just received a brand-new Liberator and flew it from England to Ludwigshaven deep into Germany. We were hit by flak going into the target, which took out one engine, but we dropped our bombs and started home.

"We started losing altitude immediately and got so low over France that we could see German soldiers shooting at us with their rifles. We could have jumped, but the crew elected to stay with her and try for a water landing in the English Channel. We had lost two more engines and just as we reached the channel, our last engine died.

"The recommended ditching procedure at that time was to 'tail drag' the plane into the water. Since too many planes had broken in half with this method, I decided to 'grease her in' with the wheels up. We made contact with the water as smoothly as we could, but it was like hitting a brick wall. It slammed me into the instrument panel and the co-pilot shot up through the top, leaving a big hole. I floated up and out that hole.

"The radio operator dove into the plane and released the dinghies, but before we could get to the co-pilot, he had drowned because he couldn't swim.

"The plane floated for 45 minutes. The record up to then had been five minutes. Sometime during the first night, the flight engineer died; we said the Lord's Prayer and slipped him into the sea. We were picked up 48 hours later by an English fishing boat.

"It was determined that tail dragging a B-24 into the water was the cause of their breaking in half, so the brass sent me around to various bases to lecture the pilots on *my* method of ditching.

"I felt greatly honored when General Jimmy Doolittle awarded me the Distinguished Flying Cross for this action."

S T A R S

Captain Roy McCaldin

Roy and I had been boring holes in the Arizona skies with our home-built airplanes for a long time before I became aware of his exciting last mission as a B-17 pilot. Roy had never mentioned it, but I discovered an alcove devoted exclusively to him while visiting the world-famous Pima Air Museum in Tucson.

"Roy, I just found out that we have something in common. We are both members of the Caterpillar Club. When did you join?"
"On my last raid—March 18, 1945 over Berlin."
"Well, I beat you by almost a year. Of course, Charles Lindbergh, General Jimmy Doolittle and President George Bush beat *me*."

The Caterpillar Club is an exclusive organization that was established back in the '20s by Leslie Irvin, the fellow who invented the ripcord method of opening a parachute in free-fall. From that time on, anybody who was forced to "hit the silk" to save his life became a member. At that time all parachutes were made of silk so the silkworm caterpillar—was responsible for the name of the club.

"Okay, Roy, you're on. Tell us about your initiation into the club."

"I was a 21-year-old second lieutenant flying as command pilot on my sixth mission. I was in the 422nd Squadron, 305th Bomb Group, 8th Air Force. The raid was on the marshalling yards in Berlin, Germany.

"The day started like all the others—in pitch darkness. The charge of quarters came in, routed us out of bed and we went down to breakfast in the dark. After breakfast, some trucks took us down to the flight line for our briefing. We all went in and sat down. Somebody yelled 'attention' and Colonel McDonald walked in, stepped up onto the stage, pulled the drape and there was a long string line from England all the way over to Berlin, which was 600 miles away.

"After being briefed on weather, flak areas and everything, we got back into the trucks and went out to the airplane. We started the engines at 0700, just as dawn was breaking. We taxied out to the runway and took off in 30-second intervals. Our group was flying 36 ships that day, so it took us about 18 minutes to get off. Gasoline was very critical and the first guy off had burned 18 minutes more fuel than the last. The guy ahead of me was just breaking ground when I got the green light and started down the runway.

"Soon we were all up in the overcast and flying IFR (Instrument Flight Rules). It really made me pay attention to my airspeed because there was a guy 30 seconds in front of me and another B-17 30 seconds behind flying the same course, same altitude and same everything.

"We all held it at 150 miles per hour indicated and broke out of the overcast still in good position. Then we flew to a beacon five miles away, made a turn and came back over the field climbing at 300 feet per minute. We flew back and forth this way until we were 10,000 feet over the field.

"This all had to be very carefully planned because there were 33 bomb groups all doing the same thing over East Anglia that morning. There were also fighters and other aircraft in the sky at the same time, so we had to stay right on course and time to avoid midair collisions.

"The high squadron was 500 feet above us and the low squadron was 500 feet below, forming a box pattern over England so the timing would be right on the button when we passed the English coast. We were always climbing.

"We left the coast at about 12,000 feet and then when we crossed the channel over France, still climbing across the enemy lines, we got to about 21,000 feet. The intelligence officer had been right and when we crossed the enemy lines, they didn't have any anti-aircraft guns available.

"We continued into Germany still climbing while making several course changes to make the Germans wonder where we were going.

"Shortly before reaching Berlin, we were at the bombing altitude of 27,000 feet. About 20 minutes before we got to the target, a little stream of oil started coming out of the number one engine. It was coming out behind the cowl flaps and that meant bad trouble. I told my co-pilot to keep his eye on that oil pressure gauge and 'as soon as it dropped, to feather the engine.

"The oil gave out all too soon, and we had to feather it immediately. We cut the engine, then rotated the prop so the edges faced forward to cut down drag. The prop governor was oil-driven and if it wasn't feathered, the engine would run out of oil and we *couldn't* stop it—it would run away with us.

"Then we had a decision to make. I chose to continue the raid because we were only about 20 minutes short of our target by this time, and I wanted credit for the mission. The problem was, we couldn't keep up with the formation at that altitude with the heavy bomb load so we slowly drifted behind and below the group.

"Another ship close to us had also lost an engine so we weren't entirely alone. I tried to call our little friends, the P-51 boys, but my radio was out. By the time those who were ahead of us got to the target, we were about two miles behind them, and a little below.

"We could tell when they were over the target because of the smoke from their bombs and the flak that was coming up to meet them.

"We got to the target and our togglier released the bombs at the first smoke trail we came across. It was the marshaling yards where trains were being loaded to go to the Russian front. Just as we released our bombs, *holy mackerel*—all *hell* broke loose! First, I lost control of the airplane. It was bucking like a wild horse. The right stabilizer had been blown away and then a big chunk of the wing came off and then here comes an Me-262 jet right over the top of us! He was so close that if I'd had a brick I could have hit him.

"My top turret gunner, Sergeant Archibald, had been banging away at him. At this time we were coming in over the target solo and the

Me-262 spotted us again in the distance and then flew in to our vapor trails right behind us so we couldn't see him. He stalked us by coming right up the vapor trails and came out in the clear for a 6 o'clock-level firing run. He blew away the right stabilizer and that's what caused the airplane to start bucking. I couldn't control it.

"Pieces of the elevators were flapping and when they blew off, I got control of the plane again with what remained of the left elevator. Then he shot up the right wing and got the number three and four engines. They were lopping and not getting much power and then there was an explosion. I thought we were going to blow up and have to jump.

"During the explosion the co-pilot had the best position to see what was happening. Archibald, the top turret engineer-gunner, had been shooting at this guy and he also saw the damage and explosion. He knew he should go out ahead of the co-pilot so he jumped right over Berlin.

"I called the rest of the crew and told them to just hang on until we got to the Russian lines at the Oder River, about 25 miles away.

"We got to the lines and were down to 7,000 feet. The plane was just barely controllable. Then we were greeted with flak. The first burst was right on the nose. We made a gentle turn to the left and the second burst was just off the right wing, so I made a gentle turn to the right. The third burst was off the left wing. I decided not to turn back and it's a good thing I didn't, because the whole sky turned black with flak right where we would have been.

"We got away from the ack-ack guns without being hit again. We were still descending and it was time to get out of the airplane. I sent the crew back into the waist where it would be easier to jump, and then remembered that I had my parachute under my seat. I was standing on the left rudder pedal and had the wheel cranked almost all the way over to keep the airplane level and couldn't get my chute on.

"I called on the intercom for help and waved at the crew. They thought I was giving the signal to jump so four of the guys went out. Powers, the radio operator, had his head-set on and knew what the problem was and he grabbed King, the togglier and told him. King came scooting back up through the bomb bay. He was a real hero because he took off his chest pack parachute to get through the bomb bay. He jumped into the co-pilot's seat and held the airplane level so I could get my chute on.

"By now we were in clouds and still descending rapidly, so I stepped down into the nose access crawl space. Powers went out the waist, King went out the nose hatch and I let go of the controls. The plane started to roll and I knew I had to get out before the bottom of the plane became the *top* of the airplane.

"I stepped between the two seats but didn't step far enough back behind the seats when I jumped into the companion way, and caught my ripcord on a loose piece of gear and the chute popped open. I grabbed two armfulls of silk, dove out the nose hatch head first, threw out my arms and the chute blossomed.

"The first thing I heard was the sound of the airplane in the clouds. It sounded like a freight train going by, and then the next sensation was caused by the snow. It looked and felt like I was going up instead of down because I was descending a lot faster than the snow was falling.

"I came out through the bottom of the clouds and saw my airplane *Naughty Virgin* hit the ground. It didn't scatter very far because it had impacted at a fairly steep angle. I spotted the other two chutes just as I hit the ground. It knocked the stuffing out of me, and when I got my wind back, I walked over to a road and found Johnnie, our radio operator, sitting in a car full of Russians—the Russians were in it and on it—all *over* it!

"Johnnie Powers had seen the Russian's car going down the road while he was still descending under his parachute. After landing, he started waving his arms, but it was unnecessary because they had seen him and were rushing over to him. They all had guns and Johnnie stiffened to attention and raised his hands as high as he could.

"We had been briefed on what to say to a Russian in a case like this and Johnnie shouted, 'Ya Amerikanski—ya Amerikanski!' until he was hoarse.

"I walked up to them and they all waved in a very friendly way. I had been issued a silk U.S. flag that was folded up in my chest pocket. It was connected to a string around my neck. On the back of the flag was a message in Russian and Polish that said, in essence, that 'I'm an American—a good guy—take me to your leader.'

"We had been told not to reach into our pockets for anything in front of a Russian. I forgot about that and started reaching inside my flying suit. Then I realized that all these Russians who had been waving also had tommyguns, and they were suddenly all pointing at my gizzard, so I stopped this maneuver and pulled on the string and the flag and message came out of my flying suit.

"The Russians looked at it and seemed more interested in the quality of the silk than the message. Anyway we all had a friendly back-slapping time and were friends again.

"I held up three fingers to try to let them know there were three of us and one was yet to be found. We started back across the field to some woods looking for King. We heard small arms fire going on all this time.

"King was really a first-rate soldier. Not only did he save my life in the airplane, but he also did the right thing when he landed. He hid his gun in a small group of trees, buried his chute under some brush and took off running to evade anyone who had seen him land. He wasn't sure he was behind Russian lines and the small arms fire worried him.

"King took off running in a straight line away from the shooting. The only thing he did wrong was go in the direction he chose, because he ran through an irrigation canal that had ice on it. It was about twelve feet wide, and he fell through the ice before reaching the other side.

"King broke on through the ice and kept wading. When he got across he kept running to some bigger woods and buried himself under some trees. He kept hearing the gunfire and decided to hold his position. Then he heard us calling and came out from hiding and found that we were, in fact, behind the Russian lines. We soon learned that some Russian soldiers had been hunting game in the woods.

"The 'Russkies' took us to their field headquarters, which was a large farmhouse. I tried to explain to their commandant what had happened by using gestures and he seemed to understand. I used a couple of words that pleased him—'bombed Berlin.' We were then great buddies because he knew that any bombing of Berlin would cut down on supplies and weapons facing the Russian army.

"After telling the commandant that we had bombed Berlin, we told him all about baseball, football, cowboys, Indians, Hedy Lamarr and General Doolittle.

"We went down into the basement of this farmhouse that looked something like a rathskeller and they poured some vodka or maybe it was a potato whiskey because we could see some of the potato floating in it.

"I had had only a few beers in my life—I wasn't much of a drinker. We'd had breakfast that morning around five o'clock. I thought two of my crew were dead, didn't know where four of them were and had lost an airplane. It had been kind of a bad day. It was around two in the afternoon and one glass of that potato whiskey or vodka was all I could handle.

"It was the custom to drink with them and an insult if you didn't. The Russkies tossed down the water glasses of vodka like we would a shot. Then they would thump their chests and say, 'Daroga—daroga! (Good - good!)'

"They saw me sitting there unable to rise for the second round of drinks. They held up their glasses and said 'Stalin, Roosevelt, Churchill.' They were toasting our leaders.

"I couldn't make it but my bombardier and radio operator made the second round. The Russkies would try to get me up and kept pointing to my second lieutenants bar. We had a secret weapon that day—Johnnie Powers. Johnnie stood up and poured the third round of water glasses of drinks and began to say a few *Stalins* trying to get them up for another toast. They couldn't get up, so good old Johnnie Powers, our radio operator, saved our faces that day.

"After drinking the toasts, the colonel wanted to feed us. We tried to tell him we had just eaten but we *had* to eat again, because when *he* eats, *everybody* eats. The colonel was completely bald and was fat and sloppy. Johnnie said, 'He seems to be quite pleased with himself, doesn't he?'

"After awhile, when we were feeling a little better, we got into a GI truck that had some of the debris from our airplane in the back and drove eastward, away from the front. We went to a little town where we were put up in the Mayor's house and they were very kind to us.

"They gave us a nice dinner. I was awfully thirsty by this time but the Mayor said the water was 'Nyet.' I understood that, so we had to learn to drink tea that had been boiled. They put us up in their guestroom and the three of us slept on one bed with a great big thick down cover. The guy in the middle cooked and the guy on each side froze, but we were glad to be alive and have a place to stay.

"The next morning we got aboard a horse-drawn cart and continued eastward, arriving at a town where there was a railroad. We were then picked up by the Russian police. They wanted to know what we were doing there, if we were Americans and who sent us.

"Finally it was straightened out, and we got on the train and rode east to the town of Leszno. We were picked up again by the police, and once they were satisfied we were who we said we were, they took us to the commandant's house, which was a large place with a garden on the side that was in a state of total disrepair. We went inside and explained to the commandant what had happened.

"He had a Polish gardener who spoke excellent English, so the communication was good here. That evening we were given a room along with some Russian soldiers. There were cots along the wall and a bunch of tommyguns. The soldiers wanted to know something. We tried gestures and charades but didn't get anywhere. Finally the Polish interpreter came in and solved the language barrier. They wanted to know if President Roosevelt spoke Russian. They were disappointed when I said I really didn't know.

"They looked at my wool shirt and wanted to know how much it cost. In dollars it was meaningless, and how many you could buy in a month was also totally meaningless because I guess their money was worthless.

"After we had a nice chat, they gestured that we would get three of the cots. By the time we went to bed, none of the tommyguns were left leaning against the wall. They were about 95% sure we were Americans, but not sure enough to leave the guns with us.

"We stayed there until their general at the front told us what to do next. In the meantime, we started exploring. There was a German tank right out in front of the building and we looked inside. The awfullness of war suddenly became apparent. That tank smelled *real* bad. The bodies still hadn't been removed and were decaying.

"The next morning, the commandant, through the interpreter, said they had captured a German Heinkel 111 bomber and asked if we wanted to fly it back to England. I said, 'Sure.' My two sergeants were quiet but this is as close to insurrection as they came because when we were alone, they said, 'What did you really think you were doing?' I told them that it may have been a bluff, and I had to *call* their bluff. If it *wasn't* a bluff and we got the airplane and could start it, we would fly it to the front and whichever side didn't shoot at us, that's the side we'd fly over going south toward Turkey or someplace, land it and start walking again.

"It *was* a bluff because the airplane deal didn't come through. The next afternoon we walked into town to see the village and somebody yelled at us. 'Hey, Yanks, wait for me.' It was a P-51 pilot, Al Peterson, in a one-horse buggy with a Polish driver. The P-51 pilot had a broken foot. He had gone down the same day we did while he was strafing a German air field. Al said he had been going pretty fast because after he was hit, he was able to coast several miles with a dead engine before he crash-landed his airplane. He broke his foot in the crash but got out and started walking and then hitchhiking.

"The P-51 guy teamed up with us. The next day the commandant called me in and said that we were to continue on our way the best we could, and he gave me two handwritten letters. One was written in Russian and the other in Polish on school-children's tablets. The letters said we were good guys and to help us on our way as we headed for the American embassy in Moscow.

"School tablets! How simple! In *our* outfit, everywhere we turned there was something to sign, write or file. It had to be typewritten and all in triplicate! The Russians were too busy fighting a war to wade through this kind of nonsense.

"Then they gave me a canvas bag with about ten feet of sausage in it. We went down to the train and boarded. It was about 2 o'clock in the afternoon. We waited many hours before starting. The train was packed. The people who take the Long Island railroad in rush hour out of New York City, have an idea what it was like except our train was *really* packed. We couldn't move!

"We left late that evening and about dawn the next morning the train stopped. I had to go in the worst way possible, so I pushed my way to the glassless window. I stood at the window and took my turn relieving myself. By this time I realized that other guys were relieving themselves, but they were on *top* of the train and there must have been a long line up there.

"We stopped in the city of Poznan, Poland and were picked up by the Russians again. They finally decided we were Americans and introduced us to a Polish professor who spoke English. The professor took us on a walking tour of Poznan.

"On some streets, the damage was complete. Narrow paths had been cleared through the debris, wide enough for walking. The Germans had done a systematic job of destruction as they retreated.

"We were taken to an old castle that had been a German strong point. The castle was completely surrounded by Russian soldiers, and a German detachment was still inside. The Russians had given them the option of coming out and being shot or staying inside and dying by starvation.

"We were taken back to the town and went to Lodz, Poland. Again, we were picked up by Russian police. The commandant wanted to practice his English for awhile and then gave us nice hotel rooms. Here we waited for two days for an American C-47 Gooneybird to fly us to Poltava, Russia.

"Poltava was a base being used by the Americans for shuttle bombing. At this time the American-Russian diplomacy was fraught with disaster. It was so miserable that after the war, Glenn B. Infield wrote a book about it called *The Poltava Affair*.

"For one thing, because of a diplomatic breach, no American planes could be flown out of Poltava and there were a lot of them there. It took two weeks to resolve the problem.

"A B-17 had crash-landed on the field and had been patched up enough to get it back into the air. They gave it to us and we flew it to Foggia, Italy.

"We taxied to the ramp and parked. The crew and I had a short business meeting and decided that the airplane was unfit to fly again. It was government property and *parked* on government property so we left it sitting there and walked out the front gate.

"We found an infantry replacement depot where they gave us new clothes and our first shower in weeks. Then we started hitch-hiking to Naples by truck. From here we hitched a ride on a B-17 to Marseilles, France and got a ride back to England where I reported to the Escape and Evasion officer in London. It was V-E day. He sent me back to my squadron."

Author's Notes:

On Roy's March 18, 1945 Berlin raid, up to 36 German jet fighters at a time attacked the B-17 formation. Before the battle ended, 36 Fortresses went down and 6 were so badly damaged by the jets and flak that they crashed behind the Russian lines. Five P-51s were also lost that day.

In October, 1994, while our flying club was having its annual competition, about twenty of us were flying over our target and dropping bombs (water-filled balloons) one at a time. Suddenly, Roy McCaldin came roaring down the runway at about 10 feet in his antique DeHaviland and salvoed a dozen water balloons along the target. The crowd cheered—they were surprised and excited!

After Roy landed and joined us, I said, "When was the *last* time you salvoed your bombs on a target, Roy?"

"It was over Berlin on my last mission on March 18, 1945. By the way, I just got my DFC for that Berlin mission."

It is quite amazing, but Roy was awarded the Distinguished Flying Cross for this mission but didn't know it was valid until September, 1994. He knew that his squadron commander had sent in a recommendation to have him awarded the DFC, but it was at the end of the war and the office personnel had finished typing the final clean-up orders with the DFCs listed in the front.

Roy speculates that the "minimum wage" fellows at headquarters were too lazy to retype everything to place his name up with the rest of the DFC recipients, so they just put him on the bottom with those who were getting air medals.

In 1992, when an author was doing research for his book on Roy (which was not completed), he read the orders where Roy's name should have been listed as a DFC recipient. This touched off further investigation. A civil service employee, another "minimum wager," said that since Roy was 49 years late in pursuing the matter, she recommended turning him down.

Retired Major General Sandy Vandenburg, a friend of Roy's, reviewed the records. He sent a letter to Arizona Senator John McCain requesting a file review. "It was clear—the DFC had been awarded in June, 1945, so Roy has finally added this impressive medal to his collection.

STARS

United States Secretary of the Treasury Lloyd Bentsen

We asked Secretary Bentsen to tell us about one of his unforgettable missions. We knew he had flown B-24s out of Italy but were not sure which outfit he was in.

"My unit was the 717 squadron of the 449 Bomb Group. We were stationed close to Taranto at a little village named Grottaglie."

"What was your age and rank, Mr. Secretary?"

"I was a 23-year-old major in 1944 when this mission almost ended in disaster. I was the 717 squadron commander and was leading a bomb run of B-24s over Austria when we lost two engines. Flames were shooting out of one of them.

"The target was a railroad marshalling yard in Vienna. We had dropped our bombs when the 88 mm anti-aircraft guns got us. The sky was *full* of flak. By the time I got the plane back under control, we had lost several thousand feet. We threw everything we could out of the plane to lighten the load and tried to keep up with the formation. Still, we couldn't keep up and fell behind.

"It would have taken eleven hours round-trip from our base to Vienna but it was now obvious we wouldn't even get back across the Adriatic Sea.

"We continued to lose altitude, so I asked my navigator to find a place to set down so we wouldn't have to bail out. He advised me that there was an island named Vis that was available in case of an emergency. This island had been changing hands in the past, but the navigator was under the impression that at the present it was in allied hands. I told him I hoped he was right because whichever side had it, we were going for it anyway because there was no way we would get back to Italy."

"When did this happen, Mr. Bentsen?"

"In February, and the Adriatic was freezing cold. If we had bailed out into the water, we probably wouldn't have lasted more than five minutes. We managed to reach the (then) Yugoslav coast and found the island with an emergency strip, but only at the last moment, because we were at a very low altitude.

"I had to make a very low turn to line up with the runway and because of the hills surrounding it, my landing was rough and I washed out the nose gear."

"Were you in friendly territory?"

"At this point I wasn't sure. As soon as the plane slid to a stop, I saw some women coming toward us wearing grenade belts. I climbed out of the plane and walked toward them hoping they were friendly.

"A man about my age emerged from the group and walked up to me.

"I said, 'Don't I know you?'

"He looked at me and said, 'Sure, you're Bentsen! I used to sack groceries for your mother at a grocery store in McAllen, Texas.'"

STARS

Lieutenant William S. Martin

I found Bill Martin in Golden, Colorado. He had been involved in the last aerial combat as the war in Europe was winding down. He and his pilot buddy, Lieutenant Duane Francies, were flying their Army L-4 observation plane at the time. Their 65 horsepower L-4 was the Army's version of the small Piper J-3 Cub in which many of us started our military flight training in the late 1930s and early 1940s.

Bill's story is interesting in two respects—the *last* aerial combat in the European Theater of World War II involved his Army observation plane, and the *first* aerial combat in World War *I* was also with observation planes in the same theater.

"Bill, how long had you and Lieutenant Francies been an aerial observation team before your engagement with the German?"

"We'd flown on a lot of missions together since we crossed the Ruhr River. In fact, our plane was getting quite old and beat up, and to get a new one, it had to be unflyable. The first pilot of the plane, Bob Nichol, had crashed it several times without being seriously injured.

"This problem was solved, one morning, when I climbed into the back seat and Duane took the controls in the front. We were in a small field, but Duane thought he could make it so he gunned the engine and got to the end of the field before we were airborne. He tried to go through an open gate in the fence but hit a post and we came to a screeching halt. It tore up the plane, but we weren't hurt. Duane just sat there for a few seconds, turned around in his seat and said, 'Well, Bill, now bet I'll get a new plane.' "

"What outfit were you with?"

"We were air observers with the 71st Field Artillery Battalion of the 5th armored division. I had been a forward observer for all our action from the time we landed at Omaha Beach in France until we crossed the Ruhr River. The Germans blew up a dam there in February, 1945 delaying our advance for a short time. We had three forward observers, but I was the only lucky one—the other two had been replaced twice by that time. Our battalion commander figured I had used up all my good luck, so he assigned me to 'C Battery' as the assistant executive officer. This gave me more time to go on air missions."

"You must have had a lot of close calls. Does one stand out in your mind?"

"Yes. I'll never forget this one. I took Staff Sergeant Sally Wisnower and Corporal Hiles Karlowsky with me in a jeep to go ahead and see what was happening. We knew that a task force had been sent in the direction of Le Mans, France. When we got to a village near there, we slowed down because there was a group of men in the street. We assumed they were *our* men, so we stopped to talk with them. I was answered by *one* word—'Heil!' I yelled at Karlowsky who was driving and said, '*They're Jerries,* let's go!'

"The corporal floorboarded the gas pedal, and we raced past the surprised Jerries through town until we got to the protection of a railroad underpass. He turned the jeep around and roared back past the Jerries again to get to our own lines. By this time the Germans had figured out who we were and started blasting away at us with machine guns and burp guns from doorways and roof tops. They even got in one round from an anti-tank gun. Luckily we were moving so fast they didn't have time to re-load and fire another round at us.

"When we got back to our combat headquarters, we examined the jeep and found one flat tire and several bullet holes in the vehicle. One hole was only a fraction of an inch from the gas tank."

"What had happened to the task force that was supposed to be on the road?"

"They had turned off the main road and were out of sight."

"When did you have your battle with the German observation plane?"

"It was at 1300 hours on April 11, 1945, near Vesbeck, a very small village in Germany. We were flying at 800 feet over endless lines of troops and vehicles of the U.S. 9th Army and the British 2nd Army. Below us we saw a swarm of troops, guns, tanks and trucks. The armies had crossed the Rhine river a month earlier and were storming toward Berlin. We had watched the breakout developing from our 'balcony' since they crossed the Rhine."

"What was your mission that day?"

"We were flying our little Cub named *Miss Me* forward to be the 'eyes' of our division, which was leading the tank columns to the Elbe River, the last major water barrier before reaching Berlin. The Elbe was 45 miles from the city and about halfway between the Elbe and Berlin was a narrow river called Havel, which winds down from the north, then bends up into the western part of the city.

"We knew this was the final offensive because the scene below us was overwhelming! All the roads, including the autobahn, were choked with tanks, fuel trucks, heavy artillery, ambulances, armored cars, self-propelled guns and *everything* required for a final push. I wouldn't have been surprised if there had been a mess kit repair outfit with them!

"While we were over the German lines we would sometimes break the monotony by buzzing the Jerry dispatch riders in their motorcycles and side-cars. We would shoot at them with our .45 automatic pistols and wouldn't hang around to see if we got one but they sure went flying out of their bikes! It was really a foolish thing to be doing so we always forgot to mention it in our reports. Of course our main mission was to scout for our division and locate German strong points. I would then radio their positions down to our artillery battalion who relayed them to the tankers."

"How close to Berlin would you get before turning back?"

"We'd get close enough to see the smoke stacks. We spotted a steady stream of German refugees heading west toward our lines. They were anxious to surrender to the allies before they were caught and imprisoned by the Russians. We could easily see that they were carrying their belongings on their backs and many were herding farm animals ahead of them. While we were close to Berlin, we checked the main roads and landmarks leading into the city. Our reports gave the tankers a 'picture' of what was up ahead."

"So you gave your guys a tour director's preview of the road to Berlin?"

"Yes, but one of the most unbelievable decisions of the war had been made that we would not go to Berlin. We were ordered to stay at the Elbe River and let the Russians take the city from the east. We were all angry at General Eisenhower for stopping our rapid advance. Some of the guys had even painted, 'On to Berlin' on their tanks."

Lieutenant Martin and his buddies were not the only ones who didn't understand Ike's 'hold at the Elbe' order. Not even our top-ranking field generals knew why and only a handful of the allied highest-ranking bureaucrats were aware of the reason for the 'stop order.'

Over a year before our troops arrived at the Elbe, our allied leaders —Roosevelt, Churchill and Stalin—made plans for the division of Germany after the war. Berlin was to be in the Russian zone. The plan was actually developed by the British and called "Operation Eclipse." Shortly after the plans and maps were completed and locked up, the Germans got their hands on them and started making their own plans accordingly.

We also learned that Eisenhower flew into a rage when he discovered that the area east of the Elbe, which included Berlin, had been given to the Russians for post-war occupation. He and General Omar Bradley at first wanted to go across the Elbe and see if they could beat the Russians to Berlin, but decided that since the allies would have to back away and give all that territory back to the Russians after the war, it would be unwise to sacrifice the lives of 100,000 or more of our troops just to say we had deprived the Russians of the big prize.

"Getting back to your air battle, how did it happen?"

"We had finished checking the real estate ahead of our tanks and were going back to land on a field near them when all of a sudden we spotted a German Fiesler Storch observation plane skimming the tree tops heading toward Berlin."

"This Storch, was it a small plane like yours?"

"It was a little larger. Storch is German for stork. It got its name because it had tall, thin landing gears."

"And you jumped him?"

"Yes. Duane and I spotted him at the same time and we both yelled, 'Let's get him!' We had the advantage of altitude, so we dived down on him and got so close we could practically touch the white swastikas on his black wings and tail. I got on the radio and reported that we were going into combat with an enemy plane. The guys on the ground probably couldn't believe what they were hearing.

"As Duane was continuing his dive, I was busy getting my .45 out of its holster. Our door was already open because we had been taking pot-shots at Jerry motorcycles. The door was on the right side. The top half was lifted up and latched under the wing and the bottom half was hanging down. We made a circle over the Storch and started blasting away at him with our .45 automatics.

"The German pilot started side-slipping and circling to the right. He was probably surprised and confused and didn't know what was happening. We emptied our ammo clips and shoved in some new ones. We got to within a few feet of him and blasted away at his windshield. By this time, old Jerry knew what his problem was and started to take evasive action. He banked steeply and dug his right wing tip into a fence, which caused him to cartwheel into a pasture. I had kept a running account of our battle over the radio from the time we first spotted him until he was on the ground. I yelled on the radio, 'We got him! We got him!' Later we found out that Lieutenant Colonel Washburn, our battalion commander, thought I'd said, 'We got hit! We got hit!'

"Duane sat *Miss Me* down near the wreck and we ran over to it. When we got there, both men were out of their plane. The observer was limping like he had a sore foot, and the pilot had dived behind a big pile of sugar beets. I ran back to our plane, grabbed a 30-caliber carbine and fired a warning shot, which brought the pilot out with his hands in the air. These fellows looked just like kids."

"So you had two prisoners on your hands."

"Yes. I kept the pilot covered with my carbine while Duane took a look at the wounded observer. He removed the Jerrie's boot and one of our .45 caliber slugs fell out. The wound wasn't serious, so Duane bandaged his foot. The German kept repeating, 'Danke. Danke. Danke.' The pilot wasn't hurt but had superficial cuts on his head made by the collapsed windshield. We had fired a lot of shots at that plane but could find only four bullet holes in it. Well, we hadn't been trained for aerial gunnery.

"Duane and I laughed and said we'd probably go down in history books as being the only guys who brought an enemy plane down with a couple of colt .45s and would get credit for being involved in the last dogfight in the European Theater. By this time aerial warfare had ceased to exist there."

"What did you do with your prisoners?"

"An armored column was on the road across the field. It stopped and First Lieutenant Bud McNees came over and took them off our hands. Before he did, however, he cut the swastika off the tail of the German plane to keep as a souvenir. At a reunion 45 years later, Bud handed that swastika to me and said, 'Here, Bill, this should be yours. After all, *you* brought him down.' Recently I gave the swastika to the curator of the Colorado National Guard Museum, who is preparing a display about me. The display covers my military career from the beginning up to my retirement from the guard as a colonel."

"Were you and Duane given commendations for this action?"

"Not at this time, but we were given an air medal for every 35 logged missions. A mission could be logged only when we were airborne for two or more hours. I flew 60 missions but got two air medals to add to the Bronze Star Medal I'd been awarded for a previous action. Twenty-one years later, Duane was awarded the DFC for that action."

"And the war in Europe ended on May 7, 1945, just under a month from your aerial episode."

"Sure did."

Authors Notes:

The first and the last—a genuine coincidence! The first was in the fall of 1914. The French and Germans were both flying small fragile wood and fabric observation planes over the front lines. Many of the rival pilots had become friends while they toured the pre-war air race circuits and simply waved to each other as they went about their observation duties. After all, flying at that time was hazardous enough without adding the extra danger of shooting at each other.

Rolland Garros was France's most famous air-circuit pilot and was performing at an air show in Berlin when the war started. He and the other pilots were being entertained at a banquet that evening but he knew that after the party, he would be detained and imprisoned. Garros pretended he was drunk and went into the bathroom where he crawled out of a window and made his way to the airport. There were some German mechanics near his plane, but they had no reason to believe he would take off in the darkness.

Garros crawled into his cockpit and asked one of the mechanics to spin his propeller. The mechanics, thinking Garros was only going to tune-up his machine, gave the blade a couple of whirls. The engine sputtered and roared into life, and he was off into the blackness. At that time, night flying was unheard of.

Garros got back to France, joined the army as a pilot and started flying a Morane-Saulnier observation plane that resembled a modern-day ultralight "puddle jumper."

Garros always carried an army revolver with him on his observation flights. One morning while he and the Huns were both performing their observation duties at the front, the hot-tempered Garros burst into a rage because he had been thinking about a newspaper article that said the Germans were claiming he had attended their air show as a spy.

As Garros grew angrier, he flew up alongside a German Aviatik observation plane carrying two Huns who started waving cheerily. While they flew wing-tip to wing-tip, Garros pulled his revolver out of its holster, steadied it on the edge of his cockpit and squeezed off six rounds at his enemy. The startled Germans, though uninjured, were outraged as they few back to their base. There were no bullet holes in their plane, but they were mad and grabbed a rifle and hurried back to the front to find him.

At this point, aerial warfare was born and both sides became not only observers, but fighters. Rolland Garros continued flying his Morane-Saulnier and taking pot-shots at his enemy until on the afternoon of April Fool's Day in 1915, he got a kill, making him the undisputed father of air-to-air combat.

STARS

Sergeant Dan Piedmont

Dan Piedmont was shot down during "Black Thursday," in the biggest and bloodiest air battle of World War II. He is lucky to be here to tell about it.

"Dan, all the World War II history books contain descriptions of that October 14, 1943 blood bath. Tell us about it."

"I was a staff sergeant in the 8th Air Force flying out of Thurleigh, England. My crew position was at the left waist gun on a B-17. I was on both Schweinfurt raids. The second one became famous in the history of the war as the 'Black Thursday' raid. We lost 60 B-17s and 600 crew members. Half were killed and half taken prisoner.

"This was my tenth mission and at the briefing that morning everybody groaned when they told us we were going to hit Schweinfurt again.

"The weather was so bad and foggy that we didn't think we would ever get off. We finally got the go from the tower and took off in 30-second intervals on instruments. By the time we were over Germany, it was a beautiful sunny day.

"Things were going pretty well for us until our escort left to go back to England and refuel. We had P-38s, P-47s, P-51s and even some Spitfires with us. As soon as they left, the German Luftwaffe came up and the big air battle started.

"We were hit by a rocket that almost tore our wing off. As a result, the pilot couldn't take evasive action. Then one engine caught fire before we hit the target. We pulled out of formation and dropped our bombs hoping we could keep up with the formation with a lighter load. This didn't work and we kept falling behind.

"The Kraut fighters were now swarming all over the sky. The tail gunner kept screaming to the pilot, 'They're coming in—they're coming in! Bounce it—bounce it!' The pilot replied, 'I can't. I'm afraid the wing will come off.'

"This went on for a few more minutes and finally we got the bail-out order. It doesn't take a lot of nerve to bail out of a burning B-17 when you've seen them blow up before the crew got out. We were at 25,000 feet and on oxygen but none of us took our little bail-out oxygen bottles with us because we had seen them go right up through a parachute when they open.

"I dove out and pulled the ripcord. I wondered why I wasn't swinging back and forth like a pendulum, which was the characteristic of chutes. I looked up and saw that my canopy was full of holes. When I snapped the chest pack onto my harness before jumping, I hadn't noticed that it had been hit by machine gun fire.

"Having a damaged parachute, I came down fast and landed hard in a tree, which broke my fall. Branches broke off all the way to the ground, and I was on my back when I stopped. I got out of the harness as quickly as I could and didn't bother to try to get the chute out of the tree because I could hear them coming through the forest after me. I was lucky. German soldiers got to me before the civilians did. The civilians would have probably killed me.

"I was put into solitary confinement and interrogated time after time after time, but all they got was my name, rank and serial number. The German intelligence knew almost as much about me as I did myself anyway.

"Several days later we were crammed into boxcars with no toilet facilities. There was straw on the floor. Occasionally the train pulled off a siding as the tracks up ahead were being bombed.

"It took three days to reach our prison camp where I was to remain for the next 19 months. The camp was in Krems, Austria and it was the infamous Stalag 17. Most people are now familiar with it because of the books and movies that came out after the war. The popular T.V. series, 'Hogan's Heroes' was also based on life in Stalag 17. We referred to ourselves as 'Krieges,' an abbreviation of the German word 'Kriegsgefangenenkartel. This mouthful meant, 'Prisoner of War.'

"Living in Stalag 17 was not fun at all. We couldn't have survived without the American Red Cross. We could live on a Red Cross parcel —one parcel per man per week. A lot of times the parcels didn't arrive because the railroads were bombed and we had to exist on what the Germans fed us.

"The contents of each parcel were:

> *Powdered milk (Klim) 16 oz. 1 can*
> *Spam 1 can*
> *Corned Beef 1 can*
> *Liver Paste 1 can*
> *Salmon 1 can*
> *Cheese 1 can*
> *Margarine 16 oz. 1 can*
> *Biscuits—K-ration*
> *Nescafe Coffee 4 oz. 1 can*
> *Jam or Orange Preserves 1 can*
> *Prunes or raisins 1 can*
> *Sugar 8 oz 1 box*
> *Chocolate 4 oz 2 bars*
> *Soap 2 bars*
> *Cigarettes 5 packs*

"In the morning they gave us some hot water, and that was it. If we had coffee, we were lucky. If we had hidden a piece of bread, we had the bread. At noon we usually had some thin rutabaga soup with insects and bugs floating around in it, but it tasted pretty good.

"In the evening they usually gave us a potato that had been buried in a manure pile to keep it from freezing. We devoured those, skins and all. Once in a while they'd give us meat. We had blood sausage with hair sticking out of it. One time one of the Kriegies found a tooth in it. He took the tooth to a fellow who had been a dentist before the war.

'Where did you get the dog's tooth?' the dentist asked.

"We got a hot shower every six months. They called it delousing. They shaved our heads and deloused our clothes and barracks but in a few days we were lousy again.

"The first winter we were there, we had a few lumps of coal to keep us warm. The second winter we had no fuel at all. We wore our clothes 24 hours a day and huddled in bed trying to stay warm.

"The Germans could be very cruel. They would call us out for roll call and dogtag check and would keep us standing out in the cold for a couple of hours in the snow, rain and mud.

"Nobody ever escaped from Stalag 17. Two boys attempted it one night. They were crawling over the snow and got up to the barbed wire fence where they started snipping the wire. We believe there were informers among us because as soon as they started cutting the wire, the flood lights came on and the guards opened fire with their machine guns. The men started crawling back to their barracks and a guard walked over to them and shot both of them in the head and said, 'Let this be a lesson to you.'

"A lot of tunnels were started but as soon as they were ready to break through beyond the barbed wire, the Germans would be there with their dogs. The German schutzhunds, or police dogs, were vicious. They would come through our barracks and we would have to get up on the top bunks to keep from being attacked.

"Since we had no fuel the second winter, all night long you could hear the guys ripping boards off the barracks to feed the fire. Of course the Germans didn't like that very much.

"The American public was misinformed about what was going on in our prison camp. As an example, there was a cesspool in the middle of our compound and one day a crazy GI jumped in and was swimming around in it. A German with a camera took his picture. For a distance it looked like a cement swimming pool.

"This picture made its way back to the States with the caption, 'American POW having a good time in the swimming pool.' The propagandists also said we were playing hockey, which of course wasn't true. One day two truck loads came in. We thought they were food parcels. They were hockey sticks. We broke them up and burned them for heat.

"The main topic of discussion was always food. Here we were *starving* and food was on everybody's mind. A guy from the south would talk about all the great southern dishes and someone from the west would talk about barbecue. We would talk about food until we actually drooled.

"We had a chaplain whose name was Father Kane. The Germans brought him in just so we could have some kind of church services. We fixed up a little chapel in one of the barracks and men of all denominations attended. The services were well-attended because I think most of us realized we were still alive because of divine intervention.

"After a few months we started getting letters and packages from home. The letters were pretty well cut up by both American and German censors. The American censors stamped the letters and the Germans put GEPRUFT on the letter. This meant censored.

"The few parcels from home had been ransacked by the Germans. They loved American cigarettes—the good brands like Lucky Strike and Camels. They didn't bother the 'off-brands' like Wings and Twenty Grand. I didn't smoke, so I'd trade a pack of cigarettes to the Krauts for a potato or an onion.

"When the Red Cross parcels came in, the Germans would take their bayonets and puncture every tin can so we couldn't hoard them to be used in an escape. If we were careful we could live a week with them.

"Toward the end of the war there would be four of us on one parcel meant to feed one man. Then there would be periods when the railroads were bombed and we didn't get any parcels at all. We do owe a lot to the Red Cross.

"Our compound was surrounded by a double-barbed-wire fence and about 40 feet inside the barbed wire fence was a single strand of wire called the warning wire. Between the single wire and the barbed wire was no-mans-land. Nobody stepped in there or even put their hand over there or you would be shot at. We played ball and if a ball went over there, you had to get the guard's attention in the tower and ask for permission to retrieve the ball.

"There were Russian POWs in the compound next to ours. It was pitiful. They had no order. No form of government at all. In our barracks we had one of our guys called the 'barrack-enchef' or barracks chief, who was in command. He supervised the distribution of food to make sure we all got an equal share.

"We used to watch the Russian compound as the Germans brought in large wooden tubs of slop and set them down on the ground. The Russians would all come running over for food. The stronger ones would get the slop and they would push the weaker ones away, and as a result, we saw many of them die and be carried out everyday. They were dying like flies. The dead were wrapped up in brown paper and buried out in the woods.

"Sometimes a guy with a good arm was able to throw a package of cigarettes over into the Russian compound, but they would all dive on it and it would end up scattered over the ground as just loose tobacco. One day a package of cigarettes landed in the no-man's-land area of the Russian compound. They dived over to retrieve it and were shot by the guards.

"We kept up with the news from the outside world in various ways.

Most of our news came from gunners who were shot down. Somehow we got ahold of a radio and listened to BBC, the British Broadcasting Company. While we were listening to the radio, we had lookouts on each end of the barracks so when the Germans came through they always found us doing something else and not listening to the news. We were all excited when it was D-day. We got a little bit of news from home, but not too much, because of censorship.

"We tried to stay fit by walking around the compound every day and some of the men worked out, but when you are on a near-starvation diet, you don't feel much like strenuous exercise.

"Our dishes were tin cans. Sometimes in a package from home there would be eating utensils, but the Germans removed the spoons, and forks, and so forth, to prevent us from making weapons or escape tools.

"We had some good German guards and some who were a pain in the neck. We liked one of the guards. He was a very likable fellow we called 'Big Stoop' because he looked like Big Stoop in the funny papers. He would come through the barracks in the morning to get us out of bed for roll call and instead of using his bayonet like some did, he would get a can of water and pour it on us. We had a good rapport with Big Stoop. He was one of the guards who was allowed to live after we were liberated. Some of the bad guards would come through the area with the dogs to keep us moving. We moved!

"Some of the boys tried to escape by hiding under the garbage in the garbage wagon but were discovered as soon as they went out the gate.

"We could see women working out in the fields. They had a 'honeywagon' full of human waste and they would dip it out and pour it on the rutabaga plants or cabbage or turnips or whatever they were growing. This was their fertilizer. The vegetables that came to us in the pails of slop were fertilized from the honeywagon.

"We wore our stocking caps 24 hours a day because our shaved heads would get cold. They shaved our heads not only to keep the lice down, but in case we escaped they would be able to see our bald heads bobbing up and down.

"Toward the end of the war we could hear the Russians shelling Vienna, which was not too far away, probably about 40 miles from us. As soon as our guards heard that, they told us to get ready to move out. They told us to take everything we could carry but didn't say where we were going.

"We left the compound and made a three-week forced march west to the American lines. They wanted to surrender us to the American forces rather than the Russians because they were afraid the Russians would machine-gun them.

"That forced march was worse than being in prison. We walked, walked and walked and at night we slept in ditches or a barn if we were lucky. For food, we'd go through fields and scratch around for a potato or something. Sometimes the guards would allow us to walk up to a farmhouse and ask for a slice of bread. Some of the farmers were very nice. They would give us food.

"We would march for seven days and rest one day because the guards needed the rest also. Most of us were miserable with dysentery. The Germans tried to stop our dysentery by giving us powdered charcoal.

"While we were on our forced march, we would meet people under German guard walking in the opposite direction. They were all dressed in black and had long beards and their eyes were sunken back in their heads. They were starving. I asked one of the German guards who they were.

"He said, 'They are German Jews.' I asked what they were doing with them. He said, 'We're just marching them and marching them and marching them until they fall and then we shoot them and roll them into the ditch.'

"These Jews had probably had the same clothes on for months and we could smell them when we met them. They smelled worse than *we* did, if that was possible.

"We finally reached Patton's troops in a forest. The first American GIs we saw drove up in a jeep. There were two of them. They had a bushel of fresh eggs on the back seat. They said, 'Help yourselves.' We all started grabbing eggs and it turned out to be one big omelet. We ate them raw.

"The rest of Patton's outfit came and they were a bunch of real tough soldiers. The first thing they asked us to do was point out the guards who had been mean to us. About half of them were pointed out. They took those guys back in the woods and we heard their guns firing. They came back without the German guards. The rest of the guards like Big Stoop were saved. We didn't want anything to happen to Big Stoop.

"About half of the guards were older men from the Luftwaffe and they were nice to us. The rest were regular army guards and they were the mean ones.

"We were taken in GI trucks to a place in France called Camp Lucky Strike. We stayed there a week or so and were given clean uniforms. They fed us on soft bread with the crusts cut off, eggnog and boneless chicken. This is all we could eat for awhile and we could only go through the line once. They didn't want us to overload our stomachs. A couple of guys sneaked through again and became violently ill.

"We especially enjoyed the white bread. The Germans fed us a slice of black bread once a day and there was always a lot of sawdust in it for filler.

"We left by truck for LeHavre and were put on boats. We were next on the priority list after the sick and wounded. The name of the ship was *The Marine Robbin.* It was so crowded that half of us had to stay up on deck while the other half slept below. We switched around every night. Finally we landed in good old New York City.

"Did you make a career in the Air Force?"

"No. I was offered another stripe if I stayed in, but I'd had enough."

STARS

Lieutenant Colonel Orville Doughty

Orville L. Doughty retired from the Air Force as a lieutenant colonel. I met him at the Titan Missile Silo, which belongs to the Tucson Air Museum Foundation. He is the coordinator of this facility.

All Titan Intercontinental Ballistic Missiles were deactivated in the U.S., but this silo is open to the public for tours. It is walking distance from my home. Before this silo was deactivated and taken off the Soviet's target plan, I thought that buying green bananas might be a waste of money.

Orville kept copious and detailed notes in a journal furnished in a Red Cross package. I'm glad he did, because he is now able to tell his experience as a POW.

"Go ahead, Orville."

"We checked the schedule for the 20th of December, 1943, for mission number 111. It had been posted at 4 p.m., and we had until 6 p.m. to confirm that we'd be able to fly it. We had to have an aircraft that was in commission and at least a nine-member crew available.

"Mission number 111 was shown on the board to be the Eleusis Airdrome in Athens, Greece, which was a frequently flown mission and usually turned out to be a milk-run. The Germans had a group of Ju-88s stationed there, and their primary purpose in life was to keep us from getting a good night's sleep. When their airdrome was in good shape, along about nightfall, here they'd come. So when we had about

30 airplanes available, we'd go over and 'dig post holes' on their runway just to put them out of business for awhile.

"On this particular day, the Second Bomb Group had a free day from the master plan, so we were delegated to go to Athens with 30 B-17s and dig post holes.

"My plane, number 736, was in commission and the crew members were available. Eight planes from the 96th Bomb Squadron were to participate. The briefing was to be at 6 a.m., so, early to bed.

"The next morning, December 20th, our wake-up call came at 5 a.m. We had our usual breakfast of greasy bacon, dehydrated eggs and toast, which we had become used to for five months. No doubt all the other airmen in the Foggia, Italy area were treated to the same. After breakfast we dressed for flight and my bombardier and navigator went with me to the 2nd Bomb Group Mission briefing at 6 o'clock. The co-pilot and the rest of the crew went to our plane, *Pomona Prodigal* for pre-flight.

"We had just moved up to Foggia Number Two from North Africa a week or two before this mission. We didn't have all of our maintenance equipment yet, and I had a bit of a brake problem. This was bad enough but to make matters worse, at Foggia the taxiways ran up and down hill.

"Going downhill, it was sometimes difficult to keep the plane going slow enough to dodge some of the vehicles. I scared the heck out of a bunch of Italians when our wing-tip sliced across the slats on one of their trucks that was too close to the taxiway. The natives weren't hurt, but they learned to keep their distance from B-17s when they were taxiing.

"Eleusis airdrome is just north-west of Athens. Our load was 12 500-pound general purpose demolition bombs. We were given the usual briefing on the route map, the bomb altitude, climb altitude, our departure instructions and how we would form up. The weather officer gave us his best guess and then the briefers wished us luck and went back to bed.

"We started engines, taxied and took off on time and started forming up. Instead of circling during the form-up, the lead aircraft made 'S' turns while we fell into position. Our formation this particular day called for two waves. The first wave was a three squadron 'V'—18 aircraft—and the second wave had two squadrons in 'V's with 12 aircraft.

"My aircraft, number 736, was flying in the number two position of the last squadron in wave two. This position was referred to as 'Purple Heart Corner' or 'Coffin Corner.' We didn't have the protection of other 17s around us to keep German fighters away, so they would pick on the guys in our corner.

"Early in the climb-out we exercised our guns and they all checked out okay. Since we were sitting way back in the corner and the guys up ahead were also checking their guns, there seemed to be a lot of brass flying by us. We tried to stay spread out because a 50 caliber cartridge case flying out of a window can easily punch holes in airplanes.

"We leveled off at a cruising altitude of about 20,500 feet, where we were flying over scattered to broken cloud cover, and as we neared the coast of Greece, it became almost solid for a way.

"Everything was going according to plan until we neared the I.P. We were all pretty much relaxed, because we'd been here before and seldom had too much trouble with flak or fighters. After all, this was supposed to be a milk-run.

"It also made us feel good that we had quite a number of P-38s flying top cover for us. We felt pretty comfortable until we approached the I.P. and began seeing German fighter aircraft in the area and flak was popping up ahead of us.

"The I.P. is the initial point where we turn inbound to the target. It is the departure point for timing and everything for your bomb run. The I.P. was about six minutes out from the target, and the formation lined up on the bomb run with squadrons stacked into the sun for better fighter protection. This put our number 736 at the bombing altitude of about 21,500 feet. The time was close to 1 o'clock.

"While the reports indicated we'd have no flak until just about 'bombs away,' I wasn't too sure about that. I remember having to feather two engines that were hit by flak, and trying to stay on the bomb run and being behind and a bit below the rest. I also remember the bombardier saying, 'If you can stay on course for another minute or so, I'll still get the bombs on the target.' We did!

"By this time the formation was pretty much ahead of us. Major Buck Ainsworth, in the lead aircraft, called and wished us luck. He apologized for not being able to wait for us. I know the call was for us, because I went by the code name 'Doc.' I heard him say, 'I'm sorry, Doc. I just can't wait for you. Good luck.'

"We were now vulnerable to fighters, and an Me-109 got on our tail and shot up our number four engine. Later I discovered that a P-38 had taken the 109 off our tail but by that time the damage had already been done. So much for the milk-run!

"Now our problem was to get out over the Adriatic Sea and try to get back to Italy. Harry Dillon was my navigator, and he did a wonderful job. Harry took us down through a mountain pass through two layers of overcast while giving me constant heading changes and got us safely over to the Adriatic.

"At this point it looked like we had about three options. One was to try to get back across and crash-land on the heel of Italy. The second was to try to get up the Albanian coast as far as we could and either crash-land or bail out. The third option was to ditch in the Adriatic, which would be quite a dangerous operation with part of our engines out and very rough seas.

"As we left the target area we jettisoned all of our weapons and loose equipment to lighten the aircraft as much as possible. In doing this, Lieutenant Llewellyn, the bombardier, was pushing a .50 caliber out the nose hatch and it went off and shot him in the right arm. The bullet went in at his wrist, followed the bone up through his right arm and came out above his elbow. Naturally he had quite a bit of pain so our navigator shot him with morphine and we went on.

"This made ditching the least desirable of our options because of his injury. He probably wouldn't make it in the water. We decided to follow the coastline north to the shortest overwater way west to the heel of Italy.

"We were still letting down when we ran into the overcast at about 7,500 feet, and with only one good engine and part of another, we couldn't stay above the overcast. The navigator told me it was nip and tuck with the top of the hills at that point, so I elected to try to start my number one and two engines. This didn't work very well since I had shut them down because of a lack of oil, and I hoped they would operate long enough to get us to the coastline. They ran for a minute or so and froze up.

"We broke out of the overcast at about 3,500 to 3,000 feet and saw scattered clouds below us down to about 2,000 feet. We tried to hold at this altitude but the number three engine was getting pretty hot. This was the only engine still running at this time. The others had been shut down.

"At this time we were just off the west coast of the island of Corfu. A few minutes later, I made the decision to crash-land on the beach if I could find a spot.

"As I was turning in toward the island, I saw a sandy beach that appeared to be smooth. Then number three froze up. It shuddered a couple of times and locked up tight. We had just run out of engines, altitude, airspeed and ideas all at the same time.

"We became a four-engine glider. I ordered the crew to their ditching stations, the co-pilot was sending out may-day calls, and we landed, wheels up, on undulating sand dunes. It was probably one of the smoothest landings I had ever made, and I was thankful that no-body was hurt.

"I'm sure the good Lord was with me because when I leveled out, we cleared one sand dune, coasted down above another one, landed right on top of a second sand dune and slid down the backside of that one to a dead stop.

"The next few minutes were pretty hectic. We exited the aircraft and were met by a Greek patriot who informed us that German soldiers were just over the hill. We elected to get out our life-raft just in case we could get off shore. This didn't work out and it's probably a good thing we couldn't get into the water, because we would have been sitting ducks trying to get over the breakers.

"I elected to burn the *Pomona Prodigal*. We didn't have to worry about the Norden bombsight, because we had thrown it out to lighten the aircraft. We opened the drain cocks under the wing tanks and the gas puddled on the ground. We fired a Very pistol into it. The Very is a flare pistol with a pretty good-sized cartridge. The fire engulfed the plane immediately.

"About this time the German soldiers arrived, and I had been so busy, I hadn't had time to get scared. I guess I was pretty relaxed in getting out of the airplane.

"A German lieutenant came up to us and the first thing he said was, 'Nix pistola?' The first thing that came to my mind was that this guy reads the same comic strip I used to read—the Katzenjammer Kids. Then he said, 'For you das kriegs kaput,' which in German meant, 'The war is over for us.'

"This was by no means a one-man effort. I had the best-disciplined, best-trained and most cooperative crew that anyone could ever be blessed with. In short, they were marvelous, and I couldn't thank them enough for their outstanding performance.

"From a flying standpoint, my 32-combat-mission tour was over. And on a milk-run! And now, none of us had much control over the immediate future.

"After we were officially captured by the very polite Germans, we were marched away and spent that night on Corfu. As we marched away from the beach, I looked back and the only thing I could see was the vertical stabilizer with a great big yellow 736 standing amongst a big skeleton.

"We spent the night in a sort of impromptu barracks the German Luftwaffe was using. The following day we were flown to Athens in a Ju-52, which resembled an old Ford tri-motor from the '30s. We were taken out to Eleusia Airdrome, the field we had bombed, and given a meal in their mess hall. We talked to some of the German GIs. One thing I remember is one of the fellows couldn't speak any English, but he pulled out his mess kit to show me. The knife and fork had been broken in two and there was a big dent in the botton of his mess kit. He kept saying, 'Bommin, bommin.' He laughed and shook my hand.

"After the meal, we were taken into a hotel in Athens and put in rooms with guards on the doors. That afternoon the guards took us out for exercise. We walked up the hill to the Parthenon and in broken English, they told us all about it. We walked back down the hill and off to our right was the biggest Coca-Cola sign we ever saw.

"I began to realize that the German soldiers were just average guys like ourselves and were more interested in discussing general things than the war. They were just doing their jobs and were as anxious to get home as we were.

"The following day we were taken in another Ju-52 to an inland place called Salonika, which was a temporary holding place for shot-down prisoners of war. The next morning a guard came to the room I shared with my co-pilot and said that the Hauptman, or captain, wanted to see me.

"I went to his office, and he introduced himself and asked me how I was and said, 'Let's go over to the club and have coffee and meet some of the other officers.' I thought he meant some American officers. It was a German officer's club, and they were all Germans.

"We sat around with a lot of small talk and no mention of missions or anything like that. He told me he had been a flak captain and an artillery captain during Rommel's North African campaign. He said he had spent considerable time in the United States and at the present time he was temporarily in charge of this camp while waiting for a new assignment back in the Fatherland.

"After coffee and some Danish we went back to his office. He sat down behind his desk and offered me a chair in front of his desk. We talked a little more about where he had been in the United States. He mentioned my father's name and occupation. He said, 'You're from the Second Bomb Group, we know that, and you're from the 96th Squadron, we know that. This was your 32nd mission, we know that. In fact we have a dossier here on your entire crew.'

"The Hauptman said that they already knew a lot of things about us and he wouldn't bother asking a lot of questions. 'There is one thing we don't know, however,' he said. 'We know you moved from Maskall, North Africa up to Manfredonia in Italy on (he gave the date) so you see we know just about everything about you, but I'd like to know what base you were stationed on.'

"I said, 'I'm sorry, Sir, I can't tell you.' He said, 'That's all right, I'm pretty sure I know where it is anyhow,' and he reached behind him to a wall map and placed his thumb exactly on Foggia Number Two. Our base! I neither confirmed it or denied it, but I'm sure the look on my face was all the answer he needed.

"After a little more small talk I was taken back to my quarters. We stayed in Salonika over Christmas Day. On Christmas morning one of the German guards knocked on the door. We opened the door, and he handed us a fir branch and wished us a merry Christmas. That was kinda like a Christmas tree.

"A little later a Greek girl came in with a tray of cookies. That was the highlight of our Christmas. A few days later we walked with another American crew to the rail yard and were loaded into a boxcar with wooden benches and no heat. We were told they were taking us to Germany.

"We got down the road a piece and the train came to a halt. We stayed there for quite some time. The guards said, 'Tito, Tito.' They were trying to tell us that the underground had interrupted the rail service a bit. Tito at that time was the leader of the resistance.

"After the damage up ahead was cleared, we proceeded up through the Albanian Alps toward Germany. It was New Year's Day. Several of the German guards came into our boxcar, and they had a bottle of schnapps with them that they shared with us. We sat there and drank schnapps, which kinda kept us warm on New Year's Eve.

"The snow was pretty deep, and they had taken our shoes away from us to make sure we wouldn't try to jump off the train and escape. When we got to Vienna, Austria, they stopped in the marshalling yards and had the Red Cross come in to check us. I had 13 blisters on one foot and 12 on the other. The rest of my crew was in similar shape.

"The treatment for these frost blisters was the standard old blue ointment that they used to put on. A few years after the war was over, I still had purple ankles.

"We got going again and arrived in Frankfurt. We were taken on a street car out to their interrogation camp, called Dulag Luft, where we were put into solitary. At this point my crew was split up. My interrogation was very brief because the Hauptmann from our last interrogation had told them he knew more about me than I did.

"They had a mess hall set up there, and we got some pretty good food for a few days. We were issued Red Cross parcels, which contained a razor, toothbrush and pajamas.

"We talked with other Americans, and on a raid just a few weeks before, a good friend of mine and his crew had been shot down, and I had seen them go down. My crew had reported there were nine parachutes, and they saw the aircraft crash into a mountainside. I walked into the mess hall and here was Lieutenant Stead, the pilot of the aircraft. He looked pretty well beat up with several scars, but very much alive. He explained that he had got the rest of the crew out but didn't have time to get out himself. The plane crashed through some trees and slid down the mountain in the snow and came to rest. When he came to, he found himself in a hospital where the Germans had taken him.

"I might mention here that Lieutenant Llewellyn, who had been shot in the arm, was taken to a hospital and given great treatment. When I saw him again about a month later at Stalag One, he had nothing but kind words about how the German hospital staff had treated him.

"When we were split up, all the officers were taken to Stalag Luft One up by Barth on the Baltic in Germany, and as far as I know, the enlisted men were sent to Stalag 17B, which was a famous camp.

"While we were on our train ride, we were in the marshalling yard in Berlin one night, when the RAF came over on a bomb raid. We thanked God that the RAF didn't do precision bombing like we did. Their bombs went off all around us but none of them hit us.

"We got to Stalag One the next day and were met by a German intelligence officer by the name of Adolf Von Mueller. One of our navigators whose name was also Adolf Mueller, recognized him at the same time the German recognized him. Our guy spelled his name 'Miller.' The German said, 'It's good to see you again, Adolf.' Our navigator said, 'Wish I could say the same, Sir.'

"It turns out that the German intelligence officer, Major Von Mueller, had operated a photo lab in Santa Barbara, California, which was Miller's home town. Miller had done business with Von Mueller at his photo shop.

"After interrogation we were allowed to go to any barracks that had room for us. A friend of mine who was already there said, 'Get barracks three—get barracks three.' This fellow said, 'We all got out but Stead, our pilot. He didn't make it.' I replied, 'I've got news for you. Stead's at Gulag Luft. I saw him in the mess hall down there, and he *did* live through the crash, and he'll be up here as soon as the hospital releases him.'

"We were in the south compound and by the time we arrived, there were about 800 prisoners. When the war was over, there were over 8,000 men there.

"The barracks were set up in rooms, and we had about 30 men in our room. We had roll call every morning and every afternoon. We fell out for roll call and the Germans counted us. At dusk they closed and locked the shutters so we were locked in for the night.

"We each got a Red Cross food parcel about every two weeks. There would be a can of Spam, some margarine, soda crackers, prunes and raisins, plus five packs of cigarettes. This was supplemented by German rations, which were black bread and barley soup with insects in it. We used to kid about being first in line so we'd get some live meat in the soup.

"When the food parcels came in, we would each take the cigarettes and candy bar out. The candy was called a 'D' Bar and it was like a baker's solid chocolate bar. These were personal items. The rest of the items went into our combined or community property. We cooked from that accumulation of rations. The camp was organized and run by the POWs. We had our own committees, such as the escape and evasion committee and policy committee. We had our own camp commander and barracks commander. These were all recognized by the Germans as being a good means of keeping control.

"We needed a purpose, some sort of a routine. Americans can adjust to *anything*. We made our own eating utensils out of tin cans. We had a clandestine radio, and we kept up with the news. Our news committee kept the latest news posted on the wall inside a barrack. It was so good that the Germans used to come over and look at our map. We'd see *their* map once in a while and the only difference would be in the front lines. We would show that the First Army had pushed forward from point X to point Y, and when we looked at theirs, it would show that we had had a strategic retreat from point Y to Point X.

"We had some sports equipment that was provided by the Red Cross from Switzerland. We played baseball and horse-shoes. Some of the guys put on plays and musicals and they were pretty good.

"A buddy of mine, Bill Meehan, and I formed a thing we called the Kriegie Construction Company. We had both been in the construction business before the war, the architectural business, that is. We were both studying to be architects so we designed homes for some of the other Kriegies.

"We used any kind of paper scraps we could find and a stub of a pencil about an inch long. We designed homes for the Kriegies to use when they got home after the war. Recently one of the guys wrote to me that he had used the basic idea of the plan I drew for him and now had a nice home. It kept me busy.

"Other busy work was digging tunnels. *Everybody* dug tunnels. We had a sophisticated air blower machine made out of tin scraps. The Krauts liked this because it kept us busy and out of trouble and when the tunnels were about finished they knew about it from their seismographs and they were always there to meet us.

"We would harass the Germans as much as we thought we could get away with in other ways besides digging tunnels. Just helped pass the time.

"We had a small group of Russian prisoners in the camp, and they weren't treated very well. The Russians had all been issued German top coats. A German top coat is nothing but a tent without pegs. It hangs almost to the ground and you see a fellow wearing one and you think, boy, if you stuck a peg here and another there, he is all set for tonight.

"The Russians were all big guys and they had the biggest top coats you ever saw. There was a knock on our door one day and I opened it. Here was this big Russkie with his big top coat, and he wanted to come in. I let him in, and he wanted to know if we had cigarettes. We fixed him up with a cigarette, and he said, 'You want wood?' About that time, he opened up his big top coat, and he had a big cedar fence post under his coat. So he gave us the fence post.

"We really needed that fence post because in our barracks we had built a stove out of old scraps but it took a little more than our weekly ration of coal to keep it operating. Most of the barracks had had the wooden sub-flooring taken out of them and used for kindling. So anytime we could get hold of anything like this fence post, we were in business.

" 'How do you cut up a fence post to get it into our little stove?'

"Our barracks commander sent word over to the German camp commander that we needed a carpenter to do some repair work in the barracks. They sent Henry, the camp carpenter over with his buck saw, and we gave him some cigarettes. We pointed to the fence post, which we had hidden under a bunk and asked him if he could cut it up into 12-inch lengths. He said, 'Ya' and started cutting it up. About this time the base commandant walked in and poor old Henry thought he'd had it, but the major just laughed and let it go at that.

"The camp was actually run by our senior officers. Colonel Hubert Zemke was a fighter ace who had been shot down and Colonel Frances Gabreski was also an ace. Hubert Zemke was the ranking Air Force colonel, so he was the head guy.

"A month before I graduated from flying school in class 43-A, my wife, Myrna, and I were married in Roswell, New Mexico and there were nine cadets who were at our wedding. Two years later in December of 1944, eight of those nine cadets were all in Stalag Luft One. The ninth one had been shot down but got with the underground and walked out. Small world.

"I was walking in the compound one afternoon and ran into a fellow from my hometown. I asked him when he was shot down and what outfit he was with. He said he was in the Second Bomb Group, 96th Bomb Squadron. He said he was with a replacement crew for a crew that was shot down on the 20th of December. He was my replacement! Like I said, small world.

"We saved the prunes out of the Red Cross packages. We managed to get a bit of yeast from the Krauts and started fermenting some wine. It was potent stuff! We had a deal among ourselves and all the rooms in the barracks. For example, room three on such-and-such a day was going to open their wine and the latrine in the barracks would be reserved for them that night.

"We had some pretty good cooks in our camp, some of the Kriegies. We'd take the big crackers that were in the Red Cross parcels and grind them up into flour and use it to bake cakes with.

"From January, 1945 until the end of the war in May our Red Cross packages were kind of disrupted. The railroads were so shot up they couldn't get through. The Germans weren't deliberately starving us, because they didn't have much food for themselves. We got just a little bit of bread. They had a big rutabaga cart that they would bring in, and dump rutabagas on the ground. Our rations from the 4th of January to the end of the war were perhaps a rutabaga per day per man.

"Quite a few of our guys got pretty thin before we got out of there. In fact I weighed 105 pounds, which was at least 25 pounds under my normal weight.

"As I mentioned, we had pretty good maps of what was going on and the Krauts would look at our maps with interest. They could see that the Russians were getting close on the east, and the Americans were closing in from the west. Finally we were happy to wake up one day and hear the guns firing at Rostoff not too far away from us.

"The Germans forecast that the Russians would be on us at a certain day so the German commandant called Colonel Zemke and the other senior officers into his office and said, 'We're going to move west. We want no part of the Russians. You're welcome to take your troops and go with us.' Colonel Zemke said, 'No Sir, our Kriegies are not in shape physically to stand a forced march. We'll wait for the Russians.'

"That night the German guard patrol of about 12 soldiers with rifles came up to the American commander, saluted and handed him their rifles. Then the patrol from the next post marched up and handed our commander their rifles. Finally all the guard posts were manned by Americans and the Germans were without rifles. The Germans were very formal and cooperative.

"The day we were liberated, a Russian colonel riding the biggest white horse I ever saw, came up to the gate. He was met by Colonel Zemke. The Russian asked how we were and about our food. The next thing we knew, they came up to the gate driving a couple of dozen cattle into the compound and said, 'They're yours.' We had steaks for a day or so.

"We were kept in the camp for 17 days after liberation while the Russian and American diplomats negotiated on getting us away from the Russians. The Russians wanted to take us back to Russia. There was considerable 'horse-trading' going on for awhile.

"We were free to do more or less what we wanted to do but it was strictly military. We had to have a pass to leave the compound and if we overstayed, we were AWOL. Several of us went over to the nearby flak school. Then next to the flak school was one of the most horrible scenes I've ever seen. It was a concentration camp populated primarily with French people. They were nothing but skeletons that were barely alive. We took food from our camp over to them. Where we had double barbed-wire fences, they had doubled barbed-wire *electric* fences. If anybody grabbed hold of the fence-too bad!

"Then beyond the concentration camp was the airfield that supported the flak school. We knew it was there, because we had seen British Mosquito bombers coming in bombing and strafing the place.

"We had a unique monetary system while we were still under German control. One 'D' bar was worth 50 Lucky Strike or Camel cigarettes. One-*half* of a D bar was worth 100 Wings cigarettes. My buddy and I charged 150 cigarettes for a house plan while we were running our Kriegie Construction Company.

"On the final day, we were told we were going to be moved to Camp Lucky Strike in France. We were flown out by B-17s and C-47s. At Lucky Strike, we were issued new uniforms and started to look like humans again.

"Camp Lucky Strike was being run by the Army, not the Army Air Corps, and we soon learned they weren't like us. They were not giving us enough to eat in the chow line. One day General Eisenhower broke into the line a few men ahead of me and asked if we were being treated all right. Ike was told that we were not getting enough to eat. He went over to the mess people and said, 'Give them anything they want.' So we ate pretty good for a few days.

"Some of us left in a B-17 and landed at Orly Airport in Paris. We had a problem getting transportation out of Orly, so we took a bus to Le Bourget Airfield, where Lindbergh landed back in 1927. We got on a B-17 and flew to England. In London our orders were cut and then we went to Northampton and boarded the *Queen Elizabeth* for home.

"After we were liberated, I read the debriefing report of our last mission. Some of the statements made by various pilots who returned to base were:

Missing Air Crew Report : Aircraft #42-97736—96th Squadron; 2nd Lt. Orville L. Doughty, 0-2056204, Pilot:

'On the bombing mission over Eleusis Air Base at Athens, Greece, we were nearing the target when the tail gunner called and said 736 was in trouble. We fell behind 736, Lieutenant Doughty's plane, to give him coverage in case of fighter attack. We had seen them toss out their bomb sight, ammo and guns. Doughty called and said the ceiling was 3,500 feet. We dropped down to that altitude but couldn't find him. We tried to call Doughty but couldn't reach him. We circled around Corfu Island at just under 3,000 feet for 15 minutes but didn't find him. We proceeded back to base.'

'About 1243 hours, just off the target, I observed aircraft 736 with its number one engine feathered. A few minutes later I saw him feather number two. He was 10 miles south-west of Lake Inias. This is where he dropped out of formation.

'Just off the target I saw that 736 had feathered his numbers one and two. I called Major Ainsworth and got permission to drop back to cover him. We flew on his right wing and was in constant radio contact with him until he crashed. Doughty had told us that his crew was okay but the engines were giving him trouble. He gave his heading and air speed. He called 909 and said he would have to land in the water. I switched to 'D' channel and heard him calling 'May day' until just before he landed on the beach.' "

STARS

Captain Cecil E. Manning

Cecil Manning of Lake Providence, Louisiana, was another "guest" of Stalag Luft One. Even though he was behind the wire for 14 months, he doesn't remember running into Orvil Doughty.

"Cecil, you are the only fighter pilot I've talked to who dropped out of the sky in a P-51 Mustang and became a POW. How did you end up there?"

"Well, I enlisted in the Royal Canadian Air Force (RCAF) on July 9, 1941 and got a lot of very good training there. As soon as we were ready for combat, we were shipped to Ireland and from there to England.

"We flew Spitfires and Hurricanes with the American Eagle Squadron and had some very good fights with the Germans.

"In 1942 when the U.S. Air Force came over, we were ordered to join them. I transferred to the Fourth Fighter Group and flew their P-47 Thunderbolts for nearly a year. Then we got the newer P-51 Mustangs. We felt right at home in them because they were a lot like the Spitfires.

"On March 4, 1944, we escorted our bombers on their first daylight raid on Berlin. We mixed it up a little with the Krauts over there but got back okay. A buddy and I were ordered to drive to London and broadcast a message to the American people. We assured our radio audience that we had bombed Berlin and would continue to do so in the future.

"I had flown for several months on 90 to 100 missions. On March 6, we pulled the biggest daylight bombing raid of the war and, of course, we flew cover for the bombers. The target was Berlin.

"Over Berlin we really mixed it up with the German fighter pilots and shot them out of the air. I got two and damaged some others. We started home and could see a large body of water ahead of us—the Zuider Zee in Holland.

"Somebody got on the radio and reported seeing a few Me-109s below us, so I said, 'Let's bounce 'em and get one apiece and then outrun the others home.' So we went down on 'em. When we reached them, we saw some more P-51s engaging 'em, so we pulled back and started home.

"A fellow in my squadron called and said he was havin' trouble. Somebody said, 'Yeah, you're smokin' pretty bad.' He said, 'Yes, I'm goin' to get out. I want one of you guys to call my wife and tell her I got out okay.'

"I then glanced at my instrument panel and saw the oil pressure needle lyin' on the peg. I called our leader, Colonel Blakesley, and said, 'Colonel, my oil pressure is down on the peg.' He said, 'Yeah, you're smokin' pretty bad. Just ride it on down and we'll keep the Jerries off of you.' I don't really know what caused the problem. We had been fightin' some twin-engine night fighter Me-210s. They had rockets under their wings and a gunner in the rear. I know one of those boys put some holes in my wing, because I could feel them and see them but I'm not sure that's what got me.

"Anyway, I was on fire and it got pretty hot so I thought it was time to get out but it took a little effort. We'd been told to set the trim to nose-heavy, get unstrapped, roll it over on it's back, pull up and we'd drop out. Since my engine wasn't running, when I rolled it over on it's back, it fell with me and I only got about half-way out. I got back in and straightened it up. This time I climbed out and got away from the plane the old-fashioned way.

"I thought I was over the Netherlands because I'd seen the Zuider Zee, but I wasn't. I was still over Germany. I landed in a field where a fella was herdin' some sheep. I got my little phrase book out, went up to him and said, 'You Dutch?' He said, 'Ya, ya.' I said, 'Well that's good' so I turned to the Dutch section of my little book and pointed to the phrase that said I was an American flyer and needed a little help.

"He said, 'Nix, nix!' I hadn't realized that when I asked him if he was Dutch he had said, 'Ya' because Dutch meant *German.*

"Some people with rifles came across the field and joined us. They searched me and told me to come with them into town. Most of this conversation was with gestures, of course. On the way into the little village, about a hundred people joined us. I was hobblin' along because I'd hurt my right hip when I landed on a fence in that field with the sheep. It was hard to walk carryin' my chute, so I finally got a guy pushing his bicycle to let me put my chute on it.

"A woman caught up with us and pulled on my sleeve and using broken English she said, 'Do you know Mister Kroger?' I said, 'No, I don't know Mr. Kroger.' She said, 'You *must* know Mr. Kroger, he's in your country and has lots of grocery stores, and I used to work for him.'

"I said, 'Oh, yeah, I know about the Kroger stores.' She said, 'Well, I was workin' for him and came back over here to get married and in the meantime the war broke out, and I'm still here. We have been told that Mr. Roosevelt is doin' a bad job over there.' I said, 'Don't you go on believin' all that. It's *not true*—I'm *tellin'* you!'

"We arrived at the city hall of the Burgermeister's office or whatever, and they went through all the junk in my pockets I'd not been able to get rid of and asked a lot of questions. I told them I didn't understand what they were saying, and besides, I didn't know what that stuff was in my pockets or how it got there. I wasn't goin' to tell them *anything* but my name, rank and serial number.

"We started walking again and came to a farmhouse. They knocked on the door, and I think they told the woman who came to the door, that I was an American and needed some supper. They took me inside, sat me down and fed me. They had some pretty good food out there in the country—bread and butter, jelly and honey. The woman pushed a bowl of sugar over to me and a soldier said, 'Nix, don't give him your sugar.' She said, 'This is *my* house and I'll give him sugar if I want to!'

"We walked several more miles and came to a big building. They put me in there and later they shoved another guy in. He smelled pretty bad and was shook up and bruised. He told me he had started to jump out of a bomber when he noticed that another crewman didn't have a parachute. So he told the fella he'd hold him. He grabbed the guy and jumped. When the chute opened the poor guy was jerked away and fell. He felt pretty bad about that.

"We stayed in jail there for three or four days and finally a truck came over and picked us up and carried us to a railroad and put us into a 40 and 8 boxcar. We rode that thing day and night. The Brits would shoot at us nights and the Americans days.

"Finally we got up to the Baltic Sea and then on to Stalag Luft One. Orvil Doughty has already told about our life there so I'll skip that and mention a coincidence that happened 50 years later.

"My wife and I had a German exchange student in our home for a year. When she got home, she asked us to visit her on her 18th birthday, so we went to Germany and spent a month there.

"Her father knew a lot of people who were still living in the area where I went down during the war. He even found the woman who jerked my sleeve and asked if I knew Mr. Kroger. She was in her eighties. We went into her house and had a *great* visit. Wonderful people. Small world!

STARS

Sergeant Herman Meyer

"Herman, how were *you* treated as a Kriegsgefangenenkartel?"

"I was sent to England the first of April, 1945 and assigned to the 388th Bomb Group, 561st Squadron located at Knettishall, not too far from Cambridge.

"We got there when the weather broke and flew every day from the first day I was there. On the sixth of April we flew out of Knettishall at 4 o'clock in the morning.

"I was the waist gunner and was also the designated armament man on the ship. Just before takeoff, Sergeant Vawter, the ball turret gunner, said he was having trouble with the solenoids on his two guns. I had to check them out so I turned on the switches and found one solenoid defective.

"I removed the solenoid and told Vawter to go over to the shack and get a new one, in case I couldn't adjust the defective one. I went up in the airplane and got a screwdriver and came down and adjusted the solenoid. Between the time I was gone from the ball turret and got back to it, without my knowing, someone had put some ammo in the chambers of both guns.

"I tried out the solenoid and both guns went off. Since we were on the ground, the guns were 90° to the plane—pointing straight out toward the next plane where the crew was getting ready. Boy was I shook up!

"Lieutenant Hickman, my pilot, and I ran over there and as we were running, somebody else pulled the triggers and the firing started again. Two guys were hit in the other airplane and their plane was shot up pretty bad. It took all the communication out of it and, of course, it had to be grounded.

"That night when we got back from the mission, the general called the pilot and me in to find out what the deal was. The general then told the MPs to arrest me. As Lieutenant Hickman and I were walking out the door the general said, 'Hey Lieutenant Hickman, are you on a mission in the morning?' And he said, 'Yes, Sir.'

"The general said to the MPs, 'Let him go on the mission tomorrow and as soon as he gets back here, I want you to put him in the brig.' Well, as it turned out, we never got back from our mission on the 7th of April.

"We took off from Knettishall and headed for the German air base at Kaltenkirchen, which was a little north of Hamburg. We could have been over water on the whole mission but flew over France and Germany to help the morale of the troops on the ground. When we turned north toward the target, the Luftwaffe hit us with about everything they had. The war was nearing an end and this was to be the last big shot the Krauts made.

"We flew along with a battle going on constantly. There were bullet holes all over the airplane. At 1 o'clock the fighters were really heavy. At about five after one an Me-109 made a dive into our tail, knocking all the tail surfaces off. We had no control of the plane and it started in a spiral toward the ground, so we had to get out of the plane. We later learned that the Me-109 that hit us also went down and no parachute was seen.

"With the centrifugal force of the spinning plane, we had a hard time getting out. I headed out the back door and as soon as I left the plane I thought, man, I've messed up because the pilot might get it back under control and go back to England, but as it turned out, that didn't happen.

"I was the first one out of the plane and was heading for the clouds when I remembered what we had been told in briefing. The clouds were supposed to be at 6,000 feet and we had been shot down at 16,000 feet, so I had to fall 10,000 feet before getting to the clouds. I hoped the weather man was right about the cloud level.

"German pilots were shooting the fellas hanging under their canopies, and we knew we'd have to fall into the clouds before pulling the rip-cord so they would have a hard time hitting us. I pulled just as I hit the clouds. As soon as the chute opened, I looked at my watch. That seemed to be very important to me. It was ten minutes after one. That was a pretty scary experience for a 20-year-old farm boy from Wisconsin. I didn't know what was down below.

"I landed okay and heard the plane hit the ground with one heckuva roar, because all our bombs were still on board. 6,000 pounds. The Germans were waiting for us when we hit the ground. I landed in a small clearing in the middle of a forest not too far from Hamburg near the village of Luneburg.

"I was captured right away. Lieutenant Hughes and Sergeant Martin were killed by the Germans as soon as they landed. The tail gunner, Sergeant Wetzel, was killed when the Me-109 rammed the tail. A ball turret gunner can't wear his chute in the ball so Sergeant Vawter's chute was up in the plane. It had been shot so full of holes that when he put it on, jumped and pulled the rip-cord, it streamered out and didn't open.

"The pilot, bombardier, radio man and I got together after we were captured, and we were put in a little jail in the village of Luneburg. It was three stories underground and the cells were about six feet long and three feet wide. There were a lot of these little one-man cells along a hallway. There was a five-watt lightbulb hanging in the hallway.

"When they took us out, they told us we had been in solitary confinement for nine days. I called them a liar and said I was in there for 31 days. I figured out later that I had slept sometimes for a short time and thinking I had slept all night, I put another mark on the wall when I woke up. These were the worst nine days I'd ever spent in my life, because I was alone and I like to talk to people.

"They took us out of Luneburg and marched us through Hamburg. Before they did that, though, they told us if we wanted to get out of solitary, we'd have to tell them everything we knew. I sure didn't know much because I'd only been overseas for six days, and I really didn't know what outfit I was in.

"When we walked through Hamburg, we saw *one big shamble!* We later learned that the hot winds created by the fires had reached 200 miles per hours and 100,000 people had been killed. The Germans said *we* were the cause of this. We told them *we* hadn't started the fire, we were just mopping up.

"Lieutenant Hickman, our pilot, got hurt pretty bad when he bailed out, so the three of us had to carry him most of the way. We couldn't get any transportation because all the trucks, trains and everything had been destroyed by the bombing.

"We marched through Hamburg and *finally* got a train, which took us to Stalag Luft One.

"There were five compounds at the Stalag. Three were for American officers, one was for British officers and one for American and British enlisted men. There were probably 12,000 prisoners there.

"We were interrogated by English-speaking German officers. When I gave my name, rank and serial number, the officer talking to me gave me hell for fighting against the Fatherland. My name, Meyer, is German. I told him I didn't *have* a Fatherland, I had a *Motherland*— America. I did admit that my grandfather had come from Germany, but my dad and I were American citizens.

"We didn't have much food. Real thin soup and a couple of boiled potatoes twice a day while we were in solitary confinement at Luneburg, but here, at Stalag Luft One there were some Red Cross packages with cigarettes and candy. The Germans didn't have much food for themselves, so naturally they didn't give *us* much.

"Lieutenant Hickman and Lieutenant Wolfe were sent to the Officer's compound and Staff Sergeant Purdue, Staff Sergeant Eisenhower and I went to the enlisted men's compound.

"During the day we sat around playing cards and planning an escape. We used cigarettes for money at cards. When President Roosevelt died on April 12, 1945, the Krauts really thought they had it made. They couldn't understand that somebody was ready to step right into his office and keep the country going.

"I only spent 36 days in the prison camp. They never did mistreat us and when the war came to an end, Colonel Zemke was the camp commander and Colonel Frances Gabreski was our compound commander. Gabreski had become a top fighter ace before becoming a POW.

"When the Russians started advancing toward the prison, the German guards all took off running toward the American lines because they didn't want to be taken by the Russians. Then Colonel Zemke and Colonel Gabreski put allied officers in the guard towers.

"When the Russian colonel got into the camp, he was furious with Zemke and Gabreski and made us tear the towers and fences down immediately. We all went into Barth and this was the first freedom for some of the British who had been there for five or six years.

"Barth is right on the coast of the Gulf of Finland and was just a short distance from Sweden. Russian soldiers were all over the place with their wagons and horses. Each wagon had a load of hay on it with plenty of vodka and soldiers who all had their own women with them. It was just a drunken orgy and I knew right then we were in trouble.

"There was a bunch of German civilians at the coast waiting for passage to Sweden—old men, women and children. Some had babies in strollers. At least 200 of these people had been shot in the head by the Russians. They had even executed the babies. They cut the women's fingers off to get their rings. I knew right then we would never be able to get along with the Russians.

"We went to the airfield, which was all bombed up and started repairing the runways, because we had gotten a message from England that they would send B-17s and C-47s over to get us. We worked very hard to get the runways serviceable, because we were anxious to get back to England.

"The planes finally came and took our officers out. When all the officers were gone, they forgot about us enlisted men, and we had to walk back through Germany and France to the coast where small airstrips and camps had been set up.

"These were POW assembly camps named after American ciga-rettes—Lucky Strike, Phillip Morris, Camel and so forth. I reported to Lucky Strike and was flown from there back to England.

"The enlisted men didn't get back to the States for two months. The officers went home immediately.

"Bob, there's a B-17 pilot who saw my plane go down. Want his address?"

"Sure do."

"His name is Noah Thompson."

STARS

Lieutenant Noah Thompson

I took Herman Meyer's story to Noah Thompson.

"Noah, I'd like to hear your version of what happened to Herman's plane."

"I was flying my 17th combat mission that day. I was a first lieu-tenant and aircraft commander. We had been briefed to hit the Kaltenkirchen airfield, which was north-west of Hamburg.

"The weather was bad that morning and we were delayed for a few hours. We finally took off at 0900 hours with our group of 36 B-17s.

"About 45 minutes before we turned on our IP, we were attacked by 50 to 75 German fighters—Me-109s and Fw-190s. Our P-51s were escorting us and were out working the fringes of the formation. All of a sudden I saw a 109 flying into our formation. He was close! I could see the swastika on his tail.

"Everybody snapped to attention. The interphone came alive with, 'Bandits in the air! Bandits coming in from everywhere!' They started making passes and came in shooting! Our gunners were in action and the P-51s were picking them off on the fringes trying to keep them out of our formation.

"Planes, mostly enemy, were blowing up all over the place. A Focke-Wulf 190 came in and flew right into Lieutenant Bare's plane. It cut his plane right in two. The front half went into a flat spin and went down. The tail half went end-over-end as it went down.

"About 15 minutes later, an Me-109 came in and rammed into the tail of Lieutenant Hickman's plane, the plane Herman Meyer was on. Hickman pulled up into a stall, then winged over and started spinning. The tail section was just a mass of jagged metal hanging down. The tail gunner couldn't have survived.

"These both looked like rammings but we couldn't believe the Germans were deliberately doing this. I thought the first time that the German pilot had been killed and slammed into Bare's plane. But the second one, the one that hit Herman's plane *was* deliberate because the pilot made no attempt to pull away before hitting the plane.

"A total of eight of our B-17s were rammed that day. This ramming tactic was being used by the Japanese Kamikaze squadrons but the Germans hadn't been known for this."

"In April, 1991, Oberstleutnant Ulrich Saft of the German air force wrote to me. He enclosed a 3 1/2 by 5 inch photograph of the grave of the Me-109 pilot who rammed the plane Herman Meyer was in. The headstone resembles a propeller blade and has the pilot's name, birth and death dates on it—Fritz Meya—26.11.1919—7.4.1945.

The grave is located in Wendhausen, which is near Luneburg, where Herman Meyer was held in solitary confinement."

STARS

Anonymous POW

An ex-POW, who spoke on condition of anonymity, was asked to listen to the tapes from the four POWs and add anything of interest they may have overlooked. Here are his comments:

"There were inequities among POWs. One of them was the pay our officers received from the Germans. The enlisted men were not paid. Lieutenants received 50 Reichsmarks per months ($20.00), the captains were paid 75 RMs ($30.00) and majors and above got 100 RMs ($40.00). The U.S. government agreed to reimburse Germany after the war.

"English officers were also paid and they used some of the money to pay 'batmen' or enlisted men servants. I asked Sergeant Dan Piedmont if the American officers had 'dog robbers'—our equivalent of the British batmen. He said that every enlisted man in their camp was given the opportunity to 'dog rob' for our officers and not one man was interested. So unlike the British officers, *our* brass had to make their own beds, wipe the mud off their shoes and clean their latrines.

"The American officers did donate one-third of their Reichsmarks to a central fund, however, which was used for sports equipment, books, educational material, medical supplies and other things for the benefit of the enlisted men. This amounted to thousands of dollars.

"In addition, the amount of mail sent home each month was determined by rank. Generals could send five letters. Lower-ranking officers were allowed to send three letters, and the enlisted men only two letters.

"Thousand of American POWs got a head start on their college educations by attending classes in the German camps. The Young Men's Christian Association (YMCA) provided books, blackboard and other instructional material and the Germans gave permission to use various rooms in the barracks for classrooms.

"College credit was given for the courses that had qualified teachers and the proper facilities. Some of these were for languages, law, accounting, mathematics and music. Future U.S. Attorney General Nicholas Katzenback studied law while he was a POW.

"Each compound had a library with thousands of volumes. The YMCA and Red Cross provided many of the books and thousands of prisoners received both educational volumes and books of fiction from home.

"As we learned on the convoy from England to North Africa, in time of danger and stress men frequently became interested in religion. It was especially true in the German POW camps. Services were held for all faiths in classrooms and in the compound theaters. Chaplains for numerous denominations were available and usually preached to full houses. Chaplains also counseled the men on a wide variety of problems. One distraught fellow told his chaplain that he had received a 'Dear John' letter from his girlfriend. He had left his truck and his power of attorney with her. She married another guy and the happy couple were using his truck and spending the money in his savings account.

"There were, of course, many 'Dear John' letters. Most were grim and pathetic. Some, although not very amusing to their recipients, were humorous. A prisoner received one of the shortest 'Dear Johns' in history: 'Darling, I have just married your father. Love, Mother.'

"In addition to the books and athletic equipment provided by the YMCA, they also sent musical instruments and theatrical supplies. One trombonist found a secondary use for his instrument when he decided to become a 'moonshiner.' He collected the dried fruit in the Red Cross boxes and traded cigarettes to the German guards for yeast.

After he had fermented the brew, he distilled it in a large Klim (milk) tin with half a football bladder wired to the top. He fastened the neck of the bladder to the mouthpiece of his trombone, which he then placed under cold running water. The product *dynamite*.

"The main entertainment was card playing and gambling. This went on day and night and as the others said, cigarettes were used for money. Many of the POWs, however, fashioned checks for their state-side banks, even when toilet paper was the only means for doing so. A very high percentage of these POW checks were later honored by the banks when they returned home.

"Most of the American prisoners were forced into a basic sense of honor because if they were caught stealing from another POW, they were severely punished by their comrades. The Germans as a whole were honest. The quickest way to irritate a German guard was to make a remark about his questionable honesty. They were highly disciplined and when ordered not to pilfer the Red Cross boxes, they obeyed without question even though they coveted the soap and cigarettes. Some POWs believed this was due to the high German morals and others suspected that they feared severe punishment.

"Former POW Dan Piedmont stated the Germans would puncture the tin meat cans so they couldn't be saved for use during an escape. One of the POW chemists discovered that the meat would not spoil for several days, but when the tin started to turn blue due to a chemical reaction, it was about ready to spoil."

The first part of the interview with our nameless ex-POW seemed to indicate that they received good treatment. He later tried to balance this, however, by saying that for the most part, they received inhumane treatment. "We went hungry. All of us lost weight and were often too weak to exercise or walk very far. Our barracks were so overcrowded that some men went crazy. Our sanitation facilities were sickening and unhealthy. We didn't have enough clothing and bedding. Many of the sick and injured were ignored by the Germans and received no medical assistance.

"We lived in constant fear because we were repeatedly shot at inside the compound and some of the POWs were murdered in cold blood. One POW was standing in a doorway and was killed by a guard for no apparent reason.

"Escape was always our number one priority. We knew that digging tunnels was usually a waste of time as far as escaping was concerned, but it caused the Germans no end of expense and trouble. We felt that this kept the Germans busy and perhaps in having to maintain a larger staff at the compounds, they were not out shooting the allies. It was good for morale also because we felt that we were contributing to the war effort even though we were behind the wire."

Author's Note:

In writing this book, I made every effort to double-check and verify inputs from other sources. The only item I could not verify was the POW officer's pay by the Germans. The former POW who gave me this information referred to his detailed fifty-year-old notes (some coded) but I cannot confirm or deny this information.

However, when I researched the 97 articles of the Geneva Convention of July, 1929, relative to the Treatment of the Prisoners of War, I found the duties and responsibilities of everyone concerned from capture to liberation of prisoners of war, and learned that provisions in international law permits a country holding officer prisoners to pay them with the assurance that reimbursement from the prisoner's government will be handled after the war. So this information is probably accurate.

According to the Geneva Convention articles, treatment of the POWs by Germany shows they placed themselves *above* international law. The combatants in the ancient holy wars were inspired by a devotion to God. German combatants were inspired by a devotion to *their* god—Hitler. Japanese soldiers also looked at Emperor Hirohito as a god so no doubt our prisoners also suffered in their POW camps.

The writers of the 1929 Geneva Convention could not have predicted that during the next war, World War II, enemy soldiers would land and be captured far from the battlefields because of the extensive use of airpower. We all dreaded the thought of landing near a target we had just attacked. We all hoped to be captured by the well-disciplined military—not the civilians, who were not accustomed to the self-control of the military.

Especially vicious and tough were the uniformed children of the Hitler Youth movement. We dreaded running into them as much as we did the civilians.

The civilians of *any* country who lose their homes and loved ones to enemy action are not going to pay much attention to the Geneva Convention—if indeed they even know of its existence.

A story made the rounds while we were in England that a Luftwaffe bomber crew parachuted into the English countryside near the city of Bedford, not far from our air base, and was immediately captured by the police. As they were being marched to the jail in

Bedford, a mob of angry civilians attacked them with garden tools. Later, when the Germans were safely inside the jail, a policeman apologized to the German crewmen. "Sorry old chaps, we're usually very nice people."

After World War II, a cynical statesman, now long forgotten, said, in reference to the Geneva Convention, "The way to international hell seems paved with 'good' conventions."

SWASTIKAS

Marion D. Swetzer

Most World War II Luftwaffe veterans I tried to find were either dead or reluctant to talk about their experiences. The ones who *did* cooperate refused to answer many of the more sensitive questions. That seemed to indicate the "brain-washing" they received a half-century ago had been very effective.

Marion D. Swetzer, from Stuttgart, Germany was able to shed some light on the plane-ramming situation.

"Marion, was this ramming thing one of Hermann Goering's ideas?"

"No, historical records show that Oberleutnant Lange wrote to Field Marshall Erhart Milch, Goering's deputy, and suggested it. Lange said he would be satisfied to die if he could take at least seven of the enemy with him. This was about a year before the decision was made to ram. Goering gave them permission to go ahead with the project but then stayed out of it."

"A school for ramming was set up?"

"Yes, I have read that it was started in 1944."

"But Goering had little to do with it?"

"Not a whole lot. Actually by this time Goering was hated by everybody in the Luftwaffe. They said he was indecisive and had no backbone. Major Gottlieb Kuschke and Colonel Heigl got things started. Later Major Otto Koehnke was put in charge of the Elbe group."

"Elbe? Isn't that a river in your country?"

"Yes. Elbe was a code name."

"How did they manage to attract student pilots for a dangerous mission like this?"

"The Luftwaffe was getting desperate and asked for volunteers for 'special and dangerous operations.' Three hundred volunteered and half of them were chosen. There were a lot of 'blue bloods' among the volunteers but only men from the lower middle class were selected. They were all normal, average young boys between the ages of 18 and 23. Most were under 20."

"Were the volunteers led to believe there was a chance to survive?"

"Not really. They were told to try to ram with a wing and then bail out. In fact the canopies of their Me-109s and Fw-190s were modified to make it easier to eject. Each volunteer had to sign a statement that he was aware he would probably die."

"Do you think it's possible that the B-17 named *All American* was deliberately rammed over the Tunisian desert a year or so earlier? The crew told me they thought the pilot was probably killed *before* his plane rammed them."

"It's quite possible. A few pilots *had* rammed. Some said it was suicide and they took this way of bringing their lives to an end by going after B-17s."

"Where was the training school for ramming located?"

"I'm not sure. It was highly secret. The students were isolated. They couldn't leave the area or talk to anybody. They couldn't even write letters."

"Obviously the instructors had no ramming experience."

"No, but one pilot had 'jumped the gun' and rammed a bomber. He bailed out and came to the school to talk about it. He couldn't offer any methods or tactics, however.

"Major Koehnke didn't have any ramming experience, of course, but told his pilots to make a diving, firing attack on the B-17s and if this failed to bring them down, they were to ram them behind the wing in the waist gun area and bail out if they survived. I read that 80% of the ramming pilots died in a very short period of time."

"So there were survivors?"

"Yes. In fact the Americans had a ramming pilot in a POW camp."

"Did he tell his story during interrogation?"

"He boasted that he was a perfect example of a brave Nazi. He said he was proud to do it for the Fatherland.

"Nine Soviet pilots, desperate to make a dent in the Luftwaffe onslaught, rammed German aircraft during the first days of the offensive. One pilot, Boris Kobzan, survived four rammings by bailing out."

SWASTIKAS

Alfred Seufert

Mr. Seufert lives in Wurzburg, Germany. During World War II he flew bombers and fighters. Toward the end of the war he flew Messerschmidt 262 jet fighters.

"Mr. Seufert, what were you flying at the start of the war?"
"I was flying bombers—Heinkel-111s. At the very beginning I flew 27 missions over France before they surrendered. On the second day of the war we were attacked by French fighters. My He-111 had 14 hits. After we returned to our station, we had the ground crew paint circles around the bullet holes as 'trophies' of our engagement. We were very proud of them and happy to have survived."
"Were the French pilots good fighters?"
"Fairly good. In fact, while we were bombing a target near Lyon, the French fighters helped to *decimate* our staffel (squadron) of 30 planes. The French anti-aircraft guns accounted for a lot of our losses also. This is because we were flying low."
"Did you fly in the Spanish civil war?"
"I was supposed to have been used in the Spanish activities but that did not happen because I was sent to East Prussia for further training. By the time I had completed my training, the Spanish war was over. I was very young at the time."
"When you finished in France, you started bombing England, didn't you?"
"Yes. I was on the first three raids over London. On all three our target was the oil tanks along the Thames River. Our positions in the bomber formations were decided by a lottery. On our first raid, I was in the lead staffel. We suffered a lot but the *entire* 9th staffel was shot down. On 5-9-40, we flew 100 machines to London and only 18 were fit to be used again."
"Were most of your casualties from British fighters or anti-aircraft fire?"
"About half-and-half. It got so bad that before take-off, we would sit on the ground near our planes and talk about who might not come back."
"Didn't you have fighter protection?"
"Yes, we usually did. Things seemed to go wrong a lot though. As an example, one time we were delayed getting airborne and our fight-

ers had gone up ahead to meet us. By the time we started crossing the English Channel, our fighters were returning because they were low on fuel. We had to face the Spitfires and Hurricanes alone over the channel and my plane was one of only 18 out of 42 that got to London."

"And over London you were probably under ack-ack fire, weren't you?"

"On this particular mission—no. The Spitfires and Hurricanes were all over us. My plane was hit in one engine, which slowed us down, making us an easy target. I was wounded in the leg and one of my gunners nearly lost an arm. Only one man on my five-man crew wasn't hit.

"We wore steel helmets on these raids and really expected to be shot down. When we got back to the channel, four Me-109s arrived to engage the British. This gave us some hope that we might survive.

"By this time, however, we had one man dead, three wounded and only one *not* wounded. We got back and were treated in the hospital."

"Were all of your missions over England?"

"No. I spent two years on the eastern front. Most of our losses were from Russian flak—not fighters. We all had a great fear that we would become prisoners of war in Russia. Some of our reconnaissance photos showed German prisoners laying in the snow with no clothes on. We all knew how fiendish the Russians were and we would rather be prisoners of the English."

"Obviously you were lucky and didn't fall into Russian hands."

"Yes, I *was* lucky. On 8-13-41, we were brought down by Russian ack-ack. Only two of us on our plane had parachutes—my navigator and myself. The other three didn't. We jumped and landed near a dense wooded area and started to run with the Russians right behind us.

"We hid in the woods and heard the Russians thrashing around and shouting. My navigator was so badly burned he looked like a Negro. He didn't have time to stop running or complain, though. It had been hard to bail out because the entire plane was on fire and we were surrounded with flames.

"Throughout that afternoon and night we could hear the Russians looking for us. We kept going west away from the noise they were making and finally got to one of our Panzer divisions and were saved. This was my 113th mission."

"After having flown so many missions on the eastern front, were you reassigned to the west?"

"No, I was sent right back to bomb Russia and flew missions every day. The Russian fighter pilots were not very good and we didn't worry much about them, but their ack-ack was *very* good.

"I was shot in the knee and landed back in the hospital, My cast was finally removed and I was sent to Vienna to join a new staffel. Then the continent was invaded and we found ourselves fighting a lot of Americans. They shot many of our crewmen as they were parachuting down. This was the only bad action by Americans I witnessed."

"Were you aware of the Jewish situation?"

"We all knew how the Jews were being treated but I, for one, did not approve. I had a Jewish girlfriend."

"When did you switch from bombers to fighters?"

"Toward the end of the war I started flying the new jets—the Me-262s. On my fourth flight I was attacked by two American Mustangs while I was practically clipping the treetops trying to land on my field. The landing was fast and hard and while still rolling I opened the canopy and jumped out on the wing and fell to the ground. The Mustangs made two more attacks on me as I was crawling behind a pile of rocks. This saved my life, but I had a 50 caliber bullet in my leg."

"General Adolf Galland commanded the jet units didn't he?"

"Yes. I became one of his flight leaders. In one engagement I had to jump out of an Me-262 jet on a night flight. I was very lucky and lived to celebrate with a few drinks."

"I know that Galland was taken prisoner. When did that happen?"

"The Americans got to Munich and he was captured there while we were moving east. I escaped and spent six weeks hiding in a little hut. While walking on the road to Westheim I was stopped by the Americans and put in jail. There I met an old friend who had flown Fw-190s. We had to sleep in the open and weren't given much to eat."

"How old are you, Mr. Seufert?"

"I was born May 17, 1919. I want to say that your bomber and fighter crews did their jobs well. We admired them. I felt a lot better when I left bombers and became a fighter pilot. Actually I requested to be trained as a reconnaissance pilot but was turned down and put into fighters. This suited me fine because I no longer had the responsibility of several crewmen."

"Mr. Seufert, I must admit that one of my heroes was one of *your* pilots, General Adolf Galland, and I'm going to try to locate him for an interview. Did you know him very well while he was your commanding officer?"

"Not really. But I sat next to him recently on his last birthday celebration in Brandenberg-Briest, which is a few kilometers west of

Berlin. It was a high honor for me. He is an outstanding individual with a great personality. During the celebration he and the rest of us talked about how much we disliked Goering. Galland told us that Goering was not unaware that he was despised.

"Galland is quite a ladies' man. Several years ago he put a notice in the newspaper that he had sent his 'partner' on her way. I do not know if he is still alive but if he is I'll help you find him. He would be in his 80s."

"Finally, what did you know about the pilots who were trained to ram our B-17s?"

"Nobody has ever asked me that question. It was only a rumor. Simply a rumor."

"Thank you, Mr. Seufert."

Author's Note:

Galland was a product of secret German training that side-stepped the Versailles Treaty, and he learned to fly in Italy. At that time he was a civilian.

He used to irritate his boss, Herman Goering, by telling him that he wanted to equip his boys with British Spitfires when Goering asked him what he needed.

SWASTIKAS

Lieutenant Ulrich Sigel

Ulrich Sigel (named changed by request) of Langenhagen, Germany, was a first lieutenant in the Luftwaffe during World War II and had flown his bomber on many raids over England.

"Mr. Sigel, the British tell us there were more of your Heinkel-111 bombers over their country than any others. Is this because it was a new airplane in mass production?"

"No, it wasn't new. We used them in the 1930s in the Spanish Civil War. It was a good machine, though, and production continued long after that.

"This is the plane I flew. It was a medium bomber, twin-engine, slender, fast and had long tapered wings. A *beautiful* machine."

"How many crewmen did you have on the He-111?"

"Five. Three in the nose compartment and two aft of the wing."

"Hitler gave Spanish dictator General Francisco Franco some of the planes your country used against the Loyalists didn't he?"

"Yes. We left a couple of Me-109 staffels (squadrons) and some tri-motor Ju-52 transports in Spain. I heard they were still being used as late as the '70s."

"Then you flew in the Spanish Civil War?"

"No. I flew He-111s *later* in the *world* war. I was out of Germany for awhile, though, during the Spanish war. Some of us were sent to South America on a rotation basis to fly Ju-52s and Ju-86s. We were in Brazil, Columbia and Bolivia. I flew from Bolivia."

"What was the mission of the Luftwaffe in South America?"

"We were training in that tropical area to be ready in case the Panama Canal should be bombed."

"This is the first time I've heard of it."

"Well, your *government* knew about it. Your spies found out that Germany was training pilots and crews for the bombing of the canal. Hitler and Goering had larger plans than that. They were going to send 3,000 bombers over to Brazil from Africa and wanted to use them to proceed north a step at a time and eventually hit Washington."

"And Hitler would send troops over to work with the Luftwaffe?"

"Of course! Certainly! And there were already two million Germans in South America and even more Italians."

"And you say that Luftwaffe pilots were already being trained in South America?"

"Yes—not only being *trained,* some were flying the aircraft of the Columbo-German Aerial Transport Company and going to within two hours flying time from the Panama Canal."

"Was this aerial transport company owned by Germany or Columbia?"

"Neither. It was owned by one of *your* companies."

"It was an *American* company?"

"Yes, Pan American Airlines owned it."

"*Pan Am?* How did *they* acquire the airline?"

"Who knows—they probably made an offer that couldn't be re-fused."

"But the Columbo-German Aerial Transport pilots were *civilians,* weren't they?"

"Yes, they were civilians but had been Luftwaffe trained and were all in the air force reserve. Some of them were our national heroes from W.W.I."

"*Incredible!*"

"And I understand that your government *and* Pan Am kept this ownership a secret from your people and *most* of your highest officials."

"That doesn't surprise me. I've found that our bureaucrats keep us in the dark about a *lot* of things. So you trained in the jungles?"

"Yes, the jungle training was very important. And having to learn to take off and land at 2700 meters (approximately 9,000 feet) was a real experience since we were all sea-level pilots."

"How old are you, Mr. Sigel?"

"I am 79 years of age."

"The British say that your Heinkels bombed one of your own unprotected cities by mistake early in the war."

"Nein! Nein! They are not telling the truth! They are referring to Freiburg, but *they* bombed it."

(Mr. Sigel still wanted to believe the false stories put out by his propaganda ministry at that time.)

"Mr. Sigel, I was in London when some of your chaps bombed it. Will you tell us what it was like from *your* point of view?"

"I was on many London raids. Here is a typical one: Our geschwader (group) left our base in Lille, France about 11 p.m. Soon we saw the whitecaps of the English Channel in the moonlight. We were at about 3,500 or 4,000 meters (approximately 12,000 feet) to be above the barrage balloons hanging over the city. We could see London many kilometers away because of the fires started by a geschwader of Heinkels before us. Then the searchlights started probing the sky over the city.

"When we got close to London we could easily see the flowing Thames River snaking its way through it. We followed the river to the Royal Arsenal and dropped our 500-kilo (approximately 1,000 pound) bomb, which was shackled beneath the fuselage. We continued down the blazing river to the Surrey docks and dropped some incendiaries. We then turned north to the Saint Paul's Cathedral area and released the rest of our incendiaries. Of course, their anti-aircraft guns kept peppering us as we were heading away from the city toward the channel. Then their night fighters attacked us and we saw their blazing tracers streaking all around us."

"The British say you flew over Coventry and bombed a *hat* factory, the *only* factory in that city."

"*Nein! Unwahr, falsch!* (No, not true.) There were *many* aircraft parts factories in and around Coventry so we *gutted* it."

"Is your artificial leg a result of the war?"

"Yes. On my last raid over London, one of their flak bursts tore into my cockpit and injured my leg so badly it had to be removed as soon as we got back to our station."

"Did you have fighter escorts on your raids?"

"Not all the way to the targets but our twin-engine Me-110s would engage the Spitfires and Hurricanes and later the American night fighters over the channel. The Me-109s were not used very often for night flying because they had no gyrocompasses or artificial horizons necessary for instrument flying."

"Your injury probably took you out of the war, didn't it?"

"Nein, nein. *All* of us served in one capacity or other until death or the end of the war. After being released from the hospital I was sent to the aircraft production office in Berlin. General Erhard Milch was the chief. Milch was a personal friend of Field Marshall Goering and actually, second in command. None of us liked Milch. He was a schweinehund! And he was a *Jew!* He would go out of his way to punish someone for absolutely no reason just to show his power and authority, I suppose.

"Milch was a *Jew,* can you believe it? His mother was Aryan but his father was a *Jew!* Goering needed him so he asked Milch to denounce his father. He did but that did not satisfy Hitler. Goering then forced Milch's mother to sign a false statement saying that his father was actually an Aryan who had been friendly with her during her Jewish husband's absence on business. No truth to it at all. At that time our top people could change *anything* they wanted to work things out their way."

"How was the Luftwaffe started?"

"As you know, Luftwaffe means 'air weapon.' It came into being because of the work of two officers—Field Marshal Herman Goering and Lieutenant General Wolfram von Richthofen. Goering had flown in World War One and Richthofen was a cousin of Menfred von Richthofen, our famous 'Red Knight of Germany.' "

"Wasn't General Adolf Galland your top ace?"

"No, Major Erich Hartmann was. He had over 350 kills and Galland had only 103 kills."

"This is *very* impressive compared to the American kills."

"Yes, that is because unlike *your* pilots, *we* flew until we were either dead or injured so badly we couldn't climb back into a cockpit."

"Galland is still alive, isn't he?"

"I think so. He became the commander of all the Luftwaffe fighters. He was a cigar smoker so he had a cigar smoking Mickey Mouse painted on the side of his Me-109 below his cockpit. During the Battle of Britain *alone* he got 57 kills."

"So Galland wasn't a newcomer to the Luftwaffe?"

"No. He flew in the Spanish Civil War where he developed the incendiary fragmentation bombs. They exploded with fire much like the napalm bombs did later on."

"We have heard that General Galland flew jets near the end of the war."

"Not only *flew* them, he commanded Jagelverband 44, an Me-262 staffel. He recruited 50 of the most battle-toughened pilots to fly the new jets. A lot of them were convalescing in the Luftwaffe pilot's rest home. They were anxious to sacrifice their lives, if need be, to fly the jets."

"Does this mean the jets were used for ramming?"

"Ramming? Of *course* not! There was *never* any ramming!"

"Getting back to Major Hartmann, your ace of aces. Can you tell us more about him?"

"Hartmann flew a black-nosed Me-109. He had 825 aerial combats and shot down 352 enemy planes. So many of his victories were Russians on the Eastern Front that they called him, 'The Black Devil of the Ukraine.' The Russians placed a 10,000 ruble price on his head. He was *never* hit by enemy fire but was forced down 16 times only because he was hit by the debris from his destroyed enemy aircraft.

"At the end of the war, Major Hartmann surrendered to the Americans who promptly handed him over to the Russians. They kept him in their prison camps for ten years. Then the Russians offered him a position in the Soviet East German Air Force. He refused and was sentenced to 25 years hard labor. In 1955 a political exchange was made and he was released. Later, he commanded the *West* German Air Force. In the 1960s he visited *your* country and flew an F-106 supersonic fighter."

"Did you have an ace in the North African Theater or Operations?"

"Oh, *yes*. Hans Jochim Marseille was a *great* ace in North Africa. He flew Me-109s and in only 12 months he had 158 kills! Most of his victories were over enemy fighters. He was returning from a Stuka escorting mission when his 109 caught on fire. He tried to stay with it for a few more minutes so he could get back to our lines but the fire got so bad, he opened the hood, rolled over and fell out. The slipstream blew him back into the tail and he fell to the desert with his parachute unopened. His score at the time of his death was around 200 enemy fighters and bombers."

"Your pilots seemed to have had very high scores."

"Yes, in fact, 103 pilots had more than 100 kills, 13 had over 200 kills and two had over 300 each."

"Do you have the figures on your final wins and losses?"

"Yes, 265,000 Luftwaffe members were killed or reported missing in action and 213,000 were wounded during the war. *Our* wins were *impressive*. We destroyed 70,000 Allied aircraft while losing only 62,500."

"This is a little off the subject, but it has been of interest to historians: What is *your* version of the Nazi SS massacre at Oradour-sur-Glane?"

"*Das ist alles! Dankeschoen!*"

That is all—Thank you," brought the interview to an abrupt end. After a half century, there were still some "sore spots" that Mr. Sigel did not care to discuss. Mr. Sigel's great-nephew, who was the interpreter, said he had talked more about the war during the interview than he had in 50 years but that some of the questions had disturbed him.

The Stuka mentioned earlier was equipped with sirens attached to its fixed landing gear, which were called, "Trumpets of Jericho." Combined with the screeching of air rushing through the slatted dive brakes, the high-pitched scream of the sirens added an extra element of terror to their attacks. Our "ground-pounders" estimated that the Stukas made their dives at about an 80 degree angle at 350 miles per hour with deadly accuracy.

SWASTIKAS

Walter R. Boehner

Mr. Boehner lives in Denver, Colorado.

"Mr. Boehner, let's start with the only information we have about you. You were an ace at age *17?*"

"Yes, actually I was almost 18 when I got my fifth one."

"And I understand you were the youngest ace on *either* side. How did you start flying at such an early age?"

"Well, my father was a businessman in Cordoba, Argentina. He was an international meat exporter and had his own airplane.

"When I was only eleven or twelve years old, he started taking me on business trips around South America and taught me to fly. When I was twelve, he was letting me do the pre-flights, take-offs and landings. He did the navigating—I did the rest."

"What kind of plane were you flying?"

"A Bellanca."

"How did you get started flying in the Luftwaffe?"

"I really became interested on a trip to Columbia. We met some Luftwaffe pilots there who had just come over from the Spanish war. They were flying Ju-52s but told us about the modern bombers and fighters that were being used in Spain."

"Did they tell you how they got to Spain and how many others were sent there?"

"Yes. General Erhard Milch recruited them and asked them to 'volunteer' for duty with the Spanish Nationalists, who were fighting the Spanish Republicans. The Italians were also flying with the Nationalists and the Russians were fighting with the Republicans.

"Generals Goering and Milch were anxious to become involved because it would be the first wartime activity for the young Luftwaffe and they could evaluate the effectiveness of our men and machines under wartime conditions. They called this action *Operation Magic Fire* and named the group of airmen *The Condor Legion*. Nearly all of the recruits were Nazis. *I* was never a Nazi, by the way.

"About 3,500 men were sent to Spain and later the number grew to 5,000."

"We've been told that General Adolf Galland flew in Spain."

"Oh yes, he flew over 300 sorties in his Me-109. In fact, Galland was the developer of 'carpet bombing.' "

"What did the Italians fly?"

"They flew Fiats—bombers and fighters. I was told that our machines were far superior to theirs."

"Okay, how did *you* get into the Luftwaffe?"

"I was traveling in Europe with my father, who was developing markets for beef. We were in Germany when the war started and were detained. We were given our choice of working in an industrial plant or becoming soldiers. My father, who was thirty-nine years old, went to work in a munitions plant. I was only fifteen—almost sixteen, but had many hours logged as a pilot, so I volunteered to become a Luftwaffe pilot."

"And you were accepted?"

"Yes. I was sent to a primary training base near Bonn where I trained for five months. I remember the cold weather there more than anything else. They would get us out of bed before daylight and have us run to a nearby river, where they had broken the ice, and make us jump in. We would then run back to our barracks and get dressed for breakfast. After awhile it wasn't too bad. It was supposed to toughen us up. And it *did!*"

"Is this where you learned to fly the Me-109?"

"No, it was at an advance training base midway between Bonn and Berlin. Actually, we were at Bonn for about five months and at the fighter training base for seven months. This is where we flew the 109s and learned fighter tactics and gunnery. We had two machine guns in the cowl and one 20mm cannon in each wing. At this point, I became a flight sergeant."

"Did you then go against the Americans?"

"No—the *British*. My first five kills were British—four Hurricanes and one Spitfire. My last kill was just two weeks before my eighteenth birthday. By the end of the war I had nine kills."

"So you flew on the western front."

"I spent some time on the eastern front. We were sent there on a rotation basis. While there, I did a lot of tank busting, which was close to the front lines. The ack-ack fire was terrible, but we seldom saw a Russian fighter."

"Did you ever get an American?"

"I don't think so."

"You're not sure?"

"I shot at everything in the sky that didn't have swastikas on their tails."

"Well, at this late date it really doesn't matter. Thank you, Mr. Boehner."

SWASTIKAS

Lieutenant Hans Fischer

I could not find a Ju-88 pilot who had dropped bombs on us in North Africa. Fortunately, however, I located a Ju-88 commander, Hans Fischer, who dropped bombs *near* us in Italy. After giving me a warm, friendly greeting at the door of his Swiss chalet, we spent a relaxing afternoon telling war stories.

"Hans, I feel a lot more comfortable seeing you sitting across from me in your living room instead of somewhere *above* me."

"Yes, the war is long over and there is no reason to be mad at each other anymore."

"How many different types of planes did you fly and how many crewmen did you have?"

"I only flew the Junkers-88 aircraft, which we used for both level and dive-bombing. The crew consisted of the pilot, navigator, radio operator and a gunner. There was no bombardier. The pilot did the bombing."

"Where was your gunner located?"

"He would lie in a bathtub-shaped pod under the fuselage and fire his gun to the rear. I could never understand why we had a gunner. His pod caused a drag that slowed us down and another thing, we flew only at night and when the gunner fired tracers at night-fighters, they could tell by the fire *exactly* where we were."

"I was not aware that Ju-88s were used as dive bombers."

"We started using them because the Stukas were too slow and couldn't carry a large bomb load. One of my most frightening missions was on a dive-bombing trip. I started the dive at 4,000 feet and had my eye glued to the sight. The navigator was supposed to call out our altitude, but didn't for some reason, so I kept diving. I glanced up away from the sight for a split second and saw the ground rushing up at us. The thought raced through my mind that we were going right into the target but I pulled back on the control column with all my might and we just *barely* missed the ground. I think all four of us soiled our britches."

"The reason I was anxious to talk to a Ju-88 pilot is because Ju-88s were used against us down on the desert in Africa. They came over every night and dropped 500-pound bombs."

"Are you sure they were 500-pounders? It's more likely they were 200 or 250-pound bombs, which were more effective on airfields. The 500-pound and larger ones were used primarily on ships, buildings, and bridges."

"Well, from the shape of the shrapnel we picked up, we assumed they were 500-pounders. Anyway, they *scared* us to *death!* We used to say, 'Well, it's about time for Jerry to arrive,' or 'The Krauts are on their way.' "

"Yes, we knew you were calling us Krauts. We felt it was a bit demeaning. We called the Americans 'Amis' and the British 'Tommys.' "

"I don't recall that you ever bombed our airfields in the Foggia area."

"No, but we knew you were flying out of Foggia. We flew out of Pordenone, which is about 50 miles north-west of Venice. Of course we usually flew nights because of your fighters. Our main targets were around Rome and south of there. We went after trains, roads, bridges and so forth. We flew many missions to Anzio Beach where the American and British beachheads were. At Anzio the flak was so intense that it looked like we were flying into a huge ball of fire. It was

"I was over the Thames River docks in my He-111."
—Lt. Ulrich Sigel photo

"A photographer in another He-111 caught my bombs falling on London." —Lt. Ulrich Sigel photo.

My crew. I'm second from left. — Lt. Hans Fischer

My Ju-88 on a bombing mission. — Lt. Hans Fischer

one of the most frightening experiences I had. We were concentrating on the ships in the invasion force and we got ack-ack from them as well as from shore.

"That wasn't the only danger in flying in Italy. There were high mountain ranges and I used to have nightmares about flying into them."

"Did you stay in Italy or were you sent to the west when D-Day happened?"

"We were sent to Melbrook, which is near Brussels, Belgium as soon as the invasion started. I was sleeping one night. About three in the morning I was awakened and told to grab anything I could take with me because we were moving our whole base to Belgium. We knew there would be allied fighters around so we flew as low as we could."

"Then you flew missions against the invasion forces?"

"Yes, every night. We would take off at Melbrook and fly 100 meters (300 feet) above the ground to evade radar detection until we got to Cherbourg. From Cherbourg, we started climbing to our bombing altitude, which was 4,000 meters (12,000 feet). We had set up some huge searchlights that pointed in the direction of the invasion beaches —our target.

"That first night we experienced the *worst* anti-aircraft fire I'd ever seen. Worse than at Anzio. We lost our squadron commander and three other crews. I got back but the plane was riddled with ack-ack shrapnel. This went on night after night."

"Before the invasion started, General Eisenhower promised our troops that they wouldn't see any German aircraft overhead."

"Well, Eisenhower was right in *one* respect. Your troops didn't see us overhead because we were always there at *night*. The only daylight bombing was from *your* planes. In fact, I met a retired U.S. Army colonel. He was on the beach and was wounded by shrapnel from a bomb—one of *your* bombs, not ours. He said that American bombs were being released a little short and were killing a lot of your troops."

"What was your primary target at the beaches?"

"The ships. We bombed them and dropped mines. On one mission I was ordered to carry a huge 2,000 kilo (4,000 pound) mine under a wing. It wouldn't fit in the bomb bay. We were supposed to arm it with a wire leading to the cockpit and drop it in the water. Before we took off we were told, 'Make sure you arm it before you drop it or you'll be court-martialed.' We had to *prove* we armed it. We brought the arming wire back for proof."

"Was flak your only problem?"

"Oh, no. They sent night-fighters over to Belgium. They knew exactly where we were going to land so they had their fighters sitting up near our field waiting for us. We'd come home late at night, tired and with our wheels and flaps down for landing. This made us a slow, easy target.

"One night they jumped us. They were blasting away with their machine guns as I was trying to land. After that, we put searchlights and anti-aircraft guns out at the end of the runway to protect us."

"While you were based in France, weren't there a lot of saboteurs or French freedom fighters around to make your lives miserable?"

"There were a lot of Marquis, as they called themselves, or resistance fighters around, but they didn't bother us. I never saw one try to kill a German. Why should they? We made sure they lived well and had a lot of good food. They lived better than *we* did! I even had a lot of French girlfriends who were supposed to be Marquis."

"We were told that the French freedom-fighters played havoc with you."

"Sure. That was toward the *end* of the war when they *knew* Germany would lose. Many of them hated General Charles de Gaulle and there was even an assassination team of the French Marquis who wanted to get him."

"That's interesting, because I interviewed a man who was with the American O.S.S. He was a 'hired assassin' as he calls himself. He will not say anything beyond the point that he was only twelve minutes away from 'getting to de Gaulle.' and causing him to die from a sudden 'ear infection.' He said his orders were countermanded by the same authority that had *issued* the orders. I asked him how high the authority was and he replied, 'the highest.' I asked if President Roosevelt or Prime Minister Churchill was the 'highest authority' and he just grinned. de Gaulle was a pain in the neck . . . ."

"You were probably moving your air bases back as the allies advanced, weren't you? This happened in Algeria."

"Yes, toward the end of the war we had moved all the way back into Germany. By this time, we had very little gasoline and we didn't fly very often. I do remember flying missions against the allies as they advanced toward Paris. Then we were moved father east to Hanover. Since we couldn't fly for awhile, we hid our planes in the woods. They cut down huge pine trees and we pushed our planes in there. Then the trees were put up again with heavy chains. I don't believe any allied photo-recon planes spotted us."

"What were you waiting for?"

"We were waiting for what they called the last push, or the Battle of the Bulge. Finally we got orders to get our planes out of the woods and go back into action. I got ready for my 44th and last mission, but by then we had lost so many planes that we had to share the ones that were left.

"It was 1 a.m. Christmas Eve, 1944, when I sat down in a seat just vacated by a pilot who had returned from his mission. He had left his seat-pack parachute in the cockpit so I adjusted the harness to fit me. The other guy was very tall and the leg straps had to be drawn up. You know what would have happened if I hadn't done that, don't you? *Let's not talk about it!*"

"You said this was your *last* mission?"

"Yes, it was. Our mission was to bomb the tanks and trucks of Patton's army heading toward Bastogue. It was a clear, beautiful night.

"We flew to the border of Germany and into Belgium at 10,000 feet. We found our target, dropped our bombs and turned for home.

"We started to run out of gasoline and I knew we couldn't land in the dark, so thinking we were over Germany, I ordered the crew to bail out. I put the plane on automatic pilot and the gunner opened his hatch and jumped. Then the radio operator crawled down there and left. The navigator was next and I was the last one out."

"Didn't you have a hatch up front that you and the navigator could use?"

"We could release the canopy and it would blow off but it was dangerous because if you went out the top you would hit the rudder.

"There must have been a very strong easterly wind because instead of being over Germany, we were over Holland.

"I'll never forget that jump. It was a *wonderful* feeling. While I was dangling under my chute, I yelled at my navigator who was coming down near me and said, 'Isn't this *great?*'

"I don't remember hitting the ground. It was frozen hard and it knocked me out. Then all of a sudden I woke up and found that my left wrist was broken and my back hurt like hell. My navigator landed right in the middle of a Canadian anti-aircraft position and the other two men were never seen again. I think they must have gone through the ice on the Rhine River, got tangled in their parachutes and didn't come up.

"I got out of my parachute and headed for the nearest house. I thought I was still in Germany so I knocked on the door. A guy opened it, looked at my German uniform and said, 'You're not in Germany, you're in Holland.' I thought, 'Uh-oh.' "

"And he took you prisoner?"

"No. He slammed the door and I left there and finally found a small shed. I stayed in that shed the rest of the night and all the next day. I was *freezing!* Then at nightfall I left the shed and tried my luck at another farmhouse.

"These people were kind enough to give me some water but no food. I told them I was cold and sleepy so they let me sleep in their barn under some potato sacks.

"I knew it was too good to be true because the farmer had probably gone to the police and I heard, 'German come out.' I came out and found a Dutch policeman and a Canadian lieutenant. They took me to a small camp."

"Was this a prison?"

"No, just an interrogation facility near the front lines. We had been lectured on what to expect when we were captured. Sure enough, the Canadians followed our script. First, they offered me a cigarette. I told them my name, rank and serial number. Then they pulled rank on me. Since I was a lieutenant, they had a *captain* interrogate me.

"The Canadian captain got rough. He kept yelling at me for more information. This was the only guy who got nasty when I refused. He took me out into a dark corridor, punched me in the stomach and said, 'Now I'm going to put you up against the wall and shoot you.' I said, 'Well, go ahead.' He put his pistol back in its holster and turned me over to a group of soldiers who took me back to a hospital in Belgium."

"Earlier you mentioned that you were accused of trying to assassinate General Eisenhower. What's the story?"

"Yes, at the hospital, a British colonel, who spoke perfect German, asked me why I wanted to assassinate Eisenhower. He hammered at me for *days.* The Germans had supposedly dropped agents wearing American uniforms during the Battle of the Bulge. They were supposed to kill Eisenhower.

"The colonel thought I was the pilot who dropped them. He reasoned that they had found my plane and two crew members and that there had probably been two or possibly three more in the plane before we jumped, so the missing men were probably agents. And *where were they?* Finally, he muttered that he would probably send me to a firing squad as a spy."

"Well, you acted exactly like a good soldier—told them nothing."

"I *had* nothing to tell because I knew nothing about agents. It was here at the Belgian hospital and I knew the war was over. I saw huge trucks loaded with ammunition driving in the *daylight.* On *our* side of the lines *nothing* was moving during daylight hours because allied planes were bombing and strafing *everything* that moved.

"I forgot to tell you that when I got to the hospital. I was put in a reception room filled with Polish soldiers. When they saw my black uniform, they tried to lynch me! The Canadians finally calmed them down."

"Did you receive good treatment in the Canadian hospital?"

"Yes, very good. I was treated as well as the allied soldiers. After releasing me from the Belgian hospital, they flew me to London in a DC-3 where I spent a night or two. I heard our buzz bombs hitting there. Then I was taken to an interrogation camp outside of London where pilots, submarine commanders and so on were sent and again they hammered away at me with questions.

"They were especially interested in the mine I had dropped into the water off the invasion beach. It must have caused a lot of damage. They also wanted to know what the He-111 bombers were doing at the airfield south of Hamburg that I flew out of. Of course I didn't tell them, but we mounted V-1 buzz bombs on top of the Heinkels because we had lost all of our launching ramps. The buzz bombs were launched from the air.

"The British knew we no longer used the Heinkels for bombing or the western front because they had been replaced with faster planes. They were still being used on the eastern front against the Russians, however. They kept saying, 'We know from our recon photos that there are He-111s on that airfield. What are they doing there?'

"I was released from this nice interrogation camp and sent to another POW camp where I spent about three months in the wintertime. It was very unpleasant except for a brief stay in a place that looked like a nice motel. They put me in a lovely room where they had planted a German who I assumed they had been able to turn. This fellow talked to me and tried to find out some things I had refused to tell the interrogation officers. This had been explained to us in our lectures, and sure enough, it was happening to me."

"You spent the rest of the war in England?"

"No. We were put on a Dutch freighter in a convoy that took us to the port of Suez. We were loaded into trucks and driven for hours and hours until we saw a huge lighted area. This was a large British engineering depot south of the Great Bitter Lake in the Suez Canal. This depot supplied the entire British army in that theater of operation, and this is where the German POW camps were.

"These POW camps were divided into cages the size of football fields. There were 300 POWs in each cage and these fellows had been in the Afrika Korps during the Rommel campaign on the desert. They had no idea what was happening and when they saw me they started yelling, 'Heil Hitler! Sieg heil!' (Hail to Hitler! Hail to victory!).

"The camp was clean and well-run by the British who had been in the desert for years. We had only two water faucets and a latrine, but we had enough to eat. We had a lot of beans and I hate beans to this day.

"I had it easy because I spoke English and the camp commander of the engineering depot had me drive around with him and act as his interpreter. The rest of the German POWs were laborers. There were also some Egyptian laborers who were supervised by an ugly Egyptian who beat them unmercifully with a big stick. He treated them just like animals, but the POWs were treated well.

"I was there two years and the war had been over for some time before I was released."

"Why were you kept there *after* the war?"

"It wasn't long. My navigator stayed longer, for some strange reason, in a POW camp in England. I was released in 1946 and he was released in 1947. In 1950, German POWs from Russia were still wandering back to their Fatherland. This was *five* years after the war and they had been kept as slave-workers.

"We didn't know what the British would do with us when the war was over. A lot of rumors started circulating. One was that the German POWs would be sent to the Israelies and *they* would take care of us. Others said they were going to send us to the Russians."

"Were you a member of the Nazi Party?"

"No, I was much too young. You see, I grew up in Prague in (then) Czechoslovakia, where I was born in 1922. When the Germans came to Prague in 1939, I was 17 years old. I immediately had to become a member of the Hitler Youth. The dumbest guy in our class became the fuhrer, or leader of our group. So you see, I couldn't even *be* a member of the party because I was only 17 years old. A year later I went into the Luftwaffe."

"The other German gentlemen we interviewed were quick to say that *they* were not Nazis."

"Well, just about *anybody* will tell you that today. But they were born in Germany and probably didn't have much choice. I only became a German citizen in 1939 when Hitler took over Czechoslovakia and my parents were Austrians. A year before, the Austrians had become Germans."

"What did you do after being released from the POW camp?"

"I made my way back to Vienna by a Greek ship, train and cattle car. My mother was there living with relatives and we were reunited on Christmas Eve, 1946.

"I tried to find some of the old schoolmates who had been in classes with me before the war. A lot of them at that time were Jewish, and it's interesting that I found many more Jewish fellows who had survived the war than I did my German friends."

"Looks like we have about covered *your* war, Hans, and it has been interesting. Is there anything else you want to say before we turn the recorder off?"

"Yes. You told me how you flew as a photographer in B-17s. I want to tell you that all of us in the Luftwaffe had great respect for the American bomber crews. You always flew in the daytime and would go straight through flak fields without taking any evasive action. Of course *we* didn't do that and neither did the British."

Author's Note:

We were able to verify all of the inputs to this book except for the ones from the Germans. They seemed to be very sure of themselves, so no changes were made.

Epilogue

An epilogue should probably make a strong moral statement, and it seems that the gentlemen who told their stories—sometimes reluctantly and sometimes painfully—have done just that. They have brought out the human side of airmen who were thrown into bitter disasters not of their own making. These personal accounts have brought out the private feelings of men from *both* sides in ways that are seldom revealed in military literature.

It is the *human* side that always seems to be of interest to folks who never knew World War II. "What was it like to be in aerial combat? What went through your mind when you were captured? How did you feel . . . ?" These questions were covered here from *both* sides.

In our two trips through Germany, we learned that old Luftwaffe pilots are really *nice* guys—they had a job to do at the time and just wanted to hurry and finish and go home like we did.

All of the men whose stories have been told—the ones who wore stars and those who sported swastikas—were in total agreement that there never has been, nor ever *can* be, a good war. Wars are beyond comprehension, but the little individual battles fought by these men changed them—hardened them in a way—and will remain in their bones forever.